Pluralistic Economics and Its History

This volume is a history of economics – as it was interpreted, discussed and established as a discipline – in the 20th century. It highlights the pluralism of the discipline and brings together leading voices in the field who reflect on their lifelong work. The chapters draw on a host of traditions of economic thought, including pre-classical, classical, Marxian, neoclassical, Sraffian, post-Keynesian, Cantabrigian and institutionalist traditions in economics. Further, the volume also looks at the history of economics in India and its evolution as a discipline since the country's independence.

This book will appeal to students, researchers and teachers of economics and intellectual history, as well as to the interested general reader.

Ajit Sinha is a Professor of Economics at Azim Premji University, Bengaluru, India. He has published extensively in the area of history of economic theory. He is also the author of *Theories of Value from Adam Smith to Piero Sraffa*, *A Revolution in Economic Theory: The Economics of Piero Sraffa* and *Essays on Theories of Value in the Classical Tradition*.

Alex M. Thomas is an Assistant Professor of Economics at Azim Premji University, Bengaluru, India. His primary research area is the history of economic thought, especially classical economics.

T0320973

Pluralistic Economics
and Its History

Edited by Ajit Sinha and
Alex M. Thomas

Routledge
Taylor & Francis Group

LONDON AND NEW YORK

First published 2019
by Routledge
2 Park Square, Milton Park, Abingdon, Oxon OX14 4RN

and by Routledge
52 Vanderbilt Avenue, New York, NY 10017

Routledge is an imprint of the Taylor & Francis Group, an informa business

British Library Cataloguing-in-Publication Data
A catalogue record for this book is available from the British Library

Library of Congress Cataloging-in-Publication Data
A catalog record for this book has been requested

ISBN: 978-1-138-09003-3 (hbk)
ISBN: 978-0-367-23235-1 (pbk)
ISBN: 978-0-429-27886-0 (ebk)

Typeset in Bembo
by Apex CoVantage, LLC

MIX
Paper from responsible sources
FSC
www.fsc.org FSC™ C013985

Printed in the United Kingdom
by Henry Ling Limited

Contents

List of figures   vii
Notes on contributors   viii
Acknowledgements   xi

1 **Introduction**   1
   AJIT SINHA AND ALEX M. THOMAS

2 **History, logic and narrative in pedagogy**   13
   C.T. KURIEN

3 **Theories of activity levels and growth before Adam Smith**   24
   ALEX M. THOMAS

4 **From 'change' to 'difference': Sraffa's reinterpretation
   of classical economics**   41
   AJIT SINHA

5 **A history of Marxian economics 1960–2010: how we 'did' it**   55
   MEGHNAD DESAI

6 **Capitalism, classical political economy and Marx's
   departures**   67
   CHIRASHREE DAS GUPTA

7 **On the origins of post Keynesian macroeconomics**   85
   JOHN KING

8 **Geoff Harcourt on G.C. Harcourt, as told to Ajit Sinha**   99
   G.C. HARCOURT

9   Is there a Cambridge approach to economics?   122
    MARIA CRISTINA MARCUZZO

10 Between theory and history: the structural dynamics
    tradition   136
    ROBERTO SCAZZIERI

11 Buffer stock operations in history and economic thought   160
    ROMAR CORREA

12 History of institutional economics   171
    PHILLIP ANTHONY O'HARA

13 General equilibrium: a status report   191
    ANJAN MUKHERJI

14 Historical perspective of econometrics   210
    K.L. KRISHNA

15 Writings of Indian economic history since independence   239
    TIRTHANKAR ROY

16 On the evolution of heterodox economic thinking in India   256
    SUNANDA SEN

17 Two sides of the colonial coin: British and Indian
    women's engagements with colonialism and patriarchy   269
    SHEETAL BHARAT

    Name index   283
    Subject index   289

Figures

4.1   Primordial production relation   42
13.1 Partial equilibrium   194
13.2 Orbits of the Scarf example   197
13.3 Excess demand – the Gale example   199
13.4 Gale example with a switch in endowments   199
13.5 The Edgeworth Box   200
13.6 Excess demands for alternative values of λ   201
15.1 Articles on Indian economic history published in leading
      journals, 1961–2013   248
15.2 Articles on Indian economic history published in leading
      journals and originating in India (% of total), 1961–2013   249
15.3 GDP by major activities (Rs Billion, in 1938–1939 prices)   253

Contributors

Sheetal Bharat is an Assistant Professor at the Bengaluru Dr B.R. Ambedkar School of Economics, India. Her research interests lie in the areas of economic history and history of economic thought.

Romar Correa retired as RBI Professor of Monetary Economics, University of Mumbai, India, in 2016. He works on the tension between micro and macro.

Meghnad Desai is an Emeritus Professor at the London School of Economics (LSE), UK.

Chirashree Das Gupta is an Associate Professor at the Centre for the Study of Law and Governance, Jawaharlal Nehru University, New Delhi, India.

G.C. Harcourt is a graduate of Melbourne and Cambridge Universities. He taught mainly at Adelaide and Cambridge and is now an Honorary Professor at UNSW Sydney, Australia. He is author, co-author, editor or co-editor of thirty-three books, including thirteen volumes of selected essays and over 400 articles, reviews and chapters in books.

John King is an Emeritus Professor at La Trobe University and Honorary Professor at Federation University Australia. His principal research interests are in the history of heterodox economic thought, especially Marxian political economy and post-Keynesian economics. Recent publications include *The Distribution of Wealth* (2016; with Michael Schneider and Mike Pottenger) and *A History of American Economic Thought* (2018; with Samuel Barbour and James Cicarelli). He is currently working on a book for Edward Elgar, *The Alternative Austrian Economics*, dealing with socialist economic thought in Austria between 1904 and the present day.

K.L. Krishna is the Chairperson, Madras Institute of Development Studies (MIDS), Chennai, India. He has a PhD in Economics from the University of Chicago. His fields of specialization include econometrics, industrial economics and economics of productivity. He has been a teacher and research supervisor at the Delhi School of Economics, India, for more than 40 years and has edited several books. Dr Krishna was also the Founding Managing Editor of *Journal of Quantitative Economics* in the 1980s and 1990s.

C.T. Kurien was a Professor of Economics, Madras Christian College, India, and subsequently Director, Madras Institute of Development Studies. He is the author of over a dozen books on economics, the latest being *Economics of Real Life – A New Exposition*.

Maria Cristina Marcuzzo has worked on classical monetary theory, the Cambridge School of Economics, Keynesian economics and more recently Keynes's investments in financial markets. She has published about 100 articles in journals and books, plus authoring or editing twenty volumes.

Anjan Mukherji is a Professor Emeritus, Centre for Economic Studies and Planning, Jawaharlal Nehru University, New Delhi, India.

Phillip Anthony O'Hara has been Director of the Global Political Economy Research Unit (GPERU) since 1998. He won the Myrdal Prize for book of the year (2002) and the Kapp Prize for article of the year (2011) from the European Association for Evolutionary Political Economy (EAEPE). He is currently completing a monograph on *Principles of Institutional and Evolutionary Political Economy: Applied to Current World Problems*.

Tirthankar Roy is a Professor in the Economic History Department of the London School of Economics, UK. He works on economic history, business history, history of development policy and the classical music of India. He is the author of *India in the World Economy from Antiquity to the Present*, besides other books and articles.

Roberto Scazzieri is a Professor of Economic Analysis at the University of Bologna and Fellow of the National Lincei Academy, Italy. He studies the relationship between persistence and change in economic systems, exploring how the uneven transformation of structures shapes the economic dynamics of societies. He recently co-edited *The Palgrave Handbook of Political Economy* (2018).

Sunanda Sen is a former Professor of Economics at Jawaharlal Nehru University, India. Her research covers development, economic history, international finance, labour economics and gender studies. She has published several books and articles including *The Changing Face of Imperialism: Colonies to Contemporary Capitalism* (2018) and *Dominant Finance and Stagnant Economies* (2014).

Ajit Sinha is a Professor of Economics at Azim Premji University, Bengaluru, India. He has published extensively in the area of history of economic theory. He is also the author of *Theories of Value from Adam Smith to Piero Sraffa*,

A Revolution in Economic Theory: The Economics of Piero Sraffa and *Essays on Theories of Value in the Classical Tradition.*

Alex M. Thomas is an Assistant Professor of Economics at Azim Premji University, Bengaluru, India. His primary research area is the history of economic thought, especially classical economics.

Acknowledgements

We are extremely grateful to Azim Premji University for financially supporting the Graduate Workshop on Economics and its History held on November 17–19, 2016, in Bengaluru, India, from which the idea for this book emerged. We would like to thank our students Mridhula Mohan and Sanjana Rajasekar for help with copy editing.

Chapter 1

Introduction

Ajit Sinha and Alex M. Thomas

Over the last four decades or so, the teaching of history of economics has been slowly purged from the curricula of economics at both the graduate and the undergraduate levels. The apparent reason for it offered by the orthodoxy is that economics is a science that concerns itself with understanding what exists rather than with navel-gazing at its own achievements and failures. This attitude rests on a naive assumption that science is a linear march towards 'true' understanding and thus what is discarded by it in its forward march is necessarily 'untrue' and, therefore, there is no reason to saddle the study of its subject matter with those ideas that have proven to be 'false'. It, however, fails to recognize that there are shifts in paradigms even in pure sciences and thus one cannot read the history of science as a linear march towards 'truth'. As a matter of fact, Piero Sraffa has put forward a strong case that not only argues that there has been indeed a paradigm shift in economics since the advent of the modern economics in 1870s but that the nature of this shift has been from science to ideology.

Furthermore, it is simply incorrect to think that pure sciences or mathematics do not care about their histories. Who among us has not learnt Euclidian geometry even though contemporary mathematics and physics almost entirely deal with non-Euclidian geometry? Or for that matter, who can graduate in physics without studying Newtonian physics, even though contemporary physics is almost entirely quantum physics? The reason for it is that the mathematicians and the physicists do not allow their history to be lost – they ensure that it is taught at an early age either at the school or early college level. So, why has orthodoxy in economics been so keen on removing all traces of its own history? It is not our purpose to settle the question here. We raise this issue only to point out that the removal of the history of economics from the curriculum of economics may be (or perhaps it is most likely) due to the fear that its own history may turn out to harbour its greatest challenge. In any case, as we all know, we learn more from our failures than from our successes. Thus it makes common sense to teach our students the history of their discipline with all its 'mistakes' and twists and turns so that they have a much richer understanding of it. In the wake of the Great Recession of 2007–8, which has exposed the limitations and weaknesses of the current orthodoxy, it is incumbent on us to go back to the history of our discipline to find ideas and inspirations to build something new. It is in this spirit that we have put together this book on *Pluralistic Economics and Its History*.

It is, however, not a usual 'history of economic thought' volume with articles on various aspects of the works of classical and pre-classical economists. Instead, we encouraged our authors to reflect on the historicity of their own research agendas. The result of this has turned into a highly interesting and perhaps a unique collection of papers that ranges from some leading scholars in the profession such as Geoffrey Harcourt recounting his more than fifty years of engagement with post-Keynesian economics, Meghnad Desai reflecting on his engagement with research and teaching of Marxian economics, John King going back in search of the core of post-Keynesian economics, Maria Cristina Marcuzzo asking whether one can characterize 1960s and early 1970s Cambridge contributions as a 'school', Roberto Scazzieri reflecting back on the history of structuralist dynamics in economics, C.T. Kurien turning to the fundamental methodological distinction between classical and neoclassical economics and the problems it poses for teaching of economics, Ajit Sinha recasting Sraffa's core contribution to classical economics, Chirashree Das Gupta distinguishing Marx from classical economics, Romar Correa scrutinizing the history and economic thought underlying buffer stock operations, Phillip Anthony O'Hara providing a pluralistic history of institutional economics, Anjan Mukherji taking stock of general equilibrium theory in the light of Sonnenschein-Mantel-Debreu theorems, K.L. Krishna engaging with the history of econometrics as well as its development in India, Tirthankar Roy reflecting on the historicity of writings of Indian economic history, Sunanda Sen trying to identify theoretical foundations of the pre-Independence Indian Nationalists' writings to young scholars, Alex M. Thomas finding Keynesian themes in pre-Smithian authors and Sheetal Bharat reflecting on how differently women responded to the British Raj depending on which side of the divide they stood.

The book begins with C.T. Kurien's brief but highly penetrating analysis of the fundamental methodological divide between classical and modern economics. For Kurien, Adam Smith is classical – however, Ricardo, due to his 'Ricardian vice', gets too close to the moderns. He argues that Adam Smith neither uses inductive logic to generalize from a sufficient number of observations nor the deductive logic to arrive at universal propositions or conclusions from a set of so-called axioms. According to Kurien, Adam Smith uses, what he calls, an 'analytical narrative'. In this case logical inferences are made on the basis of commonly accepted concrete historical instances. These logical inferences develop an 'analytical narrative' of the concrete situation and is bound-up with it in the sense that these logical inferences do not make any general truth claims independently of the concrete historical situations they refer to. This, he contrasts with the modern neoclassical economics that aims at developing universal truth claims based on ahistorical 'Robinson Crusoe'. In this case, the theory attempts to reduce the whole of economics to one single principle.

Kurien, who learnt his general equilibrium theory from none other than Ken Arrow at Stanford University and who has been one of the leading economists of India for decades, thinks that it is better and natural to introduce economics to students at the undergraduate level as an 'analytical narrative' rather than as a set of abstract propositions deduced from a set of so-called axioms and unrealistic assumptions.

Next comes a chapter by Alex M. Thomas, who discovers some Keynesian notes in early classical economics. Through a textual analysis of the key texts of Richard Cantillon, François Quesnay, Anne Robert Jacques Turgot and James Steuart, Thomas argues that aggregate activity levels and economic growth in their respective theories are demand driven. He also notes that, in their work, the supply of labour adapts to the demand for labour.

This is followed by Ajit Sinha's highly unconventional interpretation of Sraffa's contribution to classical economics. Sinha revisits the theory of value in Smith and Ricardo to argue that their theories of value were rooted in the idea of *original cause* of value and their search for an 'invariable' scale of measurement of value was inherently linked with this idea. He argues that Sraffa rejected the problematic of 'original cause' – for him the theory of value related to an economy at a point of time like a snapshot of a moment. However, with the help of his analysis of the standard system and the standard commodity as the scale of measurement of value, Sraffa succeeded in proving the fundamental classical or rather Smithian proposition that distribution of income is independent of prices but prices are dependent on it.

Next comes Meghnad Desai's highly interesting reflection on Marxian economics from 1960 to 2010, of which he has been one of the major contributors himself. Desai first narrates the story of scant availability of the literature on Marxian economics in the 1960s and its subsequent growth throughout this period. Then he brings his highly penetrating insights to bear upon the major theoretical themes in Marxian economics such as the 'transformation problem', Marx's 'reproduction schemas' and the theory of business cycles and crisis, etc. – most interestingly, Desai thinks that Ladislaus Bortkiewicz had solved the 'transformation problem' in 1907!

Chirashree Das Gupta, a teacher and scholar of political economy and economic history at Jawaharlal Nehru University, argues that Marx should be essentially seen as a critic of classical economics rather than a part of it. She makes this distinction on the grounds of the visions these authors have of an ideal economy. She argues that though Smith and Ricardo held the view that a freely competitive capitalist economy was an ideal system, Marx was of the view that the capitalist system had to be overcome to establish a society of freely associated producers, which was for him the ideal society. These antagonistic ideals gave rise to opposing theories rather than a theoretical development within a paradigm.

Post-Keynesian themes are introduced by a leading commentator and contributor to heterodox economics, John King. He places post-Keynesian themes in opposition to the old neoclassical interpretation of the *General Theory* in terms of the IS-LM model. According to King, there have been three fundamental trends or approaches in the history of post-Keynesian thought. A primary move was made by Sidney Weintraub and then followed by his student Paul Davidson. In the Weintraub-Davidson approach, which King characterizes as the 'Fundamentalist Keynesian' approach, the ideas of a non-commodity money and non-ergodic expectations play the central role in explaining Keynes's non-general equilibrium results. The non-neutrality of money is a result of the future being unknowable even in probabilistic terms. Since businesses hedge against uncertainty by contracting future transactions in terms of money, demand shifts in favour of holding money lead to decline in the production of real commodities and employment, but an increase in the money supply in response to an increase in demand cannot lead to an increase in employment as money is not produced by labour like other commodities. Though King is appreciative of this approach, he criticizes Davidson for accepting the neoclassical aggregate supply/production function as well as labour demand and supply functions. King identifies the second approach with Michał Kalecki and his followers. The Keynesian dimension in Kalecki's theory is the centrality of capitalists' investment demand. Starting from a full employment equilibrium, a fall in investment demand by the capitalist class would create a realization problem for the total value of investment goods produced, leading to a fall in aggregate income and employment through the multiplier mechanism. This approach also leads to the conclusion that an increase in the profit share at the cost of the wage share in the total income could lead to a similar realization problem for the consumption goods produced, and also to a fall in investment demand via the accelerator mechanism, and hence to a fall in total income and employment. King criticizes the Kaleckian approach for not taking account of 'financial fragility' as an important aspect of modern capitalist economies. This gap was bridged by Hyman Minsky, who put financial markets at the centre of his analysis of modern capitalism – it is creditors and debtors who are the principal actors in Minsky's capitalist world rather than capitalists and labourers. Minsky uses Keynes's idea of the fundamental uncertainty of the future that cannot be reduced to probabilistic risk, an interpretation of Keynes also emphasized by Davidson, to develop his 'financial instability hypothesis'. Given the 'bull' and 'bear' cycle of expectations in financial markets, the rise and fall of the value of financial assets affects the real market through its impact on both consumption and investment demand – consumption demand is affected due to the 'wealth effect' and investment demand is affected because a fall in the price of old assets reduces the incentive to buy new assets. During the phase of a deep recession, financial institutions become so cautious that they refuse to lend even to credible borrowers even at a higher rate of interest – the point that Minsky emphasizes is that there is a fundamental asymmetry between creditors and debtors, though debtors can be forced to cut their expenditure creditors cannot be forced to increase their expenditure. Hence not only money but also debt is non-neutral, which requires a rejection of Modigliani-Millar theorem that is central to all versions of the neoclassical-Keynesian synthesis. King argues that all these three approaches were well-established by mid-1970s and though they were not mainstream macroeconomics, they were considered as 'other' respectable voices. But since the development of New Classical and New Keynesian economics, post-Keynesian voices have been pushed to the 'margins' of the profession even though post-Keynesian economics itself is flourishing.

This is followed by Geoffrey Harcourt's 'collectors' item' – a unique contribution that reflects on his highly influential and rather eclectic lifelong contribution to economics and post-Keynesian economics in particular. Harcourt's contributions to post-Keynesian economics is not obsessed with the non-neutrality of money and the question of unemployment equilibrium as is the case with a large body of post-Keynesian literature. He also brings in the question of technical change, theories of price determination and Sraffa-inspired capital theoretic critique of orthodox economics under this rubric, which has made post-Keynesian literature much richer over the years. His highly appreciated paper 'The Accounted in a Golden Age' (1965b) is a good example of his concern for empirical data and its relation to theoretical concepts. The reader will find the account of his famous survey paper on 'capital theory', published in *JEL* in 1969, and the well-known papers on growth and distribution of 1963 and 1965 particularly interesting. Harcourt candidly criticizes his latter two highly influential papers for utilizing 'representative agent' to model pricing and gives credit to Opocher and Steedman (2015) for bringing to his notice the role of intermediary goods in price determination that cannot be captured by 'representative agent' models. Throughout this intellectual autobiographical account, one learns about several great economists who influenced his thinking over the years. The chapter also contains a prodigious bibliographical list of Harcourt's work, starting with his 1953 unpublished honours thesis submitted to the University of Melbourne to his 2017 journal articles – more than 60 years of contributions!

Then Maria Cristina Marcuzzo, who is an authority on several Cambridge economists, asks this question: is there a 'Cambridge School' of economic thought? Her answer is that though there are some commonalities in their approaches, particularly their rejection of a mechanical interpretation of capitalist market economy, their overall contributions cannot be characterized as a 'school' – they are rather a 'group'. The reason for this distinction, as she puts it, 'is to convey the idea of both cohesion and sharing, rather than adhesion to a common body of doctrine'. Though Marshall was the founding father of Cambridge economics and the point of reference for the Cambridge approach to economics, the two main protagonists of Marcuzzo's story are Keynes and Sraffa. Keynes was a student of Marshall and never completely abandoned Marshallian economics. He, however, introduced the idea of 'fundamental uncertainty' and the 'non-neutrality of money' at the centre of his economic analysis of capitalist market economy, which led him to conclude that market mechanism may not necessarily lead to a full employment equilibrium and thus the economy needed to be 'managed' by setting up 'rules and *limitations*' (Keynes 1936 [1971]: 374). Marcuzzo argues that this was in line with the Marshall-Pigou tradition. Keynes's adherence to Marshallian tools of supply and demand, however, created contradiction and tension in his theory. This notwithstanding, the publication of the *General Theory* was a landmark development in the intellectual environ of Cambridge economics – Richard Kahn, Joan Robinson and Nicholas Kaldor became the most notable followers and tried to develop the Keynesian approach in different directions. Sraffa was an outsider and started from the position that the Marshallian tools of analysis needed to be rejected lock, stock and barrel. Sraffa's early criticisms (1926) of Marshall's theory of prices based on partial equilibrium and his idea of 'imperfect competition' as a possible way out had some influence on Kahn and Robinson, since they attended Sraffa's lectures on Advanced Theory of Value in 1928 – they, however, took it in directions that Sraffa perhaps did not approve of. Sraffa also did not approve of Keynes's *General Theory*, which had almost taken over the Cambridge economics scene after 1936. All this contributed to make Sraffa reluctant to share his main research project, which was to challenge the foundations of orthodox economics of his Cambridge colleagues, and therefore it more or less remained hidden from them till the publication of *Production of Commodities by Means of Commodities* in 1960 – Robinson, however, could glimpse its main message from Sraffa's 'Introduction' to *The Works and Correspondence of David Ricardo*, published in 1951, as is evident from her 1954 attack on neoclassical aggregate production function. Marcuzzo follows Garegnani's lead in interpreting Sraffa's theory of prices in which one of the distributional category, i.e., either wage rate or the rate of profits, is determined independently of prices (i.e., in a socio-historical context) but the other distributional category is determined simultaneously with prices. One of us (see Sinha 2016), however, has argued that in Sraffa's theory not one but both the distributional categories are determined simultaneously and independently of prices – the standard system and the standard commodity were the devices developed by Sraffa to precisely prove this proposition. Leaving aside our controversy, Marcuzzo goes on to document the later research agendas of leading Cambridge economists that came out of either the *General Theory* or the *Production of Commodities*. She paints a comprehensive picture of the intellectual environment of Cambridge economics from 1930s to 1970s.

Roberto Scazzieri, who has been one of the foremost theoreticians and proponents of structuralist dynamics for decades, provides us with a masterly survey of the literature from Genovesi and Steuart to Pasinetti and beyond. He emphasizes the link between economic theory and economic history that the structuralist dynamic analysis provides. On one hand Antonio Genovesi's (1765–1767) idea of 'political geometry' highlights the temporal sequence of various 'arts', such as 'fundamental arts', i.e., production directly related to nature, 'arts of improvements', i.e., mainly manufacturing activities, and 'arts of luxury', that any economy's normal development should take; it also, on the other hand, points out the proportionality in which these 'arts' must exist at any given point in history. Steuart (1767) highlights the crucial link between the 'surplus' production in agriculture to the development of manufacturing. Scazzieri detects the twin concepts of a 'natural' course of development as an analytical device along with concrete historical circumstance as a historical reality in Steuart's distinction between 'natural distribution' and 'particular circumstances'. This trend becomes more pronounced in Adam Smith's (1776 [1976]) analytical description of the 'natural' trajectory of development of any economy from agriculture to manufacturing and then finally to international commerce. At the same time Smith also realizes that this has not happened in many cases in Europe where coastal cities, through their linkages with international commerce, generated 'surplus', which stimulated local manufacturing, which in turn stimulated agriculture – hence reversing the natural course. However, for Smith such conflicting causation against its natural course always exacted a price. The idea of a 'natural' or 'normal' course of development or growth as an analytical internal causal nexus and divergence from it in the real course of history as disturbances caused by external causes gave rise to two different approaches to structural dynamic literature in modern times: one relating to the analysis of equilibrium growth paths and the other to the analysis of 'traverse', i.e., the analysis of crossing from one equilibrium path to another. Harrod (1939) inaugurated the 'equilibrium' growth path literature by highlighting the improbability of it in the real history with his double knife-edge growth path needing to equilibrate not only the average propensity to save with the given capital-output ratio but also to equilibrate the warranted rate with the natural rate. Pasinetti and Spaventa (1960) pointed out the unnaturalness of the Harrodian growth path in which economies could keep growing (if they hit the dual knife-edge) without any change to their basic variables. Obviously, a growing economy would experience changes in its savings propensities and consumption patterns along with changes in technologies, etc. Pasinetti, over the years, has worked out the path of the structural changes an economy must make on the condition that it throughout maintains full employment of labour and total capacity unitization of capital. This he calls the 'natural economy', which is independent of any particular institutional set-up in which a real economy works – interaction of the two throws light on our understanding of how and why in historical times we are faced with unemployment and under-utilization of total capacity. This line of research has been further developed by Scazzieri, Baranzini and others. Scazzieri then goes on to survey the literature on the 'traverse'. Starting from Ricardo's famous analysis of sudden changes in the patterns of international trade to Menger, Pigou, Hicks and Quadrio Curzio's contributions. Here Scazzieri brings forward the emphasis on vertical links as well as horizontal or circular links among industries and sectors in various theories. The reader is provided a truly comprehensive survey of a long and large literature.

A leading heterodox monetarist economist of India, Romar Correa, traces the historical evolution of buffer stock operations in commodities and money. He finds a pause in the narrative during the time of Franklin Roosevelt, who introduced a set of policy innovations in 1930s. Roosevelt connected with Keynes, who provided theory for those practices. Correa goes on to argue that buffer stock operations in able and willing workers is one lesson we have learnt for modern times. He recommends stock-flow-consistent modelling as the language to study the subject, although microeconomics can be a supporting dialect.

An 'all-rounder' in cricket is someone who is good at all aspects of the game and Australia has produced some very good ones over the years. One may say the same for heterodox economics. Phillip Anthony O'Hara, following the tradition of Geoffrey Harcourt and John King, is another good Australian all-rounder of heterodox economics. He presents a highly comprehensive and broad-based historical account of institutional economics. O'Hara takes the perspective of institutional and evolutionary political economy (IEPE) and thus defines institutional economics in very broad terms – mainly a theoretical perspective that studies an empirical economy rather than an 'abstract model' in terms of its historical evolution over time and the relations of agents and institutions in terms of circular and cumulative causation, which rejects reductionism. O'Hara finds traces of institutional economics in Physiocracy and classical economics and its substantial development in Marx, but it was Veblen, he claims, whose work inaugurates its formal beginning. Veblen set the stage by developing a complex analysis of the US economy at the turn of the 20th century. He situates the economy within an interacting four qualitative levels and analyzes its evolution in terms of cumulative causation. Following a detailed exposition of Veblen's work, O'Hara goes on to document institutionalist themes in the works of Keynes, Joseph Schumpeter, Wesley Mitchell, Clarence Ayres, Gunnar Myrdal and John Kenneth Galbraith, among the 'original institutionalists'; the 'French Regulation' and the 'social structure of accumulation' approaches to analyzing historical changes under capitalism; plus feminist institutionalism, radical institutionalism as well as 'new institutionalists' such as Douglass North and Elinor Ostrom. The reader is provided a truly comprehensive sketch of the long history of institutional economics.

Following this, Anjan Mukherji presents perhaps the most challenging chapter of this volume. Mukherji takes stock of the general equilibrium theory, particularly the problem of 'stability' associated with it. Mukherji has been India's foremost general equilibrium theorist for decades – he studied it (for his PhD degree) under the supervision of none other than Lionel McKenzie. Mukherji argues that the news of the death of general equilibrium theory is rather exaggerated. He first shows the reader how the partial equilibrium approach to pricing can be fundamentally misleading and wrong and not just marginally off the true result. He takes the reader through the 'stability' problem raised by Scarf (1960) and Gale (1963) and then the well-known

Sonnenschein-Mantel-Debreu theorems on excess demand. Mukherji argues that the 'instability' problem in general results from the 'miss-specification' of endowments, and that an appropriate re-allocation can take care of the instability given the equilibrium prices resulting from the original allocation. In Mukherji's words:

> What about the SMD (Sonnenschein-Mantel-Debreu) theorems then? It may be recalled that what SMD theorems show is that the properties of homogeneity of degree zero in the prices and Walras Law do not tie down the nature of the excess demand functions adequately. The result we have named, the Second Fundamental Theorem of Positive Economics, shows however, that the excess demand functions may be made to behave by redistributing endowments, without affecting equilibrium prices provided a regularity condition holds. Such a redistribution is one that will alter the volume of trades at equilibrium as well as the distribution of the gains from trade. But post-trade, the situation remains unaffected.

K.L. Krishna, one of India's senior most economists and a leading econometrician, presents a history of econometrics. In this context, Krishna takes up a few seminal works in this area and provides us with an expert commentary not only on the history of econometrics but on its historiography as well. The seeds of modern econometrics could be found in the works of William Petty, Gregory King and Charles Davenant with the use of statistical facts in their analysis of political arithmetic or their attempt to combine quantitative data with theory. Gregory King fitted a linear function of changes in corn prices on variations in corn harvest and, with the development in statistical theory, economists were quick to adopt them into economic analysis as correlation analysis was carried out as early as 1895–1896 by Yule, and as early as 1907, Benini applied the method of multiple regression to his economic analysis. But the real development and use of statistical tools for economic analysis, Krishna suggests, began only with Fisher's (1922) recasting of economic induction into its modern form. However, up till the 1940s, econometrics mainly meant innovative applied work, and it was only in 1940s that it began to develop its own theoretical side. The work of the Cowles Commission (1932–1953), mainly of Trygve Haavelmo and Tjalling Koopmans, succeeded in theoretically solving the identification problem in a simultaneous equation model and hypothesis testing but did not succeed empirically. Krishna thinks that Haavelmo's 'Probability Approach to Econometrics' (1944) marks the beginning of modern econometrics. Koopmans maintained that theory must come prior to data. Theoretical econometrics followed Koopmans' prescription during the period 1950–1970 in developing appropriate estimators. In the 1950s micro level data became widely available, which led to better recognition of social problems and programme evaluations. This presented a challenge to the traditional econometrics methods, which led to the development of microeconometrics and a more robust approach to policy evaluation. The periods of the 1950s and 1960s saw the consolidation of econometrics around the linear regression model. Development in dynamic modelling displaced simultaneity and identification problems from the centre of econometric discussions. Prior to the 1960s, development in econometrics followed advances in statistical theory dealing with non-experimental data in the linear regression model, but since the 1960s, advances in computing has relaxed the most serious constraint on applied econometrics and, due to this, empirical econometrics has seen phenomenal growth in recent years. Krishna concludes the chapter with a brief history of teaching and applied econometric research in India.

Next comes a critical survey of the history of Indian economic history by Tirthankar Roy, one of the foremost scholars of the subject today. The history of Indian economic history is now more than a hundred years old; Roy places its inception around 1900 and provides an interesting account of it to date. He contends that the early writings in this field were mostly Nationalist and ideological in nature and lacked a theoretical foundation. And though a lot of work during the period 1900–1947 engaged with economic history, it was not in its own right – it rather used economic history to shed light on some specific contemporary economic problems – Indian economic history had not yet arrived as a distinct field when India became independent. The period 1947–1960 saw some movements in the direction of positivist evidence-based historiography but still the field had not sufficiently congealed as one. This changed in the 1960s with the rise of Marxism as a global intellectual event that provided the early Nationalists' narratives with a theoretical foundation – it developed a singular global theoretical narrative in which both prosperity and poverty in different parts of the world could be explained simultaneously. However, the global discourses on India were Eurocentric and the question they were mainly concerned with was the economic inequality between nations. Hence India could be seen as a homogeneous entity that was poor and underdeveloped. Roy places the publication of Morris D. Morris's paper in the *Journal of Economic History* in 1963 and its republication in *IESHR* in 1968 as a significant event. Morris challenged the narratives based on singular causal explanations of Indian poverty and underdevelopment either in colonial exploitation or cultural backwardness. He raised the paradox of the simultaneous existence of both highly developed pockets along with vast underdevelopment in India and argued that the colonial State was too weak (in economic terms) to have made much difference in either direction. The Marxist response to Morris's challenge, according to Roy, couldn't see the forest for the trees. They read Morris as an apology for colonial rule and the debate degenerated into rather shrill pro- and anti-colonial historiography. This perhaps was one important reason why young scholars moved away from Indian economic history and Roy documents a perceptible decline in research publications in this area since 1990. Roy's own work, along with some others, picks up the problematic 'paradox' raised by

Morris and has contributed to the revival or at least survival of the field (this is not his claim – eds.). Some new developments in the area of new institutional economics, particularly the works of Douglass North, which explain the divergence in economic performances between countries or regions on the basis of some initial institutional differences, and a powerful critique of it by Pomeranz in his *The Great Divergence* (2000), have given a new boost to fresh research on Indian economic history.

Sunanda Sen then tries to provide some theoretical foundations to early Indian Nationalist writings from late 19th century to the interwar period. Sen is a leading Indian post-Keynesian economist and, on this occasion, she uses her expertise in the service of the history of Indian economic thought. She concentrates mainly on two economic issues on which the Nationalist writings were most prevalent: (i) transfers of unrequited tax revenues including sterling proceeds of India's net export earnings and 'home charges' and (ii) policies related to tariff and exchange rates. She argues that, on point (i), which was characterized by Dadabhai Naoroji and his followers as the 'drain of wealth' from India, their arguments foreshadow the Keynesian idea of 'multiplier' as they argued that these drains from the Indian budget led to the severe contraction of indigenous income. They also pointed out unfairness of the heavy tax burden imposed on Indians compared to the British and went on to foreshadow the principle of progressive taxes as fair tax policy. Naoroji and his followers rejected the explanation of Indian poverty as an outcome of inefficiency and developed a macroeconomic explanation based on the idea of the 'vicious circle of poverty'. On point (ii), Sen argues that the Nationalists demanded high tariff on imports in general to protect indigenous industrialization very much in the line with Friedrich List's perspective on 'infant industries'. By 1941, Adarkar introduced Keynesian ideas into the mix of the debate, which naturally led to the question of exchange rates as well. In this context, Sen argues that the Nationalists used the purchasing power parity theory to argue that the Indian rupee was overvalued vis-à-vis pounds sterling. She goes on to briefly discuss the issue of export of gold from India and its opposition by the Nationalists as they were interested in having a gold-based indigenous currency and wanted to keep the gold reserves for that purpose.

The book ends with two beautifully written tales of a country. Sheetal Bharat, a highly talented young economist from Bangalore, brings the gender dimension to the study of history. She looks 'at the literature produced by women who lived in colonial India to gain an understanding of the various and opposing forces at play with regard to the British occupation of India, and related aspects of these women's lives' (p. 269, this volume). We leave the reader to enjoy the rest. The reader can now see that here an attempt is made to bring together the historicity of several areas of economics as well as Indian economics. We hope that the volume will be helpful to research scholars in economics as well as interested general readers.

References

Fisher, R. A. 1922. '"On the mathematical foundations" of Theoretical Statistics', *Philosophical Transaction of Royal Society A*, 222, 309–368.

Gale, D. 1960. *The Theory of Linear Economic Models*, New York: McGraw Hill.

Haavelmo, T. 1994. 'The Probability Approach in Econometrics', *Econometrica*, 12, supplement, 1–118.

Harrod, R. 1939. 'An Essay in Dynamic Theory', *The Economic Journal*, 49(193), 14–33, March.

Keynes, J. M. 1936. 'The General Theory of Employment, Interest, and Money', in E. Johnson and D. E. Moggridge (eds.), *The Collected Writings of John Maynard Keynes*, vol. VII, London: Palgrave Macmillan, 1971.

Opocher, A. and Steedman, I. 2015. *Full Industry Equilibrium: A Theory of the Industrial Long Run*, Cambridge: Cambridge University Press.

Pasinetti, L. L. and Spaventa, L. 1960. 'Verso il superamento della modellistica aggregata nella teoria dello sviluppo economico', *Rivista di politica economica*, 50, 1749–1781, September–October 9–10.

Scarf, H. 1960. 'Some Examples of Global Instability of the Competitive Equilibrium', *International Economic Review*, 1(3), 157–172.

Sinha, A. 2016. *A Revolution in Economic Theory: The Economics of Piero Sraffa*, London and New York: Palgrave Macmillan.

Smith, A. 1776. *An Inquiry into the Nature and Causes of the Wealth of Nations*, General Editors R. H. Campbell and A. S. Skinner, Textual Editor W. B. Todd, Vol. I, Oxford: Oxford University Press, 1976.

Sraffa, P. 1926. 'The Laws of Returns Under Competitive Conditions', *Economic Journal*, 36, 535–550.

Steuart, J. 1767. *An Inquiry into the Principles of Political Economy*, Edited and with an introduction by A. S. Skinner, Edinburgh and London: Oliver and Boyd, 1966.

Chapter 2

History, logic and narrative in pedagogy

C.T. Kurien[1]

The setting

Visualize a classroom situation – an undergraduate course in economics. Among the social sciences and humanities economics is still one of the favourites: perhaps it has greater employment opportunities, or there is much discussion in the media on economic issues. The students, of course, talk about prices, certainly about demonetization if that is the latest topic of media discussion and show off their debit/credit cards. They probably discuss some of these matters too, but in the language of daily life, because these are issues of day-to-day experience. But with rare exceptions none of them aspires to be a professional economist.

The teacher, on the other hand, is a member of the economic profession, an academic whose approach to the subject is different and who speaks the language of the profession. Consider further that it is neoclassical economics that is being taught, as is the case in practically all Indian universities and colleges. The textbook is one of the most widely used, not only in the country but in most parts of the English-speaking world. (It used to be Alfred Marshall's *Principles of Economics* in the early part of the 20th century; by the middle of that century Paul Samuelson's *Economics* replaced it. I understand that the latest favourite is Gregory Mankiw's *Principles of Economics*.) There is much in common between the language of the textbook and what the students already know – prices, markets and the like. But the textbook also has diagrams, equations and other terminologies – 'equilibrium' for instance – not familiar to the students. The teacher assumes that his/her responsibility is to 'raise the level of discourse' of the students, and perhaps to bring to their notice some inter-connections that are not familiar to the untutored. He/she, therefore, places before the students what 'theory' offers, essentially explanations for what is taken for granted. Everybody knows, for instances, that an increase in demand leads to an increase in prices, but why is it so? A diagram is introduced with appropriate supply and demand curves, the equilibrium price that they determine; and how the price goes up when demand 'shifts'.

In economics, therefore, the central pedagogic problem is of the nature of narrative – the narrative of daily life *versus* the narrative of theory and it arises mainly because economics is so intimately linked up with daily life.

Two traditions in economics

To elaborate the pedagogic issue mentioned, I make a twofold classification of the many 'schools' in economics. The first is where the emphasis is on real life issues with a variety of procedures used to provide coherence to those issues, including their interconnections. This may be referred to as the 'substantive' approach. The second has its emphasis on formal aspects and logical derivations and hence referred to as the 'formal' tradition. In what follows I am relying on the history of our discipline, taking Adam Smith's *The Wealth of Nations* as the typical example of the former and neoclassical economics to illustrate the latter concentrating on one of its earliest versions given by Leon Walras and sub- sequently expounded by mid-20th-century scholars, principally by Kenneth Arrow, Gerard Debreu, T.C. Koopmans and others.

Announcing the substantive thrust of the work is the title that Smith gave to his work – *An Inquiry into the Nature and Causes of the Wealth of Nations*, a practical question that was everybody's concern when the book was written. Smith explicitly linked up the individual's desire to improve his conditions and the possibility to enhance the wealth and prosperity of society. However, this individual is no isolated Robinson Crusoe; he is part of a larger society of social classes, of the day-labourers, landlords, merchants and masters. These social classes are recognized without making any attempt to problematize the concept of 'class'. Indeed, a long list of occupations are brought in as and when required – menial servant, baker, butcher, brewer, master and workman, farmer, smith, carpenter, . . . players, buffoons, opera singers, the sovereign are all there 'real people within the constraints of existing institutions' as a recent writer has aptly put it (Deane 1978: 10). Real life activities are described in rich detail too as in the case of the pin-making. In fact, another well-known economic writer of a later generation, J.B. Say ([1803] 1971: xix) considered the *Wealth of Nations* an 'immethodological assemblage of the soundest principles of political economy, supported by luminous illustrations . . . an irregular mass of curious and original speculations, and of known and demonstrated truths!'

Though rich in descriptive accounts, Smith was not stopping there. After tracing the 'eighteen distinct operations' required to produce pins from metal wires, Smith goes on to show why the division of labour results in a much larger output of pins in a day. It results from three different circumstances: 'first to the increase of dexterity in every particular workman; secondly, to the saving of time which is commonly lost in passing from one species of work to another; and lastly, to the intervention of a great number of machines which facilitate and abridge labour, and enable one man to do the work of many' (Bk I, Ch I: 7).

Then there is the oft-quoted passage about exchange: 'Give me that which I want, and you shall have this which you want' followed by: 'It is not from the benevolence of the butcher, brewer, or the baker that we expect our dinner, but from their regard to their own interest' (Bk I, Ch II: 13). The invocation of this passage, however, is not meant to show what exchange implies, but to seek the approval of the Master that what underlies economic activity is self-interest. Two passages, one just before and the other just after the one above which give a clearer understanding of exchange as the 'propensity to truck, barter and exchange' are seldom referred to. Here is the first that comes immediately *before* the one quoted above: 'In almost every other race of animals each individual, when it is grown up to maturity, is entirely independent, and in its natural state has occasion for the assistance of no other living creature. But man has almost constant occasion for the assistance of his brethren, and it is in vain for him to expect it from their benevolence only'. The second passage from the very next page shows the connection between exchange and division of labour: 'The certainty of being able to exchange all that surplus part of the produce of other men's labour, which is over and above his own consumption, for such parts of the produce of other men's labour as he may have occasion for, encourages every man to apply himself to a particular occupation.'. So, there are three related factors that lead to exchange – the unique human propensity to co-operate with others, the division of labour that allows an individual to specialize on what he/she has the greatest capability and his/her awareness of his/her own needs. What Smith brings out by these different narratives of exchange is that it is an activity that results from the fact that the actions of an individual cannot be explained except with reference to other human beings in whose midst he/she lives, or that economic activities are essentially *societal*. Or, the subject-matter of economics cannot be spelt out in terms of the decisions of an isolated Robinson Crusoe.

The thrust on the societal nature of economics ('political economy', to be sure) can be seen throughout the *Wealth of Nations*. Here are two more examples.

> Kelp is a species of sea-weed, which, when burnt, yields an alkaline salt, used for making glass, soap, and for several other purposes. It grows in several parts of Great Britain, particularly in Scotland, upon such rocks only as lie within the high water mark, which are twice every day covered with the sea, and of which the produce, therefore, was never augmented by human industry. The landlord, however, whose estate is bounded by a kelp shore of this kind demands a rent for it as much as for his corn fields.
>
> (Bk I, Ch XI: 131)

The second is about the relationship between town and country. 'As subsistence is, in the nature of things, prior to conveniency and luxury, so the industry which procures the former must necessarily be prior to that which ministers to the latter. The cultivation and improvement of the country, therefore, which affords subsistence, must, necessarily, be prior to the increase of towns, which furnishes only the means of conveniency and luxury' (Bk III, Ch I: 337).

What is the nature of these statements? They are clearly logical derivations, but they are not merely exercises in logic. The derivations are from substantive premises which are observations from 'the nature of things'. They are also in the nature of derivations, but not generalizations derived by the inductive process based on the frequency of occurrence. In most cases, they are drawn from a single concrete instance. They make no claim to 'universality' and are, indeed, bound by the specificity of the real. They are, therefore, logical inferences from descriptive understandings of specific real-life instances, and so may be termed *analytical descriptions*.

Consider how the theme of the great work is developed. The first proposition is that the annual labour of every nation is the fund which originally supplies it with the necessities and conveniences of life. The productivity of labour depends on the division of labour. The division of labour is limited by the extent of the market. When the market spreads, it generates a commercial society where prices regulate economic activity. Prices of commodities consist of the wages, rents and profits which must be paid to produce it. The demand for those who live by wages increases with the increase in revenue and stock of the country. But the increase of stocks which raises wages tends to lower profits. Rent is a monopoly price. Wherever a person saves from his/her revenue, he/she adds to his/her capital. Capitals are increased by parsimony, and diminished by prodigality and misconduct. The greater part of the capital of every growing society is first directed to agriculture, afterwards to manufactures and last of all to foreign commerce. And so on.

Here is a chain of reasoning based not on arbitrary premises, but on the rudiments of social life, each inference then becoming the premise for a further inference, cumulatively producing a corpus of substantive understanding of the working of a reality that is becoming increasingly complex. There is no claim that the inferences arrived at are valid for all times and for all places, for, they are based on the concreteness of an ever-changing reality. The question is whether the *method*, one of inter-relating a wide range of disparate activities that human beings enter into in their pursuit of making a living (as also making a profit by some) and drawing inferences of a general nature is valid. We shall get back to this question after examining the second tradition in economics, the neo-classical tradition whose central claim is its 'universality'.

In its beginning this tradition too was contextual, the emergence in many parts of Europe of small farmers who were producing a wide range of goods, more than required for their consumption and hence entering the market to sell something and buy something else. The theoretical quest was to provide an explanation of this phenomenon of exchange and markets. It was not a complete break with the past either. Ricardo had already set the pattern. As Phyllis Deane has pointed out:

> Ricardo's technique of abstract reasoning from *a priori* postulates, his propensity for logical-mathematical rather than philosophical-historical theories had important implications for the methodology of orthodox economics away from the real world by encouraging the theorist to depend on

a type of theory which called for logical refutation rather than empirical verification.

(Deane 1978: 93)

Those considered to be the pioneers of this tradition are William Jevons, Carl Menger and Leon Walras. Jevons had noted:

As all physical sciences have their basis more or less obviously in the general principles of mechanics, so all branches and divisions of economics science must be pervaded by certain general principles. It is to the investigation of such principles – to the tracing out of the mechanics of self-interest and utility, that this essay has been devoted.

(Jevons [1871] 1970: 50)

Walras, the engineer-turned economist, was more definitive when he stated the aim was to convert economics into a 'physico-mathematical science'. As Walras was quite explicit about the science of economics, I shall concentrate on his exposition.

Science, according to Walras, had been demonstrated as the search for universals. In a scientific discourse, key terms derive their meaning in relation to other terms used in the discourse. He sets up a system of this kind. Thus, *social wealth* is defined as all things that are *scarce*. Scarce things are those that are *useful and limited in quantity*. Things limited in quantity are *appropriable*. Useful things limited in quantity are *valuable* and *exchangeable*, and so on (Walras [1874] 1954: Lesson 3).

On this basis, Walras sets up a system of exchange that takes place in a competitive market where all participants are individuals who try to maximize their utility. First, the case of exchange of two commodities by two individuals is considered.

The exchange of two commodities for each other in a perfectly competitive market is an operation by which all holders of either one, or both of the two commodities can obtain the greatest possible satisfaction of their wants consistent with the condition that the two commodities are bought and sold at one and the same rate of exchange throughout the market.

Walras then goes on to say:

The main objective of the theory of social wealth is generalize this proposition by showing, first, that it applies to the exchange of several commodities, for one another as well as to the exchange of two commodities for each other, and secondly, that it applies to production as well as to exchange. The main object of the theory of production of social wealth is to show how the principle of the organization of agriculture, industry and commerce can be deduced as a logical consequence of the above proposition. *We may say, therefore, that this proposition embraces the whole of pure and applied economics.*

(*ibid:* 143, emphasis on the last sentence added)

Menger too had arrived at the same conclusion via a slightly different route. He first established that marginal utility could explain the prices of goods and services for which there was demand from consumers that, therefore, were directly related to their wants or preferences. He further argued that means of production – or 'goods of higher order' as he called them – also came within the concept of economic goods because they too yielded consumers' satisfaction, though indirectly, through helping to produce things that do satisfy consumers' wants directly. Thus, they acquired their indices of economic significance and hence of exchange values) from the same marginal utility principle. Hence prices, established through the forces of demand via marginal utility, also governed the determination of costs (prices of the means of production) on the supply side. But since costs to the producers were income to households, the same marginal principle also automatically covered the phenomenon of income distribution. Production (or allocation of resources) and distribution, were thus seen to be two sides of the same coin. Commenting on this, Joseph Schumpeter remarked: 'The whole of the organon of pure economics thus finds itself thus unified in the light of a single principle – in a sense it was never before' (1954: 913).

Once the new theory came to the notice of other scholars, there were many attempts to demonstrate the claim of the pioneers that it was not merely 'pure theory' but directly applicable to concrete situations. Alfred Marshall's *Principles of Economics* late in the 19th century with its many pedagogic devices became and remained for a long time the best example of the application of the marginalist theory to practical problems, and entered into classrooms in many parts of the Empire. The mid-20th century saw fresh attempts to provide neoclassical theory with a fresh impetus of rigorous proof. The background may be briefly recalled. In the 1930s the socialist regime of the Soviet Union where the State had more or less complete control over the allocation of resources in production claimed that a rational allocation could be achieved without the mediation of the market. This was followed by a debate, essentially academic in nature, on the relative merits of a centralized allocation of resources and a decentralized allocation via the market responding to the preferences of the consumers. During the Second World War, the discussion remained muted, but the 'free world' returned to it during the Cold War that followed the end of the war. That led to the revival of the neoclassical tradition marked by much greater academic rigour. The famous paper by Kenneth Arrow and Gerard Debreu, 'Existence of an Equilibrium for a Competitive Economy' (1954), was a pioneer in this attempt. It was followed by a series of studies that showed the number of protective assumptions required to arrive at the conclusion that the competitive economy leads to a situation where no one can be made better off without making somebody else being worse off. These assumptions include not only that all participants are 'maximizers' of whatever they are stated to be maximizing, thus playing a role that is assigned to them by the theorists, or simply 'role-playing zombies'; that information is free and is equally available to everybody; that transactions are always between producers and consumers without the role of mediating merchants who are the most active agents in any real-life market situation; that production is subject to the law of constant returns that negates the possibility of cost per unit of production coming down when the scale of production increases; and much more. There is also a further assumption that is seldom spelt out – that of leaving out the nature of the property relations, i.e., the *ownership of resources* that influences (if 'determines' is too strong a word) the nature of consumer behaviour, the pattern of production and the sharing of the produce in real life situations.

The two traditions: two kinds of logic

To make a comparison of the two traditions, and, in particular, to examine the nature of the logic that underlies them, let me start with the neoclassical tradition that claims to be based on logic. Although the pioneers of that tradition, especially Jevons, was keen to argue that they were breaking away from the method of the classical writers, later assessment has been that it was Ricardo who initiated a new approach in political economy. Schumpeter, for instance, has said:

> His [Ricardo's] interest was in the clear-cut result of direct, practical significance. In order to get this he cut that general system to pieces, bundled up as large parts of it as possible, and put them in cold storage – so that as many things as possible should be frozen and 'given'. He then piled one simplifying assumption upon another until having really settled everything by those assumptions, he was left with only a few aggregative variables between which, given those assumptions, he set up a simple one-way relation so that, in the end, the desired results emerged as almost tautologies.
>
> (1954: 472–473)

It is this procedure of deciding on the conclusion to be arrived at and then searching for assumptions with the help of which to 'derive' that conclusion that underlies the logic that neoclassical economics relies on. The conclusion may be that, in equilibrium, the quantity supplied and demanded are equal and that that equality also shows the unique price. Or, that once the point of Pareto optimality is reached, it is not possible to improve anyone's position without making someone else worse off. These are attractive states to be arrived at. The issue then is what assumptions are necessary to lead to those conclusions. The realism of such assumptions is no issue because they are brought in for a functional purpose: the only question is whether the reasoning is valid. Thus, there are 'decision-makers' in the system, but the only decision they make (allowed to make?) is what the theorists want them to do, 'maximize their satisfaction' (whatever that means) buying or selling, or whatever. What theories of this kind state is that given the premises the conclusion follows. Formally: 'if P, then T'. The classic example is this: 'All men are mortal; Socrates is a man; hence, Socrates is mortal'. The first two statements are the Ps (postulates or assumptions) and the third is the conclusion (theory). It may be noted that the same procedure can be used to establish the opposite as well, that Socrates is immortal. All that is required is to change the first postulate. 'All men are immortal; Socrates is a man; hence Socrates is immortal'. If the intention is to uphold a conclusion, the procedure is to look for premises that will yield that conclusion.

This is both the strength and weakness of neoclassical economics. It can put forward the claim that it is a logically robust theory with 'universal' application (as Newtonian physics was claimed to be). The 'universality' of the theory gets misinterpreted, though, as a claim that it is applicable to all economies and at all times, whereas the proper meaning of 'universality' in this context is that wherever the premises are given, the conclusion follows. The progress of neoclassical economics has been achieved by scholars who have continued to search for assumptions that validate the conclusion (particularly those that are necessary to establish that the equilibrium that the theory claims is stable, unique etc.). That search sometimes leads to awkward positions as well. One of the earliest was pointed out by T.C. Koopmans fairly soon after the celebrated Arrow-Debreu paper was published. Koopmans was trying to ensure that the model of the competitive economy was not merely a mathematical exercise, but satisfied the minimum conditions of an actual economy such as the survival of the participants. 'The hardest part in the specification of the model', he stated, 'is to make sure that each consumer can both survive and participate in the market, without anticipating in the postulates what specific prices will prevail in an equilibrium' (1957: 59). Among the possibilities that he put forward was what he described as the 'hard-boiled' one 'to assume instantaneous elimination by starvation of those whose resource power prove insufficient for survival', which he did not recommend. He went on to say that the model 'would be found best suited for describing a society of self-sufficient farmers who do a little trading on the side' (ibid., 63). That proposal implies certain institutional arrangements that go against the claim of universality of the model. It also raises questions about ownership, property rights, etc. that neoclassical economics does not accommodate.

There is a further problem with the kind of approach to theory that neoclassical economics relies on. The scholars who work on it may know the crucial connection between the assumptions of the theory and the conclusion derived from them. However, the conclusion arrived at − in this instance the allocative efficiency that the market brings about − will soon be picked up by those who benefit by the manner in which markets actually function and will be used for purposes of propaganda, a case of theory becoming the supporter of ideology as has been clearly demonstrated by the neo-liberal support for a market-oriented economic policy. As Edward Fullbrook states in his recent work, 'A knowledge narrative may become *invert*, meaning that instead of being used mainly as means for explaining reality, its focus becomes itself. Turning away from the empirical phenomena that inspired it, it becomes transfixed with its own existence' (2016: 36). On neoclassical economics, Fullbrook adds,

> Neo-classical economics usually reads its models backwards. This gives the illusion that they show the behaviour of individual economic units determining sets of equilibrium values for markets and for whole economies. It hides the fact that these models have been constructed not by investigating the behaviour of individual agents, but rather by analysing the requirements of achieving a certain macro state, that is a market or general equilibrium.
>
> (*ibid.*, 95)

In passing on from the method in neoclassical economics to Adam Smith's economics we may recall the oft-quoted words of Albert Einstein: 'Pure logical thinking can give us no knowledge whatsoever about the world of experience: all knowledge of reality begins with experience and terminates in it' ([1933] 1960). As has been noted already, Smith based his economics on the experiences of real life. His vivid narratives are the day-to-day experiences of the real people of his days. What he did was to impose order on the narrative to provide coherence by bringing out the inter-connectedness of the disparate elements. There is logic in the narrative, but of a different kind from what was noted above. If postulational or formal logic is of the kind: '*If* this, then that', what may be described as *substantive logic* is of the form: '*Since* this, then that', making inferences from the knowledge of the real. What makes this possible is the inter-connectedness of the real which may lie latent, and the task of an analyst is to uncover it, polish it and present it. It is discovery, not invention. And, the discovery consists of bringing together materials that lie scattered, cleaning and ordering them, juxtaposing them with other material. Everybody knows from practical experience that if the sky is turning cloudy, rain will follow. But it requires competence of a different kind to point out that the phenomenon is also linked to the sea that is far away.

The distinction between the two types of logic can be brought out by reflecting on what the 'economy' is. Obviously, it consists of human beings with rich variety, material things of great diversity, decisions, actions and much more. Understanding it and analyzing it calls for intellectual effort. The procedure of formal logic is to reduce the variety and complexity of the entity as much as possible so that certain key relationships can be featured, i.e., to rely on the logic of concepts. The procedure of substantive logic is to bring out the inter-connections by preserving the richness and variety of the entity by focussing on the inter-relationships. It calls for much more familiarity with the actual working of the entity or the system.

Analytical narrative: the pedagogic challenge

We are back in the undergraduate classroom where we started. What kind of economics should form the basis of pedagogy? The preference of the teachers is likely to be to pass on neoclassical economics for a variety of reasons: most likely that is what they have picked up; it has the standing and prestige of a science; highly commended textbooks (including their Indian editions or Indian imitations!) are easily available. Some diluting of the science is inevitable, partly because unless the teacher had specialized in economic theory at the graduate/doctoral level he/she is unlikely to be familiar with the premises from which the conclusions of the theory are arrived at.

How helpful is this approach if the aim of an undergraduate course in economics is (as indicated at the beginning) to enable students to identify and analyze real-life economic problems? From that perspective, the approach of *analytical narrative* has much to be commended. A procedure for it must be consciously developed. During the days when I was teaching economics (1960s and 1970s) both at the undergraduate level (principles of economics) and at the graduate level (advanced economic theory), I emphasized logic in the latter but tried to develop a procedure for analytical narrative in the former. At one stage, I used (and shared with the students) three related questions to probe real-life economic issues: 'Who **owns** What?', 'Who **does** What?', 'Who **gets** What?' The emphasis on ownership was unconventional in courses in economics, especially 'Principles', but in the discussions in the classroom, it was not difficult to establish that while personal preferences certainly play a role in consumption and in the understanding the market phenomenon, economic power, arising from ownership, was more decisive in the demand for goods. Similarly, the 'Who does What?' question was used to bring out the role of merchants and intermediation in understanding markets in real life, that, however, neoclassical economics completely ignores, as also the asymmetry of information arising from it.

It follows that the pedagogic challenge at the undergraduate level is not to get students acquainted with economic theory, but to initiate them into the methods of economic analysis concentrating on real-life issues. Apart from concentrating on live, contemporary issues, the course must have two other components. The first is history, history of economic changes of the past and how they influence economic thought and analysis (including neoclassical economics in its historical context). The second is methods of collecting and processing raw material for analysis and interpreting of data that are made available. Devising a course that combines these three aspects is the pedagogic challenge in economics.

Note

1 This piece is a modified version of the inaugural talk that I was privileged to give at the workshop on 'Economics and Its History'. I draw upon my experience as a practitioner of the subject for over six and half decades as well as on my earlier writings, especially *Rethinking Economics – Reflections Based on a Study of the Indian Economy* (Sage, 1996) where I had discussed the need for economists to be 'bi-lingual'.

References

Arrow, K. and Debreu, G. 1954.'Existence of an Equilibrium for a Competitive Economy', *Econometrica*, 22, 265–290.

Deane, P. 1978. *The Evolution of Economic Ideas*, Cambridge: Cambridge University Press.

Einstein, A. 1933.'Essay on "Method of Science"', in Edward H. Madden (ed.), *The Structure of Scientific Thought*, Boston: Houghton Mifflin, 1960.

Fullbrook, E. 2016. *Narrative Fixation in Economics*, World Economic Association Book Series, Vol. 9, London: College Publications.

Jevons, W. S. 1871. *The Theory of Political Economy*, Edited by R. D. Collinson Black, London: Penguin Books, 1970.

Koopmans, T. C. 1957. *Three Essays on the State of Economic Science*, New York: McGraw Hill.

Kurien, C. T. 1996. *Rethinking Economics – Reflections Based on a Study of the Indian Economy*, New Delhi: Sage.

Mankiw, G. 1998. *Principles of Economics*, Fort Worth, TX: Dryden Press.

Marshall, A. 1890. *Principles of Economics*, London: Palgrave Macmillan.

Samuelson, P. 1948. *Economics: An Introductory Analysis*, New York: McGraw-Hill Company.

Say, J-B. 1803. *A Treatise on Political Economy*, New York: Augustus M. Kelly, 1971.

Schumpeter, J. 1954. *History of Economic Analysis*, New York: Oxford University Press.

Smith, A. 1776. *The Wealth of Nations*, London: Everyman's Library, 1991.

Walras, L. 1874. *Elements of Pure Economics, or, the Theory of Social Wealth*, Translated by William Jaffe, Homewood, IL: Richard D. Irwin, 1954.

Chapter 3

Theories of activity levels and growth before Adam Smith

Alex M. Thomas[1]

Adam Smith's 1776 book *An Inquiry into the Nature and Causes of the Wealth of Nations* is a foundational treatise in the science of political economy covering a wide range of topics, most notably, the theory of value and distribution and the theory of growth. There is a large literature on the theory of value and distribution and growth in Adam Smith, David Ricardo and Karl Marx, the three great classical economists (Dobb 1973; Eltis 1984; Bharadwaj 1989; Stirati 1994; Kurz and Salvadori 1995; Sinha 2010). The literature on pre-Smithian political economy, although growing, is relatively less voluminous (Aspromourgos 1996; Murphy 2009; Groenewegen 2002; Brewer 2010). This chapter offers a concise survey of the theory of activity levels and growth in four major pre-Smithian classical economists – Richard Cantillon, François Quesnay, Anne Robert Jacques Turgot and James Steuart. Those readers familiar with Dobb's 1973 book *Theories of Value and Distribution since Adam Smith* will recognize that it has provided the inspiration for this chapter's title.

Richard Cantillon (1680?–1734)[2]

Although Marx considers William Petty and Pierre Boisguilbert as the founders of classical political economy, it is in Cantillon's *Essai sur la Nature du Commerce en Général* (1755) that we first come across a 'system' of economic theory (Marshall 1920: 625; Schumpeter 1954: 562; Aspromourgos 1996: 112).[3] Moreover, it is in the *Essai* that we find the origin of the circular view of the economy between production and consumption (cf. Murphy 1986: 260; Thomas 2012). Cantillon divides the society into three broad classes: landowners, fixed-income earners, and 'entrepreneurs':[4]

> except the Prince and the Proprietors of Land, all the Inhabitants of a State are dependent; . . . they can be divided into two classes, Entrepreneurs and Hired people; and . . . all the Entrepreneurs are as it were on unfixed wages and the others on wages fixed so long as they receive them though their functions and ranks may be very unequal. The General who has his pay, the Courtier his pension and the Domestic servant who has

wages all fall into this last class. All the rest are Entrepreneurs, whether they set up with a capital to conduct their enterprise, or are Entrepreneurs of their own labour without capital, and they may be regarded as living at uncertainty; the Beggars even and the Robbers are Entrepreneurs of this class.

(Cantillon 1755: 55; cf. 43, 51–55)

The entrepreneurial class, which includes those with and without capital, are distinguished from the others because their incomes are uncertain.

Cantillon is emphatic that the primary use of land should be for producing necessaries to meet the customary needs of the society (cf. Aspromourgos 1996: 74–79):

As for the use to which the Land should be put, the first necessity is to employ part of it for the Maintenance and Food of those who work upon it and make it productive: the rest depends principally upon the Humour and Fashion of Living of the Prince, the Lords, and the Owner: if these are fond of drink, vines must be cultivated; if they are fond of silks, mulberry-trees must be planted and silkworms raised, and moreover part of the Land must be employed to support those needed for these labours; if they delight in horses, pasture is needed, and so on.

(Cantillon 1755: 7)

Once subsistence needs are met, land may be cultivated to meet non-necessary/luxury consumption. In Cantillon's system, '[t]he overplus [le surplus du produit] of the Land is at the disposition of the Owner', of which a fraction is paid to the State (Cantillon 1755: 7). And in his *Essai*, there is no discussion of technological progress.

To use latter-day terms, the consumption that is dependent on current income is induced and that which is independent of it is autonomous. Individuals with incomes greatly in excess of subsistence requirements can alter their consumption independently of current income by varying their saving behaviour. Moreover, the ability of individuals to engage in borrowing also contributes to the element of autonomy, of course, subject to the fact that repayments have to be made out of future incomes. In Cantillon's political economy, there is only one social class which is capable of engaging in autonomous consumption – the landowners.[5]

In Cantillon, the size and composition of aggregate demand is determined primarily by the size and composition of landowners' consumption: '[t]he Owner, who has at his disposal the third of the Produce of the Land, is the principal Agent in the changes which may occur in demand' (Cantillon 1755: 63). This is the first and direct route through which landowners' consumption affects overall consumption (both size and composition). According to Cantillon, there is a second route: indirectly through the other social classes, especially

when the entrepreneurs imitate the consumption of the landowners (cf. Aspromourgos 1997: 426–427):

> Labourers and Mechanicks who live from day to day change their mode
> of living only from *necessity*. If a few Farmers, Master Craftsmen or other
> Entrepreneurs in easy circumstances vary their expense and consumption
> they always take as their model the Lords and Owners of the Land. They
> *imitate* them in their Clothing, Meals, and mode of life. If the Landowners
> please to wear fine linen, silk, or lace, the demand for these merchandises
> will be greater than that of the Proprietors for themselves.
>
> (Cantillon 1755: 63; emphases added)

In a way, this observation by Cantillon is an early account of 'conspicuous consumption behaviour' (Murphy 1986: 259). On the other hand, labourers change
the size and composition of their consumption only out of 'necessity'.

In the economy Cantillon theorized, the commodity supplies adapt to the
commodity demands (cf. Brewer 1992: 64; Aspromourgos 1996: 84). To obtain
increased commodity supplies, there has to be increased utilization of land and/
or an increase in labour supply. Hence, both the demand for land and the
demand for labour are derived from the demand for commodities. As Cantillon writes, 'the Labourers, Handicraftsmen and others who gain their living by
work, must proportion themselves in number to the employment and demand
for them in Market Towns and Cities' (Cantillon 1755: 25; also 23). But note
that Cantillon does not have a theory of output as a whole. And nor does he
have any explicit or implicit[6] account of aggregate activity levels, which makes
it difficult to provide a definitive answer regarding the link between land utilization and activity levels (see Cantillon 1755: 23, 63, 91). However, on extending Cantillon's logic of sectoral activity levels along with his counterfactual
statements regarding land utilization and activity levels to aggregate activity
levels, it can be argued that when there is an overall increase in the volume
of consumption across sectors, it will, over time, lead to an increase in the
employment of labour (for a detailed account, see Thomas 2018).[7] However,
an increase in labour supply is possible, in a closed system without technological progress such as Cantillon's, if and only if there is an increase in the land
utilized for cultivating necessaries. And Cantillon's theory of population states
that population growth is positively related to the demand for labour and the
availability of subsistence.

The landowners vary the utilization of land based on how much of necessaries (such as corn) to non-necessaries (luxury manufactures such as 'fine linen'
and finely wrought knives and forks) are to be produced. The ratio of necessaries to non-necessaries produced depends on the subsistence requirements of the
population and the total available land.[8] Aggregate consumption and employment of labour can increase, with landowners' consumption demand playing a
leading role, until a certain proportion is reached at which point no increase

in luxury manufactures is possible without a reduction in corn cultivation (cf. Spengler 1942: 126 for such a proportion). There is no explicit mention of such a proportion in the *Essai* although the following counterfactual provides a strong hint: 'if . . . the Prince, or the Proprietors of Land, cause the Land to be used for other purposes than the upkeep of the People . . . the People will necessarily diminish in number. Some will be forced to leave the country for lack of employment' (Cantillon 1755: 73).

Among the modern commentators on Cantillon, the role of consumption in determining the *composition* of aggregate output is well recognized. However, there is no clear consensus amongst them on the link between consumption and size of aggregate output. Brewer argues that changes in consumer demand will result in a 'reallocation of resources' (1992: 196); Murphy also makes a similar observation: '[e]xpenditure determined the pattern of output in his [Cantillon's] schema, with resources being allocated to the production of commodities which the landlord wishes to purchase' (1986: 259). Similarly, Berdell points out that 'the pattern of demand determines the level of employment' in Cantillon and highlights the role of 'higher consumption standards' and 'demonstration effects' in determining activity and employment levels (2010: 215).

Cantillon observes that the setting up of manufactures especially in 'remote' or 'distant' areas 'would need not only much encouragement and capital but also some way *to ensure a regular and constant demand*, either in the Capital itself or in foreign Countries' (Cantillon 1755: 155; emphasis added). This suggests that Cantillon considers demand to be crucial in the determination of activity levels and that the provision of 'funds' ('fonds' in French) does not automatically generate a sufficient demand to validate the output. But note that Cantillon does not possess a clear understanding of capital (cf. Murphy 2015: xviii).

To sum up, in Cantillon, the thesis that emerges is that aggregate activity levels are demand determined as long as land is available; the formulation of this thesis builds on the demand-determined sectoral activity levels in Cantillon and his counterfactual statements on land availability, labour supply and activity levels. Moreover, labour supply is ultimately determined by labour demand, a chain of causation opposite to that found in marginalist economics.

François Quesnay (1694–1774)

Quesnay, the central figure in Physiocracy, advances Cantillon's conception of the economy as a circular process between production and consumption through several essays.[9] It is in Quesnay that we first come across an analysis of capital prompting Marx to label the Physiocrats as the 'true fathers of modern political economy' (Marx 1963: 44). Capital is distinguished into fixed and circulating, and profits are identified as the source of capital accumulation. Agricultural rents emerge as the net product in Quesnay's economics: '[t]he annual wealth which constitutes the nation's revenue consists of the products which, after all expenses have been deducted, form the profits which are drawn from landed property' (Meek 1962: 104). That is, by definition, net product can only be drawn from land (cf. Serrano and Mazat 2017: 8). In this excerpt, both agricultural profits and rents seem to constitute the net product.

Land is owned by the proprietary sector. It is the idea of land being able to generate a net product which gives rise to Quesnay's classification of sectors as productive and sterile.

> *Productive expenditure* is employed in agriculture, grasslands, pastures, forests, mines, fishing, etc., in order to perpetuate wealth in the form of corn, drink, wood, livestock, raw materials for manufactured goods, etc.
> *Sterile expenditure* is on manufactured commodities, house-room, clothing, interest on money, servants, commercial costs, foreign produce, etc.
>
> (Kuczynski and Meek 1972: i; '3rd edn')[10]

The outputs of the sterile sector enter as inputs into the productive sector and vice versa. This inter-sectoral relation between the productive and sterile sector is rendered explicit in the following sentence of Quesnay. 'The two classes spend in part on their own products and in part mutually on the products of one another' (Kuczynski and Meek 1972: 2; '2nd edn'); after all, the 'productive' class requires 'manufactured commodities' like tools and 'clothing'. A very brief account of the production and reproduction conditions of the economy Quesnay theorized is now in order. Landowners do not engage in production, but receive rents from leasing out land. Labourers in the agricultural and manufacturing sector earn wages which are just enough to meet their subsistence requirements. When agricultural profits are more than what is necessary for reproduction, there will be positive *net* capital accumulation in the economy assuming that (at least a part of) these profits are used for capital accumulation.

Quesnay's stationary economy is characterized by prices being at their *bon prix*,[11] with profits just sufficient for reproduction and therefore net accumulation is zero, as is the case in the *Tableau Économique* (cf. Serrano and Mazat 2017: 11). Output supplies exactly equal their demands as Quesnay assumes 'a medium situation in which the reproductive expenditure renews the same revenue from year to year' (Kuczynski and Meek 1972: I, cf. xi; '3rd edn'). In Quesnay's growing economy, the *bon prix* of agricultural and manufacturing commodities contain profits such that a positive net capital accumulation is possible. Net accumulation or investment implies an increase in agricultural capital, resulting in an increased supply of outputs (cf. Meek 1962: 243, 251; Groenewegen 1983: 7, 13, 21). As Eltis writes, the 'capital of the entrepreneurial farmer . . . determines everything else' (1984: 26, also see 25, 31 and 37). Owing to profits being greater than the minimum required for reproduction, there is net capital accumulation and hence economic growth. Moreover, on this growth path, there are no labour supply constraints nor any binding land constraints (Eltis 1984: 10). Cantillon did not conceive of any labour supply constraints either, but he is more open to the possibility of land supply as a constraint on activity levels than Quesnay.

The inter-sectoral equilibrium in the *Tableau* is characterized by the equality of outputs supplied and consumed in all the sectors (cf. Eltis 1984: 25). If the economy is growing on a steady equilibrium path, sectoral output supplies must grow in line with the growth of sectoral consumption. Quesnay appears to possess a vague idea of production and consumption growing in line with each other: '[a]n abundance of products is obtained through large advances; consumption and trade maintain the sales and market value of the products; the market value is the measure of the nation's wealth' (Kuczynski and Meek 1972: 17; '3rd edn'). A growth in net accumulation and production alone are not sufficient, as Quesnay recognizes, to ensure economic growth (cf. Barna 1976: 320).

> The interest of the cultivator is the mainspring of all economic operations and all agricultural progress: the more that products constantly sell at high prices, the more assured are the annual returns of the farmers, the more cultivation is extended, and the more revenue the land brings in, as much through the proper price of the products as through the increase in annual reproduction. And the more reproduction increases, the more the wealth of the nation is expanded.
>
> (Meek 1962: 164, 1n)

Therefore, it is clear that Quesnay grasps the positive link between profits, net capital accumulation and consumption (Meek 1962: 100).

Although Quesnay indicates the need for adequate consumption demand, he does not provide any explicit mechanisms by which the sectoral demands and supplies might equalize. On the nature of equilibrium in the *Tableau*, Meek concludes that 'the "equilibrium" depicted in the *Tableau* is hardly stable. . . . Quesnay did not imagine that there were any forces inherent in the system which would pull it back toward this "equilibrium" situation if it should happen to depart from it' (1962: 292–293). Similarly, Vaggi notes that '[i]n Physiocracy there is no automatic mechanism which guarantees that the entire production will be sold' (1987: 105, 15n). In short, Quesnay does not engage with questions relating to the stability of equilibrium in the *Tableau*.

In Quesnay's economics, it is the farmers who primarily undertake investment by taking recourse to their own saving. Perhaps owing to landowners' incomes being greatly in excess of their subsistence requirements, Quesnay recognizes that they could engage in saving. But he rightly considers landowners' savings to be a reduction of aggregate demand which has a negative impact on activity levels and growth (cf. Eltis 1984: 20).

> That the proprietors and those engaged in remunerative occupations are not led by any anxiety, unforeseen by the Government, to give themselves

over to sterile saving, which would deduct from circulation and distribution a portion of their revenues or gains.

(Kuczynski and Meek 1972: 4,
see also 3; '3rd edn'; cf. Meek 1962: 236)

No further details are provided especially with respect to the vehicles of savings or what happens to these savings eventually. According to Quesnay, 'the expenditure of wealth must necessarily precede the reproduction of wealth' (Meek 1962: 71), and leakages from the circular flow negatively affect activity levels and growth.

Workers' consumption forms an important component of aggregate expenditure. As in Cantillon, workers' consumption is evidently induced consumption (given the customary subsistence consumption per capita) whereas landowners' consumption is relatively autonomous. In the following excerpts from Quesnay, we notice that the consumption of the workers contributes towards maintaining the *bon prix* of agricultural products.

The peasant is useful in the countryside only in so far as he engages in production and makes a gain as a result of his labour, and in so far as his consumption of decent food and clothing contributes to maintain the price of produce and the revenue of property, to increase the number and ensure the gains of the manufacturers and artisans.

(Meek 1962: 83)

That the well-being of the lower orders is not reduced; for then they would not be able to contribute sufficiently to the consumption of the produce which can be consumed only within the country, and the reproduction and revenue of the nation would be reduced.

(Kuczynski and Meek 1972: 10; cf. 11; '3rd edn')

[When the] class of men [who cultivate the vineyards] . . . becomes very numerous, it widens the market for corn and wine, and maintains their market value, in the proportion that cultivation is extended and the expansion of cultivation increases wealth.

(*ibid*: 16)

While it might be tempting to ascribe underconsumptionist tendencies[12] to the above set of passages in Quesnay, these statements instead indicate the importance of a high *bon prix* in the agricultural sector and for his growth theory in general.

To reiterate, it is not clear how the growth in sectoral supplies and demands will tend to balance without making very special assumptions. The two very special assumptions are the following: (i) a decision to save is one and the same as a decision to invest whereby each farmer finances his investment entirely from his own saving, and (ii) there are no monetary leakages. However, from Quesnay's discussion of landlords' saving and workers' consumption, it is clear that the later issue of adequate aggregate demand is already implied but not consciously understood or satisfactorily theorized.

Anne Robert Jacques Turgot (1727–1781)

Turgot builds upon the economics of Cantillon and Quesnay. It is in his *Réflexions sur la Formation et la Distribution des Richesses* (1766) that we first come across the rate of profit as a return on capital and it being a permanent part of commodity prices. Turgot classifies the inhabitants of a society into three social classes: (i) productive, (ii) stipendiary and (iii) disposable; the cultivators belong to the first, the artisans to the second and the proprietors to the third social class (Turgot 1766 [1977]: 49). The cultivators and artisans, according to Turgot, fall under the 'non-disposable classes' (Turgot 1766 [1977]: 50). Much like Quesnay, Turgot labels the non-cultivators 'the sterile class' or 'the industrial or commercial class' (Turgot 1766 [1977]: 50, 90). Unlike Cantillon and Quesnay, Turgot states very clearly that the entrepreneurs in manufacturing earn profits proportional to their capital advances (Turgot 1766 [1977]: 70–71).

Capital originates 'from the accumulation of annual produce not consumed' (Turgot 1766 [1977]: 65). Capital, writes Turgot, comprises the total wealth of a nation along with the capitalized value of land: '[T]he total Wealth of a nation consists: firstly, in the net revenue of all landed estates, multiplied the rate at which land is sold; secondly, in the sum of all moveable wealth existing in the nation' (1766 [1977]: 88). In the following page, he emphasizes that '[i]t would be a very gross error to confound the immense mass of moveable wealth with the mass of money that exists in a State' (Turgot 1766 [1977]: 89), an error found in the works of the mercantilists. Both Cantillon and Quesnay also considered this an error.

How, Turgot asks, will 'the sum of all moveable wealth' increase in a State? His answer is through positive capital accumulation. And, the source of capital accumulation is saving from the annual produce.

> Whoever, either from the revenue of his land, or from the wages of his labour or industry, receives each year more value than he needs to spend, may set aside this surplus and accumulate it: these accumulated values are what is called *a capital*.
>
> (Turgot 1766 [1977]: 68; also see 64)

The only true wealth is the produce of the soil; the advances can thus grow only by the setting aside of part of what the soil produces, and part of what is not absolutely necessary for reproduction. It makes no difference whether this part is put aside by entrepreneurs of the industrious classes, or by the proprietors. . . . the entrepreneurs retain part of their profits and accumulate capitals which they use to expand their enterprises. . . . *The immediate result of thrift is the accumulation of moveable capitals*, and these capitals are only accumulated for the purpose of obtaining a revenue or annual profit, which can only be done by employing this capital.

(Turgot 1767 [1977]: 116; emphasis added)[13]

Note that it is not only the landowners and entrepreneurs who could save but also the workers who earn wages at customary subsistence levels by curtailing their consumption. As in Quesnay, entrepreneurs' saving, by way of a special assumption, is treated as one and the same as investment, thereby avoiding the need for an account of the coordination of saving and investment. Therefore, a positive saving out of profits is sufficient for economic growth (see also Brewer 1995: 629). And Cantillon's account does not contain any definitive statements on saving by the entrepreneurs although there is a discussion of landowners' saving and borrowing to undertake luxury consumption.

According to Turgot, the landowners have a passion for luxury consumption whereas it is 'especially the entrepreneurs' who engage in saving and capital accumulation.

The wage-receivers, and especially the entrepreneurs of the other classes, receiving profits proportionate to their advances, talents and activity, have, though they do not possess a revenue properly so called, a surplus beyond their subsistence; and almost all of them, devoted as they are to their enterprises, and occupied with increasing their fortune, removed by their labour from amusements and expensive passions, save all their surplus, to invest it again to their enterprise, and to increase it.

(1766 [1977]: 94)

From this passage, it is evident that entrepreneur profits are capable of being disposed in any manner without it affecting the 'simple reproduction' of the system; moreover, additional investment by entrepreneurs will lead to the system's 'expanded reproduction' (to use Marx's terms). More importantly, a part of the social surplus is realized when the entrepreneurs make profits.

How do the entrepreneurs get back their advances and a normal profit on the capital advanced? Turgot's answer: by proper sales.[14] Proper sales imply a sufficient volume of sales appropriate to production volumes and a proper sale price, which in a competitive environment will be at their 'fundamental value', a concept equivalent to the classical economists' natural price (Turgot 1767 [1977]: 120n).

As fast as . . . capital returns to him [the owner of capital] by sale of his products, he uses it for new purchases to furnish and maintain his Manufactory by this continual circulation; he lives on his profits, and lays aside what he can spare to increase his capital, and to direct it to his business, thereby increasing the amount of his advances, in order to increase his profits even more.

(Turgot 1766 [1977]: 70)

The Entrepreneurs either in Agriculture or in Manufacturing, draw their advances and their profits only from the sale of the fruits of the earth, or of the manufactured commodities ... the Entrepreneurs require that their funds should return to them immediately and regularly, in order that they may put them back into their enterprises.

(Turgot 1766 [1977]: 73)[15]

In other words, a positive net capital accumulation alone does not guarantee economic growth; it has to be validated by an equivalent growth in aggregate demand with commodity prices at their 'fundamental' levels. Despite recognizing the role of adequate demand, Turgot somewhat inconsistently maintains that the 'spirit of thrift' promotes capital accumulation and that luxury consumption has a negative effect on capital accumulation: 'The spirit of thrift in a nation continually increases the amount of capitals, luxury continually tends to destroy them' (Turgot 1766 [1977]: 81; also 84; cf. Groenewegen 1971: 336). Such a theoretical tension between investment and consumption demand is also visible in Quesnay.

Although Turgot recognizes the benefits of division of labour (see Turgot 1766 [1977], 45), he does not connect it with his growth theory in a systematic manner.[16] With the rate of profit secured as a component of fundamental price, Turgot is able to theorize, in a satisfactory manner, the process of economic growth in this sense: a positive rate of net saving (assumed equal to net capital accumulation) leads to economic growth so long as the extra production is validated by an equivalent consumption demand. However, Turgot does not pursue the possible difficulties that would arise from a deficiency of demand.

James Steuart (1712–1780)

In *An Inquiry into the Principles of Political Oeconomy* (1767), Steuart makes use of the concept of the surplus, engages more deeply with inter-sectoral relations than Quesnay and possesses a notion of demand, relatively autonomous of the current levels of income and output. Steuart defines agricultural surplus or 'net produce' as 'the quantity of food and necessaries remaining over and above the nourishment, consumption, and expence, of the inhabitants employed in agriculture' (Steuart 1767: 54). Similar to Cantillon and Quesnay, surplus is realized in land rents.

it is very certain, that all rents are in a pretty just proportion to the gross produce, after deducting three principal articles. First, The nourishment of the farmer, his family, and servants. Secondly, The necessary expences of

his family, for manufactures, and instruments for cultivating the ground.
Thirdly, His reasonable profits, according to the custom of every country.

(Steuart 1767: 53)

Notice the presence of inter-sectoral relations in this passage; necessary consumption includes commodities produced by the manufacturing sector besides
those produced by the agricultural sector (cf. Yang 1994: 10, n. 3). In Steuart,
agricultural output depends upon demand from the manufacturing sector and
manufacturing output depends upon demand from the agricultural sector (cf.
Eagly 1961: 54; Skinner 1963: 441; Yang 1994: 112–113). However, the equat-
ing of agricultural surplus with the net product places his economics closer to
Cantillon and Quesnay than to that of Turgot.

Owing to the inter-sectoral relations between the agricultural and manufacturing sectors, a growing agricultural surplus is favourable for manufacturing growth and vice versa. Apart from the necessary agricultural and
manufacturing outputs which are used up in the process of production, the
surplus outputs are mainly used for luxury consumption. In terms of incomes,
these correspond to rents and profits. Steuart writes that profits are 'either spent
in luxury, (that is, superfluity,) lent, or laid up' (1767: 53). The role of capital
advances in production is not explicit, nor is the role of profits in capital accumulation. It is evident, as Aspromourgos concludes, that 'Steuart does not have a
theory of net accumulation or saving' (1996: 143; also see Eagly 1961: 55, n. 2).

Steuart rightly identifies hoarding ('laid up' profits) – a particular form of
saving – as a possible leakage from the circular flow which would dampen
aggregate demand, and therefore lower output and employment levels (cf.
Akhtar 1979: 297; Karayiannis 1994: 47). This is not surprising given Steuart's
view of the economy as a circular process; as we have already seen, expenditure-
reducing leakages are considered harmful by both Quesnay and Turgot.

An increase in agricultural surplus alone does not guarantee economic
growth. The increase in supply must be in proportion to the demand of the
inhabitants. Steuart recognizes that

the augmentation [of agriculture] must be made to bear a due proportion
to the progress of industry and wants of the people, or else an outlet must
be provided for disposing of the superfluity.

(Steuart 1767: 40)

And that,

in proportion as foreign trade declines, either a proportional augmentation
upon home consumption must take place, or a number of the industrious,
proportioned to the diminution of former consumption, must decrease.

(Steuart 1767: 229)

He treats foreign consumption as a distinct source of aggregate demand (cf. Skinner 1963: 442; Yang 1994: 129–130, 135). The point to note is that alternative avenues of consumption are required in order to avoid a glut of supply. The two significant avenues mentioned by Steuart are exports and public expenditure. Hence, the statesman 'must do what he can, to constantly proportion the supply to the demand made for them' (Steuart 1767: 234). If agricultural production is greater than what can be consumed, it will discourage agriculture which negatively affects activity levels (Steuart 1767: 40–41). A glut in the commodity market will lead to unemployed labour and reduce the land under cultivation. Such a mechanism, as we have already discussed, is also present in Cantillon.

A disequilibrium between quantity supplied and demanded implies that 'either a part of the demand is not answered, or a part of the goods is not sold' (Steuart 1767: 190). The latter is what Steuart emphasizes – the possibility of a glut. When quantity supplied is greater than the quantity demanded,

> the balance is *overturned*; because this diminishes the reasonable profits, or perhaps, indeed, obliges the workmen to sell below prime cost.[17] The effect of this is, that the workmen fall into distress, and that industry suffers a discouragement; and this effect is certain.
>
> (Steuart 1767: 191–192)

In other words, demand deficiency, through a similar process as in Quesnay, leads to a fall in prices and profits and thereby dampens output and employment levels (Yang 1994: 104–107; cf. Karayiannis 1994: 43; Stirati 1994: 93). Since there is no automatic tendency towards full employment, the need arises for 'control' and 'management' of the economy.[18]

In the following rather lengthy but very crucial passage, Steuart explains the causal link between 'effectual demand' and agricultural surplus.

> We have said that it is the surplus produced from it [agriculture], which proves a fund for multiplying inhabitants. Now there must be a demand for this surplus. Every person who is hungry will make a demand, but every such demand will not be answered, and will consequently have no effect. The demander must have an equivalent to give: it is this equivalent which is the spring of the whole machine; for without *this* the farmer will not produce any surplus, and consequently he will dwindle down to the class of those who labour for actual subsistence. The poor, who produce children, make an ineffectual demand, and when they cannot increase the equivalent, they divide the food they have with the newcomers, and prove no encouragement to agriculture. By dividing, the whole become ill fed, miserable, and thus extinguish. Now because it is the *effectual* demand, as I may call it, which makes the husbandman labour for the sake of the

equivalent, and because this demand increases, by the multiplication of those who have an equivalent to give, therefore I say that multiplication is the cause, and agriculture the effect.

(Steuart 1767: 117)

Income, therefore, is what converts 'demand' into 'effectual demand' which is implicit in his reference to 'the poor' who lack income and therefore 'make an ineffectual demand'. Although Steuart writes that 'multiplication is the cause' of growth, this is not correct because, as Steuart himself notes, it is the 'multiplication' of people *with* the ability to pay that causes growth.

Apart from income, 'taste' can be seen as another channel capable of increasing 'effectual demand'. This, if visualized as autonomous of current incomes, becomes similar to the autonomous consumption of landlords highlighted in Cantillon. The link between taste, demand and activity levels is evident in the following excerpt from Steuart.

We cannot therefore say, that trade will force industry, or that industry will force trade; but we may say, that trade will facilitate industry, and that industry will support trade. Both the one and the other however depend upon a third principle; to wit, a taste for superfluity, in those who have an equivalent to give for it. This taste will produce demand, and this again will become the mainspring of the whole operation.

(Steuart 1767: 151)

As Akhtar also observes, '[a]n increase in the farmer's propensity to consume luxuries induces a corresponding increase in the agricultural surplus – this aspiration effect is one of the most distinguishing features of Steuart's theory of economic growth' (Akhtar 1978: 63; also see Yang 1994: 102–103; Brewer 1997: 8). The 'third principle' can be read as Steuart dimly groping towards an autonomous demand notion, which would get him close to the Keynesian causation (cf. Aspromourgos 1996: 143).

While Steuart does identify income as the crucial link which transforms demand into 'effectual demand', he does not pursue this connection further. If he had, Steuart would have been moving in the direction of a multi-sectoral model based on the Keynesian principle of effective demand wherein demand and incomes are simultaneously determined.

Conclusion

The classical economists before Smith, with the exception of Cantillon, possessed a rudimentary but clear account of the necessary role of capital accumulation in determining activity levels. The idea that demand should validate supply is present in the concept of the circular flow, found in Cantillon, but given significantly greater clarity by Quesnay and it is visible in Turgot and incomplete in Steuart. Moreover, in all these accounts, it is (aggregate) demand which is the relatively autonomous variable. That is, commodity supplies adapt to commodity demands. In addition to demand (particularly elements of consumption demand) being the autonomous element, there is a considerable discussion of taste formation in Cantillon and Steuart which would be valuable in developing a classical theory of consumption along the lines of Duesenberry's (1949) relative income hypothesis. Lastly, it must be noted that the latter-day marginalist idea of a competitive economy's tendency towards the full employment of labour is absent – with labour demand adapting to labour supply – in the works of these classical economists; as a matter of fact, they posit that labour demand determines labour supply, the reverse of the causation found in marginalist economics.

Notes

1 An early version of this chapter was presented at the Azim Premji University Graduate Workshop on Economics and its History, November 17–19, 2016, Bengaluru, India. I acknowledge Tony Aspromourgos, Ajit Sinha and Limakumba Walling for their helpful comments on a subsequent draft.

2 Parts of this section are taken from Thomas (2018).

3 However, see van den Berg (2012), who argues that examining the *Essai* alone is inadequate to understand Cantillon's economics. The scholarly approach to study Cantillon's work today is to consult van den Berg's 2015 variorum edition. Alternatively, one can use the very reasonably priced Murphy (2015) edition alongside the 1931 Higgs edition.

4 Higgs translates 'entrepreneur' as 'undertaker' but we retain 'entrepreneur', the French term, in all the quotations.

5 Cantillon also mentions State spending as a source of demand (Cantillon 1755: 175), and ascribes autonomy to the consumption of the State (see especially Part I, Chapter XIV in the *Essai* entitled 'The Fancies, the Fashions, and the Modes of Living of the Prince . . . determine the use to which Land is put in a State and cause the variations in the Market-prices of all things').

6 Aspromourgos (1997: 425, 434) convincingly argues that there exists no theory of aggregate output; that is, necessary outputs are determinate but the surplus outputs are not.

7 The effects of increased production and income of some sectors vis-à-vis other sectors are also mentioned in the *Essai*. In general, there will be a movement of entrepreneurs to the high-income sectors (cf. Cantillon 1755: 163–165).

8 Labour is not a constraint in Cantillon because labour supply adapts to labour demand.

9 The essays have been translated and published by Ronald Meek in *The Economics of Physiocracy: Essays and Translations* (1962), which also contains Meek's articles on aspects of Physiocracy.

10 In 1972, M. Kuczynski and R. Meek published an English translation of the various 'editions' of Quesnay's *Tableau Économique*.

11 According to Quesnay, if the commodities 'are sold at a price which is high enough to yield a gain sufficient to encourage people to maintain or increase their production, they are at their proper price [*bon prix*]' (Meek 1962: 93).

12 See also Meek's essay entitled 'Physiocracy and the Early Theories of Underconsumption', where he does not find underconsumptionist ideas in the analysis of consumption in Physiocracy (Meek 1962: 313–318).

13 This passage is from Turgot's paper titled 'Observations on a Paper by Saint-Péravy on the Subject of Indirect Taxation' (1767), translated in Groenewegen (1977).

14 As was discussed earlier, Quesnay tried to address this question through his concept of the *bon prix* as his *prix fundamental* does not contain profits (cf. Thomas 2015: 31–32).

15 Compare this passage of Turgot with that of Quesnay for a striking similarity:

> the more that products constantly sell at high prices, the more assured are the annual returns of the farmers, the more cultivation is extended, and the more revenue the land brings in, as much through the proper price of the products as through the increase in annual reproduction.
>
> (Meek 1962: 164, 1n)

16 Aspromourgos (2009: 142) also notes the presence of division of labour and productivity gains in Turgot and rightly points out that he does not possess an account of 'ongoing technological progress'.

17 Steuart's 'prime cost' is akin to Cantillon's 'intrinsic value' – a measure of the cost of production (cf. Aspromourgos 1996: 135–136).

18 Yang (1994: 110–111) also discusses how the introduction of machinery leads to temporary unemployment in Steuart. For a rival interpretation, see Akhtar (1978: 66), who posits that full employment is a characteristic of Steuart's political economy.

References

Akhtar, M. A. 1978. 'Sir James Steuart on Economic Growth', *Scottish Journal of Political Economy*, 25(1), 57–74.

Akhtar, M. A. 1979. 'An Analytical Outline of Sir James Steuart's Macroeconomic Model', *Oxford Economic Papers*, New Series, 31(2), 283–302.

Aspromourgos, T. 1996. *On the Origins of Classical Economics: Distribution and Value from William Petty to Adam Smith*, London: Routledge.

Aspromourgos, T. 1997. 'Cantillon on Real Wages and Employment: A Rational Reconstruction of the Significance of Land Utilization', *The European Journal of History of Economic Thought*, 4(3), 417–443.

Aspromourgos, T. 2009. *The Science of Wealth: Adam Smith and the Framing of Political Economy*, London: Routledge.

Barna, T. 1976. 'Quesnay's Model of Economic Development', *European Economic Review*, 8(4), 315–338.

Berdell, J. 2010. 'An Early Supply-Side – Demand-Side Controversy: Petty, Law, Cantillon', *Journal of Economic Perspectives*, 24(4), 207–217.

Bharadwaj, K. 1989. *Themes in Value and Distribution: Classical Theory Reappraised*, London: Unwin Hyman.

Brewer, A. 1992. *Richard Cantillon: Pioneer of Economic Theory*, London: Routledge.

Brewer, A. 1995. 'The Concept of Growth in Eighteenth-Century Economics', *History of Political Economy*, 27(4), 609–638.

Brewer, A. 1997. 'An Eighteenth-Century View of Economic Development: Hume and Steuart', *European Journal of the History of Economic Thought*, 4(1), 1–22.

Brewer, A. 2010. *The Making of the Classical Theory of Economic Growth*, London: Routledge.

Cantillon, R. 1755. *Essai sur la Nature du Commerce en Général*, Edited by H. Higgs with an English translation and other material, London: Palgrave Macmillan, for the Royal Economic Society, 1931.

Dobb, M. 1973. *Theories of Value and Distribution since Adam Smith: Ideology and Economic Theory*, Cambridge: Cambridge University Press.

Duesenberry, J. 1949. *Income, Saving and the Theory of Consumer Behavior*, Cambridge: Harvard University Press.

Eagly, R. V. 1961. 'Sir James Steuart and the "Aspiration Effect"', *Economica*, New Series, 28(109), 53–61.

Eltis, W. 1984. *The Classical Theory of Economic Growth*, London: Palgrave Macmillan.

Groenewegen, P. D. 1971. 'A Re-Interpretation of Turgot's Theory of Capital and Interest', *The Economic Journal*, 81(322), pp. 327–340.

Groenewegen, P. D. ed. 1977. *The Economics of A. R. J. Turgot*, The Hague: Martinus Nijhoff.

Groenewegen, P. D. 1983. *Quesnay. Farmers 1756 and Turgot. Sur la Grande et la Petite Culture*, Edited and translated with an introduction, Reprints of Economic Classics, series 2, no. 2, Sydney: University of Sydney.

Groenewegen, P. D. 2002. *Eighteenth-Century Economics: Turgot, Beccaria and Smith and Their Contemporaries*, London: Routledge.

Karayiannis, A. D. 1994. 'Sir James Steuart on the Managed Market', in D. Reisman (ed.), *Economic Thought and Political Theory*, Boston: Kluwer Academic Publishers.

Kuczynski, M. and Meek, Ronald. 1972. *Quesnay's Tableau Economique*, London: Palgrave Macmillan, Augustus M. Kelley.

Kurz, H. D. and Salvadori, Neri. 1995. *Theory of Production: A Long-Period Analysis*, Cambridge: Cambridge University Press.

Marshall, A. 1890. *Principles of Economics*, 8th edition, London: Palgrave Macmillan, 1920.

Marx, K. 1861–1863. *Theories of Surplus-Value* (Volume IV of *Capital*), Part I, Moscow: Progress Publishers, 1963.

Meek, R. L. 1962. *The Economics of Physiocracy: Essays and Translations*, London: George Allen & Unwin.

Murphy, A. E. 1986. *Richard Cantillon: Entrepreneur and Economist*, Oxford: Clarendon Press.

Murphy, A. E. 2009. *The Genesis of Macroeconomics: New Ideas from Sir William Petty to Henry Thornton*, Oxford: Oxford University Press.

Murphy, A. E. ed. 2015. *Richard Cantillon: Essay on the Nature of Trade in General*, Indianapolis: Liberty Fund.

Schumpeter, J. 1954. *History of Economic Analysis*, Edited by from manuscript by E. B. Schumpeter, London: George Allen & Unwin.

Sen, S. R. 1957. *The Economics of Sir James Steuart*, Cambridge: Harvard University Press.

Serrano, F. and Mazat, Numa. 2017. 'Quesnay and the Analysis of the Surplus in the Capitalist Agriculture', *Contributions to Political Economy*, 36(1), 81–102.

Sinha, A. 2010. *Theories of Value from Adam Smith to Piero Sraffa*, New Delhi: Routledge.

Skinner, A. S. 1963. 'Sir James Steuart: International Relations', *The Economic History Review*, New Series, 15(3), 438–450.

Smith, A. 1776. *An Inquiry into the Nature and Causes of the Wealth of Nations*, Edited by R. H. Campbell, A. S. Skinner and W. B. Todd, Glasgow Edition of the Works and Correspondence of Adam Smith, Vol. 2, Oxford: Clarendon Press, 1976.

Spengler, J. J. 1942. *French Predecessors of Malthus: A Study in Eighteenth-Century Wage and Population Theory*, Durham: Duke University Press.

Steuart, J. 1767. 'An Inquiry into the Principles of Political Oeconomy: Being an Essay on the Science of Domestic Policy in Free Nations. . .', 2 vols., London', in A. S. Skinner (ed.), *Sir James Steuart. An Inquiry into the Principles of Political Oeconomy*, 2 vols., Edinburgh: Oliver & Boyd, 1966.

Stirati, A. 1994. *The Theory of Wages in Classical Economics: A Study of Adam Smith, David Ricardo and Their Contemporaries*, Translated by J. Hall, Aldershot: Edward Elgar.

Thomas, A. M. 2012. 'Cantillon's Political Economy', *Economic and Political Weekly*, 47(31), 92–96.

Thomas, A. M. 2015. *Consumption and Economic Growth in the Framework of Classical Economics*, PhD thesis, Sydney: University of Sydney. https://ses.library.usyd.edu.au/handle/2123/14130.

Thomas, A. M. 2018. 'Consumption and Activity Levels in Cantillon's *Essai*', *History of Economic Ideas*, 26(1), 11–29.

Turgot, A. R. J. 1766. 'Reflections on the Formation and Distribution of Wealth', in Groenewegen (ed.), *The Economics of A. R. J. Turgot*, pp. 43–95, 1977.

Turgot, A. R. J. 1767. 'Observations of a Paper by Saint-Péravy', in Groenewegen (ed.), *The Economics of A. R. J. Turgot*, pp. 109–122, 1977.

Vaggi, G. 1987. *The Economics of François Quesnay*, London: Palgrave Macmillan.

van den Berg, R. 2012. '"Something Wonderful and Incomprehensible in Their Economy": The English Versions of Richard Cantillon's *Essay on the Nature of Trade in General*', *European Journal of the History of Economic Thought*, 19(6), 868–907.

van den Berg, R. ed. 2015. *Richard Cantillon's Essay on the Nature of Trade in General: A Variorum Edition*, London: Routledge.

Yang, H-S. 1994. *The Political Economy of Trade and Growth: An Analytical Interpretation of Sir James Steuart's Inquiry*, Aldershot: Edward Elgar.

Chapter 4

From 'change' to 'difference'
Sraffa's reinterpretation of classical economics

Ajit Sinha[1]

Introduction

Classical economists were mainly concerned with the *dynamics* of an economic system. Adam Smith was interested in measuring the 'real change' in nominal GDPs over a period of time and David Ricardo was interested in measuring changes in the rates of wages, profits and rents over a period of time. Both of them tried to relate these changes to the ultimate cause of value. In this chapter I will argue that the notions of 'change' and 'ultimate cause' were the epistemological foundations of both Adam Smith's and David Ricardo's theoretical frames with regard to the relations between values and distribution of income. The problem of the invariable scale or the 'invariable measure of value' got entangled with the notion of the 'ultimate cause', which eluded a solution. Sraffa, at an early stage, realized this problem. He decided to cut the classical theory of value from its roots in the notions of 'change' and 'ultimate cause' and establish it on an epistemological foundation of 'difference' and 'simultaneous relations'. This approach succeeds in preserving a fundamental classical proposition that the distribution of income can be separated from price determination.

Adam Smith

Adam Smith (1981 [1776]) identified the real wealth of a nation with the real goods produced and argued that the wealth of a nation would rise only if the total labour employed to produce goods rises or the productivity of labour that is employed in producing goods rises or both. Thus the cause of wealth was identified with labour and its productivity. Now, the next question was how to compare or measure the rise or fall in the real wealth of a nation over a period of time. Since the total goods produced in a nation are heterogeneous in nature, they cannot be added up together to get a homogeneous measure of real wealth and compared with each other. A comparison of their measure in terms of their total nominal value is not satisfactory because of price variations of the goods, which must be excluded in comparing the changes in real terms.

Now, instead of finding a solution to this problem in terms of index numbers, Smith tried to find a solution in the 'original or ultimate cause' of the value of a commodity. Since then the problem of the measure of 'real value', i.e., the *scale* to measure the value of commodities, got entangled with the problem of 'ultimate cause' of value in classical economics. In general, Smith analyzes production as ultimately a relation between Man and Nature. The flip side of production is the appropriation of Nature as income. The income so produced is necessarily appropriated by the labourer or divided among the population according to the positions they occupy in the process of production. It is the question of the relation that the value of a commodity forms with production on one hand and its appropriation on the other that constitutes the theoretical problematic of Smith's theory of value in the static context.

As mentioned earlier, Smith rejected comparison of nominal GDPs on the grounds of price variations of commodities, which includes the money-commodity that is used to measure the nominal GDP. This is where Smith confronts the problem of a standard of value, that is, a scale that measures wealth (or aggregate income) that itself remains unaffected by price movements over periods of time. Smith reasoned that this 'invariable measure' must lie outside the commodity set as all commodities are liable to price movements over time.

This problem takes Smith to the idea of a direct primordial production relation between Man and Nature as depicted in Figure 4.1.

In other words, the top arrow in the figure represents the 'real price' paid by the labourer for the income received. For Smith, income that is produced and appropriated belongs to the commodity set and the ratios in which commodities exchange with each other represent 'nominal price' of commodities when one commodity is used to measure the price of another. The 'real price' of a commodity, on the other hand, represents the sacrifice the labourer must make to acquire the commodity, i.e., the amount of time a labourer must work to acquire the commodity. Now, let us suppose that a labourer 'A' spends eight hours of labour to kill a beaver then the 'real price' of a beaver to A is eight hours of labour. Similarly, if a labourer 'B' takes eight hours of labour to kill two deer then the 'real price' of two deer would be eight hours of labour to B.

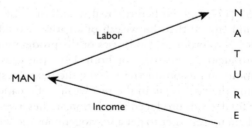

Figure 4.1 Primordial production relation. The top arrow represents Man's labouring activity against Nature and the bottom arrow represents his appropriation of Nature as the product of his labour.

Source: Author

On the assumption that both the hunters are equally skilled in killing the two animals and work with equal intensity, Smith concludes that it will be 'natural' for one beaver to exchange for two deer in this case. Here a rule for determining 'nominal price' (the price of beaver in terms of deer) is apparently found in the determination of the 'real price' of commodities separately against the sacrifice of labour:

> In the early and rude state of society which precedes both the accumulation of stock and the appropriation of land, the proportion between the quantities of labour necessary for acquiring different objects seems to be the only circumstance which can afford any rule for exchanging them for one another. If among a nation of hunters, for example, it usually costs twice the labour to kill a beaver which it does to kill a deer, one beaver should naturally exchange for or be worth two deer. It is natural that what is usually the produce of two days or two hours labour, should be worth double of what is usually the produce of one day's or one hour's labour.
>
> (Smith [1776] 1981: 65)

At this stage, Smith introduces another nodal point in the relationship between the 'real' and the 'nominal' price. Smith argues that the exchange of one beaver for two deer can also be represented as one beaver for eight hours of labour of B and two deer for eight hours of labour of A. The argument boils down to this: A's willingness to give up one beaver for two deer amounts to A's willingness to work eight hours for whoever offers two deer to him, as the 'real price' of two deer is eight hours of labour to him. Thus the 'real price' of any commodity is the amount of labour-time of others it can command:

> Labour was the first price, the original purchase-money that was paid for all things. It was not by gold or by silver, but by labour, that all the wealth of the world was originally purchased; and its value, to those who possess it and who want to exchange it for some new production, is precisely equal to the quantity of labour which it can enable them to purchase or command.
>
> (pp. 47–48)

The two definitions of 'real price' are, however, not identical. The first case, which defines 'real price' on the basis of direct expenditure of labour in production as a sacrifice, leads us to conclude that the wealth of a nation or its 'real' GDP would increase only if the total labour expenditure in the economy increases. Now, this would be a satisfactory measure for the changes in real GDP if we assume no technical change or changes in the productivity of labour. But what if GDP in terms of real goods increases due to increase in labour productivity and not just employment of labour? The first definition is not able to capture this phenomenon. However, from the point of view of the second definition, a rise in labour productivity would result in the rise in the real GDP if the command of labour by every unit of a commodity remains the same – in this case, the 'real price' of commodities remain the same but their total number increases.

This was perhaps the reason Smith felt that he had to move from the first definition to the second definition of 'real price' of a commodity and keep the 'real price' constant while measuring a change in GDP. Smith does recognize that wages also vary over a period of time and a rise and fall in wages would reflect in changes in 'real' GDP if it is measured against the command of labour.

In this case, however, he claims that those changes in GDP must be reckoned as purely nominal changes and therefore the 'current' GDP measure must be adjusted by the percentage changes in wages before comparing it with the 'base period' GDP:

> But though equal quantities of labour are always of equal value to the labourer, yet to the person who employs him they appear sometimes to be of greater and sometimes of smaller value. He purchases them sometimes with a greater and sometimes with a smaller quantity of goods, and to him the price of labour seems to vary like that of all other things. It appears to him dear in the one case, and cheap in the other. In reality, however, it is the goods which are cheap in one case, and dear in the other.
>
> (p. 51)

Now, let us suppose productivity of both the hunters double: A produces two beavers in eight hours and B produces four deer in eight hours, thus the real GDP of this economy has doubled. This will be reflected in terms of the 'real price' of beaver and deer if we maintain that both the hunters continue to receive either one beaver or two deer for their eight hours of labour. If that is the case, then we have a 'surplus output' in the system that is not appropriated by the labourers themselves. Let us suppose that a capitalist 'C' had advanced one beaver for the subsistence of A for his eight hours of labour and on that basis appropriated the two beaver produced and similarly a capitalist 'D' appropriates the four deer produced. Smith argues that in such cases when labourers themselves do not appropriate all the income produced, then the natural rule for determining 'nominal price' or exchange ratios between commodities can no longer be maintained on the basis of labour expenditure in the production of the respective commodities since the 'real price' of a commodity has no one-to-one relation with labour expenditure.

Once surplus emerges and with it a class of non-labouring individuals who appropriate the surplus, then it becomes clear that labourers may not be willing to exchange their labour directly with any particular commodity that is in possession of the non-labouring class. In that case, how can the 'real value' or 'real price' of a commodity be determined? At this stage, Smith suggests that one can conceive that wages are given in terms of 'corn', which remain fixed over time.

Now, let us assume that agriculture sector produces a homogeneous good called 'corn' and that the capitalists advance one ton of corn to hire x hours of labour on a unit of land that produces three tons of corn. Smith argues that capitalists receive their income as a percentage of their capital investment and this is determined in the context of economic growth, but at any given time it is a known datum. So, suppose the rate of profits happens to be 100%, then Smith argues that the residual one ton of corn must turn out to be the rent per unit of land. Given these three division of the total income produced, it is clear that the real value of the wages, profits and rent in this case turns out to be x hours of labour each and the total 'real value' of the GDP turns out to be 3x hours of labour. In this simple case, it is also clear that the 'real value' of one ton of corn is x hours of labour, which can be seen as made up of x/3 hours of labour as wages, x/3 hours of labour for profits and x/3 hours of labour for rent. We can complicate this case by introducing means of production. Smith argues that a production equation of any commodity, in the final analysis, can be reduced to a direct relation between Labourer and Nature and thus all capital investment can be reduced to a long series of wages. From here on, Smith generalizes this proposition by arguing that the 'real value' of any commodity is determined by adding up the direct and indirect wages, profits and rent that its production generates in terms of command of labour. It should, however, be noted that the rent of land is determined as a residual in the corn sector and reflects the productivity of land (on this issue, see Sinha 2010a):

> In the price of corn, for example, one part pays the rent of the landlord, another pays the wages or maintenance of the labourers and labouring cattle employed in producing it, and the third pays the profit of the farmer. These three parts seem either immediately or ultimately to make up the whole price of corn. A forth part, it may perhaps be thought, is necessary. In the price of corn, for example, one part pays the rent of the landlord, another pays the wages or for replacing the stock of the farmer, or for compensating the wear and tear of his labouring cattle, and other instruments of husbandry. But it must be considered that the price of any instrument of husbandry, such as labouring horse, is itself made up of the same three parts; the rent of the land upon which he is reared, the labour of tending and rearing him, and the profits of the farmer who advances such a rent of this land, and the wages of this labour. Though the price of the corn, therefore, may pay the price as well as the maintenance of the horse, the whole price still resolves itself either immediately or ultimately into the same three parts of rent, labour, and profit.
>
> (p. 68)

Let us now suppose that the productivity of labour doubles in our simple corn sector. This would imply that one ton of corn capital investment that hires x hours of labour would now produce six tons of corn. Given that the rate of profits that prevails in this economy is 100%, the total profits appropriated by the capitalists would be one ton of corn as well. Thus the rent will rise to four tons of corn per unit of land and the total real GDP would rise to 6x hours of labour. But what if productivity doubles in the industrial or non-corn sector? Now, if the productivity in the corn sector has remained the same then the rent per unit of land must remain the same. This implies that increased productivity in the non-corn sector must result in a fall in the price of the non-corn good vis-à-vis corn such that the increased output of non-corn good is completely absorbed by the fall in its 'real price'. This shows that implicit in Smith's theory is the centrality of the wage-good or agricultural sector. But this also shows that Smith's real measure of value is not able to capture all productivity gains and consequently increases in real goods production.

Let us now assume that productivity remains constant but the conventional rate of profits increases to 150%. In the corn sector, this would show up in an increased appropriation of corn by the capitalists to 1.5 tons of corn that would leave 0.5 tons of corn for rent. Since the rate of profits and rent throughout the economy must be uniform, this must result in the price of the industrial goods rising vis-à-vis corn to release some of the industrial goods from wage advances to meet the higher requirements for profits. This shows that a rise in the rate of profits at the cost of rent would cause the real price of industrial goods to rise and therefore increase the value of real GDP even though no changes in the real goods produced has taken place.

Hence Smith's invariable measure of value fails to play the role it was designed to play.

David Ricardo

Ricardo (1951 [1821]) was quick to recognize that Adam Smith's invariable scale was nothing more than replacement of precious metals such as gold or silver with corn as a unit of measure of commodity value and there was no reason to think that in the long run corn would be more stable than gold or silver. Ricardo criticized Smith for moving away from relating the theory of value with labour as an activity to income distribution. He argues that Smith was wrong in suggesting that the hypothesis that exchange-ratios of commodities are determined by the labour-time ratios spent in producing the respective commodities no longer holds once a non-labouring class arrives on the scene and demands a share in income produced. He showed that Smith's original hypothesis remains intact even if a positive rate of profits arises as long as the techniques of producing commodities have the same direct to indirect labour ratios, i.e., the industrial ratios of their total direct labour employment to total physical capital used in production, measured by the labour-time needed to produce them. Hence it is not a new share in national income that causes the original hypothesis to be modified (Ricardo 1951: 27). However, the hypothesis requires modification because in general there is no reason to assume that the ratios of direct to indirect labour-time for all the techniques of production would be the same for all the industries in the economy. And if that is the general case, then the requirement of equal rate of profits across industries for the long-term solution of the equilibrium or 'natural prices' must bring about a deviation in exchange-ratios from their labour-time ratios. This is because when the technical ratio of direct to indirect labour-time across the industries is equal then an equal percentage fall in wages would release proportionately equal income per unit of capital in all the industries to be distributed as profits. Thus the rate of profits in all the industries will remain equal without affecting the prices. However, if the technical ratios of direct to indirect labour are unequal across industries then an equal percentage fall in wages would release proportionately unequal income per unit of capital resulting in unequal rates of profits across industries if prices remain the same. Hence prices must be affected if the long-term equilibrium condition is to be maintained.

Even after acknowledging this, Ricardo, however, was not ready to abandon the labour theory of value. He argues that even though the equilibrium exchange-ratios deviate from their labour-time ratios, it could be argued that the *ultimate cause* of *changes* in exchange-ratios can be traced back to changes solely in the techniques of production or the labour-times needed to produce the commodities (Ricardo 1951: 46). In other words, Ricardo wanted to deny that changes in the distribution of the national income or the net output produced have any impact on the exchange-ratios of commodities. Ricardo, however, could see that the same cause that necessitates the modification in exchange-ratios of commodities from their labour-time ratios must also necessitate changes in the exchange-ratios of commodities when the rate of profits or wages rise or fall. So, how could he argue that it is solely the changes in techniques that explain the changes in exchange-ratios of commodities? Ricardo thought that the effect of changes in the distribution on exchange-ratios of commodities is only *apparent* and solely due to the fact that we have to use an arbitrary commodity as a standard to measure the changes in the exchange-ratios of commodities. He hypothesized that if we could find or theoretically construct a commodity that is not affected by changes in the distribution of income then it could be shown that exchange-ratios of commodities would remain unchanged in the face of changes in distribution of income when it is measured against this particular 'invariable' measuring standard. At one stage Ricardo almost identified the search for an invariable standard of value with the true theory of value itself: 'Is it not clear then that as soon as we are in possession of the knowledge of the circumstances which determine the value of commodities, we are enabled to say what is necessary to give us an invariable measure of value?' (letter of Ricardo to McCulloch, dated August 21, 1823, *Works IX*, p. 358).

This proposition of Ricardo is however logically false because changes in distribution affect relative values of commodities and thus logically there cannot be any commodity against which the relative values of commodities could remain constant in the face of changes in distribution. Evidently, Ricardo had finally come to this realization, as in a letter to James Mill, written six days before his untimely death on September 11, 1823, he states: 'I have been thinking a good deal on this subject lately but without much improvement – I see the same difficulties as before and am more confirmed than ever that strictly speaking there is not in nature any correct measure of value nor can any ingenuity suggest one, for what constitutes a correct measure for some things is a reason why it cannot be a correct one for other' (*Works IX*, p. 372, dated September 5, 1823).

But why did Ricardo try to establish that changes in what he called 'real or absolute value', i.e., exchange-value of a commodity measured against the invariable standard of value, can be traced back only to the original cause of value, which, in the final analysis, is the expenditure of labour? It is because Ricardo's project was to inquire into the *laws* that regulate the distribution of income with the progress in the *Wealth of Nations*. He argued that without the knowledge of the true doctrine of rent, for which he credits Malthus and Edward West, 'it is impossible to understand the effect of the progress of wealth on profits and wages' (Ricardo 1951: 5). With the help of his theory of differential rent, Ricardo tried to establish that the increase in the wealth and population of a nation leads to a rising trend in rent of land at the cost of rate of profits on capital. Now, if value could be determined by adding up wages profits and rent, as Ricardo interpreted Smith's theory to be, then this proposition may not be true, as a rise in rent could lead to a rise in the prices of all commodities leaving the rate of profits and wages unchanged (see Sinha 2010b for a critique of Ricardo on this point). However, if the labour theory of value is true then an extension of cultivation on less fertile land must lead to a fall in the rate of profits, if wages are held constant. On the other hand, leaving the rent constant, it can also be shown that a rise in wages must lead to a fall in the rate of profits and vice versa. For Ricardo, labour is the ultimate cause of value. Thus value should be independent of changes in distribution but changes in value due to changes in the expenditure of labour must have implications for distribution, since it is the value that constrains the relations between distributional variables. When Ricardo realized that, in the general case, prices of commodities are not given by their labour-time ratios, he thought that this was still not fatal to his project as what he needed was the ultimate cause of *change* in the values or prices of commodities, since his inquiry was focussed on the effect of changes in value on distribution due to rising difficulties in the production of agricultural goods. But once he realized that even in this case effects on values of changes in distribution cannot be removed, he blamed it on the arbitrary nature of the standard in which values or prices are measured and entertained the idea for some time that an 'invariable' standard, i.e., a standard that is not affected by changes in distribution, will simply remove all the distortions caused in prices by changes in distribution.

Piero Sraffa (1951), however, has a different interpretation of Ricardo's problem of the 'invariable measure of value'. In his highly influential 'Introduction' to Ricardo's *Principles*, which was written in collaboration with Maurice Dobb, Sraffa argues that Ricardo around 1814–1815 was working on the basic principle that 'it is the profits of the farmer that regulate the profits of all other trade' (1951: xxxi). According to Sraffa, Ricardo assumed that in agriculture both capital (including seed and wage advances) and products were the same goods, and thus a rate of profit in agriculture could be determined on the basis of the physical data without any need for a theory of value. And since, in a competitive market, an equal rate of profits must prevail, the prices of manufactures and other commodities have to be so adjusted as to allow the same rate of profits on their capital investments. In this framework, an inverse and proportional relationship between the rate of profits and the real wages can be directly observed through the microcosm of the agricultural sector. Apparently, Malthus had objected to Ricardo's reasoning on the ground that '[i]n no case of production, is the produce exactly of the same nature as the capital advanced. Consequently we can never properly refer to a material rate of produce. . . . It is not the particular profits or rate of produce upon the land which determines the general profits of stock and the interest of money' (letter dated August 5, 1814, quoted in Sraffa 1951: xxxi–xxxii). In the face of such criticism, Ricardo had to abandon his 'corn model', which opened him up to the problem of aggregating heterogeneous commodities, as the measure of capital required some device to homogenize a heterogeneous collection of goods. This led Ricardo to search for a general theory of value, which would then allow him to get a measure of the produce and capital in terms of their values. Thus the problem of value had to be solved before the question of distribution could be dealt with, as Ricardo in the early stages of the preparation of the *Principles* wrote to James Mill, 'I know I shall be soon stopped by the word price' (letter dated December 30, 1815, *Works VI*, p. 348, quoted in Sraffa 1951: xiv). Now, the labour theory of value establishes that prices are determined by technique alone and are not affected by changes in distribution. Hence, if labour theory of value could be defended as a legitimate theory of value then it can be shown that wages and profits must be inversely and proportionately related as the size of the net output remains constant when it is cut in different proportions. However, as we have seen earlier, Ricardo had to admit that in the general case values do get affected by changes in distribution, and therefore, in general, he could not establish that the size of the net output remains constant when distribution changes. It is Sraffa's contention that Ricardo maintained that such changes in the size of the net output due to changes in distribution arises solely because we take an arbitrary commodity as the standard to measure prices, and that commodity is also affected by the changes in distribution as other commodities are. He thought that an 'invariable measure of value' should ensure that the size of the net output remains constant as prices change due to changes in distribution (see Sinha 2017 for a detailed commentary on Sraffa's position on Ricardo). This brings Ricardo's problem of invariable measure closer to Smith's problem, in the sense that both are concerned with the changes in the size of the nominal GDP due to changes in distribution, but this also has no solution.

Piero Sraffa

Sraffa (1960) rejects the idea that one can *ultimately* reduce productive activity to the primordial act of production by going back and back in time. The reason for it is that if produced means of production acquired through exchange is used in producing any commodity, then no matter how far back we go in time there always will remain some *commodity residue*, and so a pure Man versus Nature situation cannot be theoretically conceived. The relevance of commodity residue becomes all important when we try to understand how the rate of profits on capital and wages are related, given a produced net income. It is clear that if one could reduce production to the primordial Man versus Nature relation then all capital investments can be reduced to a long-dated series of wage payments, and thus in this scenario the rate of profits must become infinite when wages are reduced to zero; however, if the commodity residue is taken into account then the rate of profits must reach a finite maximum when wages are reduced to zero given that some positive non-wage capital always must exist in physical form. Sraffa hypothesized that the finite maximum rate of profits of any given system of production that uses other commodities as means of production must remain constant when the rate of profits and wages vary. In other words, Sraffa hypothesized that the ratio of net output to total capital of any given economy must remain constant in the face of changes in prices due to changes in wages or the rate of profits:

> What is demanded of a model is that it should show a constant (constant with respect to variations of r) ratio between quantity of capital & quantity of product. If this can be constructed and proved to be general, a number of important 'consequences' follow.
>
> (Sraffa Papers, D3/12/16: 14, dated August 1942, quoted in Sinha 2016: 115)

Let us suppose we *observe* a simple three commodity economy after a cycle of production (a 'harvest' or an annual cycle with equal rotation time for all the industries), which is given by:

$$90 \text{ t. iron} + 120 \text{ t. coal} + 60 \text{ qr. wheat} + 3/16 \text{ labour} \rightarrow 180 \text{ t. iron}$$
$$50 \text{ t. iron} + 125 \text{ t. coal} + 150 \text{ qr. wheat} + 5/16 \text{ labour} \rightarrow 450 \text{ t. coal}$$
$$40 \text{ t. iron} + 40 \text{ t. coal} + 200 \text{ qr. wheat} + 8/16 \text{ labour} \rightarrow 480 \text{ qr. wheat}$$

In this case, the net output of the system is given by (165 t. coal + 70 qr. wheat) and the total capital investment by (180 t. iron + 285 t. coal + 410 qr. wheat). Clearly, at this stage the maximum rate of profits of the system, which is equal to net output/capital ratio (let's call it R), cannot be determined without the knowledge of prices; since the ratio (165 t. coal + 70 qr. wheat)/(180 t. iron + 285 t. coal + 410 qr. wheat) is a ratio of heterogeneous goods. Let us assume that all the industries receive their profits equal to the average rate of profits of the system, say r, which is an unknown. This can be represented in equation form as:

$$(90p_i + 120p_c + \ \ 60p_w) \ (1 + r) + 3/16 \ w = 180p_i$$
$$(50p_i + 125p_c + 150p_w) \ (1 + r) + 5/16 \ w = 450p_c \qquad\qquad (I)$$
$$(40p_i + \ \ 40p_c + 200p_w) \ (1 + r) + 8/16 \ w = 480p_w,$$

$$(180p_i + 185p_c + 410p_w) \ (1 + r) + w \ \ \ \ = 180p_i + 450p_c + 480p_w$$

where ps are the prices of respective commodities, r is the average rate of profits of the system and w is the wage rate. The system has five unknowns and three equations. Since prices are relative, one can choose any of the three prices and put it as the measuring standard by putting its value equal to one, say, e.g., $p_w = 1$ or any combination of commodities such as the net output $(165p_c + 70p_w) = 1$. Thus we have now four independent equations and five unknowns. If we take the value of w given from outside in terms of the measuring standard adopted, then we can solve for a unique set of all positive prices and the average rate of profits r (this result is ensured by Perron-Frobenius theorem). Notice that when we take $w = 0$, the solution of r that we obtain is equal to the maximum rate of profits of the system R, which is associated with a particular set of prices. Let us take $(165p_c + 70p_w) = 1$ as our measuring standard, thus the range of w is from 0 to 1. Now, as we go on changing the value of w from 0 to 1 in the above equation-system (I), we generate a series of different set of ps and rs as our solution sets. We notice that as the set of ps changes with changes in w, the ratio of net output to capital: $(165p_c + 70p_w)/(180p_i + 285p_c + 410p_w)$, or R, keeps changing as well. Thus it apparently refutes Sraffa's hypothesis, which was that the ratio of net output/means of production must remain constant with respect to changes in r or w. As we shall see later, Sraffa, however, succeeded in showing that his hypothesis is indeed correct, and the result we observed earlier is simply due to the arbitrary nature of the standard of measure we have selected.

We have seen that Ricardo had already established that if industrial ratios of direct to indirect labour were uniform for all the industries then changes in the rate of profits will have no impact on the relative prices of the commodities and the labour theory of value would correctly predict those price ratios. However, when the industrial ratios of direct to indirect labour happen to be unequal across industries then changes in the rate of profits would affect the price ratios to maintain the requirement of a uniform rate of profits in the system. The same reasoning holds for Sraffa's system of equations as well. If the industrial ratios of direct labour to means of production were equal for all the equations, then every fall in wages (starting from $w = 1$) would release just enough revenue in each industry to pay for profits at an equal rate without having to disturb the prices. However, if the proportions of the means of production to direct labour are not equal for all the industries then by the same logic prices *must* be affected, because at the old prices some industries would have a surplus of revenue and some a deficit after paying the rate of profits at the uniform rate and therefore, prices *must* change to remove these surpluses and deficits from the equations. It should be noted that the determination of equality or inequality of proportions can be made by measuring means of production by taking their values at any wage (say, $w = 1$), since when proportions are the same then changes in wages have no impact on the prices and thus on the proportions so measured. From this, it follows that if the proportions are not equal at one wage, they will not be equal at any wage.

The mathematical reasoning of the necessity of movements of prices with respect to changes in wages, when the proportions of means of production to labour are not uniform, reveals an important fact: since these 'surplus' and 'deficit' industries are results of differing proportions of means of production to labour, there would be a *critical* or *balancing* proportion of means of production to labour for which no 'surplus' or 'deficit' would emerge; i.e., if an industry that used this 'balancing proportion' of means of production to labour then in this industry the 'cause' of change in prices due to change in wages would be absent. The important point about this 'critical proportion' is that if it is a balancing proportion at one set of prices then it must remain 'balancing proportion' for all the set of prices throughout the range of w from 1 to 0. This is because by definition a fall in wages releases in this industry exactly the amount needed to be transferred to profits to pay for the new general rate of profits on the *initial prices*.

To prove this, Sraffa showed that any empirical input–output data of basic goods,[2] as we have taken earlier, can be converted to a standard system by simple algebraic manipulation. For example, if we rescale the coal industry by 4/5 and the iron industry by 4/3, we obtain a rescaled equation system (I), which is a standard system:

$$(120p_i + 160p_c + 80p_w) (1 + r) + 3/16 \, w = 240p_i$$
$$(40p_i + 100p_c + 120p_w) (1 + r) + 5/16 \, w = 360p_c \qquad \text{(I')}$$
$$(40p_i + 40p_c + 200p_w) (1 + r) + 8/16 \, w = 480p_w$$

$$(200p_i + 300p_c + 400p_w) (1 + r) + w \qquad = 240p_i + 360p_c + 480p_w$$

The standard system (I') is *unique* to the equation system (I).[3] Now, in our standard system (I'), we find that the value of the net output/capital ratio is well defined in physical terms, independently of the knowledge of prices; since (40 t. iron + 60 t. coal + 80 qr. wheat)/(200 t. iron + 300 t. coal + 400 qr. wheat) = 1/5 or 20%, no matter what ps happen to be. We call this the standard maximum rate of profits, R^*. Now, if we take our standard net output

$(40p_i + 60p_c + 80p_w) = 1$ as our standard of measure and give wages as fraction of this composite commodity, which Sraffa calls the Standard commodity, we will trace out value of all the rs associated with all the values of w from 0 to 1 independently of the knowledge of prices. This relationship is given by $r = R{\star}(1 - w)$, where $R{\star}$ remains constant with respect to changes in w and r. This shows that given w, r can be determined independently of prices as the value of $R{\star}$ is known and remains constant with respect to changes in w.

Since the equation-system (I') is derived from simply rescaling the equations of equation-system (I), both the equation-systems are algebraically equivalent. And therefore, the relationship $r = R{\star}(1 - w)$ must also hold for the equation-system (I), i.e., $r = R(1 - w)$, so long as the standard of measure for prices and the wages are taken to be the standard net product as above. Now, given w we can calculate r or given r, we could calculate w and plug these values in equation-system (I) to derive the set of prices that are compatible with the given r and w determined independently of prices. Thus with the help of the Standard commodity as the standard of measure, Sraffa establishes Adam Smith's fundamental proposition that the distribution of income is determined independently of prices and these given rates of distributional variables put constraints on prices to be such that the national income accounting must come out to be consistent with the *given* distribution of the national income. However, this standard has nothing to do with either relating changes in the national income or changes in prices to the distribution of national income or showing that the size of national income remains constant when distribution changes (see Sinha 2016 for a detailed exposition on the nature of Sraffa's theoretical contribution).

Notes

1 An earlier version of this chapter was first presented at the 'Economics and Its History' conference at Azim Premji University in November 2016 and again at the ESHET Annual Meetings at Antwerp, May 18–21, 2017.
2 A basic good is a good that goes directly or indirectly in the production of all goods.
3 See Sraffa (1960) for a proof of this proposition.

References

Ricardo, David. 1817, 1821. *On the Principles of Political Economy and Taxation*, 3rd edition, Cambridge: Cambridge University Press, 1951.

Ricardo, David. 1955. *The Works and Correspondence of David Ricardo vol. IX*, Edited by Piero Sraffa, Cambridge: Cambridge University Press.

Sinha, Ajit. 2010a. *Theories of Value from Adam Smith to Piero Sraffa*, London: Routledge.

Sinha, Ajit. 2010b. 'In Defence of Adam Smith's Theory of Value', *The European Journal of the History of Economic Thought*, 17(1), 29–48.

Sinha, Ajit. 2016. *A Revolution in Economic Theory: The Economics of Piero Sraffa*, London, New York: Palgrave Macmillan.

Sinha, Ajit. 2017. 'A Comment on Sraffa's "classical economics"', *Cambridge Journal of Economics*, 41(2), 661–677.

Smith, Adam. 1776. *An Inquiry into the Nature and Causes of the Wealth of Nations Volumes I and II*, Indianapolis: Library Fund, 1981.

Sraffa, P. 1951. 'Introduction', in *Works and Correspondence of David Ricardo, vol. 1*, Cambridge, Cambridge University Press.

Sraffa, P. 1960. *Production of Commodities by Means of Commodities*, Cambridge: Cambridge University Press.

Sraffa, P. nd. 'Sraffa Papers', Wren Library, Trinity College, University of Cambridge.

Chapter 5

A history of Marxian economics 1960–2010

How we 'did' it

Meghnad Desai

Introduction

This is not and cannot hope to be a complete history of Marxian economics. That would require a knowledge of several languages (including Japanese),
mathematics and a long life. This is why I have added a personal reference in
the title. This is an account of what it was like to 'do' Marxian economics over
the fifty years from the 1960s to now, the period that I have dabbled in Marxian
economics. It is both subjective and incomplete.

As of the early 1960s, there was not much material available for someone
wanting to do work in Marxian economics. Reading the three volumes of *Capital* plus the three volumes of *The Theories of Surplus Value* and *The Contribution to
the Critique of Political Economy* (CCPE) was possible but not often done. There
was Paul Sweezy's definitive exposition *The Theory of Capitalist Development*
(1948). It was more than a textbook of Marxian economics; it did introduce us
to the value-price transformation problem, but not to the circuits of capital or
to simple and expanded reproduction. Sweezy also edited the text of Ladislaus
Von Bortkiewicz's solution to the value-price transformation problem, which
became a key reading for the principal theme in much of the work on Marxian
economics over the next twenty-five years (Sweezy 1942).

Apart from these sources, there was not much – Joan Robinson's essay on
Marxian economics (1942) does not engage with Marx's ideas per se, but rather,
tells us about her honest attempts to study Marx from a Marshall Cambridge
perspective. Maurice Dobb's historical account of capitalist development was
taken to be an authoritative account of the Marxist version of European history.
Dobb did very little analytical writing on Marx. Ronald Meek had written a
historical account of the labour theory of value (1973). He was interested in the
history of economic ideas rather than advancing the subject of Marxian economics. Sam Aaranovitch, a lifelong member of the Communist Party of Great
Britain, came to academic economics late in his life, and told me that members
of the party were discouraged from reading *Capital* or any other work by Marx.
They read Max Beer's short account. In India, with a more intellectual tradition, we were encouraged to read Engels' *Anti-Duhring*. The Communist Party

of Great Britain had a history group, which consisted of Christopher Hill, Eric Hobsbawm, John Saville and Rodney Hilton, among others. However, there was no parallel group of economists.

One interesting aspect of doing Marxian economics is that Marx's own works became increasingly 'discovered' or translated during the 1960s and later. Thus, the discovery of young Marx was one of the major events of the 1960s, and the translation of Grundrisse of the 1970s. Marx's mathematical manuscript and his anthropological notes on Russia became available in the 1970s as well.

Works of Marxist economists, or communists who wrote about economics, was only patchily available. Lenin's *Imperialism* was indeed popular, but his earlier works such as *On the So-Called Question of the Market* (1893/1937) and later works including *The Tax in Kind* (1921) were only available in the *Collected Works* and not separately. Rosa Luxemburg's *Accumulation of Capital* 1951) had been translated into English and published with a foreword by Joan Robinson, who later authored a book with the same title. Works by Bukharin and Preobrazensky were also available but were not widely read. Bukharin is interesting because he was engaged in the debate around the scheme of expanded reproduction, in which Rosa Luxemburg was the principal author. He wrote his critical work on the leisure class and after 1917 took part in policy debates.

There was also the writing criticizing or dismissing Marx as well as non-communist and non-Bolshevik writing. Bohm-Bawerk's *Karl Marx and the Close of His System* was well known. Schumpeter's 1942 essay on Marx was another good source. We had all read about Tugan-Baranowsky and his take on the materialist conception of history. There were some articles by young American economists written in the immediate post-war period but further activity was discouraged due to McCarthyism. Lawrence Klein pointed out parallels between Keynes and Marx, and May also wrote on value theory. Paul Samuelson's was the first article by a major economist to be published in a mainstream journal. His 1957 *American Economic Review* article, 'Wages and Profits', looked at Marx's theory from the point of view of modern economics.

The big surge in writing debating and floating new ideas in Marxian economics came with the student revolts of the 1960s and the anti-Vietnam War movement. The civil rights movement in the US did not have much impact, but radical political economy became a sustained activity on American campuses in the 1970s. The Union of Radical Political Economists was formed around this time with its journal, *Review of Radical Political Economy*. Paul Baran and Paul Sweezy brought out their analysis of the American economy and society in *Monopoly Capital* (1968). For many, this was the first introduction to Marxist economics. However, it was more of a general critique of aspects of American society than a theoretical updating of Marx's analysis, incorporating monopoly elements in the value theory. Another somewhat unusual book was by a member of the German Communist Party who had migrated to the US: Paul Mattick lived in Boston and brought out his book on Marx and Keynes in 1964.

In the UK, while there was greater familiarity with Marxist and socialist writing, the ferment of student activity was in the period of the Labour governments from 1964 to 1970 and from 1974 to 1979, and did not face an antagonistic official culture as it did in America. The split in the Communist Party due to the differences over Hungary in 1956 had already spawned the *Universities and the Left Review*, which later became the *New Left Review*. The British universities had a strong Marxist tradition in history but not so much in economics. In the late 1960s, there appeared a new journal, *Economy and Society*. Bob Rowthorn, Andrew Glyn and I, among others, founded the Conference of Socialist Economists early in the 1970s and we brought out the *Bulletin of the Conference of Socialist Economists* (later called *Capital and Class*).

A controversy broke out between William Baumol and Paul Samuelson as to how seriously economists should discuss the notion of exploitation. These exchanges appeared in the *Journal of Economic Literature* in 1971 (Samuelson 1971).

One could say that for about two decades – the 1970s and 1980s – Marxian economics received much attention from mainstream economists. Morishima's book was a major factor in this. His reputation as a mainstream economist was the reason. Unlike Samuelson, who wrote short analytical accounts of what he thought Marx had done, Morishima was trying to go beyond that and relate Marx to modern economics. There was also, as Morishima explained, a lively tradition of Marxian economics in Japan. In a sense, he was responding to Japanese Marxism from the point of view of Japanese mainstream economics. One of the schools of Japanese Marxism was the *Uno School*, named after Kozo Uno. Uno did not write in English, but Tom Sekine gave an account of the Uno school in the *Journal of Economic Literature* (1975). Makoto Itoh came to the UK in the 1980s and wrote in English (Itoh 1980, 1988). The Uno methodology was to keep the different levels of abstractions strictly separate so that questions of empirical relevance would be kept separate from those of abstract theory.

John Roemer published his *Analytical Foundation of Marxian Economic Theory* in 1981. This seminal work put Marxian economics into a rigorous framework of general equilibrium and game theory. Roemer went on to work further in radical political economy in his *A General Theory of Exploitation and Class* in 1982. He has gone on to work on justice and the environment as themes in 'applied' Marxian economics.

The ferment among American campuses had led to a systematic analysis of the inequalities of American society in terms of Marxian theory. Unlike Europe, where the controversies centred around the old texts, there was an attempt to use theory for the critical analysis of the *Structure of Social Accumulation*. Samuel Bowles and Howard Gintis were the leading authors in this effort. They explored Marx's distinction between labour and labour power to explain income inequality and class formation. They studied the educational system in depth for its role in the stratification of students into different streams, as it suited their slotting into classes. This is a rich body of work, integrating Marxian concerns into a general framework, using all the tools of modern economics. There was also a lively debate about Marxism and feminism. It was based more around Engels's book on the *Origins of Family, Private Property and Law*. Engels was criticized for a paternalistic bias. There was an associated debate about the role of women's unpaid labour in the reproduction of labour power.

The best account of Marx's economics, including his entire lifelong thinking and writing on political economy, was written by Samuel Hollander, the doyen among historians of economic ideas (2008). Hollander followed it up with a full volume account of the political economy of Engels, which is the only treatment of his thought (Hollander 2011). Hollander's volume on Marx weaves a seamless account of Marx's ideas without marking a disjunction between the young Marx and the old Marx, as was done by some commentators. Similarly, Hollander is unique among the writers of political economy of Marxism in offering a careful and complete account of Engels's thought both as an economic theorist on his own, as one who predates Marx in his economic thinking, and as the companion of Marx during his life and the guardian of his work after his death.

What was Marxian economics?

Like Keynesian economics or Ricardian economics, Marxian economics has to be based on Marx's works to begin with. In Keynes's case, we begin with the *General Theory*. The central issue is that in a free market economy, there can be multiple equilibria, at least two. One of these will be the full employment equilibrium. The controversy surrounds Keynes's assertion that there can be another locally stable underemployment equilibrium. The idea that involuntary unemployment can exist with free markets was the difficult one to sustain in face of Walrasian theory. Much of the Keynesian and post Keynesian economics which survives, as much as its denial, turns on this issue.

In Marx's case, the proposition is that capitalism as a mode of production is sustained by an accumulation process built on profits, which are expropriated from the surplus value produced by living labour. This is the central proposition of Marxian economics. It is the most hotly contested and the most worked upon proposition. Proving the soundness of the proposition was the equivalent of proving the existence of an equilibrium in the Walrasian general equilibrium model. It was, in the eyes of many who were of a Left inclination, the moral proof that capitalism survived on exploitation. If the proposition was not provable, the fear was that capitalism would survive unchallenged. Mohun and Veneziani (2016), in their comprehensive analytical survey of the problem, argue that the three possible approaches to the Value Price Transformation Problem (VPTP) are descriptive, predictive and normative. By their criterion, we have to classify the profits/exploitation interpretation as a normative one. One could instead treat the VPTP as a description of the production process whereby values are transformed into prices, or use it to predict how movements in value would determine movements in price. The descriptive and predictive approaches are much more characteristic of a classical political economy than of Marx.

The demonstration of the surplus value–profit relationship became the central theme of much of the work in Marxian economics in the 1960s and 1970s. On this proposition hinged the notions of the class inequalities in a capitalist society.

VPTP

The doctrinal history of the proposition, known as VPTP, is that it is a chapter in the third volume of *Capital*, which was published in 1894, a dozen years after Marx's death, by Engels from the manuscript left behind by Marx. Chapter 9 of Volume III lays out an arithmetical example of five industries – capitals – setting out their value 'accounts' and then their price calculations. Marx failed to demonstrate his proposition. Profits could not be shown to be a 'transformed' version of surplus value. It was a muddle.

Engels had been saying sometime before the publication of Volume III, especially in his preface to Volume II, which he published in 1885 two years after Marx's death, that Marx's proof for his shattering proposition would be available in Volume III, which he was hoping to publish soon. When he wrote that in the preface to the second volume of *Capital*, Engels could not have read the manuscript notes from which Volume III was arranged. When the material was published, there was dismay. Bohm-Bawerk immediately declared that Marx had failed to prove his most radical proposition. Mainstream economics stopped taking Marx seriously after that.

There was much else in the three volumes of *Capital*. In Volume I, Marx had covered, among other matters, the nature of labour process in manufacturing, the explanation of business cycles and crises, and the history of the transition from feudalism to capitalism in Britain via primitive accumulation. Volume I was one good model, so the VPTP issue did not arise. In Volume II, there is a discussion of circuits of capital, of the problem of reducing physical durable capital to a value measure, and finally in the last part, a 'macroeconomic' tableau of national income determination and its growth path. These schemes of simple and expanded reproduction had led to a heated debate among Marxists in the years following the publication of Volume II.

There were also some predictions attributed to Marx. Chief among them were the falling rate of profit, the immiseration of the working class, the reduction of the middle class to the working class, growing centralization and concentration of capital and, of course, crises of increasing severity till the final crisis when '[t]he expropriators are expropriated' (Marx 1887 [2010]). Through the three volumes of *Capital*, there are many reflections on the nature of money.

Teaching Marxian economics

I began to teach a course titled Marxian economic theory outside the curriculum in 1969, upon the request of students who were curious about alternatives to the current system. My course was quite academic and kept away from themes such as imperialism or racism. My lectures were recorded and printed as *Marxian Economic Theory*, which came out in 1974 and was the first 'textbook' since Sweezy. It is worth listing the themes I taught as the analytical core of Marxian economics.

First was the labour theory of value, where one had to explain how in a world of voluntary contracts one could have exploitation and surplus value. This led to the transformation problem of reconciling the surplus value accruing at different rates, relative to the capital employed and the presumed equality of the (money) rate of profit. This continued to be the theme on which most debates and disputes about Marxian economics converged. Thus, Ian Steedman in his *Marx After Sraffa* pointed out that Marx's argument linking surplus value to profit is not analytically sound (1977). A controversy followed in the wake of Steedman's publication, which is covered in Fine (1986). Positive profits could coexist with negative surplus value. Michio Morishima, in his *Marx's Economics*, showed that if inequality constraints were put in stating the problem of translating values into prices, there would be no peculiar results such as what Steedman had discussed (1973). VPTP, to this day, remains the one subject on which a lot of activity of Marxian economists is engaged (Mohun and Veneziani 2016).

I taught and thought a lot about VPTP. Marx's muddle was indefensible no matter how loyal one was. However, from the beginning, I had made a distinction between values which were unobservable and prices which were. The problem was that at the visible (phenomenal) level, workers entered into a voluntary exchange of labour power for wages – a full day's wage for a full day's work. One had to go beneath the visible level to uncover the real structural relations of value, to locate exploitation. I used an analogy from econometrics. The price domain was the reduced form while the value domain was the structural form. You had to work backwards from the price domain to the value domain in order to make exploitation visible.

This was the logic of the three circuits of capital, but Marx did not use it in Volume III. The way the three circuits of capital worked was that we start with money which becomes money capital m once Mr Moneybags invests it. He converts it into labour power, which he buys along with constant capital. In the *physical* circuit, we take labour and capital and get output q. This is sold at price p. $m' = p \star Q$. $m' > m$. The difference is profit $(m' - m) = r$. Where does r come from?

Marx's argument is that the labour power L bought with wage w represents labour time expended, which is the value of labour power. The labour value equivalent of the wage is v, variable capital. There is a surplus s which is unpaid for. Total value produced is $y = c$ (value of capital used up – constant capital) $+ v + s$. The difference $(m' - m) = ₹. ₹$. Profit is the money form of surplus value s.

The problem was that Marx defined the rate of surplus value s/v and the value rate of profit $s/(c + v) = €$. Since different industries or even firms may have different organic composition of capital $= c/c + v = £$, we can see that $€ = s/v (1 - £)$. Thus, $€$ will differ from firm to firm, yet the money rate of profit $₹$ will be equal across all capitals as classical theory had already proved. How could one reconcile the two propositions?

This was the problem that Marx posed in his numerical example with five separate capitals (firms or industries). He recalculated the value inputs c and v by multiplying them with an average profit rate which he took as $S/C + V$ (uppercase letters denote aggregates while the corresponding lowercase letters are individual industry quantities). He had imposed two overall restrictions: total profit had to equal total surplus value, i.e., $S = R$, and total value produced had to equal total money value of output $Y = M'$.

In his numerical example, Marx could not satisfy the overall restrictions. He then proceeded to maintain the truth of his prediction despite the numerical mess. Bohm-Bawerk pronounced Marx's theory as a failure. In the German context, where Marx was a powerful influence for the Social Democratic Party, this was felt to be a big setback.

The answer had been given by Bortkiewicz, who was a statistician by training. He made two innovations. Marx's five separate capitals were not integrated in an input-output framework. Bortkiewicz used Marx's scheme for simple reproduction, which had such an interconnected structure as his basis. But he also realized that instead of setting $(1 + E) (c + v)$ for each capital's output, one had to price each input at its own price. The answer is then a better proof. Bortkiewicz was, however, puzzled by the two restrictions. He thought one of them to be redundant. That said, Bortkiewicz had solved the VPTP and nothing further needed to be said. I was puzzled that few economists referred to this solution.

It took me several years of teaching the subject before I realized the significance of the double restriction. The identity $S = R$ is obviously required if one wishes to argue that profits come from surplus value. The condition that total output in value terms is equal to total money value of output $Y = M'$ is just a condition to bridge the value accounts with the price accounts. It is a way of normalizing by saying one hour of labour expended, which is one unit of value equals one dollar (Desai 1998).

In subsequent debates, some have argued that the purpose of VPTP is to calculate equilibrium prices. This, however, can be done at the level of the physical circuit as is done in input-output tables without bothering about value quantities. In any case, prices are visible. You can show their logic of interdependence via an input-output table, but it does not need the surplus value-profit connection.

The debates about VPTP continue. For some people, the answer is a Holy Grail – find it and you can destroy capitalism. Walking along the Strand in London, I was eagerly approached by someone who had heard me lecturing in the New School in New York. He asked breathlessly, 'I hear you have finally solved VPTP. Is that true?' He was disappointed when I told him that it had been solved by Bortkiewicz. Marxists are reluctant to accept this because they do think that it is a key to the end of capitalism!

Dynamics of capitalism

The second theme on which there is some debate in the old literature but not the new one is the result in Marx's example of the scheme for expanded (extended) reproduction, which showed a two-sector capitalist economy converging to balanced growth in perpetuity (*Capital* Volume II, Chapter 23). This contradicted the prediction of a crisis-ridden capitalism, or of a falling rate of profit. The publication of Volume II set off a controversy which is surveyed by Rosa Luxemburg in her *Accumulation of Capital*. Luxemburg denied that Marx's solution of the realization problem was plausible, assuming that there would be the problem of insufficient demand and offered her solution in terms of the third department – armaments or luxury consumption.

I did some work on this, as is shown in *Marxian Economics* (1979), which is the expanded and revised version of the 1974 book. I still think it is an unsolved problem as to why capitalists do what they do in Marx's schema. Morishima praised it as the fastest converging two-sector growth model, but did not question how Marx had miraculously arrived at the right solution, which was untypical of capitalists (investing a constant proportion of surplus value and keeping the organic composition of capital unchanged). Joan Robinson told me that there is no problem as these are steady states. People do what they do because they have always done so. On this one occasion, Frank Hahn, who was present when I gave a seminar at Cambridge, agreed with her. I still wanted to know the underlying logic in terms of actual or expected profitability which drove these capitalists.

Three circuits

The third topic I taught is the discussion of the three circuits of capital from Part I of Volume II. This is, in my view, crucial because it brings together the value domain, the physical input–output domain and the money costs and profits domain in their intersecting movements. Realization problems, such as that in the scheme of expanded reproduction (SER), cannot be discussed without bringing the money circuit in. Marx does not tackle the money circuit in his scheme. Rosa Luxemburg, in her critique of the SER, raises the question, 'Where does the money come from?', i.e., for Department I, capitalists make investments before they sell the output. But she neither mentions the circuits of capital, nor tries to out the SER in the circuits framework. This is an area which needs much more research.

Marx's model of the business cycle

In *Capital* Volume I, Part VII, Marx puts forward a model of the business cycle in terms of the struggle for shares between capital and labour. As the pace of accumulation speeds up, there develops a labour shortage. That leads to a rise in the share of wages and a decline in the profit share. After a while, capitalists adopt more capital-intensive techniques which throw labour out. Wage share declines and profit share goes up, but this only speeds up accumulation, and the economy is back in its cycle.

Richard Goodwin, in a brilliant five-page article, embodied this model in a two-equation structure based on the predator-prey model of the fish populations of Volterra and Lotka (1967). One of those equations concerns the real wage bargain which is a linearized version of the Phillips curve, though Goodwin takes the percentage employed rather than unemployed as his first equation. This equation defines the growth rate of real wages which is one part of the growth of the wage share. He then assumes that all profits are invested, that the capital-output ratio is constant and that labour productivity grows at a constant exogenous pace. The second equation is then the relation of the growth of the employment rate as a function of the profit share, expressed as one minus the wage share.

Thus two variables, wage share and employment percentage, are captured in their dynamics, in two nonlinear differential equations. The property of the model is that while an equilibrium exists which defines the wage share (and thereby the profit share, and given the constancy of capital-output ratio, the rate of profit) as well as the proportion employed (the natural rate of employment), the economy never reaches equilibrium but perpetually cycles around it.

Goodwin's model is an elegant formulation of Marx's model, though it does have a constant capital-output ratio (no rising organic composition). The profit rate cycles but has no long-term downward trend. The cycles can be short or long depending on the values of the parameters. Goodwin does not quote Marx nor does he engage in an exegesis, yet it is a powerful way of translating Marx in a dynamic model.

I did extensive work extending the model: adding money-wage bargain, inflation and a variable capital-output ratio (Desai 1973). There is a large literature extending the Goodwin model (Goodwin et al. 1984). I also did empirical work on it with UK data (Desai 1984). The model goes on being developed even now (refer Flaschel and Luchtenberg 2012).

Quantitative Marxism

A topic which I did not teach in the 1970s but did encourage students to do research in is 'quantitative Marxism'. There is not much work of a quantitative sort in this area. Andrew Glyn and Robert Sutcliffe did write a seminal article in the *New Left Review* predicting the crisis of the 1970s using the concept of rate of profit in a Marxian framework. They later elaborated it in a full-length book (Glyn and Sutcliffe 1971, 1972). This was a brilliant example of the predictive power of Marxian theory. Some years earlier, Ernest Mandel had written an analysis of the post-war Keynesian boom in the *Socialist Register*, the annual collection of articles edited by Ralph Miliband and John Saville. Mandel foresaw the slowdown of the boom forthcoming, using the long cycles analysis. This was not seen at the time but proved prescient (Mandel 1964). Mandel also wrote *Late Capitalism*, which was the major source of Marxian analysis of contemporary capitalism (Mandel 1978 [1976]).

There is a continuing research programme in quantitative Marxism by the French economists Dumenil and Levy. They have examined the trend and cycles in profitability in the US using national income accounts to extract Marxian measures of the rate of profit. It is a large corpus of work which points out the downward trend in profitability over the last fifty years (see Dumenil and Levy 2014 and the references therein).

Conclusion

Not much work is being done in Marxian economics. That impression may be due to my own diversion from that activity. The value price transformation problem remains fascinating, like the existence of equilibrium in Walrasian theory. A credible solution of the value price transformation problem is the Holy Grail that will prove that profits come from surplus value generated by workers and from no other source. We await a rigorous proof.

References

Baran, Paul A. and Sweezy, Paul M. 1966. *Monopoly Capital*. New York and London: Monthly Review Press.

Bellofiore, R. ed. 1998. *Marxian Economics: A Reappraisal: Essays on Volume III of Capital Profit, Prices and Dynamics*. Hampshire: Palgrave Macmillan.

Bellofiore, R. and Vertova, G. 2014. *The Great Recession and the Contradictions of Contemporary Capitalism*, Cheltenham: Edward Elgar.

Bohm-Bawerk, E. 1948. *Karl Marx and the Close of His System*, Translated and edited by Paul Sweezy, London: Augustus Kelly.

Bowles, Samuel and Gintis, Herbert. 1976. *Schooling in Capitalist America: Educational Reform and the Contradictions of American Life*, New York: Basic Books.

Desai, Meghnad. 1973. 'Growth Cycles and Inflation in a Model of the Class Struggle', *Journal of Economic Theory*, 6(6), 527–545.

Desai, Meghnad. 1974. *Marxian Economic Theory*, London: Gray-Mills.

Desai, Meghnad. 1979. *Marxian Economics*, Oxford: Martin Robertson.

Desai, Meghnad. 1984. 'An Econometric Model of the Share of Wages in National Income: UK 1855–1965', in Goodwin et al. 1984.

Desai, Meghnad. 1989. *Lenin's Economic Writings*, London: Lawrence and Wishart.

Desai, Meghnad. 1991. 'Methodological Problems in Quantitative Marxism', in Dunne, pp. 27–41.

Desai, Meghnad. 1998. *Profits, Prices and Values in Bellofiore, Volume II*, pp. 3–14.

Dobb, Maurice. 1946. *Studies in the Development of Capitalism*, New York: Monthly Review Press.

Dumenil, G. and Levy, D. 2014. 'The Crisis of the Early 21st Century: Marxian Perspectives', in R. Bellofiore and G. Vertova (eds.), *The Great Recession and the Contradictions of Contemporary Capitalism*, Cheltenham: Edward Elgar, pp. 26–49.

Dunne, Paul. ed. 1991. *Quantitative Marxism*, Cambridge: Polity Press.

Feinstein, Charles. 1967. *Socialism, Capitalism and Economic Development: Essays in Honour of Maurice Dobb*, Cambridge: Cambridge University Press.

Fine, B. 1986. *The Value Dimension: Marx Versus Ricardo and Sraffa*, London: Routledge and Kegan Paul.

Flaschel, P. and Luchtenberg, S. 2012. *Roads to Social Capitalism: Theory, Evidence and Policy*, Cheltenham: Edward Elgar.

Goodwin, R. M. 1967. 'A Growth Cycle', in C. H. Feinstein (ed.), *Socialism, Capitalism and Economic Growth: Essays Presented to Maurice Dobb*, Cambridge: Cambridge University Press.

Goodwin, R. M., Krueger, M. and Vercelli, A. 1984. *Nonlinear Models of Fluctuating Growth*, Berlin: Springer Verlag.

Glyn, Andrew and Sutcliffe, Robert. 1971. 'The Collapse of UK Profits', *New Left Review*, 66, March–April.

Glyn, Andrew and Sutcliffe, Robert. 1972. *British Capitalism, Workers and the Profit Squeeze*, London: Penguin.

Hollander, Samuel. 2008. *The Economics of Marx: Analysis and Application*, Cambridge: Cambridge University Press.

Hollander, Samuel. 2011. *Friedrich Engels and Marxian Political Economy*, Cambridge: Cambridge University Press.

Itoh, Makoto. 1980. *Value and Crisis*, London: Pluto.

Itoh, Makoto. 1988. *The Basic Theory of Capitalism: The Forms and Substance of the Capitalist Economy*, London: Palgrave Macmillan.

Lenin, Vladimir Ilyich. 1893, 1937. 'On the So-Called Question of the Market', reprinted in Desai, 1989, *The Tax in Kind in Desai*, 301–338.

Mandel, Ernest. 1964. 'The Economics of Neo Capitalism', in R. Miliband and J. Saville (eds.), *Late Capitalism*, London: Verso.

Mandel, Ernest. 1978. *Late Capitalism*. Translated from the German by Joris De Bres. Atlantic Highlands, NJ: Humanities Press, Inc., 1976.

Marx, K. 1887. *Capital*, Translated from the third German edition by Samuel Moore and Edward Aveling and edited by Frederick Engels, Vol. 1, Ch. 32, p. 715, New Delhi: Leftword, 2010.

Mattick, Paul. 1969. *Marx and Keynes. The Limits of the Mixed Economy*, Boston: Extending Horizons Books.

Meek, Ronald. 1973. *Studies in the Labour Theory of Value*, Second Edition, London: Lawrence and Wishart.

Miliband, R. and Saville, J. eds. 1964. *The Socialist Register 1964*, New York: Monthly Review Press.

Mohun, Simon and Veneziani, Roberto. 2016. *Values, Prices and Exploitation: The Logic of the Transformation Problem*. Unpublished, Queen Mary University of London.

Morishima, Michio. 1973. *Marx's Economics*, Cambridge: Cambridge University Press.

Robinson, Joan. 1942. *An Essay on Marxian Economics*, London: Palgrave Macmillan.

Roemer, John. 1981. *Analytical Foundations of Marxian Economic Theory*, Cambridge: Cambridge University Press.

Samuelson, Paul. 1957. 'Wages and Interest: A Modern Dissection of Marxian Economic Models', *American Economic Review*, 47, 884–912.

Samuelson, Paul. 1971. 'Understanding the Marxian Notion of Exploitation: A Summary of the So- Called Transformation Problem Between Marxian Values and Market Prices', *Journal of Economic Literature*, IX(2), 399–431, June.

Sekine, Thomas. 1975. 'Uno-Riron: A Japanese Contribution to Marxian Political Economy', *Journal of Economic Literature*, 13(3), 847–877, September.

Steedman, Ian. 1977. *Marx After Sraffa*, London: New Left Books.

Sweezy, Paul M. 1942. *The Theory of Capitalist Development*, New York: Oxford University Press.

Sweezy, Paul. 1948. *The Theory of Capitalist Development*, New York: Monthly Review Press.

Chapter 6

Capitalism, classical political economy and Marx's departures

Chirashree Das Gupta[1]

The rise of disciplines in Europe, particularly classical political economy (CPE henceforth) and moral philosophy, was coterminous with the rise of capitalism and had intellectual concerns that were fairly recent. Scholarship emanating from Europe was mainly concerned with explanations of phenomenon that constituted the 'brave new world' of capitalism. In the current conjuncture, CPE (with emphasis on the works of Adam Smith and David Ricardo) has again begun to find a place in syllabi after more than three decades of wilful neglect. The same syllabi also often (though not always) retains a section on Marx in which Marx is read as one of the classical political economists. In this chapter, we argue that Marx's theorization of capitalism marked a sharp methodological departure from CPE rather than continuity. Our formulation is that CPE in the tradition of Smith and Ricardo was based on a utopian view of capitalism as a market system. Our contention here is that Marx's utopia, in sharp contrast to that of CPE, was one in which the power of capital and that of the capitalist nation-State would have to be dissolved to create a society of associated producers. This is quite distinct from the market utopia of capitalism that CPE was premised on. This is the central argument of the chapter.

At the outset, it must be stated that this chapter is *not* a reconstruction of either CPE or Marxist political economy in the light of later developments for examples interventions of the 20th century from the liberal Marxist and Sraffian paradigms. Nor is it an ambitious exercise to critically locate every argument in CPE and Marxist political economy in its historical context and compare the two. A large literature already exists which has done that in great detail. This chapter is focussed solely on the historical and philosophical premises of the distinctive analytical methods of classical political economy and that of Marx.

The first section of this chapter locates the rise of CPE as a discipline in its combination of methods towards its explanation of the past and present of production, circulation and exchange, through an examination of Adam Smith's work with a primary focus on *Wealth of Nations* (*WON* henceforth) in the construction of the utopia of the market system as the institutional basis of capitalism. The second section discusses David Ricardo's continuities and departures within the paradigm of CPE. The third section of the chapter examines Karl Marx's problematic and methodological departures from CPE in the construction of his utopia. It explores Marx's explanation of the imperatives of the institutional basis of the expanded reproduction of the capitalist system.

The world of Adam Smith's utopia

For Smith, the significant social changes due to the rise of capitalism in the second half of the 18th century in Europe entailed several distinctive features, namely (i) commoditization of land, labour and products of labour, (ii) emergence of money as the universal medium of circulation and exchange, (iii) a distinctive new class society based on a particular set of private property rights and (iv) the simultaneity of extensive poverty and expanding wealth. In *WON*, Smith is particularly concerned with the changing nature of political and economic power. This is evident in his critique of the grant of the monopoly charters and the changing relationship between the church and the State.

Smith's thesis was premised on three foundational propositions, the first being that the sole source of value creation is labour. Every product consists of material that was the product of 'prior' labour and application of living labour to this 'prior' labour. It is from this thesis that capital in Smith's conception is accumulation of 'prior labour'.

The second thesis is based on a conceptualization of history as two states of nature. The first is what Smith calls the 'rude state of society' which is imagined as a hunter/gatherer society. All examples including that of the deer and the beaver to establish the basis of exchange value is based on this conceptualization of the past. The second is the advanced state of society, which for Smith is his present, i.e., rising capitalism, whose defining characteristic for Smith is a market-society. Thus for Smith, history is an abstraction with two typified states of nature. History in terms of its actual course and conjunctures has little or no role in explaining social change.

It is this historical abstraction in the particular reading of material history by CPE that leads to an apparent conflict in Smith's exposition of the first thesis. Embodied labour in a good is the sole determinant of exchange value in the rude state of society. But in the advanced state of society, Smith proposes that labour commanded in a commodity constitutes the basis of exchange value. There is no explicit explanation as to why the labour embodied or materialized in a commodity should be necessarily equivalent to labour commanded in the advanced state (Dasgupta 2009). This was precisely Ricardo's departure point from Smith.

The third thesis is based on the premise of 'self-interest' (self-love in Smith's parlance) as the *natural* basis of human behaviour. This is developed in the *Theory of Moral Sentiments* to argue that all emotions and actions which apparently defy self-love, e.g., empathy, pain or happiness for others, and philanthropy or altruism are all manifestations of self-love because in the end it brings pleasure, satisfaction and fulfilment to the self (Smith 2002). Thus, all human behaviour and action is reducible to self-love. All social relations thus are based on 'self-love' conceived as 'natural behaviour' specific to humans (Smith 1937, 2002). This reduction of all human behaviour to self-love in the *Theory of Moral Sentiments* (Smith 2002) is thus the precepts of neoclassical methodological individualism as the basic organizing tenet of society.

In *WON*, despite the methodological holism that Smith attempts throughout in his analysis, this behavioural assumption of self-love is the foundational explanation of human action in production, reproduction and exchange. Thus division of labour (DOL henceforth) as the basis of production in advanced societies is based on this 'original principle' of human nature:

> It is not from the benevolence of the butcher, the brewer, or the baker that we expect our dinner, but from their regard to their own interest. We address ourselves, not to their humanity but to their self-love.
>
> (Smith 1937 Book I Chapter 2)

The other 'natural' propensity of human beings is to 'truck, barter and exchange' and this propensity forms the basis of the social DOL:

> This division of labour . . . is . . . the necessary . . . consequence of a certain propensity in human nature . . . the propensity to truck, barter, and exchange one thing for another.
>
> (Smith 1937 Book I Chapter 2)

Given these natural propensities, every human society experiences an expansion of wealth through creation of surplus commodities because of productivity increases due to DOL (presupposing accumulation of stock), which then give rise to exchange. The first and foremost difference between the rude and advanced state of society is largely quantitative according to the extent of DOL and the extent of exchange (markets) – both of which are linked by cumulative circular causation. The second difference lies in the extent of use of money solely as a medium of exchange in which the demand and supply of money is regulated by the demand and supply of commodities. The third difference between the two states is indicated by the accumulation of capital ('stock' in Smith's parlance) – where the genesis of capital is *prior* accumulation of labour values. Thus the difference between those who do not own capital and those who do lies in savings propensities and levels of industriousness (Smith 1937 Book II Chapter 3). So implicitly it is 'hard work' and savings proclivities that create the class of accumulators whom Smith calls the 'owners of stock'. This is evident in the following passage:

> the principle which prompts to save is the desire of bettering our condition, a desire which, though generally calm and dispassionate, comes with

us from the womb, and never leaves us till we go into the grave. . . . An augmentation of fortune is the means by which the greater part of men propose and wish to better their condition . . . the most likely way of augmenting their fortune is to save and accumulate some part of what they acquire, either regularly and annually, or upon some extraordinary occasions.

(Smith 1937 Book II Chapter 3)

The owners of stock, in Smith's account are an unsavoury class who exploit workers inhumanly. However their deployment of their stocks of capital drives the creation and expansion of commodities in the advanced state of society and hence they are crucial as a class in the expansion of the wealth of nations. Workers constitute the other class that is crucial to the expansion of the wealth of nations as they are the creators of labour values materialized in commodities. Their conditions of material existence depend on the demand for their labour in the advanced state of society as well as the cost of subsistence (Smith 1937 Book I Chapter 8).

The increase in the stock of capital by increasing the demand for labour raises the wages of labour. It also increases labour productivity, and so a smaller quantity of labour produces a greater quantity of work. DOL accounts for this increase in labour productivity due to the proclivity for innovation:

More heads are occupied in inventing . . . machinery for executing the work of each, and it is, therefore, more likely to be invented . . . many commodities, therefore . . . come to be produced by so much less labour than before.

(Smith 1937 Book I Chapter 8)

DOL leads to incremental and continuous innovation both in technology and labour organization and hence ensures continuous increases in productivity and increasing returns to scale. Wage increase (if achieved by workers) does not necessarily lead to a rising cost of employment. This continuous increase in productivity compensates for rise in wages as less labour is required to produce the same goods. Also, as long as continuous DOL leads to innovation of new commodities, there is continuous labour absorption as labour supply adapts to labour demand in the longer term. Thus the process of expansion of wealth of nations in itself entails a harmonious process.

The wealth of nations expands through surplus creation due to DOL and the realization of the surplus by extension of internal and external markets. This continuity of the process of expansion is driven by competition in the market and hence all barriers to mobility of labour and capital need to be done away with. In this process of extension of markets, population growth is a positive function of expansion of wealth in sharp contrast to the later Malthusian and neo-Malthusian arguments of the 19th and 20th centuries.

According to Smith, who does what in a society based on DOL is social rather than natural:

> The difference between the most dissimilar characters, between a philosopher and a common street porter, for example, seems to arise not so much from nature as from habit, custom, and education.
>
> (Smith 1937 Book I Chapter 2)

This is where we find the cognitive dissonance in Smith's thesis. While talent is social and the basis of DOL, self-interest driving the system of DOL-based exchange is natural. Thomas (2018) elucidates Smith's emphasis on early childhood education. Thus, Adam Smith stands firmly on the side of 'nurture' as opposed to natural or progenical claims to talent. In sharp cognitive contrast, however, the sexual division of labour in social reproduction is largely natural for Smith. Harkin (2013) has argued that women are largely absent from Smith's analysis. She argues that Smith's 'distinctive conception of women's experience' is exceptional and non-normative'. For Smith, the value of women's role in social reproduction is a direct function of the rate of expansion of the wealth and population of nations. Smith illustrates this by the following anecdotal comparison of the marriage market for widows with young children in the US and Europe in the late 18th century.

> a young widow with four or five young children, who, among the middling or inferior ranks of people in Europe, would have so little chance for a second husband, is there [US] frequently courted as a sort of fortune. The value of children is the greatest of all encouragements to marriage.
>
> (Smith 1937, Book One Chapter VII)

While men are implicitly the driving force in the expansion of the economy, the instrumentality of women's role in social reproduction and children's role in the process of production is largely determined by rates of accumulation.

The differences of expansion of wealth among nations are explained by the potential of (i) extension of DOL; (ii) expansion of markets; (iii) social barriers on mobility – e.g., caste in India, restrictions by the Church under the feudal order in England etc.; (iv) existence of trade barriers with examples from China and Egypt and (v) the existence of monopoly charters.

However, it is the level of 'industriousness of societies' which essentially explains the difference between the West and the rest. Colonialism based on monopoly charters is a barrier to expansion but not colonialism per se. In fact, the expansion of market society through colonizing 'civilizing missions' inculcates this virtue of industriousness in the 'lazy native' (Smith and Toye 1979). Colonial trade in general in Smith's reading was mutually beneficial:

> What goods could bear the expense of land-carriage between London and Calcutta? Or if there were any so precious as to be able to support this

expense, with what safety could they be transported through the territories of so many barbarous nations? Those two cities, however, at present carry on a very considerable commerce with each other, and by mutually affording a market, give a good deal of encouragement to each other's industry.

(Smith 1937, Book One Chapter III)

In Smith's exposition, society is equivalent to the nation. Thus the nation is assumed to be the trans-historical basis of organization of society. Here emerges the second question on Adam Smith's historical method. Was the nation also the basis of organization of the 'rude state' of society or is it only a characteristic of the 'advanced state'?

In this conception of the social system of the 'advanced state of society', the nation is presumed as a state of nature, while the State is what the State does (Byres 1997) – namely national defence, maintenance of law and order and administration of justice, and infrastructure (transport and communication) development in the form of public institutions with a particular emphasis on professional and general education and public works (Smith 1937).

Capitalists collude among themselves and also mobilize the institutions of the State on their behalf whenever there is any mobilization by workers for their rights. There is an explicit hint at both the class basis of the State and the organized power of employers in the following passages:

> Masters are always and everywhere in a sort of tacit, but constant and uniform combination, not to raise the wages of labour above their actual rate. . . . We seldom, indeed, hear of this combination, because it is the usual, and one may say, the natural state of things. . . . Masters, too, sometimes enter into particular combinations to sink the wages of labour even below this rate. These are always conducted with the utmost silence and secrecy, till the moment of execution. . . . Such combinations, however, are frequently resisted by a contrary defensive combination of the workmen. . . . But whether their combinations be offensive or defensive, they are always abundantly heard of. . . . The masters . . . never cease to call aloud for the assistance of the civil magistrate, and the rigorous execution of those laws which have been enacted with so much severity against the combinations of servants, labourers, and journeymen. The workmen . . . very seldom derive any advantage from the violence of those tumultuous combinations . . . generally end in nothing, but the punishment or ruin of the ringleaders.

(Smith 1937, Book One Chapter VIII)

In Book Five, Chapter I, Smith further argues:

> Wherever there is great property there is great inequality . . . and the affluence of the few supposes the indigence of the many. . . . It is only under

the shelter of the civil magistrate that the owner of that valuable property . . . can sleep a single night in security . . . he can be protected only
by the powerful arm of the civil magistrate. . . . The acquisition of valuable
and extensive property . . . requires the establishment of civil government.
Where there is no property . . . civil government is not so necessary.

In fact, the strongest assertion hinting at the class basis of the State appears in
the same chapter where Smith observes:

Civil government, so far as it is instituted for the security of property, is in
reality instituted for the defence of the rich against the poor, or of those
who have some property against those who have none at all.

Thus, for Smith, the protection of private property is the *raison d'être* of the
existence of the State. However, this functionalist view of the State does not
offer a theory of the State and more importantly the specific form of the State
under capitalism – namely, the nation-State.

Thus capitalism in Smith's opinion is essentially a market-system propelled
by 'social' talent with incremental innovation and 'natural' self-interest in which
the liberal State with all its functional roles is required for the protection of
private property. This formulation of the 'market utopia' based on natural laws
derived from history as two states of abstraction is the hallmark of CPE.

Ricardo's departures from utopia to dystopia in CPE

David Ricardo's *Principles of Political Economy and Taxation* was primarily a
response to Adam Smith within the tradition of CPE. Ricardo started with the
following observation:

It cannot then be correct, to say with Adam Smith, 'that as labour may
sometimes *purchase* a greater, and sometimes a smaller quantity of goods, it
is their value which varies, not that of the labour which purchases them;'
and therefore, 'that labour *alone never varying in its own value*, is alone the
ultimate and real standard by which the value of all commodities can at all
times and places be estimated and compared;'– but it is correct to say, as
Adam Smith . . . said, 'that the proportion between the quantities of labour
necessary for acquiring different objects seems to be the only circumstance
which can afford any rule for exchanging them for one another;' or in
other words, that it is the comparative quantity of commodities which
labour will produce, that determines their present or past relative value,
and not the comparative quantities of commodities, which are given to the
labourer in exchange for his labour.

(1817: 12)

Ricardo after setting up this poser was unable to reconcile the question that had been Adam Smith's point of entry – i.e., determinants of both the absolute and relative value of commodities. This argument has been argued to be misplaced as it is clear in Smith's exposition that labour embodied is equivalent to labour commanded only in the rude state of society in which the only form of income is the return to labour (Sinha 2010). However, abandoning the question altogether of absolute value, Ricardo argued that every exchange entailed relative labour values indicated by relative prices. This formulation within CPE was based on an analysis of isolated and discrete exchange in an abstract two-commodity world. Further in his last paper on absolute and exchangeable value, Ricardo moved even further into abandoning labour theory by expressing price in terms of the 'average commodity' (De Leo 2017).

The second modification that Ricardo made to Smith's thesis was on the question of the determination of the wage level. His argument was that cost of social subsistence affects profits and hence competition was the solution to holding wages low. This was the basis of his intense advocacy for the repeal of the Corn Laws and the Poor Laws.

> Like all other contracts, wages should be left to the fair and free competition of the market and should never be controlled by the interference of the legislature.
>
> The clear and direct tendency of the poor laws, is in direct opposition to these obvious principles: it is not, as the legislature benevolently intended, to amend the condition of the poor, but to deteriorate the condition of both poor and rich; instead of making the poor rich, they are calculated to make the rich poor; and whilst the present laws are in force, it is quite in the natural order of things that the fund for the maintenance of the poor should progressively increase, till it has absorbed all the net revenue of the country.
>
> (Ricardo 1817: 67–68)

The third departure in Ricardo's thesis was in the nature of innovation. Ricardo, who was writing at the conjuncture of the Industrial Revolution, saw innovation consisting of discrete giant leaps with technological inventions. This was at odds with Adam Smith's idea of innovation being incremental and continuous.

The fourth and the most decisive departure lay in Ricardo's hypothesis that capitalism as a system stagnates because the return from additional unit use of land tend to decrease. Second, the wage shares and profit shares that constitute the main part of the national product are at conflict which in turn generates social conflict,

> and that however abundant capital may become, there is no other adequate reason for a fall of profit but a rise of wages.
>
> (Ricardo 1817: 214)

So, continuous cheapening of commodities through free trade *is* essential for social reproduction with low levels of conflict. It is on these grounds that Ricardo argued that colonial trade based on these principles is mutually beneficial even if one country out of the two involved in the exchange is at a 'competitive disadvantage'.

These formulations of CPE are contingent on strong assumptions. First, each production period is self-contained. This assumption is similar in both Smith's and Ricardo's conceptualizations. Hence, philosophically time is linear and discrete. The difference between two discrete and linear time periods is explained in terms of additions to capital and labour. Second, in the conception of the economic system, wage advances are the only form of capital and the wage rate is assumed to be constant in a given time period. So aggregate wages are identical with capital and thus it is possible to envisage a given capital-labour ratio in every time period (Dasgupta 2009).

The labour of social reproduction has no consideration in the working of the system. Wages, while socially determined, respond to change in cost of subsistence. There is no concept of either unpaid labour or unpaid work in the creation and distribution of value in capitalism.

The capitalist is supposed to accumulate, urged by the prospect of expected profit. The additional wage fund available at the beginning of a period is dependent on total profit accumulated from the previous period (Dasgupta 2009). This determines additional labour that can be employed at the given wage rate. There is a tendency for the wage rate to rise but the population catches up and hence supply of labour adjusts to demand. As accumulation proceeds, employment increases and more output gets added but at a diminishing rate in Ricardo's conceptualization.

The distributive outcomes follow from this growth process. According to Smith, the *natural level* of wages and profits rise and fall within their minimum and maximum levels depending on the rate of growth of the economy (Sinha 2010) which is in turn determined by the extent of competition that drives expansion of markets and scope of productivity increase based on DOL in the 'advanced state of society'.

According to Ricardo, the share of wage rises because aggregate wage increases in the same proportion as employment, aggregate output increases less than proportionately due to diminishing returns. The share of profit declines in the same proportion as the rise in wage share in both Smith and Ricardo's formulations (Sinha 2010). So the rate of profit would fall as the economy progresses. Even aggregate profit would fall at advanced stages of the system.

This is the limit to growth that is endogenous to capitalism and constitutes Ricardo's dystopia of a stagnating system. As profit rates decline, the urge to accumulate also declines. The wage fund will also be declining as consumption propensity of the capitalist is perverse. Capital ceases to grow and, with it, the population. The economy reaches a stationary state. Technology improvement can counter this process but only temporarily because labour saving machinery increases the capital–labour ratio. Labour productivity would also be declining as there are diminishing returns to increasing employment.

Social reproduction in this perspective is merely a quantitative question of how subsistence can be made as cheap as possible through mass production and imports. Any role of the State to either expand welfare or to subsidize production can solely be reliant on increased rates of taxation. Since social reproduction has to be as cheap as possible, any enhanced rate of taxation is implicitly a cut in the investible fund available for the next time period. Moreover, any taxes on trade in subsistence goods also leads to an increase in the wage share as 'home-made' subsistence would be more expensive which would directly lead to rise in the wage share of the economic product. Thus taxes are a drain on society and particularly on capitalists in Ricardo's conception. Smith largely is also of the same view but at the same time believed strongly in limited intervention by the State in building public institutions and especially funding public education. Thus Smith, unlike Ricardo, is inclined towards an optimal rather than a minimal level of taxation.

What unites Smith and Ricardo is the question of the best measure of value that would reconcile the value–price relationship. Thus the preoccupation was with the best way of 'measuring' value and whether labour could be an invariable standard in this process of measurement. Sraffa (1951) had interpreted Smith's thesis as an 'adding up' theory of the three primary components of price. This leads us to suggest that the 'labour theory of value' in CPE is a theory of measurement and this preoccupation with measurement in the end leads to subsequent abandonment of CPE's foundational thesis of labour as the source of creation of value in Ricardo's later writings.

Based on these premises, the second and third quarter of the 18thcentury marks CPE's analysis of the capitalist utopia of the expanding free 'market society' driven by self-interest–induced competition in the creation and distribution of value. On the other hand, internal debates within CPE followed in the next fifty years as the world of capitalism changed drastically between 1700 and 1820s. By the 1840s and 1850s, capitalism was hit by protracted crises, challenges to the institutions of capital accumulation, the rise of class conflict and workers' militant mobilizations, along with revolts against slavery, racism and patriarchy (Hobsbawm 1992;Davis 1981). This gave rise to competing ideologies of anarchism, syndicalism and socialism along with the first articulations of feminism. The answer in history came in the form of rival imperialist expansion in the form of the 'new world' of capital (Hobson 1902; Hilferding 1981; Lenin 1916). Nation-states were at the heart of this imperialist expansion of the 'world system' and yet CPE did not have an adequate theory of the nation state. But was there an adequate theory of the market-system and the institutions of capitalism in the transition from utopia to dystopia? Marx's answer was in the negative.

Marx's utopia and his critique of CPE

Marx's *Capital* was exactly what its subtitle claimed: a critique of political economy. Marx in his entire life time of work summarily rejected many of the philosophical premises and methods of CPE, though his rejection of the later positivist departures from the same by those whom he referred to as the 'vulgar economists' was in toto. This difference in his critique of vulgar economics and CPE is clearly laid out in *The Poverty of Philoshophy* and in the *Theories of Surplus Value*.

In *The Poverty of Philosophy*, Marx posits his critique of 'vulgar economists':

> Economists express the relations of bourgeois production, the division of labour, credit, money, etc., as fixed, immutable, eternal categories . . . what they do not explain is how these relations themselves are produced, that is, the historical movement which gave them birth. . . . The economists' material is the active, energetic life of man. . . . But the moment we cease to pursue the historical movement of production relations . . . the moment we want to see in these categories no more than ideas . . . independent of real relations, we are forced to attribute the origin of these thoughts to the movement of pure reason. How does pure, eternal, impersonal reason give rise to these thoughts . . . to produce them?
>
> (Marx 1955, Chapter Two)

Further, in the *Theories of Surplus Value*, Marx lays down his critique of CPE:

> Classical Political Economy seeks to reduce the various fixed and mutually alien forms of wealth to their inner unity by means of analysis and to strip away the form in which they exist independently alongside one another. . . . Classical economy is not interested in elaborating how the various forms come into being, but seeks to reduce them to their unity by means of analysis, because it starts from them as given premises. But analysis is the prerequisite of genetical presentation and of the understanding of the real, formative process and its different phases.
>
> (Marx 1971, Part III)

Thus, Marx's critique of political economy was of the entire philosophical method and not just its methodological parts. The material historicity of social systems in general and capitalism in particular (as opposed to CPE's historical abstractions discussed in earlier sections and the ahistoricity of vulgar economics that Marx refers to in the *Poverty of Philosophy*) was Marx's entry point into his debates with and departures from political economy in the analysis of capitalism. Marx's problem consisted of the following: what constitutes value in a generalized system of circulation of commodities in historical time in a specific kind of class–divided society where the producers of commodities (workers) are not the owners of the commodities they produce? Marx sets up this problem with five questions as his entry point. First, what are the historical specificities of capitalism (in sharp contrast to CPE's historical abstractions)? Second, how is value created and distributed in capitalism? Third, why and how are social relations of capital specific in space and time? Fourth, what is the relationship between social reproduction and social production in particular societies in specific time periods? Fifth, why do nation-states exist, or, in other words, what is specific to the system of nation-states under capitalism?

The major departure from the metaphysics of CPE in Marx is the philosophical perspective of the dialectics of historical materialism. This is indeed the methodological turning of CPE 'on its head'. Marx argues in Chapter 2 of *The Poverty of Philosophy* that 'you have the logic and metaphysics of political economy . . . you have the economic categories that everybody knows, translated into a little-known language . . . so much do these categories seem to engender one another, to be linked up and intertwined with one another by the very working of the dialectic movement' (1955). With this methodological break, Marx puts forward the theory of surplus value as opposed to CPE's formulations around the measurement problematic of the labour theory of value.

In doing so, Marx takes head on the question of 'prior' accumulation in Adam Smith's thesis with a detailed material historical account of the bloody history of primary accumulation and colonialism in Part Eight of *Capital*, Volume One (Marx 1970). While tribute and accession were the two main channels in the explanation of ownership of property and consequent proprietary rights in Smith's *Lectures on Jurisprudence* (1982), Marx's account starting from the enclosure movement captures the violent pursuit of accumulation from the 15th to the 19th century in Europe in which the gory history of colonialism is central to this objective. The role of law and the State in legalizing expropriation of peasants, pauperization, subjugation, extermination and annihilation of entire peoples, and the creation of a huge mass of property-less proletariat are elucidated (Marx 1970). But, unlike Cantillon (2010), it is not only violence, conquest and the use of arms by the State that explains primary accumulation. What remained unaddressed in CPE was the question of the modes of appropriation of proprietary rights for direct appropriation in the form of M-M'. While Marx shows that both capital and profit are older than capitalism, in Marx's analysis, the nation-State in capitalism is central as a terrain in the aid of primary accumulation. Taxation, transfers and various means of settlements of international payments are shown as means by which private wealth is garnered through State facilitation (Marx 1970). This formulation on one hand contests Smith's 'prior accumulation' to be a product of industriousness and savings propensities. But it also makes two other inter-connected departures. It shows that capital as self-valorizing value M-M' can take two forms – one is the route of capitalist accumulation which consists of M-C-C'-M' but the other is rentier forms of M-M'. The second is primary accumulation, which is not confined to just explaining the pre-history of capitalism. The argument is that both forms of accumulation run through the history of capitalism.

Marx's second critical departure from CPE was based on the lacunae that CPE takes profit as a given, and does not tell us how profits are created and distributed to give capital the character of self-valorizing value through the production and circulation of commodities. Marx's entry point lay in the formulation of the uniqueness of not labour but labour power as a commodity (Marx 1970). This distinction between labour and labour power is the second paradigmatic departure from CPE.

He dwells upon the distinction of money as money and money as capital in *Capital* Volume I in which capital in money form has the characteristic of self-valorizing value (M–M') through generalized circuits of circulation that constitutes both production and exchange. In this conception, capital is a social relation rather than physical embodiment of labour value. This is his third conceptual departure point. It is in the money–commodity relationship and its fetishism that Marx rejects CPE and formulates the historical specificity of capital relationships in capitalism.

It is the 'hidden abode of production' in which social relations of capital create the conditions of production of surplus value. If indeed the wage contract entailed a full compensation to labour and all material in the form of constant capital had to be paid for by the capitalist in the production process, where would profits come from? It is here that the social power of capitalists as owners and controllers of constant and variable capital (as opposed to CPE's conception of fixed and circulating capital) and hence by default all means of production under capitalism subjugates the working class in the institution of the market in which the wage contract entails the selling of labour-power and its variable utilization by capitalists as labour-time. It is the variability of this labour-time which is a direct function of the power of capital over labour that explains the raison d'être of both the existence of the capitalists and the creation of surplus value. Thus time in capitalism has a specific dimension – the length and intensity of the 'working day' which explains the creation of absolute and relative surplus value. Workers work to socially reproduce themselves (at subsistence) for part of the working day which constitutes socially necessary labour time (SNLT). The rest of the day that constitutes surplus labour-time in which the intensity of labour is uncompensated, and is constituted by unpaid labour. This is the source of the creation of surplus value through deployment of surplus labour time by the institutions of capital. The lesser the component of SNLT, the more is the possibility of extraction of unpaid labour for production of surplus value. This is not simply a function of cheapening of subsistence (as in CPE), but it is constituted by the direct power of the capitalist over the worker. Thus, social reproduction and production for profit are outcomes of the same material conditions. Marx argues explicitly in the Grundrisse that, in capitalism, social reproduction is subsumed to the needs of production for profits. Moreover, the role of patriarchy and other sources of oppression are endogenous to the nature of class society and the material basis of production and reproduction and not exogenous as in CPE(Marx 1973). This is evident in Chapter 8 of the Holy Family on the discussion on sexual exploitation of masters of their servant as well as in Engels's later exposition on the family, private property and the State, along with the role of women and children in the production process in capitalism in *Capital* Volume I (Engels 1884; Marx and Engels 1956; Marx 1970).

The product of surplus labour time accrues as surplus value, which, when realized by exchange, would materialize as profit. Thus, the extent of power of the capitalist to appropriate surplus labour time derives from the extent and form of ownership and control of capital and in the compression of expenditure on what CPE regarded as 'unproductive labour' (which according to Marx is crucial to the realization of profits but a deduction from the surplus value). Profits materialize only with the realization of surplus value through the generalized system of circulation of commodities through the extended circuits of reproduction (Marx 1956). Competition between capitalists is a crucial determinant of the extent of the realization of surplus value but the rate of surplus value (exploitation) depends on the power of capital over labour in the production process. This constitutes a theory of profit that is missing in CPE, and is his fourth major departure from CPE.

Marx traces the rise of the joint stock company and the banking system in *Capital* Volume III. He elaborates on how the institutions that emerge in historical time in the form of the banking and financial system in capitalism mops up the entire savings of society to put it at the disposal of capitalists for conversion into 'social capital' (Marx 1986). However, the very same process also triggers the subordination of industrial capital by banking capital and small capital by the big which later Marxists would develop into the theories of imperialism. In Volume III of *Capital*, Marx clearly elucidates the tendency of monopoly in capitalism as opposed to CPE's envisioning of capitalism as a system based on competition of small individual capitals (Marx 1986). This is Marx's fifth departure from CPE.

In this formulation, the limits to competition between capitalists through the tendencies of concentration and centralization of capital lead to disproportionality and overproduction. It is in these outcomes of the process of concentration and centralization of capital that Marx locates the potential of periodic crisis that is inherent in capitalism (Marx 1956, 1986). Each such crisis originates in production and leads to creation of avenues of primary 'rentier' accumulation in which M–C–C'–M' becomes subordinated by rentier forms of M–M' circuits (Marx 1986). Thus financialization is a symptom of crisis and not the cause unlike Keynes' formulation. This theory of crisis is Marx's sixth departure as opposed to CPE.

The last significant departure lies in Marx's argument of the impossibility of a universal theory of the nation-State that abstracts away from the historical method (Das Gupta 2016). Marx and Engels traced the relationship between the 'development of the bourgeoisie' in Europe and the 'corresponding political advance of that class' as follows:

> An oppressed class under the sway of the feudal nobility, an armed and self-governing association in the medieval commune; here independent urban republic (as in Italy and Germany), there taxable 'third estate' of the monarchy (as in France), afterwards, in the period of manufacture proper, serving either the semi-feudal or the absolute monarchy as a counterpoise against the nobility, and, in fact, cornerstone of the great monarchies in general, the bourgeoisie has at last, since the establishment of Modern Industry and of the world market, conquered for itself, in the modern representative State, exclusive political sway.
>
> (Marx and Engels 1998: 37)

This was an analysis historically rooted in the transformations of European states with the emergence of capitalist relations as dominant and the bourgeoisie as the key ruling class. Marx in the third volume of *Capital* also pointed to the historical specificity of State formations and its relationship with social relations by arguing:

> It is always the direct relationship of the owners of the conditions of production to the direct producers ... which reveals the innermost secret, the hidden basis of the entire social structure, and with it the political form of the relation of sovereignty and dependence ... the corresponding specific form of state.
>
> (Marx 1986: 791)

Similarly, in the *Critique of the Gotha Programme*, Marx argued that while one can generalize about 'present society' across national boundaries, it is impossible to do so about the 'present state'. Thus, whereas a 'capitalist society' could be found in all 'civilised countries' and 'varies only in degree of development, the form of the State changes with each country's border' (Marx 1968: 312) and differs between the Prusso-German empire and Switzerland and was 'different in England from that in the United States' (Marx 1968: 312).

Every attempt to define the class nature of the capitalist State, which abstracts from the historical origins and trajectories of that State, conflicts with historical materialism (Mandel 1969). This is Marx's methodological starting point on the question of the role of the nation-State in capitalism. However, he also recognizes that the nation-State universally has been an indispensable instrument in the process of capitalist development, not only because the military power of European nation states has carried the dominating force of capital to every corner of the world, but also in the sense that nation states have been the conduits of capitalism at the receiving end too (Wood 2003).

The modern nation-State and the modern market system are seen generally in the liberal paradigm as separate institutional domains of political and economic power, respectively. However, the State plays an economic role (that CPE partially captures). Marx's significant departure lay in illustrating that capital plays a crucial political role in subjugation and disciplining through the institutions of the market either because of the needs of the stomach or 'fancy', i.e., through a commodity fetish (Mandel 1969;Marx 1970).

Marx's paradigmatic departure from CPE thus is constituted by the perspective that oppression and exploitation would be impossible to end without ending the regime of capital and profits. It is this emancipator perspective that led Marx to formulate his utopia. It was one in which the power of capital and that of the capitalist nation-State would be dissolved to create a society of associated producers – 'something that cannot be easily emulated . . . from past experience quite distinct from the market utopia of capitalism that CPE was premised on' (Roy et al. 2015: 6). The reorganization of social reproduction with the promise of emancipation from patriarchy – the end of the tyranny of family, private property, capital and the nation-State – and the conscious political attempt of collectivism rather than individualism forming the basis of new 'individualities' were the revolutionary departures of this utopia (Das Gupta 2017).

Thus the usual dominant approach (in the teaching of economics, history and other social sciences) of classifying Marx as a classical political economist subverts and subsumes the radical revolutionary departure that Marx signified in the making of a 'new' political economy as a method. This is irrespective of what one's ideological perspective maybe on classical political economy, Marx and/or of Marxist/Marxian political economy.

Note

1 The author acknowledges with gratitude the valuable comments and suggestions received from Surajit Mazumdar, Satyaki Roy, the editors of this volume and an anonymous reviewer.

References

Byers, T.J. 1997. 'Introduction', in T. J. Byes (ed.), *The State, Development Planning and Liberalisation in India*, Oxford: Oxford University Press.

Cantillon, R. 2010. *An Essay on Economic Theory*, Albama: Mises Institute.

Dasgupta, A.K. 2009. *The Collected Works of A. K. Dasgupta Volume I: Two Treatises on Classical Political Economy*, New Delhi: Oxford University Press.

Das Gupta, C. 2016. *State and Capital in Independent India: Institutions and Accumulation*, New Delhi: Cambridge University Press.

Das Gupta, C. 2017. 'Revolution, Emancipation and Social Reproduction', paper presented at the conference on 150 years of capital and 100 years of Russian Revolution, South Asia University, November 4.

Davis, A. 1981. *Women, Race and Class*, London: The Women's Press.

De Leo, M. 2017. '"Absolute Value and Exchangeable Value": A Key Element in Ricardo's Theory of Value', *Contributions to Political Economy*, 36(1), 61–80, July 1.

Dobb, M. 1973. *Theories of Value and Distribution Since Adam Smith*, Cambridge: Cambridge University Press.

Elson, D.1979. 'The Value Theory of Labour', in Elson, D. ed., *Value: The Representation of Labour in Capitalism*, Atlantic Heights, NJ: Humanities Press.

Engels, F. 1884. *The Origin of the Family, Private Property and the State*. Marx/Engels Selected Works, Volume Three. www.marxists.org/archive/marx/works/1884/origin-family/. Last accessed on 30 November 2017.

Fanon, F. 1963. *The Wretched of the Earth*, New York: Grove Press.

Harkin, M. 2013. 'Adam Smith on Women', in C. J. Berry, M.P. Paganelli and C. Smith (eds.), *The Oxford Handbook of Adam Smith*, Oxford: Oxford University Press.

Heilbroner, R.L.1985. *The Nature and Logic of Capitalism*, New York: W.W. Norton.

Heilbroner, R. L. and Milberg, W. 2008. *The Making of Economic Society*, New Jersey: Pearson Prentice Hall.

Hilferding, R. 1981. *Finance Capital: A Study of the Latest Phase of Capitalist Development*, London: Routledge & Kegan Paul.

Hobsbawm, E.J. 1992, *The Age of Revolution 1789–1848*, London: Abacus.

Hobson, J.A. 1902. *Imperialism: A Study*, New York: James Pott & Co.

Lenin, V.I. 1916. 'Imperialism: The Highest Stage of Capitalism', in V.I. Lenin (ed.), *Selected Works*, Moscow: Progress Publishers, Vol. 1, pp. 667–766, 1963.

Lindbolm, C. E. 2001. *The Market System: What It Is, How It Works and What to Make of It*, New Haven: Yale University Press.

Mandel, E.1969. *Excerpts from Marxist Theory of the State*, Pamphlet with an introduction by George Novac, Pathfinder Press.www.marxists.org/archive/mandel/1969/xx/state.htm. Last accessed on 14 November 2017.

Marx, K. 1955. *The Poverty of Philosophy*, Moscow: Progress Publishers, www.marxists.org/archive/marx/works/1847/poverty-philosophy/index.htm. Last accessed on 29 November 2017.

Marx, K. 1956. *Capital, Vol. 2*, Moscow: Progress Publishers.

Marx, K. 1968. 'Critique of the Gotha Programme', in K. Marx and F. Engels (eds.), *Selected Works in One Volume*, London: Lawrence and Wishart.

Marx, K. 1970. *Capital: A Critique of Political Economy, Volume 1*, London: Lawrence and Wishart.

Marx, K. 1971. *Theories of Surplus-Value*, Moscow: Progress Publisher. www.marxists.org/archive/marx/works/1863/theories-surplus-value/. Last accessed on 13 December 2017.

Marx, K. 1973. *Grundrisse*. Penguin Books. www.marxists.org/archive/marx/works/1857/grundrisse/index.htm. Last accessed on 12 December 2017.

Marx, K. 1986. *Capital*, Vol. 3, reprint, London: Lawrence and Wishart.

Marx, K. and Engels, F. 1956. *The Holy Family or Critique of Critical Criticism*, Moscow: Foreign Languages Publishing House.

Marx, K. and Engels, F. 1998. *The Communist Manifesto*, London: Verso.

Milonakis, D. and Fine, B. 2009. *From Political Economy to Economics: Method, the Social and Historical Evolution of Economic Theory*, London and New York: Routledge.

Ricardo, D. 1817. *On the Principles of Political Economy and Taxation*, London: John Murray.

Roy, S., Mazumdar, S. and Das Gupta, C. 2015. *Socialist Experiences and Methods in Social Science*, Mimeo.

Sinha, A. 2010. *Theories of Value from Adam Smith to Piero Sraffa*, New Delhi and London: Routledge.

Smith, A. 1937. *An Inquiry into the Nature and Causes of the Wealth of Nations*, Random House. www.marxists.org/reference/archive/smith-adam/works/wealth-of-nations/index.htm. Last accessed on 12 December 2017.

Smith, A. 1982. *Lectures on Jurisprudence*, Indianapolis: Liberty Fund.

Smith, A. 2002. *Theory of Moral Sentiments*, Cambridge: Cambridge University Press.

Smith, S. and Toye, J. 1979. 'Introduction: Three Stories About Trade and Poor Economies', *The Journal of Development Studies*, 15(3), 1–18.

Sraffa, P. ed. 1951. *The Works and Correspondence of David Ricardo*, Volume I, Cambridge: Cambridge University Press.

Thomas, A.M. 2018. 'Adam Smith on the Philosophy and Provision of Education', *Journal of Interdisciplinary Economics*, 30(1), 105–116.

Weber, M. 1927. *General Economic History*, New York: Greenberg.

Wood, E.M. 2003. *The Empire of Capital*, New Delhi: LeftWord.

Zinn, H. 1980. *A People's History of the United States*, London and New York: Longman.

Chapter 7

On the origins of post Keynesian macroeconomics

John King

The ambiguity of the *General Theory*

The pre-history of post Keynesian economics begins just over eighty years ago. John Maynard Keynes was surprisingly ambivalent about the doctrinal (and political) implications of his intended masterpiece, *The General Theory of Employment, Interest and Money*. In a frequently cited letter in 1935 to George Bernard Shaw, he made a very strong claim about its likely impact: 'To understand my state of mind, however, you have to know that I believe myself to be writing a book on economic theory which will largely revolutionise – not, I suppose, at once but in the course of the next ten years – the way the world thinks about economic problems' (1973: 492). And in 'Concluding Notes' to the book itself he foreshadowed 'the euthanasia of the rentier, and, consequently, the euthanasia of the cumulative oppressive power of the capitalist to exploit the scarcity-value of capital', and called for 'the somewhat comprehensive socialisation of investment' as 'the only means of securing an approximation to full employment' (Keynes 1936: 376, 378). 'In some other respects', however, Keynes argued, 'the foregoing theory is moderately conservative in its implications', since 'no obvious case is made out for a system of State Socialism which would embrace most of the economic life of the community'. Indeed, he believed, once full employment had been achieved 'the classical theory comes into its own again from this point onwards' (*ibid.*, pp. 377, 378). All this in three pages!

The *General Theory* was a poorly structured and, in some ways, also a poorly written book, which left many questions unanswered and many theoretical issues unresolved. Keynes was aware of the problems that this posed, writing a summary and clarification of the arguments for his American readers (Keynes 1937) and promising to produce a set of 'footnotes' to the book dealing with the more important criticisms that had been made. Under different circumstances these 'footnotes' might have been expanded into a substantially revised second edition. Keynes's ill health – he suffered a severe heart attack in 1937 – and his focus on public service during the Second World War prevented him from even beginning work on a revised edition of the *General Theory* before his death in 1946.

The similarities between Keynes, Alfred Marshall, Knut Wicksell and even Léon Walras were noted by several reviewers (King 2002: 15–18), leading J.R. Hicks to describe the *General Theory* as 'a useful book but it is neither the beginning nor the end of Dynamic Economics' (1937: 159). As Keynes had (almost) conceded, it set out nothing more *general* than 'the Economics of Depression' (*ibid.*, p. 152). Hicks was one of the originators of what came to be known as the (old) neo-classical synthesis, with what soon became the textbook IS-LM model at its core (King 2018). The (old) Keynesian school saw its (old) neo-classical synthesis as a systematic and coherent reconciliation of Keynes and neo-classical macroeconomics. (The 'old' is needed to distinguish both the school and the synthesis from the New Keynesian school, and the associated new neo-classical synthesis, which emerged half a century later). The IS-LM model itself was a genuine multiple discovery, suggesting that its interpretation of Keynes as champion of a new form of general equilibrium theory was very much 'in the air'. And Keynes himself showed some sympathy for it, even in the version set out by Oskar Lange, a Polish socialist then working in the US and as such about as unlikely to attract Keynes's intellectual sympathy as anyone then alive (King 2002: 31).

The Fundamentalist Keynesians

The IS-LM model was one of the three components of the old neo-classical synthesis (hereafter ONS), and the only one to be developed within a year or two of the publication of the *General Theory*. The other two components made a delayed appearance. IS-LM provided a clear neoclassical framework for the determination of real income (and hence for the determination of output and employment) and the rate of interest in the short period. Eventually the Solow-Swan growth model extended the analysis to the long period, and the Phillips Curve offered an explanation of wage (and therefore also price) inflation in terms of the extent of excess supply in the labour market. One of the most prominent pioneers of post Keynesian economics, the American Sidney Weintraub (1914–1983), was an advocate of the ONS until the late 1950s, when inflation accelerated in the US with no apparent tightening of the labour market, leading him to argue that cost-push inflation had become important but had been neglected in the ONS, which focussed entirely on demand-pull inflation (these terms were widely used in policy discussions at the time). Weintraub himself became a vocal supporter of a market-based incomes policy to complement demand management in controlling inflation, using the taxation of excessive wage increases to stiffen employer resistance to trade union demands (Wallich and Weintraub 1971).

His student and subsequent colleague Paul Davidson (b. 1931) took issue with the theoretical basis of the ONS at a more fundamental level. Davidson rejected what he termed the three 'classical axioms' that the old Keynesians had incorporated into their models. None of these axioms, he maintained, was consistent with Keynes's analysis in the *General Theory*. The first, the *ergodicity* axiom, was required to support the notion of rational expectations, but it was totally unrealistic and could not be reconciled with Keynes's recognition of the importance of fundamental uncertainty in the economy. The second, the axiom of *gross substitutability*, entailed that unemployment was due to wage rigidity and could thus be reduced by cutting real wages. The third, the *neutrality of money* axiom, restored the classical dichotomy between real and monetary variables, making output and employment a function of real factors (only) and the inflation rate a function of the quantity of money (only).

To illustrate what he regarded as the authentic Keynesian macroeconomic model, Davidson drew the aggregate demand/aggregate supply model in *Z, N* space that Keynes himself had described, but not drawn, in the *General Theory*, in which the level of employment is determined in the product market, by the principle of effective demand, not in the labour market (Davidson and Smolensky 1964; Davidson 1972). The actual real wage is indeed higher than the real wage that would prevail at full employment, but full employment can be achieved only by an increase in effective demand, not simply by reducing the real wage. The rate of interest does not play a central role in Davidson's analysis: it may have some influence on the level of investment, and hence on effective demand, but it is much less important than it is in the IS-LM model.

There are still some significant neoclassical elements in this 'Fundamentalist Keynesian' macroeconomics. Davidson's aggregate supply curve is Marshallian in inspiration, and is derived from a standard aggregate production function, and he never showed any interest in the 'neo-Ricardian' critique of marginal productivity theory that was mounted by Piero Sraffa and his Cambridge (UK) colleagues (Harcourt 1972). The associated labour supply and labour demand functions are also essentially neoclassical in nature. But in some ways Davidson's approach was more radical than it appears to be. First, he was always a strong critic of 'imperfectionism', the claim that has been at the heart of the new neoclassical synthesis since the 1980s – that imperfect competition in the labour market (and the resulting downward wage rigidity) is a necessary condition for the principle of effective demand to operate. This, Davidson maintained, is a fallacy. Second, his analysis is essentially macroeconomic, like that of Keynes, and cannot be reduced to propositions about microeconomics. It points to a serious fallacy of composition at the heart of the 'microfoundations' project that would later unite the New Keynesians and New Classical economists (King 2012). Third, as we have seen, Davidson's non-ergodicity axiom denies the validity of the 'rational expectations' hypothesis that underpins New Classical theory, since this hypothesis cannot be reconciled with fundamental uncertainty.

The Kalecki version

The Polish theorist Michał Kalecki (1899–1970) was self-taught in economics, working first as an engineer and then as a business journalist before becoming a full-time economic researcher (Toporowski 2013). He worked in Britain and North America for almost two decades after 1936 before returning to Poland, where he spent the rest of his life as an academic economist and government adviser. In addition to his work on the macroeconomics of capitalist economies Kalecki wrote extensively on development economics and the economics of socialism, leading Geoff Harcourt to describe him as 'the greatest all-round economist of the twentieth century' (2006: 163).

Although never a Communist, Kalecki was a lifelong socialist with a strong interest in some (but not all) aspects of Marxian political economy. Thus he always emphasized the *class* nature of capitalist society, carefully distinguishing the conflicting interests and the very different behaviour of capitalists and workers. He also stressed the instability of the capitalist economy, and the central role of *political* as well as economic conflict in determining economic outcomes. But Kalecki was an undogmatic and in many ways unorthodox Marxist, who took no interest in the labour theory of value or in Marx's analyses of the falling rate of profit, dialectics or the materialist theory of history. He read little, and cited very few sources. As an economic theorist, then, Kalecki was very much a minimalist, but he anticipated some key elements of Keynes's *General Theory* and arguably improved on them in several important respects.

The principle of effective demand in a two-class society is based on the proposition that 'workers spend what they get; capitalists get what they spend' (this formulation is often attributed to Kalecki, but it has never been traced to a published source). Workers live from one pay packet to the next, saving (and dis-saving) little or nothing. Capitalists do save, but it is their expenditure that is crucially important for the behaviour of the economy. The algebra of Kalecki's income-expenditure model is very simple (Kalecki 1954). To simplify the analysis (without seriously compromising it) we assume a closed economy with no government. Income (Y) accrues to workers in the form of wages (W) and to capitalists in the form of profits (P). Aggregate income is equal to total expenditure on consumption by workers (C_w) and capitalists (C_c), plus investment spending by capitalists (I). Thus

$$Y = W + P = C_w + I + C_c \tag{1}$$

If workers do spend all that they get, so that their saving is zero, then

$$W = C_w \tag{2}$$

so that

$$P = I + C_c \tag{3}$$

In equation (3) causation runs from right to left, that is, from expenditure to income: aggregate profits equal the sum of capitalists' spending on investment and consumption. As for Keynes, investment expenditure plays a crucial role, and the most important factor in the determination of investment decisions is the expected profitability of new investment projects. Kalecki's emphasis on class relations leads him to identify a potential contradiction here, since any tendency for the profit share (P/Y) to rise at the expense of the wage share (W/Y) will reduce consumption and may well also lead to a decline in investment via the accelerator mechanism. Thus the constant pressure to reduce wages may be bad for profits, not for any individual capitalist but for the class as a whole.

There are some important implications for economic policy. Kalecki was not a revolutionary socialist, and unlike many more orthodox Marxists he did not expect the capitalist economy to break down because of its profoundly contradictory nature. But he did identify some very serious problems that would confront a reformist social democratic government that attempted to apply Keynesian principles of demand management to create and sustain full employment. The most significant of these problems was political rather than narrowly economic. Capitalists had always relied on unemployment to maintain their power over the working class, and they would therefore see full employment in peacetime as a threat to discipline in the factories (Kalecki 1943). They could also be expected to have ideological objections to the growth of government expenditure, and to any increase in government influence over the economy more generally, that the adoption of Keynesian macroeconomic policies would generate. Kalecki noted that these objections applied more strongly to civilian than to military spending, and he thus anticipated the 'military Keynesianism' of the Cold War era (Toporowski 2016).

Towards the end of his life Kalecki came to acknowledge what he termed the 'crucial reform' of advanced capitalist economies that had taken place after 1945 (Kalecki and Kowalik 1971; King 2013a). The combination of a commitment to full employment (and the fiscal and monetary policy measures that were needed to implement it), strong trade unions, tight labour market regulation (via collective bargaining and/or government action) and a comprehensive welfare state had allowed real wages to rise at the same rate as productivity, so that the wage share remained constant and the economic contradictions of pre-1939 capitalism had been overcome. This was the so-called golden age of capitalism, or what the French still refer to as the 'trente glorieuses' (thirty splendid years), 1945–c. 1975.

There was never a Kaleckian school of economics, at least not in his lifetime. Kalecki became an academic economist, with students and academic colleagues, only after his return to Poland in 1955, and his relationship with the Communist regime was always somewhat precarious. He did influence some Western theorists, including the dissident Austrian writer Josef Steindl, whose *Maturity and Stagnation* (1952) established him as Kalecki's most important disciple. Kalecki's influence can also be seen in the analysis of *Monopoly Capital* by the independent American Marxists Paul Baran and Paul Sweezy (1966). But arguably his most important advocate was the eminent Cambridge Keynesian

Joan Robinson, who shared both his sceptical view of neoclassical economics and his sympathetic but critical approach to Marxism and promoted his ideas throughout the English-speaking world.

One major question that is missing in the Kaleckian model is any serious discussion of financial fragility. Kalecki was not greatly interested in the macroeconomics of money and finance. His most significant treatment of financial markets had a microeconomic focus, with the phenomena of 'borrowers' risk' and 'lenders' risk' used to explain why oligopoly rather than monopoly was the typical market structure; the risks associated with increased debt made firms unwilling and/or unable to borrow enough to take over the entire industry (Kalecki 1971: 105–109). Kalecki died in 1970, before the process of 'financialization' had really begun and five years before Hyman Minsky published his first major book, *John Maynard Keynes* (1975). As we have seen, he was not a great reader, and it is entirely possible that he had never encountered Minsky's work (the only two references to the American theorist in volume II of Kalecki's *Collected Works* were both made by his editor, Jerzy Osiatynski). At all accounts, Kalecki's penetrating analysis does need to be complemented by that of Minsky.

Hyman Minsky and the financial instability hypothesis

Hyman Philip Minsky (1919–1996) was born to working-class parents in Chicago, where he studied undergraduate economics before moving to Harvard. There he wrote his PhD dissertation on the integration of money and finance into Keynesian models of the business cycle. At Harvard he came under the influence of Joseph Schumpeter, whose emphasis on the importance of innovation was to have a great influence on his later work. Minsky was also influenced by Irving Fisher, whose debt deflation interpretation of the Great Depression would also form part of that work. Minsky taught at Brown University (1949–1957), the University of California at Berkeley (1957–1965) and finally at Washington University in St. Louis (1965–1990). Here he was also associated with the Mark Twain Banks, which he described as 'my laboratory'. On a personal note, I still have strong memories of two seminars that he gave at the University of Melbourne in 1988, where he spoke for almost an hour and a half without, apparently, pausing for breath. Minsky awakened my latent interest in post Keynesian economics and thereby determined the course of the second half of my academic career. He was, quite literally, unforgettable.

His underlying vision of American capitalism placed financial markets at the centre of his analysis; labour, industry and production did not interest him very much (see King 2013b, on which I draw heavily in this section). In Minsky's 'Wall Street vision', the crucial economic relationship is that between investment banker and client, not factory-owner and worker. His 'representative agent' is neither a classless consumer (as in mainstream economic theory) nor an industrial capitalist (as in Kalecki), but a financial capitalist. Borrowing and lending are the crucial transactions, not buying consumer goods or selling labour power.

Minsky's *financial instability hypothesis* (FIH) explained why the system is vulnerable to financial crises, why nevertheless a catastrophe like the Great Depression had not happened again, and what must be done in order to prevent a recurrence. For Minsky, financial markets are inherently unstable. In a world characterized by fundamental uncertainty rather than by quantifiable risk, the expectations of lenders and borrowers fluctuate in what seems to be a regularly repeated cyclical process. As the economy begins to emerge from a cyclical downturn, depressed expectations give way to increasing confidence, which grows into exuberance and excitement in the boom phase of the cycle before collapsing into renewed despair.

These mood swings are reflected in financial transactions, as caution is replaced first by optimism and then by euphoria. In the early stages of an upswing, *hedge finance* is the general rule: borrowers are able to make both their scheduled interest payments and the necessary repayments of principal from the cash flows generated by their activities. Eventually *speculative finance* becomes more typical, and profit flows prove to be sufficient only to meet interest charges and at best a proportion of principal repayment commitments. As the boom nears its end, *Ponzi finance* appears, with borrowers unable even to pay interest without incurring further debts in order to do so. (Here Minsky invoked the memory of the early 20th-century Italian-American swindler Charles Ponzi; a century later Bernie Madoff would achieve notoriety – and a lengthy prison sentence – for similar fraudulent behaviour). *Financial fragility* now increases rapidly, and soon the cycle turns down in a spiral of bankruptcies, 'fire sales' of assets at greatly reduced prices, falling profit expectations and declining profit flows, before confidence recovers and the entire process begins all over again.

Minsky identifies three ways in which financial events affect the real economy. First and foremost, changes in asset prices lead to changes in both consumption and investment spending. Consumption depends on wealth as well as income, so that increases in asset prices induce agents to increase their consumption expenditure, and vice versa, reinforcing the accelerator mechanism that links the level of investment to the rate of change of consumption spending. Investment is also heavily dependent on the price of existing assets relative to newly produced capital goods. When asset prices collapse, due to the 'fire sales' required to meet financial commitments, the incentive to buy new capital goods falls; the reverse is true when asset prices are rising.

The second way in which financial conditions affect aggregate expenditure, and therefore influence output and employment, is through changes in expectations. Indeed, the financial instability hypothesis is in a sense a theory of cyclically *irrational* expectations, as speculative finance gives way to Ponzi finance and then, after the credit crunch, to hedge finance once more. The third channel through which finance affects output and employment is critical in the crisis and depression phases of the cycle. This is *credit rationing*. When the bubble bursts even solid credit-worthy borrowers will be denied finance, irrespective of the interest rates that they are prepared to pay, and will be forced to reduce their expenditure accordingly.

All this has a further important implication: the *non-neutrality of debt*, and hence the rejection of the Modigliani-Miller theorem that is central to the ONS and to all subsequent developments in mainstream macroeconomic theory. A fundamental asymmetry is involved: debtors can be forced to cut back on their expenditure, but creditors cannot be forced to increase spending. In effect this takes the non-neutrality of *money* one stage further than Keynes and the Fundamentalist Keynesians had done. After the global financial crisis of 2007–8 this might seem to be a very obvious point, but before then it was denied or ignored by the great majority of orthodox macroeconomists.

While Minsky believed that capitalism could and must be reformed, he was under no illusion that the business cycle could be abolished or economic instability eliminated. Thus he advanced what might be termed a financial market regulation vulnerability hypothesis (FMRVH), according to which entrepreneurial agility, which was repeatedly demonstrated by financial innovation, demanded from the regulators both eternal vigilance and constant attention to institutional reform. The profits available from the evasion or avoidance of financial regulation are so enormous that efforts to do so will be continuous, substantial and often successful. 'A fundamental flaw exists in an economy with capitalist financial institutions, for no matter how ingenious and perceptive Central Bankers may be, the speculative and innovative elements of capitalism will eventually lead to financial usages and relations that are conducive to instability' (Minsky 1977: 22; cf. Minsky 1986: 287, 333). Thus the authorities need to be constantly alert, but they will not always succeed. Minksy would not have been at all surprised by the innovative practices, novel institutions and new asset types that were implicated in the global financial crisis, which has often been interpreted as a vindication of both the FIH and the FMRVH. Note, however, that there is no suggestion of stagnation in Minsky's work, since he regarded innovation and dynamic change to be inherent features of the modern capitalist economy.

What is missing from Minsky's analysis? First, until 1977 he had no clear analysis of capitalists' financial *resources* to set against his very well developed model of their financial *commitments*. When he finally adopted the Kaleckian income-expenditure model, set out in the second section, he was able to fill this very important (and frequently criticized) gap in his model (Minsky 1977). Second, and this omission persisted until his death in 1996, he had little or nothing to say about working-class finances. In effect he followed Kalecki in (implicitly) assuming that workers spend every dollar that they receive in wages pretty well as soon as they are paid, neither saving nor incurring any substantial debts. Even his identification of a new stage of 'money manager capitalism' (Wray 2009; Whalen 2017) did not seriously alter this assumption, since it was too focussed on relations between capitalists, not on the relationship between capital and labour.

Post Keynesian economics in the 1970s – and in 2019

These three post Keynesian schools of thought were clearly recognizable by the mid-1970s. The essence of Fundamentalist Keynesianism was set out in 1972 in Davidson's *Money and the Real World*. Kalecki's approach was advocated by Joan Robinson and other theorists of the Cambridge (UK) school, for example in the ambitious introductory text that she co-authored in the following year (Robinson and Eatwell 1973; King and Millmow 2003). The book-length version of Minsky's arguments appeared two years later in his *John Maynard Keynes* (1975).

As we have seen, there were serious differences between the three schools on major points of theoretical concern. But they all agreed on the six core principles set out by A.P. Thirlwall (1993: 335–337). First, employment and unemployment are determined in the product market, not the labour market. Second, involuntary unemployment exists, and it is caused by deficient demand, not labour market imperfections. Third, the investment-saving relationship is crucial to any post Keynesian model, and causation runs from investment to saving, and not vice versa.

Fourth, a money economy is fundamentally different from a barter economy, so that money matters. In Marxian language, it is necessary to distinguish capitalism from simple commodity production, or what Keynes termed a 'cooperative economy'. In the latter, the commodity circulation process takes the form C-M-C, the exchange of a commodity (C) for money (M) in order to obtain another commodity of equal value (C). In capitalism, however, it takes the form M-C-C'-M', the exchange of money (M) for capital goods and human labour power of equal value (C) in order to produce different commodities of greater value (C' > C) and sell them for profit (M' > M). The difference between C' and C, which is equal to the difference between M' and M, is the surplus value generated by the performance of surplus labour in the production process. Although he was no friend of Marxism, Keynes himself used this formula in an early draft of the *General Theory* (Keynes 1982: 81).

Fifth, the quantity theory of money is wrong. Money is not neutral, and debt matters, so that the Modigliani-Miller theorem is also false; it does make a difference if new investment is financed by borrowing. Sixth, capitalist economies are driven by the 'animal spirits' of investors, which means that the profit expectations of entrepreneurs are crucial, while utility maximization over a lifetime by classless consumers is not. These six principles are sufficient to establish the principle of effective demand and to demonstrate that Say's Law is wrong. Active fiscal and monetary policies are needed to maintain full employment, and an incomes policy is required to combat inflation.

In the early to mid-1970s these principles were not so alien to mainstream macroeconomics as they would soon become. In a recent book on the history of American economics two colleagues and I distinguished the mainstream from 'other voices' and 'crosscurrents' in economic thought, which itself was treated as if it were a normal statistical distribution. The mainstream represents the median, plus or minus one standard deviation, while 'other voices' are found between one and two standard deviations away and 'crosscurrents' occupy the outer fringes, more than two standard deviations from the median (Barbour et al. 2018: x). For the period ending in 1973, post Keynesian economics was one of the 'other voices', along with institutionalism and behavioural economics. In the subsequent period, down to the present day, post Keynesianism has been moved to the 'crosscurrents' section of the chapter, which it now shares with Marxian, Austrian, feminist and ecological economics, along with institutionalism, leaving the 'other voices' section to more respectable schools like neuroeconomics and complexity theory (ibid., pp. 187–93, 225–33).

Evidence in support of these classifications is not hard to come by. J.K. Galbraith was elected president of the American Economic Association for the calendar year 1971, and he arranged for Joan Robinson to give the Richard T. Ely lecture at the annual meeting of the AEA in New Orleans in the December of that year (Robinson 1972). Her lecture, on 'the second crisis of economic theory', was very well received, but it was also the last occasion on which any economist so far from the mainstream would be honoured in this way. Through to the mid- to late 1960s Davidson, Minsky and Weintraub were still able to publish in the leading economic journals, with Davidson having a paper in *Econometrica* as late as 1968. But these opportunities soon dried up, as mainstream economics displayed increasing hostility towards post Keynesian and other forms of unorthodox ideas and refused to publish their work. In 1978 the newly established *Journal of Post Keynesian Economics* began to meet the need for a separate and distinct outlet for post Keynesian ideas. It followed a number of other heterodox journals, which included the *Review of Radical Political Economics* (which began publication in 1969), the *Review of Social Economy* (1972), the institutionalist *Journal of Economic Issues* (1973) and the more ecumenical *Cambridge Journal of Economics* (1977). By the end of the century the term 'heterodox economics' was in widespread use as a loose collective description of these various 'cross-currents' (Lee 2009).

In 2018 there were flourishing societies of post Keynesian economists in many parts of the world, including France, Germany and the United Kingdom – though not, surprisingly, in the US, where the *Journal of Post Keynesian Economics* remained, as it had begun, the property of the company that published it (for many years Myron E. Sharpe Inc., and more recently Taylor & Francis). New journals with a post Keynesian emphasis commenced publication in the 21st century: the *European Journal of Economics and Economic Policies* (formerly *Zeitschrift für Ökonomie/Journal of Economics*) in 2004 and the *Review of Keynesian*

Economics in 2013. In Australia the journal *Economic and Labour Relations Review*, edited from the University of New South Wales, is an important outlet for post Keynesian ideas, which were given a major boost by the return of Geoff Harcourt to his native land. The two-volume *Oxford Handbook of Post-Keynesian Economics* that he co-edited remains the best scholarly summary of its subject-matter (Harcourt and Kriesler 2013a, 2013b). In Australia and elsewhere, post Keynesians continue to enjoy relatively friendly relations with other dissident schools of thought, including institutionalists and radical Marxists, though whether these contacts are close enough to constitute a single, united, coherent heterodox economics remains contentious (King 2013c).

In terms of macroeconomic theory, the three distinct post Keynesian schools discussed in previous sections can still be identified (King 2015). Fundamentalist Keynesian ideas continue to be promoted in the English-speaking world by theorists such as Mark Hayes (2006), while a strong Kaleckian flavour is evident in the work of Eckhard Hein (2017) and Özlem Onaran and Engelbert Stockhammer (Onaran et al. 2011; Stockhammer 2017). Hyman Minsky's influence has never faded, becoming quite pervasive in the aftermath of the global financial crisis (Whalen 2017). As noted earlier, in some ways Kalecki's ideas are complementary to those of Minsky, and there have been several attempts in recent years to combine them. A shift in the distribution of income away from capital and towards labour would generate 'wage-led growth' along Kaleckian lines, and it would also reduce the dangers inherent in the increase in working-class debt that has resulted from the increased inequality of recent decades and would have been understood by Minsky, even if he failed to anticipate it (Hein and Truger 2017; Lavoie and Stockhammer 2013; Obst et al. 2017). It is too early to say whether such a Kalecki-Minsky synthesis will succeed in bringing together the various post Keynesian schools, and there are (of course) very substantial obstacles to the achievement of wage-led growth in the real world (King 2019), but these are promising developments in the world of ideas.

At all events, the gulf between post Keynesian and mainstream macroeconomics is greater in 2019 than it has ever been. The new neo-classical synthesis is advocated by many who claim to be 'New Keynesians', but in many respects it is fundamentally anti-Keynesian, with full employment taken as the norm and downward wage rigidity seen as the cause of demand-deficient unemployment. The widely used and very elegant dynamic stochastic general equilibrium (DSGE) models aim to reduce macroeconomics to microeconomics, but – quite apart from the methodological objections to this procedure – it turns out that they cannot even account for the use of money in a capitalist economy (Rogers 2013). For all the continuing disagreements among the post Keynesians, they concur in their rejection of all this. Some years ago I suggested that 'continued survival as an embattled minority appears to me to be the medium-term fate of Post Keynesian economics' (King 2002: 259; original stress deleted). It seems that on this question at least I was quite right.

References

Baran, P. A. and Sweezy, P. M. 1966. *Monopoly Capital*, New York: Monthly Review Press.

Barbour, S., Cicarelli, J. and King, J. E. 2018. *A History of American Economic Thought*, London and New York: Routledge.

Davidson, P. 1972. *Money and the Real World*, London: Palgrave Macmillan.

Davidson, P. and Smolensky, E. 1964. *Aggregate Supply and Demand Analysis*, New York: Harper & Row.

Harcourt, G. C. 1972. *Some Cambridge Controversies in the Theory of Capital*, Cambridge: Cambridge University Press.

Harcourt, G. C. 2006. *The Structure of Post-Keynesian Economics: The Core Contributions of the Pioneers*, Cambridge: Cambridge University Press.

Harcourt, G. C. and Kriesler, P. eds. 2013a. *The Oxford Handbook of Post-Keynesian Economics. Volume I: Theory and Origins*, Oxford: Oxford University Press.

Harcourt, G. C. and Kriesler, P. eds. 2013b. *The Oxford Handbook of Post-Keynesian Economics. Volume II: Critiques and Methodology*, Oxford: Oxford University Press.

Hayes, M. 2006. *The Economics of Keynes: A New Guide to the General Theory*, Cheltenham: Edward Elgar.

Hein, E. 2017. *Stagnation Policy in the Eurozone and Economic Policy Alternatives: A Steindlian/ neo-Kaleckian Perspective*, Dusseldorf: Hans-Böckler Stiftung, FMM Working Paper No. 5, July.

Hein, E. and Truger, A. 2017. *Opportunities and Limits of Rebalancing the Eurozone via Wage Policies: Theoretical Considerations and Empirical Illustrations for the Case of Germany*, Dusseldorf: Hans-Böckler Stiftung, FMM Working Paper No. 6, July.

Hicks, J. R. 1937. 'Mr. Keynes and the "classics": A Suggested Interpretation', *Econometrica*, 5(2), 147–159, April.

Kalecki, M. 1943. 'Political Aspects of Full Employment', *Political Quarterly*, 14(4), 322–331, October–December.

Kalecki, M. 1954. *Theory of Economic Dynamics: An Essay on Cyclical and Long-Run Changes in Capitalist Economy*, London: Allen & Unwin.

Kalecki, M. 1971. *Selected Essays on the Dynamics of the Capitalist Economy*, Cambridge: Cambridge University Press.

Kalecki, M. and Kowalik, T. 1971. 'Observations on the "crucial reform"', *Politica ed Economica*, 2–3, 190–196, reprinted in J. Osiatýnski (ed.), *Collected Works of Michał Kalecki. Volume 1. Capitalism, Business Cycles and Full Employment*, Oxford: Clarendon Press, pp. 466–476, 1990.

Keynes, J. M. 1936. *The General Theory of Employment, Interest and Money*, London: Palgrave Macmillan.

Keynes, J. M. 1937. 'The General Theory of Employment', *Quarterly Journal of Economics*, 51(2), 209–223, February.

Keynes, J. M. 1973. *The Collected Writings of John Maynard Keynes, Volume XIII*, London: Palgrave Macmillan and Cambridge: Cambridge University Press for the Royal Economic Society.

Keynes, J. M. 1982. *The Collected Writings of John Maynard Keynes, Volume XXVIII*, London: Palgrave Macmillan and Cambridge: Cambridge University Press for the Royal Economic Society.

King, J. E. 2002. *A History of Post Keynesian Economics Since 1936*, Cheltenham: Edward Elgar.

King, J. E. 2012. *The Microfoundations Delusion: Metaphor and Dogma in the History of Macroeconomics*, Cheltenham: Edward Elgar.

King, J. E. 2013a. 'Whatever Happened to the Crucial Reform?' in R. Bellofiore, E. Karwowski and J. Toporowski (eds.), *Economic Crisis and Political Economy. Volume 2 of Essays in Honour of Tadeusz Kowalik*, Basingstoke: Palgrave Macmillan, pp. 29–41.

King, J. E. 2013b. 'Hyman Minsky and the Financial Instability Hypothesis', in G. C. Harcourt and P. Kriesler (eds.), *The Oxford Handbook of Post-Keynesian Economics*, New York: Oxford University Press, pp. 218–230.

King, J. E. 2013c. 'Post Keynesians and Others', in F. S. Lee and M. Lavoie (eds.), *In Defense of Post-Keynesian and Heterodox Economics: Response to Their Critics*, London and New York: Routledge, pp. 1–17.

King, J. E. 2015. *Advanced Introduction to Post Keynesian Economics*, Cheltenham: Edward Elgar.

King, J. E. 2018. 'The Keynesian School and the Neoclassical Synthesis', in H. Bougrine and L-P. Rochon (eds.), *A Short History of Economic Thought: Major Contributions Since Adam Smith*, Cheltenham: Edward Elgar.

King, J. E. 2019. 'Some Obstacles to Wage-Led Growth', *Review of Keynesian Economics* 7(3).

King, J. E. and Millmow, A. 2003. 'Death of a Revolutionary Textbook', *History of Political Economy*, 35(1), 105–134, Spring.

Lavoie, M. and Stockhammer, E. eds. 2013. *Wage-Led Growth: An Equitable Strategy for Economic Recovery*, Basingstoke: Palgrave Macmillan and the International Labour Office.

Lee, F. 2009. *A History of Heterodox Economics: Challenging the Mainstream in the Twentieth Century*, London: Routledge.

Minsky, H. P. 1975. *John Maynard Keynes*, New York: Columbia University Press.

Minsky, H. P. 1977. 'Banking and a Fragile Financial Environment', *Journal of Portfolio Management*, 3(4), 16–22, Summer.

Minsky, H. P. 1986. *Stabilizing an Unstable Economy*, New Haven, CT: Yale University Press, Second Edition, New York: McGraw-Hill, 2008.

Obst, T., Onaran, Ö. and Nikolaidi, M. 2017. *The Effects of Income Distribution and Fiscal Policy on Growth, Investment and Budget Balance: The Case of Europe*, London: Greenwich Political Economy Research Centre, Greenwich Papers in Political Economy No. 43.

Onaran, Ö., Stockhammer, E. and Grafl, L. 2011. 'Financialisation, Income Distribution and Aggregate Demand in the USA', *Cambridge Journal of Economics*, 35(4), 637–661, July.

Robinson, J. 1972. 'The Second Crisis of Economic Theory', *American Economic Review*, 62(2), Papers and Proceedings, 1–10, May.

Robinson, J. and Eatwell, J. 1973. *An Introduction to Modern Economics*, London: McGraw-Hill.

Rogers, C. 2013. 'The Scientific Illusion of New Keynesian Monetary Theory', in G. C. Harcourt and P. Kriesler (eds.), *The Oxford Handbook of Post-Keynesian Economics*, New York: Oxford University Press, pp. 167–187.

Steindl, J. 1952. *Maturity and Stagnation in American Capitalism*, Oxford: Blackwell; Second Edition, New York: Monthly Review Press, 1976.

Stockhammer, E. 2017. 'Wage-Led Versus Profit-Led Demand: What Have We Learned? A Kaleckian-Minskyan View', *Review of Keynesian Economics*, 5(1), 25–42, Spring.

Thirlwall, A. P. 1993. 'The Renaissance of Keynesian Economics', *Banca Nazionale del Lavoro Quarterly Review*, 186, 327–337, September.

Toporowski, J. 2013. *Michał Kalecki: An Intellectual Biography. Volume 1: Rendezvous in Cambridge 1899–1939*, Basingstoke: Palgrave Macmillan.

Toporowski, J. 2016. 'Multilateralism and Military Keynesianism: Completing the Analysis', *Journal of Post Keynesian Economics*, 39(4), 437–443, Summer.

Wallich, H. C. and Weintraub, S. 1971. 'A Tax-Based Incomes Policy', *Journal of Economic Issues*, 5(2), 1–19, June.

Whalen, C. 2017. *Understanding Financialization: Standing on the Shoulders of Minsky*, Annandale-on-Hudson, NY: Levy Institute of Bard College, Working Paper No. 892, June.

Wray, L. R. 2009. 'The Rise and Fall of Money Manager Capitalism: A Minskian Approach', *Cambridge Journal of Economics*, 33(4), 807–828, July.

Chapter 8

Geoff Harcourt on G.C. Harcourt, as told to Ajit Sinha

G.C. Harcourt[1]

When Ajit Sinha asked me to write an essay on my main contributions to post-Keynesian economics, I had not fully taken on board Vela Velupillai's shy-making chapter on me (Velupillai 2017) in Bob Cord's *Palgrave Companion to Cambridge Economics*, Volume Two. Now that I hope I have, it has helped me to sharpen my focus, so that I may put forward here an historical narrative on my contributions.

I start by arguing that I took a post-Keynesian approach long before I knew what post-Keynesian economics was. Thus, in my honours thesis at the University of Melbourne (Harcourt 1953), I tried to examine the systemic consequences of the dominant market structure in the economy being K.W. Rothschild's oligopolists whose guide to action was based on Clausewitz's principles of war (Rothschild 1947). Especially important was Rothschild's argument that the pursuit of secure profits was on a par with the pursuit of maximum profit.[2]

The particular issue I examined was Keynes's argument (Keynes 1936: 100) that 'financial prudence' – writing off the book values of existing fixed assets well ahead of the need for expenditure to replace them – had a contractionary and deflationary impact on aggregate expenditure and the levels of activity and employment. Keynes assumed a dominant market structure of free competition. I looked at the profit and loss accounts, balance sheets and funds statements of a selection of Australian quoted public companies over the years of the Great Depression to see whether their experiences matched inferences I had drawn from my theoretical discussions – overall, they did not. Nevertheless, this began my now long-standing and sustained interest in the connections between market structures and systemic behaviour.

Thus, in my Cambridge PhD dissertation (Harcourt 1960), I coupled the basic model of the economy as a whole of Joan Robinson's *The Accumulation of Capital* (1956) with the pricing models of the seminal work of John Grant and Russell Mathews on inflation and company finance in Australia (1957, 1958). They examined how the use of historical cost accounting principles to set prices and measure incomes for dividend and tax purposes affected overall prices and economic activity in a period of inflation. They contrasted their findings with what would have happened, had replacement cost accounting principles been used for the same purposes.

In effect, my PhD dissertation was to do a 'Grant and Mathews' for the UK. I used the five-year series of profit and loss accounts, balance sheets and funds statements of UK quoted public companies for the years 1949–1953 developed in the 1950s at the National Institute for Economic and Social Research in London. Using a Marchand calculating machine, I converted the raw historical cost data into replacement cost figures by estimating stock appreciation and depreciation in replacement cost terms. The main findings may be found in Harcourt (1958, 1959, 1961).

My analysis certainly fits under the rubric of post-Keynesian economics, starting from Joan Robinson's succinct definition: 'To me, the expression *post-Keynesian* has a definite meaning; it applies to an economic theory or method of analysis which takes account of the difference between the future and the past' (1978; *CEP*, V, 1979: 210, emphasis in the original).

There is, though, one major flaw in the models – too great a use of representative agents to model pricing and other behaviour, a flaw recently forcefully brought home to me when I read Arrigo Opocher and Ian Steedman's *Full Industry Equilibrium* (2015). One of their most important emphases concerns the role of intermediate, as opposed to final, products in the setting of prices, a role that cannot be caught in representative agent models (see Harcourt 2017a).

I certainly made this error in two of what Vela and others regard as among my most important contributions: my critique (Harcourt 1963) of Nicky Kaldor's theories of distribution and growth of late 1950s vintage (Kaldor 1955–1956, 1957) and my alternative positive take on the same issues in a two-sector model of distribution and employment in the short period (Harcourt 1965a). The account of how prices are set in both the consumption goods ('bread') and investment goods ('steel') sectors is flawed by this neglect.[3]

In his 1950s and early 1960s phase, Kaldor argued that a capitalist economy could not sustain an equilibrium rate of growth over the long period unless it was operating at full employment. I asked the question: if this constraint is imposed on the economy in both the short period *and* the long period, in both of which Kaldor argued in his 1957 paper, his 'Keynesian' macroeconomic theory of distribution (Kaldor 1955–1956) operated, what pricing policies in the different sectors of the economy would allow his macroeconomic theory to go through? In his theory, investment led and saving responded, the marginal propensity to save out of profits was greater than that from wages. Most importantly, prices were assumed to move in such a way relatively to money wages that planned investment, initially imposed exogenously at the amount and share of full employment income that would allow the economy to grow along Harrod's natural rate of growth, would be realized through Kaldor's distribution mechanism establishing the distribution of income that allowed a corresponding amount and share of saving to occur.

In the 1963 article, I analyzed a number of possible scenarios, most of which implied that price-makers in the consumption goods sector set prices in markedly different, often unbelievable, ways from their counterparts in the investment goods sector, the unintended consequences of the full employment constraint.[4]

In 1962 when I was in my first period of teaching at Adelaide University, Peter Karmel, the George Gollin Professor of Economics and head of the Department of Economics, very kindly asked me to review Wilf Salter's classic *Productivity and Technical Change* (Salter 1960) for the *Economic Record*. In the event, I wrote a review article (Harcourt 1962). Salter's book, together with related papers, had a profound effect on my thinking then and ever after. Many of my subsequent papers include applications and developments of his analysis and insights.

In the 1950s and 1960s Salter and my greatest Australian mentor and friend, the late Eric Russell, were influencing the formation of wages policy in Australia through their evidence on behalf of the unions to the annual Basic Wage Case held before the Australian Conciliation and Arbitration Commission, and through their academic publications. I mention this because it is essential background to the discussion of my 1965 two-sector model paper.

The immediate stimulus which led to me writing the paper was hearing Bob Solow's 1963–1964 Alfred Marshall lectures on the short- and long-period theories of distribution and growth of two mythical creatures, 'Joan' and 'Nicky'.[5] I brought together the influences of Keynes, Joan Robinson, Nicky Kaldor, Piero Sraffa, Wilf Salter, Eric Russell and, as I now realize, most of all, Michał Kalecki, on the structure of my thought.

The two sectors were, of course, the consumption and investment goods sectors. I had price-making behaviour in both sectors, equations for the setting of money wages, analysis of the choices of technique that followed Salter's analysis in the equations describing investment decisions and I attempted to avoid the obstacles surrounding the theory of accumulation and capital emanating from Joan Robinson's and Piero Sraffa's writings. Putting all these influences together, I derived the characteristics of the rest states of employment and the distribution of income in the short period.

I read the paper on a nostalgic return to Piero Sraffa's and Robin Marris's research students' seminar at which some well-known research students – Ken Arrow, Richard Kahn, James Meade, Joan Robinson and Bob Solow – were present. The paper was the immediate reason for Kahn asking me to join the 'secret seminar' and Joan Robinson asking me whether I was interested in applying for the Cambridge lectureship then being advertised. This was something which, not even in my wildest dreams, I would have thought of doing as Cambridge was then, if not the best economics faculty in the world, certainly up with the leading ones. In the event, I was appointed and also elected a Fellow of Trinity Hall.[6]

I realized subsequently that in the paper I had established for one period the characteristics of a model which when/if extended to following periods in all probability would have produced a growth cycle akin to Goodwin (1967) and Kalecki (1968). At the time, I asked Jim Mirrlees (we were both then teaching at Cambridge) to collaborate with me on the extension; he said 'no' immediately. I then asked Joe Stiglitz. Joe, then a graduate student at MIT, had been sent by Paul Samuelson and Bob Solow to learn in person about the other (I would say real) Cambridge. Joe lasted a week – a long time in his intellectual life – before he too said 'no'. I hope it is realized what good judgment I showed in my choice of joint authors. At the moment I am hoping to work with Bob Marks, my colleague at UNSW, who is a whiz kid simulator, in order to carry out the proposed extension of the model.[7]

The paper was published in the *Economic Record* in early 1965, only to virtually disappear without a trace. So I was delighted when Robert Dixon (1988: 247), wrote that 'This much underrated paper is one of the major building blocks of post-Keynesian economics'.

Probably my second best-known paper (the first is the June 1969 *JEL* survey of capital theory, Harcourt 1969) is 'The Accountant in a Golden Age', Harcourt (1965b). Before I went on leave to Cambridge in 1963, Harold Lydall, who had succeeded Peter Karmel in the George Gollin Chair, showed me his calculations of accounting rates of profit in different scenarios, the values of which did not match their corresponding economic rates of profit (defined as Keynes's *mei/mec* or internal rates of return). The disparities puzzled him and he asked me to examine why they happened.

So I let the accountant loose in Joan Robinson's Golden Age where, because expectations are always realized, expected and actual rates of profit are equal to one another. I made up a number of scenarios in which companies used different methods of depreciation, had different patterns of expected quasi-rents associated with their planned investment expenditures, were static or growing, and had different proportions of real and financial assets in their balance sheets. As I could not solve the models analytically, I used simulations on the then pioneer computers at Cambridge. I found that the disparities were mostly due to which method of depreciation was used, to the quasi-rents patterns, but also to the other influences listed previously.

I read the paper at the weekly Faculty, Department of Applied Economics seminar, at which Ken Arrow (who had helped me obtain some of my results), Bob Solow, Frank Hahn, James Meade, Joan Robinson, Richard Kahn and other faculty and DAE colleagues were present. It made something of a mark, so much so that Frank Hahn was subsequently to say that if I were ever to be made a Life Peer, I should take the title of Lord Harcourt of Depreciation.

The paper was published in *Oxford Economic Papers*. A pleasing byproduct was the start of my friendship with David Henderson, then at Oxford, who refereed the article. He asked me to come to Oxford to discuss it with him, telling me that it was the only paper he had ever suggested should be made longer, in order to make it read more clearly!

The nearly four years I spent in Cambridge in 1960s were amongst the happiest and most productive of my working life. The 1960s was the Golden Age of university teaching worldwide, so the environment was just right for ideas to flourish. I was able to develop many ideas that initially occurred in the also wonderful environment of Adelaide. The only paper that I ever published in *R.E. Studs* (Dennis Robertson called it 'The Green Honour'), Harcourt (1966a), arose from Robin Matthews, then review editor of the *Economic Journal*, asking me to review Minhas's (1963) classic, *An International Comparison of Factor Costs and Factor Use*. His book had at its analytical centre the CES production function already made famous in the literature by Arrow, Chenery, Minhas and Solow (ACMS)'s 1961 *Review of Economic and Statistics* article, 'Capital-labor Substitution and Economic Efficiency'.

ACMS's empirical work required using international data on averages and totals to estimate marginals, to wit, the values of the elasticities of substitution of capital for labour of Salter's 'best practice' isoquants. My paper was a satirical one, not an exploration of sources of bias in econometric estimations.[8] I asked: suppose we grant all simplest neoclassical assumptions *except* the absence of vintages; what biases could this introduce into empirical estimations? I made up a number of possible different but, I hoped, plausible histories (Bob Solow [1997] is not so sure) and applied the econometric specifications of ACMS to reveal significant biases in the estimates of the relevant parameters, biases that could either overstate or understate the 'true' values. In effect, I had coupled Joan Robinson's criticisms of the aggregate production function (Robinson 1953–1954) with Salter's work on vintages to tackle the puzzles I had identified. For good measure, I also applied the findings of 'The Accountant in a Golden Age' to point out the limitations of using data embodying accounting conventions.

Another offshoot from 'The Accountant in a Golden Age' was an article in *Oxford Economic Papers* (Harcourt 1966b) on the then practice of basing bonuses for managers in the Soviet Union on accounting rates of profit which affected the choice of techniques in their investment decisions.

These interests led me to possibly the most explicitly post Keynesian papers I have written: a series in which I investigated the impact of 'real world' investment-decision rules – the pay-off or pay-back criterion, the accounting rate of profit rule – on the choice of techniques. I compared the outcomes with those obtained by applying neoclassical theoretical procedures. At the time, these were increasingly being taught in leading business schools.

One of the papers arose from Aubrey Silberston, then Chair of the Cambridge Faculty, getting me invited to an IEA conference in Nice which was chaired by John Dunlop (Harvard) and Nikolay Federenko (an academician in the Soviet Union). (They also edited the volume of the conference, Dunlop and Federenko 1969.) At Nice twenty economists from behind the Iron

Curtain lived it up in bourgeois decadence/splendour with twenty bourgeois economists from UK and American economics departments.

In the paper, as well as making the above comparisons, I also examined the choice of technique resulting from using the recoupment period criterion of socialist planners.[9]

At the conference I became friends with two wonderful people, Shirley Almon and Ronald McKinnon. Discussions with them led to my most maths-intensive paper, 'Investment-decision Criteria, Investment Incentives and the Choice of Technique' (Harcourt 1968), published in the *Economic Journal* in early 1968. (I received the acceptance letter from Charles Carter, then the editor, on the day Joan and I left Cambridge in December 1966 to return to Adelaide.) In the paper I analyzed the effect on the choice of technique of different rules and different investment schemes – accelerated depreciation, investment allowances, cash grants, then all the rage in the UK.[10] The core finding was that, with orders of magnitude likely to be met in the 'real world', the pay-off criterion resulted in more investment-intensive, less labour-intensive techniques being chosen than would be chosen by any other method.[11]

Alongside writing these papers were two other major projects: first, writing the first draft of my first book, *Economic Activity*, co-authored with Peter Karmel and Bob Wallace (Harcourt et al. 1967); it is an introduction to the economics of Keynes. Second, I met Vincent Massaro soon after both of us arrived in Cambridge in September 1963. We teamed up to read Piero Sraffa's (1960) classic, *Production of Commodities by Means of Commodities*, not allowing ourselves to go onto the next sentence until we were convinced we had understood the last. (Vince often went to natter in Italian with Piero, which proved a great help.)

Our joint effort resulted in two papers, a note on Sraffa's sub-systems published in the *Economic Journal* in 1964 and a review article of *Production of Commodities . . .* published in the *Economic Record*, also in 1964. We claim that both of these are definitive because they were not submitted for publication until Piero, a hard task master, had approved every word. Reading Sraffa's book while writing the national accounts chapter of *Economic Activity* forcefully brought home to me the intricate 'inter-relationship' between the national expenditure, national production and national income creation of Keynes's analysis with the production interdependence analysis of the structure of Sraffa's book. I believe this insight to be one of the major contributions of the sub-systems note. Sraffa's influence may also be seen in the two-sector model article. Getting on top of Sraffa's analysis was probably the most difficult intellectual work out of my life. It is therefore humbling to realize that I was absorbing an end product that had started as a blank page for the author.

Subsequently I was either commissioned to write or wrote a number of evaluations of Sraffa's contributions and influence. I single out two which, though written before the Sraffa papers in the Wren Library at Trinity were fully open to scholars (to this one anyway!), I believe still have some merit. The first is 'On Piero Sraffa's Contributions to Economics' (Harcourt 1983) in Peter Groenewegen and Joseph Halevi's *Altro Polo Italian Economics Past and Present*. The second (Harcourt 1986a) evaluates Sraffa's influence on Joan Robinson's contributions to economic theory, published in the *Economic Journal*.

I think *Economic Activity* has stood the test of time as an exposition of the economics of Keynes. My most distinguished pupil at Cambridge, Mervyn King, attended lectures based on it in 1966. (After a fine career as an academic economist, he became Governor of the Bank of England – and Lord King.) Three times in semi-public he has praised the lectures and the book as ideal introductions to Keynes.

My best-known article is 'Some Cambridge Controversies in the Theory of Capital' (Harcourt 1969). It is the survey article in the second issue (June 1969) of the newly formed *Journal of Economic Literature* edited by Mark Perlman. Mark had Australian connections, having written his PhD at the University of Melbourne. He was in Melbourne in 1968 when the person he had commissioned to write a survey of capital theory pulled out. Wilfrid Prest, the professor from my undergraduate days in Melbourne, suggested to Mark that he commission me to write it because Prest, a dour Yorkshireman, said I was good at explaining other peoples' ideas. Perlman came to Adelaide for a day and talked me into writing the survey. At that time, I was heavily involved in anti-Vietnam war activities – Australia was one of only two 'respectable' allies of the Americans in that most immoral of wars. My comrades in the anti-war movement generously allowed me to reduce my time with them in order to write the survey.

Initially I was so overwhelmed by the huge and difficult literature involved that I despaired until I decided to write working papers on segments of the literature and circulate them to twenty-one friends, both those for and those against the Cambridge, UK, arguments. This procedure allowed me to get the first draft to Perlman by December as he had requested. The survey has sub-headings which reflect their origins in the working papers:

1   Malleability, fossils and technical progress,
2   Solow on the rate of return: tease and counter-tease,
3   A child's guide to the double-switching debate,
4   The rate of profit[s] in capitalist society,
5   Conclusion,
6   Technical addendum: Wicksell effects – real and price, positive, neutral and negative – exposed.

Apart from the referees (who included Paul Samuelson, thumbs up, and Joe Stiglitz, thumbs down), the friends who sent me comments are listed in the opening footnote. The second footnote contains Dharma Kumar's wonderful quip that 'Space was a device to stop everything happening in Cambridge', her response to Bergson's definition of time as a device to stop everything happening at once. I quote the rather inconclusive conclusion, parts of which nevertheless have been borne out.

> We break off in midstream and few issues are settled. A key one relates to marginal productivity and its role in distribution, about which . . . there is a complete cleavage of opinion on the significance of the double-switching results for the issue. I suspect, though, that in the future, the battles will centre more around the *relevance* of equilibrium analysis and of maximising behaviour, for it is the *general methodology* of neoclassical analysis, rather than any particular result, which basically is under attack. As a betting man I know on whom I'd put my money; but then as a God-man, I have never expected virtue to triumph this side of the grave. In closing, I might say that some of my best friends are neoclassicals and I hope that they remain so!
>
> (Harcourt 1969, 1986b: 190, emphasis in original)

Subsequently I received a Leverhulme Exchange Fellowship, which allowed me to spend the Australian University long vacation of 1969–1970 at Keio University in Japan. There, working at an intensity I've never been able to again, I wrote the first draft of a book with the same title as that of the survey; it was published by Cambridge UP in 1972. For the next ten years I rarely submitted a paper for publication because I kept being commissioned to write on aspects and developments of the Cambridge-Cambridge debates (Harcourt 1973, 1975a, 1975b, 1976, 1977, 1979a).

As I regard the raison d'etre of economics is the policy outcome that theory and applied work lead to, I would nominate the 1975 Shann Memorial Lecture, *Theoretical Controversy and Social Significance: An Evaluation of the Cambridge Controversies* (Harcourt 1977), as the most important of these. In it I set out the approach to policy formation implied by what most of the profession regard as abstract esoteric considerations. I also think 'Non-neoclassical Capital Theory' (Harcourt 1979a) and 'The Cambridge Controversies: Old Ways and New Horizons – Or Dead End?' (Harcourt 1976) are significant: the first, because it tries to bring out in a clear manner, the main differences between the mainstream approach and the classical/post Keynesian approach to capital theory; the second, because it further develops the most important themes in the 1969 survey and 1972 book, and reactions, con and pro, to them. Mark Perlman thought it a superior article to the survey (which he admired) and despite the unacceptable behaviour of George Bortis (then editor of the *AER*) when, on Mark's recommendation, I submitted a draft to the *AER* (see Harcourt 2012a: 261–265). It was subsequently accepted for publication in *OEP*. Finally, I wish to record that, while I must stress that I was the most junior of partners in the project, I think the recently published article in *History of Political Economy* in 2017, 'Joan Robinson and MIT', authored by Harvey Gram and myself, is the definitive statement on the deepest issues unearthed in the controversies.

Jon Cohen, who became my closest Canadian friend during the two semesters (1977, 1980) I spent at Toronto, introduced me to Avi Cohen (no relation) and we became close friends from then on. Amongst many other things, Avi is a wonderful historian of economic theory who has taken a special interest in capital theory debates over the ages. I learnt an enormous amount from him, and when in the early 2000s Timothy Taylor, the managing Editor of *Journal of Economic Perspectives (JEP)*, asked me to write a retrospective article on the Cambridge-Cambridge debates, I asked that Avi be a joint author, otherwise I would be taking credit for Avi's great influence on what I would write. As a result we published 'Whatever Happened to the Cambridge Capital Theory Controversies?' in *JEP* in 2003 and a much fuller version of our joint themes in the article in our Introduction (2005) to the three-volume selection of readings on capital theory, edited by Christopher Bliss, Avi and I, and published by Edward Elgar. We documented recurring themes in capital theory over the ages from the 19th century on, now again emerging in the reactions to Thomas Piketty's extraordinary best seller on the causes of inequality in income and wealth (Piketty 2014, see, for example, Harcourt and Tribe 2016, in Hudson and Tribe 2016). Piketty's core theoretical model is the neoclassical aggregate production function and he does not protect his flanks adequately, if at all, from the Cambridge, UK, critique of the model.

There is another notable exception to this decade of mostly non-submission, the 1976 *Kyklos* paper with Peter Kenyon, 'Pricing and the Investment Decision'. I think this is regarded as a key paper in the post-Keynesian literature. It had a long gestation period, dating back to 1966 when I submitted to an Oxford journal my first attempt to set out the link between price setting and planned investment expenditure in oligopolistic industries dominated by price leaders. It was unsuccessful because of a major logical flaw in the argument, associated with inconsistent time periods. This was picked up by an unsung hero of modern economics, G.B. Richardson, who refereed it. When Peter Kenyon came to Adelaide in the early 1970s to do a master's degree, I suggested that he work on the issues and literature associated with this puzzle, especially Al Eichner's and Adrian Wood's important contributions (Eichner 1973, 1974; Wood 1975).[12] When Peter gave a progress report on his research in 1974, the solution to the error Richardson had pointed out literally flashed into my mind. I sketched the theory that evening and suggested to Peter that he put the scholarship around it, which led to the paper that was published in *Kyklos* in 1976. I do think the paper is a major contribution to post-Keynesianism as it is the first analysis in historical time of the simultaneous determination of the size of the mark-up and the rate of planned investment expenditure in which the size of the mark-up is determined by the need for internal funds, retained profits, to finance that part of investment expenditure not financed from external and other sources. Adrian's most elegant analysis is explicitly set in logical time and Al's theory of investment – he derived it from Keynes's Chapter 11 – is flawed for the reasons identified by Abba Lerner, Michał Kalecki, Joan Robinson and

Tom Asimakopulos (see Harcourt 2006, Chapter 4). I believe our paper over-comes these limitations.[13]

The 1970s were characterized by stagflation and Milton Friedman's and others' successful attack on Keynesian theory and policies (but not on the economics of Keynes, see, for example, Freedman et al. 2016). In Australia, led by Eric Russell, a number of us fought a rear guard action against Friedman, Hayek, Lucas and their surrogates, providing in effect comprehensive post-Keynesian package deals of policies to restore and sustain full employment and reduce inflation. I set out the gist of these in 'The Social Consequences of Inflation' (Harcourt 1974) and in Prue Kerr's and my chapter 'The Mixed Economy' in the North/Weller volume *Labor* (1980). Prue's and my chapter is also the source of the draft I wrote on 'Economic Policy and the Future of Australia' that became Discussion Paper No. 6 of the Australian Labor Party's (ALP) National Committee of Enquiry into why the ALP had done so badly in the 1975 and 1978 federal elections and what could be done about this (Discussion Papers 1979).[14] My proud boast is that Bob Hawke implemented my proposals a good half hour after he became prime minister in 1983.

The 1970s also saw me start on what I believe to be one of my most important contributions to understanding post Keynesian economics: the writing of intellectual biographies. They took two forms: those derived from publications in the public domain and papers in archives, and oral histories based on interviews with the economists concerned. The first essay I wrote arose from a request from Angus Wilson (who was the public orator at the University of East Anglia [UNE]) to send him some background material on Joan Robinson whom Ed Nell, then at UNE, had persuaded the university to give an honorary degree. I wrote a paper, 'Portrait of a Lady', and sent it to Wilson. A colleague at Adelaide read the paper in our Working Paper series and told me how much she liked it. This gave me the confidence to keep on writing such essays, even after a most distinguished Indian economist later dismissed them as 'mere chit chat'.

The final version of the paper was published in 1979 in the Biographical Supplement of *The International Encyclopedia of the Social Sciences*, volume 18, edited by David Sills (Harcourt 1979b). When I wrote the first draft of the concluding chapter of the biography of Joan that Prue Kerr and I jointly authored (Harcourt and Kerr 2009), I was still able to draw heavily on this first essay.

In the early 1980s I also suggested to Paul Davidson, then the joint editor of the *Journal of Post Keynesian Economics*, that we should publish a series of oral history articles on the founding mothers and fathers of post Keynesianism. He enthusiastically agreed and I wrote a number of them over the coming years.

I started with Lorie Tarshis (Harcourt 1982a, 1982b), who had become a dear friend following meeting him at Stanford in 1965, and then subsequently spending two semesters (1977 and 1980) at the Scarborough Campus of the University of Toronto (known as Scarberia by all of us who worked there, twenty miles from downtown Toronto, out in the boondocks). Lorie was then head of a department there, containing a remarkable group of mostly young economists.

Other oral histories I wrote are on George Shackle, Kenneth Boulding, Dick Goodwin and Dick Stone (Harcourt 1981a, 1983, 1985, 1995: 153–159, respectively). I gathered together both oral histories and other essays and tributes in *Post-Keynesian Essays in Biography: Portraits of Twentieth Century Political Economists*, which was published by Macmillan in 1993, courtesy of their remarkable economics editor, Tim Farmiloe.

I left Adelaide, Paradise on Earth, in September 1982, returning to Cambridge to a lectureship in the faculty and a fellowship at Jesus, so starting twenty-eight wonderful years in Heaven on Earth. My major research project was to write the intellectual history of Joan Robinson and her circle, to try to set out their lasting contributions. My principal collaborator in this task was Prue Kerr. Between us we have written, often together, over a hundred essays on this theme, published a number of edited volumes and introductions to volumes, for example Harcourt and Kerr (2002); Kerr with Harcourt (2002a, 2002b; Harcourt and Kerr (2013). The overall project was brought, if not to an end then certainly to a peak,[15] with our biography of Joan, published in 2009 in Tony Thirlwall's series with Palgrave Macmillan, *Great Thinkers in Economics*.

There were at least two major detours on the way: first, Peter Riach (whose idea it was) and I edited *A 'Second Edition' of The General Theory*, 2 volumes, published by Routledge in 1997. The quotes around *Second Edition* signal that it is not that, but that our aim was to get the contributors to write about what Keynes might have written in 1938–1939 if his heart attack in 1937 and then the onset of war had not prevented this; and why they had worked on the particular aspects of *The General Theory* that they had in the post-war period. All the contributors are/were eminent scholars of Keynes and not all were post Keynesians, notwithstanding the inference that they were in Roy Weintraub's disparaging review in the *Economic Record* (1998). Roy has a thing about post-Keynesians. I think it fair to regard the volumes as making an important contribution. Certainly Hirofumi Uzawa thought so when he wrote the Foreword to the 2005 Japanese translation and so did Bernard Corry, who wrote a perceptive and favourable review in *The Manchester School* in 2000. Tony Thirlwall (1999) wrote an excellent review article of the volumes in the *Journal of Post-Keynesian Economics*, writing convincingly as JMK, as had a number of the contributors.

Another detour was to write a book for Cambridge University Press based on my decades of teaching post-Keynesian themes and growth theory in Adelaide and Cambridge. The book is entitled *The Structure of Post Keynesian Economics: The Core Contributions of the Pioneers* (Harcourt 2006). John King said it should have been the *Cambridge Pioneers*. He is probably right but I don't feel too guilty about this since their American counterparts are quite capable of blowing their own trumpets while often airbrushing the original Cambridge pioneers, and especially Kalecki, from history. I list the chapter headings to show what issues are covered:

1   Introduction: why post-Keynesian economics and who were its Cambridge pioneers?
2   Post-Keynesian macroeconomic theories of distribution

Kaldor's 'Keynesian' theory
Kalecki's 'degree of monopoly' theory
Kalecki's review of Keynes' *General Theory*
The eclecticism of Joan Robinson
Hahn's finest hour: the macroeconomic theory of employment and distribution of his PhD dissertation[16]

3   Post-Keynesian theories of the determination of the mark-up

Wood's 'Golden Age' model
The choice of technique in the investment decision: orthodox and post-Keynesian approaches
Harcourt and Kenyon's model in historical time
Why is internal finance to be preferred? Kalecki's theory of increasing risk

4   Macroeconomic theories of accumulation

Keynes' theory: right ingredients, wrong recipe
Lerner's internal critique
Kalecki's, Joan Robinson's and Asimakopulos'[s] Keynesian critique
Joan Robinson's banana diagram

5   Money and finance: exogenous or endogenous?
6   The complete model: its role in an explanation of post-war inflationary episodes
7   Theories of growth: from Adam Smith to 'modern' endogenous growth theory

Introduction
Smith and Ricardo
Marx
Harrod
Solow-Swan
Kaldor, Mark 1
Joan Robinson (as told to Donald Harris)
Goodwin's eclecticism
Pasinetti's grand synthesis
Kaldor, Mark 2
Endogenous growth theory

8   Applications to policy

The vital link between 'vision' and policy
'Package deals': a solution to the Kaleckian dilemma?
Appendix 1: biographical sketches of the pioneers: Keynes, Kalecki, Sraffa, Joan Robinson, Kahn, Kaldor

John Maynard Keynes, 1883–1946
Michał Kalecki, 1899–1970
Piero Sraffa, 1898–1983
Joan Robinson, 1903–1983
Richard Kahn, 1905–1989
Nicholas Kaldor, 1908–1986

Appendix 2: the conceptual core of the post-Keynesian discontent with orthodox theories of value, distribution and growth

The volume was generously endorsed by people whose judgment and respect I value: Stephanie Blankenburg, Wylie Bradford, Duncan Foley and John Nevile.[17]

Joan and I returned permanently to Australia in 2010. I was made most welcome at the School of Economics, UNSW Australia (now Sydney) where I am an Honorary Professor. There, I finished a project I had begun three or four years earlier. It is in effect the culmination of my life's work: *The Oxford Handbook of Post-Keynesian Economics*, 2 volumes, published by OUP in 2013 and co-edited with Peter Kriesler. Peter and I were delighted that the *JEL* which, once Mark and Naomi Perlman had retired, had refused to review any of my books (or ask me to review other people's books), had Steve Pressman (2014) review it, as it turns out, most favourably. Reneé Prendergast (2013) also wrote a deeply thoughtful and positive review in the *Economic and Labour Relations Review*, as has Philip Armstrong (2017) in the *Review of Political Economy*.

Before I go down the home straight, I want to mention that over the years I have been asked to give some well-known public lectures in Australia and Cambridge. They include the 1975 Shann Memorial Lecture *Theoretical Controversy and Social Significance* (Harcourt 1977), the 1978 Academy Lecture 'The Social Science Imperialists' (Harcourt 1979b, 1982a), the 1982 G.L. Wood Memorial Lecture, Melbourne University, 'Reflections on the Development of Economics as a Discipline' (Harcourt 1984), the 1982 John Curtin Memorial Lecture (ANU) 'Making Socialism in Your Own Country', published in Sardoni (1992), the Second Annual Donald Horne Address (1992) 'Markets, Madness and a Middle Way', published in Harcourt (2001a, Ch. 16), 'University Ideals and the Market', the Third Halford Cook Memorial Lecture, Queens' College, Melbourne, 1996, published in Harcourt (2001a, Ch. 22), the Seventh Colin Clark Memorial Lecture, Queensland University, 1997, 'Economic

Theory and Economic Policy: Two Views' (Harcourt 2001a, Ch. 23), and the 1997 Kingsley Martin Memorial Lecture, Cambridge, 'Two Views on Development: Austin and Joan Robinson' (Harcourt 1998, 2001b, Ch. 23). As may be seen from the titles, I spoke on broad, often wide-ranging themes, somewhat akin to what Frank Hahn called his 'blah blah' papers, which were often wise reflections and were certainly more readable than his 'serious' technical papers.

In 2016, with Joseph Halevi, Peter Kriesler and John Nevile, I published with Palgrave Macmillan four volumes of *Post-Keynesian Essays from Down Under: Theory and Policy from an Historical Perspective*. I had proposed to Palgrave Macmillan that I bring out with them a tenth volume of selected essays in order to get into double figures as any cricketer (but not golfer) would wish to do. Peter Kriesler pointed out to me that since I had joined him and John Nevile at UNSW in 2010, we had published a number of joint papers, and that he and John, and he and Joseph, had written many joint papers over the past thirty years or more – hence there resulted these four volumes of selections of their essays from those years and selections of mine published after publication of the last two volumes of my selected essays in 2012 (Harcourt 2012a, 2012b). We do hope that readers of the volumes agree with Gay Meeks's endorsement of Volume III, *Essays on Ethics, Social Justice and Economics*: 'Searching for gold, you must look down under. There are riches for the questioning economist perplexed by unjust policy outcomes of seemingly neutral analysis'. I must confess that I near the end of the account of my contributions by saying 'au revoir', not 'adieu', as Peter tells me we have already accumulated enough new essays for possibly three more volumes.

In my *Selected Essays*, I have tried to include only essays that I think make a contribution. They include some speculative essays, for example, Harcourt (1981b, 1982b), in which I discuss the concept of centres of gravitation in the writings of Marshall, Sraffa and Keynes. I examine whether the three authors are incompatible bedfellows in their understanding and use of the concept. I also run a hobby horse, the difference between the concept of period and that of run, as they are so often regarded as the same concept. To me, 'period' is a theoretical concept under the control of the analyst using it, whereas 'run' is an historical happening, period (see Halevi et al. 2016, Chapter 2).

I close by mentioning my roles as joint editor of journals and book series, all of which I would argue have contributed to getting post Keynesian themes into the public domain. I was joint editor of *Australian Economic Papers* for about twenty years, 1962 to 1982. I published papers of mavericks who were then struggling to get their papers published elsewhere, as I recount in '*AEP* and Me: A Short(ish) Memoir' (Harcourt 2014). The most important article ever published in *AEP* was the first translation in full from Polish into English by Ferdinando Targetti and Bogna Kinda-Hass (1982) of Kalecki's remarkable review of Keynes's *General Theory* (Kalecki 1936). It establishes conclusively that he independently discovered the principal propositions of the *General*

Theory, set, moreover, more appropriately in the framework of Marx's schemes of reproduction rather than within Keynes's Marshallian approach.

I have also been associated one way or another with the *Cambridge Journal of Economics* since it started in 1977 (see Blankenburg 2014 for an evaluation of my contribution). Since coming to UNSW, I have taken a significant interest in the school's local journal, the *Economic and Labour Relations Review (ELRR)*, of which I am Obituary Editor (as I was of the *Economic Journal* for eight years, 1990–1998). As I've grown older – I am now eighty-seven – the number of obituaries and tributes I have commissioned or written myself have grown exponentially. In the last two years alone, I have written tributes to Stan Wong (2016), John Whitaker (Harcourt with Neil Hart 2016), Ken Arrow (2017b) and John Grieve Smith (2017c). A Symposium on Inequality in Honour of Tony Atkinson was published in *ELRR* in March 2018. Avi Cohen, Peter Kriesler and Jan Toporowski and I are general editors of Palgrave 'Studies in the History of Thought', a series published by Palgrave Macmillan. The most important item in the series is Jan's great intellectual biography of Kalecki, the first volume of which was published in 2013. The second volume has just been published. I was/still am a series editor of 'Aspects of Political Economy' for Polity Press. The most important volume in the series is Dick Goodwin's magnum opus (co-authored with Lionello Punzo), *The Dynamics of a Capitalist Economy: A Multi-Sectoral Approach* (1987).

I have also edited or contributed chapters to a number of *Festschrift* volumes and have written well over 100 review articles or reviews; see Repapis (2014) for an evaluation of what he argues these have contributed.

Finally, over the years, I have written several surveys of post-Keynesian economics. The first grew out of a paper I was asked to present to a seminar at the Reserve Bank of Australia in the early 1980s. I also gave it at a seminar at Monash University. I asked someone what the listeners there thought of it; he replied: 'You must realize, Geoff, half of them think you are a sociologist'. It was published as 'Post-Keynesianism: Quite Wrong and/or Nothing New?' in the series Thames Papers in Political Economy in the Summer of 1982 (Harcourt 1982c). I still think it is worth a read. The most cited (and criticised) survey, 'Post-Keynesianism: From Criticism to Coherence?' was written with Omar Hamouda and published in the *Bulletin of Economic Research* in 1988. The last and I think the most comprehensive is 'Post-Keynesian Thought' (Harcourt 2001c). It was commissioned by Orley Ashenfelter for Smelser and Baltes's *International Encyclopedia of the Social and Behavioural Sciences*.

Alex Thomas, Ajit's joint editor, mentioned that there were chapters in their volume on Indian economic thought and suggested that I discuss my *Economica* review article (Harcourt 2012c) of A.K. Dasgupta's three volumes of collected works (Patel 2009). Dasgupta was a sage, a deep thinking and original theorist, an outstanding historian of economic theory – his *Epochs of Economic Theory* (Dasgupta 1985) is a classic – an Indian patriot who contributed massively, directly and indirectly, to policy making in India. Most of all, he was an inspiring teacher; he rightly regarded teaching as the top priority of an academic economist.

I regard my tribute to Krishna Bharadwaj (Harcourt 1993–1994, 1995), one of the finest and most loveable persons I ever knew, as one of the best essays I have written. Finally, I was privileged to write with my great friend and colleague of many years, the late Ajit Singh, a tribute (Singh and Harcourt 1991) to another outstanding Indian patriot and scholar, Sukhamoy Chakravarty.

Alex also suggested I write a paragraph on my approach to the teaching of the history of economic theory. I try, first, to put past greats in the context of their own times, to spell out their niches in their societies and their personalities. I then try to set out the relevance of their contributions to our times. So Bob Heilbroner is clearly the greatest influence on what I try to do.

To conclude: I thank Ajit and Alex for asking me to write this chapter on my favourite subject. Looking through my CV, I am sad that I have had to leave out some of my favourite essays. But I have surely already tried the patience of the editors and any readers, so I now sign off.

Notes

1   I thank but in no way implicate Joseph Halevi, Prue Kerr, Peter Kriesler, Vela Velupillai and the editors of the volume for their comments and suggestions on a draft of this chapter.
2   Years later I coupled this insight with John Hicks's 1950s distinction between snatchers and stickers in imperfectly competitive markets (Hicks 1954; 1983). Snatchers try to maximize immediate short-term profits regardless of this behaviour's impact on customers' goodwill and so profits in the long term. Stickers forgo some immediate gains in order to secure lasting relationships and profits.
3   I am in good company; the same criticism may be made of the arguments in Michał Kalecki's remarkable review of Keynes's *General Theory* (Kalecki 1936), and Joan Robinson's exposition of Kalecki's analysis of capitalism (Robinson 1977, see also Harcourt 2017a).
4   For the history of the trials that the paper went through before finally being published in *Australian Economic Papers* in June 1963, see Harcourt (1995, 2012a). For those who like that sort of thing, there is a brawl by brawl account of the exchanges that occurred when I gave the paper at Nicky's research students seminar at King's in early 1964, the day before I went down with a severe attack of adult mumps; see Harcourt (2002).
5   Only the real Joan was there in person; the real Nicky was visiting Australia.
6   As I felt I had a moral obligation to return to Adelaide – I was on leave from there – I obtained three years leave without pay in order to accept the Cambridge posts.
7   Bob, who goes in for this sort of thing, discovered that we are related to each other, as we are also to Karl Marx.
8   One referee recognized this, the other thought it to be an attempted econometric exercise that failed miserably. Thankfully, Mike Farrell, then the relevant editor of *R.E. Studs*, accepted the advice to publish of the first referee.
9   My paper (Harcourt 1967) was the first ever paper by a bourgeois economist published in *Czchoslovak Economic Papers* (I met the editor at the conference); it was also Chapter 14 of Dunlop and Federenko (1969).

10 A much longer version of the paper was obtainable from the Cambridge faculty office and I understand there was a file at HM Treasury named 'Harcourt'.

11 I thought I had established this ordering as a general result for all relevant values but Jim Mirrlees kindly had a look at my maths and found that I had a sign wrong in a crucial partial derivative. All was not lost, however, because following up using 'real world' magnitudes led to further useful insights.

12 We all forgot an original pioneer, Jim Ball, whose take on the issues was hidden away in his 1964 book *Inflation and the Theory of Money*, an inexcusable lack of good manners on my part as I reviewed his book in the *Economic Journal* (in 1965).

13 For the sad story of how long it took to get the paper in its final form published, see Harcourt (2012a, Ch 21).

14 I was the economist on the Committee; ten Discussion Papers were published in 1979.

15 Prue wrote the chapter on Joan (Kerr 2017) for Bob Cord's *Palgrave Companion to Cambridge Economics*.

16 This was a tease of Frank, not a serious evaluation.

17 Peter Kriesler said to add the favourable view expressed to him by Joseph Halevi, one of the most wide-ranging and deep-thinking economists I have ever met.

References

Works by G.C. Harcourt referred to in the text

Unpublished dissertations

Harcourt, G. C. 1953. *The 'Reserve' Policy of Australian Companies During the Depression: A Study of Oligopoly in Australia Over the Period 1928 to 1934*, unpublished Honours thesis, University of Melbourne.

Harcourt, G. C. 1960. *The Finance of Investment, Taxation, Depreciation and Retained Profits in Selected United Kingdom Industries, 1949–1953*, unpublished PhD dissertation, Cambridge University.

Books

Harcourt, G. C. 1972. *Some Cambridge Controversies in the Theory of Capital*, Cambridge: Cambridge University Press, Italian Edition, 1973; Polish Edition, 1975; Spanish Edition, 1975; Japanese Edition, 1980. Reprinted in the Gregg Revivals Series (Mark Blaug, editor), 1991.

Harcourt, G. C. 1982a. *The Social Science Imperialists. Selected Essays. G.C. Harcourt*, Edited by Prue Kerr. London: Routledge and Kegan Paul. Reprinted in the Routledge Library Editions Series in 2003.

Harcourt, G. C. 1986b. *Controversies in Political Economy. Selected Essays by G.C. Harcourt*, Edited by O. F. Hamouda, Brighton: Wheatsheaf Books Ltd.

Harcourt, G. C. 1993. *Post-Keynesian Essays in Biography: Portraits of Twentieth Century Political Economists*, Basingstoke, Hants: Palgrave Macmillan.

Harcourt, G. C. 1995. *Capitalism, Socialism and Post-Keynesianism. Selected Essays of G.C. Harcourt*, Cheltenham, Glos: Edward Elgar.

Harcourt, G. C. 2001a, *Selected Essays on Economic Policy*, London: Palgrave Macmillan.

Harcourt, G. C. 2001b. *50 Years a Keynesian and Other Essays*, London: Palgrave Macmillan.

Harcourt, G. C. 2006. *The Structure of Post-Keynesian Economics: The Core Contributions of the Pioneers*, Cambridge: Cambridge University Press.

Harcourt, G. C. 2012a. *The Making of a Post-Keynesian Economist: Cambridge Harvest*. Houndmills, Basingstoke, Hampshire: Palgrave Macmillan.

Harcourt, G. C. 2012b. *On Skidelsky's Keynes and Other Essays: Selected Essays of G. C. Harcourt*, Houndmills, Basingstoke, Hampshire: Palgrave Macmillan.

Harcourt, G. C., Bliss, Christopher and Cohen, Avi J. eds. 2005. *Capital Theory*, 3 vols, Cheltenham, UK and Northhampton, MA: Edward Elgar Publishing Limited.

Harcourt, G. C., Karmel, P. H. and Wallace, R. H. 1967. *Economic Activity*, Cambridge: Cambridge University Press, Italian Edition, 1969.

Harcourt, G. C. and Kerr, P. 2009. *Joan Robinson*, Houndmills, Basingstoke, Hampshire: Palgrave Macmillan.

Harcourt, G. C. and Kriesler, P. eds. 2013. *The Oxford Handbook of Post-Keynesian Economics. Volume 1: Theory and Origins. Volume 2: Critiques and Methodology*, New York: Oxford University Press.

Harcourt, G. C. and Riach, P. A. eds. 1997. *A 'Second Edition' of the General Theory*, 2 Vols, London: Routledge. Japanese translation with a Foreword by Hirofumi Uzawa, 2005.

Articles

Harcourt, G. C. 1958. 'The Quantitative Effect of Basing Company Taxation on Replacement Costs', *Accounting Research*, 9, 1–16.

Harcourt, G. C. 1961. 'Pricing Policies and Earning Rates', *Economic Record*, 37, 217–224.

Harcourt, G. C. 1963. 'A Critique of Mr. Kaldor's Model of Income Distribution and Economic Growth', *Australian Economic Papers*, 1, 20–36.

Harcourt, G. C. 1965a. 'A Two-Sector Model of the Distribution of Income and the Level of Employment in the Short Run', *Economic Record*, 41, 103–117.

Harcourt, G. C. 1965b. 'The Accountant in a Golden Age', *Oxford Economic Papers*, 17, 66–80.

Harcourt, G. C. 1966a. 'Biases in Empirical Estimates of the Elasticities of Substitution of C.E.S. Production Functions', *Review of Economic Studies*, 33, 227–233.

Harcourt, G. C. 1966b. 'The Measurement of the Rate of Profit and the Bonus Scheme for Managers in the Soviet Union', *Oxford Economic Papers*, 18, 58–63.

Harcourt, G. C. 1967. 'Investment-Decision Criteria, Capital-Intensity and the Choice of Techniques', *Czchoslovak Economic Papers*, 9, 65–91, reprinted in Dunlop and Federenko, 1969, 190–216.

Harcourt, G. C. 1968. 'Investment-Decision Criteria, Investment Incentives and the Choice of Technique', *Economic Journal*, 78, 77–95.

Harcourt, G. C. 1969. 'Some Cambridge Controversies in the Theory of Capital', *Journal of Economic Literature*, 7, 369–405.

Harcourt, G. C. 1973. 'Las Parabolos Neoclasicas y la Funcion Agregade de Produccion', *Cuadernos de Economica*, 46–62, June.

Harcourt, G. C. 1974. 'The Social Consequences of Inflation', *Australian Accountant*, 520–528, October.

Harcourt, G. C. 1975a. 'Capital Theory: Much Ado About Something', *Thames Papers in Political Economy*, 1–16, Autumn. Spanish version 'Las Controversias de los Economistas i un Mar de Irrelevancias?' *Economia*, 1974, 27–53.

Harcourt, G. C. 1975b. 'The Cambridge Controversies: The Afterglow', in M. Parkin and A. R. Nobay (eds.), *Contemporary Issues in Economics*, Manchester: Manchester University Press, pp. 305–334.

Harcourt, G. C. 1976. 'The Cambridge Controversies: Old Ways and New Horizons – or Dead End?' *Oxford Economic Papers*, 28, 25–65.

Harcourt, G. C. 1977. 'The Theoretical and Social Significance of the Cambridge Controversies in the Theory of Capital: An Evaluation', *Revue d'Economie Politique*, 87, 351–375 (The 1975 Shann Memorial Lecture). Reprinted in Jesse Schwartz (ed.), *The Subtle Anatomy of Capitalism* (California: Goodyear 1977, pp. 285–303).

Harcourt, G. C. 1979a. 'Non-Neoclassical Capital Theory', *World Development*, 7, 923–932.

Harcourt, G. C. 1979b. 'The Social Science Imperialists' (The 1978 Academy Lecture, November 1978), *Politics*, 14, 243–251.

Harcourt, G. C. 1981a. 'Notes on an Economic Querist: G.L.S. Shackle', *Journal of Post Keynesian Economics*, 4, 136–144. A longer version is the Introduction to Stephen F. Frowen (ed.), *Unknowledge and Choice in Economics* (London: Palgrave Macmillan, 1990), xvii–xxvi.

Harcourt, G. C. 1981b. 'Marshall, Sraffa and Keynes: Incompatible Bedfellows?' *Eastern Economic Journal*, 7, 39–50.

Harcourt, G. C. 1982b. 'An Early Post Keynesian: Lorie Tarshis (or: Tarshis on Tarshis by Harcourt)', *Journal of Post Keynesian Economics*, 4, 609–619.

Harcourt, G. C. 1984. 'Reflections on the Development of Economics as a Discipline' (The 1982 G.L. Wood Memorial Lecture, June 1982), published in *History of Political Economy*, 16, 489–517.

Harcourt, G. C. 1982c. 'Post Keynesianism: Quite Wrong and/or Nothing New?' *Thames Papers in Political Economy*, 1–19, Summer. Reprinted as chapter 6 in Philip Arestis and Thanos Skouras (eds.), *Post Keynesian Economic Theory: A Challenge to Neo-Classical Economics*, Brighton: Wheatsheaf Books, 1985.

Harcourt, G. C. 1983. 'A Man for All Systems: Talking to Kenneth Boulding', *Journal of Post Keynesian Economics*, 5, 143–154.

Harcourt, G. C. 1984. 'The End of an Era: Joan Robinson (1903–83) and Piero Sraffa (1898–1983)', *Journal of Post Keynesian Economics*, 6, 466–469.

Harcourt, G. C. 1985. 'A Twentieth Century Eclectic: Richard Goodwin', *Journal of Post Keynesian Economics*, 7, 410–421.

Harcourt, G. C. 1986a. 'The Influence of Piero Sraffa on the Contributions of Joan Robinson to Economic Theory', *Supplement to the Economic Journal*, 96, 96–108.

Harcourt, G. C. 1992. 'Markets, Madness and a Middle Way', *The Second Annual Donald Horne Address*, Melbourne, 1992, also published in *Australian Quarterly*, 64, 1992, 1–17 and in a revised version, in 'Viewpoint', *The Cambridge Review*, 114, 1993, 40–45.

Harcourt, G. C. 1993–1994. 'Krishna Bharadwaj, 21 August 1935–8 March 1992: A Memoir', *Journal of Post Keynesian Economics*, 16, 299–311, reprinted in Harcourt, 1995, 160–171.

Harcourt, G. C. 1996, 2001a. 'University Ideals and the Market', The Third Halford Cook Memorial Lecture, Queens' College, University of Melbourne, May 1996, 1–11. Revised version, *The Cambridge Review*, 117, 1996, 35–39. Also in *Journal of Economic and Social Policy*, 3, 1998, 28–35.

Harcourt, G. C. 1997. 'Economic Theory and Economic Policy: Two Views' (The Seventh Colin Clark Memorial Lecture) in Joanilio Rodolpho Teixeira (ed.), *Issues in Modern Political Economy* (University of Brasilia), 15–47. Also in *Economic Analysis and Policy*, 27, 1997, 113–130.

Harcourt, G. C. 1998. 'Two Views on Development: Austin and Joan Robinson', *Cambridge Journal of Economics*, 22, 367–377.

Harcourt, G. C. 2001. 'Post-Keynesian Thought', in N. Smelser and P. Baltes (eds.), *International Encyclopedia of the Social and Behavioural Sciences*, Oxford: Elsevier, 13375–13379.

Harcourt, G. C. and Cohen, Avi J. 2003. 'Whatever Happened to the Cambridge Capital Theory Controversies?' *Journal of Economic Perspectives*, 17, 199–214.

Harcourt, G. C. and Gram, Harvey. 2017. 'Joan Robinson and MIT', *History of Political Economy*, 49, 437–450.

Harcourt, G. C. and Hamouda, O. F. 1988. 'Post Keynesianism: From Criticism to Coherence?' *Bulletin of Economic Research*, 40, 1–33.

Harcourt, G. C. and Kenyon, P. 1976. 'Pricing and the Investment Decision', *Kyklos*, 29, Fasc. 3, 29, 449–477.

Review articles

Harcourt, G. C. 1962. 'Review Article of W.E.G. Salter', *Productivity and Technical Change, Economic Record*, 38, 388–394.

Harcourt, G. C. 2012. 'The Collected Writings of an Indian Sage: *The Collected Works of A.K. Dasgupta*. Edited by Alakmanda Patel, 2009', *Economica*, 79, 199–206, reprinted in Harcourt, 2012b, 189–196.

Harcourt, G. C. and Massaro, V. G. 1964. 'Mr Sraffa's *Production of Commodities*', *Economic Record*, 40, 442–454.

Notes

Harcourt, G. C. 1959. 'Pricing Policies and Inflation', *Economic Record*, 35, 133–136.

Harcourt, G. C. 2014. '*AEP* and Me: A Short(ish) Memoir', *Australian Economic Papers*, 53, 255–259. Erratum printed in *Australian Economic Papers*, 54, 2015, 61.

Harcourt, G. C. 2016. 'Stanley Wong (23 July 1947–30 April 2016): A Tribute', *Economic and Labour Relation Review*, 27, 559–561.

Harcourt, G. C. 2017a. 'A Note on an Important Implication of the Conceptual Aspects of *Full Industry Equilibrium*', *Metroeconomica*, 22–23. https://doi.org/10.1111/meca.12182.

Harcourt, G. C. 2017b. 'K.J. Arrow (23 April 1921–21 February 2017): A Personal Tribute', *Economic and Labour Relations Review*, 28, 352–355.

Harcourt, G. C. 2017c. 'John Grieve Smith (2 November 1927–13 February 2017): A Memoir and a Tribute', *Economic and Labour Relations Review*, 28, 356–357.

Harcourt, G. C. and Hart, N. 2016. 'John Whitaker (39 January 1933–25 January 2016): A Memoir and a Tribute', *Economic and Labour Relation Review*, 28, 173–174.

Harcourt, G. C. and Massaro, V. G. 1964. 'A Note on Mr Sraffa's Sub-Systems', *Economic Journal*, 74, 715–722. (Reprinted in French in Gilbert, Farcarello and Phillipe de Cavergne (eds) *Une nouvelle approche en économie politique? Essais sur Sraffa*, Paris: Economica 1997, 53–61).

Harcourt, G. C. and (Raja) Junankar, P. N. 2018. 'Symposium on Inequality in Honour A.B. Atkinson', *Economics and Labour Relations Review*, 29, 3–58.

Chapters in books

Harcourt, G. C. 1967. 'Investment-Decision Criteria, Capital-Intensity and the Choice of Technique', *Czechoslovak Economic Papers*, No. 9, 65–91 and Chapter 14 of John T. Dunlop and Nikolay P. Fedorenko (eds.), *Planning and Markets* (New York: McGraw-Hill, 1969), 190–216.

Harcourt, G. C. 1975. 'The Cambridge Controversies: The Afterglow', in M. Parkin and A. R. Nobay (eds.), *Contemporary Issues in Economics*, Manchester: Manchester University Press, 1975, pp. 305–334. (Reprinted in French as "Les controversies cambridgiennes après la tourmente" in Gerard Grellet (ed.), *Nouvelle critique de l'èconomie politique* (Paris: Calman, Levy, 1976, pp. 35–76).

Harcourt, G. C. 1979. 'Robinson, Joan', in David L. Sills (ed.), *International Encyclopedia of the Social Sciences. Biographical Supplement*, 18, New York: The Free Press, pp. 663–671.

Harcourt, G. C. 1983. 'On Piero Sraffa's Contributions to Economics', in Peter Groenewegen and Joseph Halevi (eds.), *Altro Polo Italian Economics Past and Present*, Frederick May Foundation for Italian Studies, University of Sydney, pp. 117–128.

Harcourt, G. C. 1995. 'G.C. Harcourt. Cambridge University', in George Sheppard (ed.), *Rejectec. Leading Economists Ponder the Publication Process,* Arizona: Thomas Horton and Daughters, pp. 73–77.

Harcourt, G. C. 2001c. 'Post-Keynesian Thought', in N. Smelser and P. Baltes (eds.), *International Encyclopedia of the Social and Behavioural Sciences*, Oxford: Elsevier, 11849–11856.

Harcourt, G. C. 2002. 'Battling with Nicky', in Karl Sabbagh (ed.), *A Book of King's. Views from a Cambridge College*, London: Third Millenium Publishing, pp. 98–100.

Harcourt, G. C. and Cohen, Avi J. 2005. 'Introduction: Capital Theory Controversy, Scarcity, Production, Equilibrium and Time', in Christopher Bliss, Avi J. Cohen and G. C. Harcourt (eds.), *Capital Theory, Volume 1*, Cheltenham, UK and Northampton, USA: Edward Elgar Publishing Limited, xxvii–lx.

Harcourt, G. C. and Kerr, P. 1980. 'The Mixed Economy' Chapter 14, in Jane North and Pat Weller (eds.), *Labor*, Sydney: Ian Novak, pp. 184–195.

Harcourt, G. C. and Kerr, P. 2002a. Introduction to the Palgrave Archive Edition of Joan Robinson, *Writings on Economics*, 7 vols, Houndmills, Basingstoke, Hants: Palgrave Macmillan, pp. v–xxxi.

Harcourt, G. C. and Kerr, P. 2002b. General Introduction to *Joan Robinson. Critical Assessment of Leading Economists*, 5 vols, Edited by Prue Kerr with the collaboration of G. C. Harcourt. London: Routledge, pp. 1–32.

Harcourt, G. C. and Kerr, P. 2013. '"Introduction" to Joan Robinson', in *The Accumulation of Capital*, third Edition, in the Palgrave Classics in Economics Series, Basingstoke, Hampshire, UK: Palgrave Macmillan, vii–xxx.

Harcourt, G. C. and Tribe, Keith. 2016. 'Capital and Wealth' Chapter 2, in Pat Hudson and Keith Tribe (eds.), *The Contradictions of Capital in the Twenty-First Century: The Piketty Opportunity*, Newcastle on Tyne: Agenda Publishing Ltd., pp. 13–28.

Other works referred to in the text

Arestis, P., Palma, G. and Sawyer, M. eds. 1997. *Capital Controversy, Post-Keynesian Economics, and the History of Economic Thought. Essays in Honour of Geoff Harcourt*, London and New York: Routledge.

Armstrong, Phil. 2017. 'Review of G.C. Harcourt and Peter Kriesler (eds), The Oxford Handbook of Post-Keynesian Economics, two volumes', *Review of Political Economy*, 1–7. https://doi.org/10.1080/09538259.2017.1352132.

Arrow, K. J., Chenery, H. B., Minhas, B. S. and Solow, R. M. 1961. 'Capital-Labor Substitution and Economic Efficiency', *Review of Economics and Statistics*, 63, 225–250.

Australian Labor Party National Committee of Inquiry. 1979. *Discussion Papers 1–10*, Bedford Park, SA: APSA.

Ball, R. J. 1964. *Inflation and the Theory of Money*, London: Allen & Unwin.

Blankenburg, S. 2014. 'Introduction', *Cambridge Journal of Economics*, 38, 1295–1305.

Cohen, A. J. and Harcourt, G. C. 2003. 'Whatever Happened to the Cambridge Capital Theory Controversies?' *Journal of Economic Perspectives*, 1, 199–214.

Cord, R. A. ed. 2017. *The Palgrave Companion to Cambridge Economics*, 2 vols, London: Palgrave Macmillan (published by Springer Nature).

Cord, R. A. and Hammond, J. D. eds. 2016. *Milton Friedman: Contributions to Economics and Public Policy*, Oxford: Oxford University Press.

Corry, B. 2000. 'Review of Harcourt and Riach 1997', *Manchester School of Economic and Social Studies*, 68, 67–68.

Dasgupta, A. K. 1985. *Epochs of Economic Theory*, New Delhi: Oxford University Press.

Dixon, R. 1988. 'Geoff Harcourt's *Selected Essays*: A Review Article', *Economic Analysis and Policy*, 18, 245–253.

Dunlop, J. T. and Fedorenko, N. P. eds. 1969. *Planning and Markets: Modern Trends in Various Economic Systems*, New York: McGraw-Hill.

Eichner, A. S. 1973. 'A Theory of the Determination of the Mark-Up Under Oligopoly', *Economic Journal*, 83, 1184–1200.

Eichner, A. S. 1974. 'Determination of the Mark-Up Under Oligopoly: A Reply', *Economic Journal*, 84, 974–980.

Feinstein, C. H. ed. 1967. *Socialism, Capitalism and Economic Growth: Essays Presented to Maurice Dobb*, Cambridge: Cambridge University Press.

Freedman, C., Harcourt, G. C., Kriesler, P. and Nevile, J. W. 2016. 'How Friedman Became the Anti-Keynes', Ch. 32 of Cord & Hammond, 2016, 607–630.

Goodwin, R. M. 1967. 'A Growth Cycle', in Feinstein (ed.), 1967, 54–58.

Goodwin, R. M. and Punzo, L. F. 1987. *The Dynamics of a Capitalist Economy: A Multi-Sectoral Approach*, Oxford: Polity Press.

Grant, J. McB. and Mathews, R. 1957. 'Accounting Conventions, Pricing Policies and the Trade Cycle', *Accounting Research*, 8, 145–164.

Grant, J. McB. and Mathews, R. 1958. *Inflation and Company Finance*, The Law Book Company of Australasia.

Halevi, J., Harcourt, G. C., Kriesler, P. and Nevile, J. W. 2016. *Post-Keynesian Essays from Down Under: Theory and Policy from an Historical Perspective*, 4 vols, Houndmills, Basingstoke, Hampshire: Palgrave Macmillan.

Hicks, J. R. 1954. 'The Process of Imperfect Competition', *Oxford Economic Papers*, 6, 41–54, reprinted as 'Stickers and Snatchers', Ch. 12 of John Hicks. 1983. *Classics and Moderns. Collected Essays on Economic Theory*, vol. III, Oxford: Basil Blackwell, 163–178.

Hudson, Pat and Tribe, Keith. eds. 2016. *The Contradictions of Capital in the Twenty-First Century. The Piketty Opportunity*, Newcastle upon Tyne: Agenda.

Kaldor, N. 1955–1956. 'Alternative Theories of Distribution', *Review of Economic Studies*, 23, 83–100.

Kaldor, N. 1957. 'A Model of Economic Growth', *Economic Journal*, 67, 591–624.

Kalecki, M. 1936. 'Pare uwag o teorri Keynesa' (Some Remarks on Keynes' Theory), *Economista*, 3.

Kalecki, M. 1968. 'Trend and Business Cycle Reconsidered', *Economic Journal*, 78, 263–276.

Kerr, P. 2017. 'Joan Violet Robinson (1903–1983)', Ch. 30 of Cord. 2017, 673–704.

Kerr, P. ed. with the collaboration of G. C. Harcourt. 2002a. *Joan Robinson. Critical Assessments of Leading Economists*, 5 vols, London: Routledge.

Kerr, P. 2002b. 'General Introduction' to Kerr with Harcourt (2002a), 1–32.

Keynes, J. M. 1936. *The General Theory of Employment, Interest and Money*, London: Palgrave Macmillan.

Minhas, B. S. 1963. *An International Comparison of Factor Costs and Factor Use*, Amsterdam: North Holland.

Opocher, A. and Steedman, I. 2015. *Full Industry Equilibrium: A Theory of the Industrial Long Run*, Cambridge: Cambridge University Press.

Patel, A. ed. 2009. *The Collected Works of A.K. Dasgupta*, 3 vols, New Delhi: Oxford University Press.

Piketty, T. 2014. *Capital in the Twenty-First Century*, Translated by Arthur Goldhammer, Cambridge, MA and London: The Belknap Press of Harvard University Press.

Prendergast, R. 2014. 'Review of Harcourt and Kriesler 2013', *Economic and Labour Relations Review*, 25, 355–362.

Pressman, S. 2014. 'Review of Harcourt and Kriesler 2013', *Journal of Economic Literature*, 52, 853–855.

Repapis, C. 2014. 'The Scholar as Reader: The Last 50 Years of Economic Theory Seen Through G.C. Harcourt's Book Reviews', *Cambridge Journal of Economics*, 38, 1517–1540.

Robinson, J. 1953–1954. 'The Production Function and the Theory of Capital', *Review of Economic Studies*, 21, 81–106.

Robinson, J. 1956. *The Accumulation of Capital*, London: Palgrave Macmillan, Second Edition, 1965, Third edition, 1969, Palgrave Classic Economics Series 2013.

Robinson, J. 1977. 'Michał Kalecki on the Economics of Capitalism', *Bulletin of the Oxford Institute of Economics and Statistics*, 39, 7–17.

Robinson, J. 1978. 'Keynes and Ricardo', *Journal of Post Keynesian Economics*, 1, 12–18, reprinted in *C.E.P.*, V, 1979, 210–216.

Rothschild, K. W. 1947. 'Price Theory and Oligopoly', *Economic Journal*, 57, 299–320.

Salter, W. E. G. 1960. *Productivity and Technical Change*, Second Edition, Cambridge: Cambridge University Press, 1966.

Sardoni, C. ed. 1992. *On Political Economists and Modern Political Economy. Selected Essays of G.C. Harcourt*, London and New York: Routledge.

Singh, A. and Harcourt, G. C. 1991. 'Sukhamoy Chakravarty, 26 July 1934–22 August 1990', *Cambridge Journal of Economics*, 15, 1–3.

Solow, R. M. 1997. 'Thoughts Inspired by Reading an Atypical Paper by Harcourt', Ch. 35 of Arestis et al., 1997, 419–424.

Sraffa, P. 1960. *Production of Commodities by Means of Commodities. Prelude to a Critique of Economic Theory*, Cambridge: Cambridge University Press.

Targetti, F. and Kinda-Hass, B. 1982. 'Kalecki's Review of Keynes' *General Theory*', *Australian Economic Papers*, 21, 244–260.

Thirlwall, A. P. writing as Keynes, J. M. 1999. 'Reviewing Harcourt and Riach (1997)', *Journal of Post Keynesian Economics*, 21, 367–386.

Toporowski, J. 2013. *Michał Kalecki: An Intellectual Biography. Volume 1: Rendezvous in Cambridge 1899–1939*, Basingstoke and New York: Palgrave Macmillan.

Toporowski, J. 2018. *Michal Kalecki: An Intellectual Biography. Volume 2: By Intellect Alone 1939–1970*, Basingstoke and New York: Palgrave Macmillan.

Uzawa, H. (2005). Foreword to the Japanese Translation of Harcourt and Riach (1997), vii–x.

Velupillai, K. Vela. 2017. 'G.C. Harcourt (1931–)', Ch. 45 of Cord. 2017, 1003–1026.

Weintraub, E. R. 1998. 'Review of Harcourt and Riach (1997)', *Economic Record*, 74, 322–324.

Wood, A. 1975. *A Theory of Profits*, Cambridge: Cambridge University Press.

Chapter 9

Is there a Cambridge approach to economics?

Maria Cristina Marcuzzo

Introduction

'*Cambridge* capital controversy', '*Cambridge* monetary theory of business cycle' and '*Cambridge* equation' are some of the geographical references used to characterize the economic theories and approaches that developed in Cambridge (UK) between the 1920s and the 1960s. The question that then arises is which are, if any, the shared aspects in these developments that point to the idea of a Cambridge approach to economics.

I have been arguing for some time that the group of economists renowned as representatives of the 'Cambridge school' (Keynes, Sraffa, Kahn and Joan Robinson) or the 'Cambridge Keynesians' with the inclusion of Kaldor, as they are also named (see Pasinetti 2007) should be best defined as a 'group' rather than a 'school'; the reason behind the distinction is to convey the idea of both cohesion and sharing, rather than adhesion to a common body of doctrine. The implication is that 'the Cambridge approach to economics' is an alternative to neoclassical economics, but is not as cohesive and a fully fledged system of thought; it is rather a legacy with many threads. Several aspects of method, 'style' and content of the economics associated with the Cambridge tradition, and often traced back to Marshall, make it well recognizable, when compared with the so-called mainstream economics and other schools of thought. This is what will be presented in this chapter, drawing on my previous works (Marcuzzo and Rosselli 2005; Marcuzzo 2012).

The Cambridge group

The Cambridge group's profile should be seen against the framework provided by Marshall – the founder father of Cambridge economics – to whom institutionalization of the subject at the University was due. Be it in the form of criticism, refinements or extension, the approach taken by Marshall towards the multifarious aspects of economic life was taken by this group as a point of reference. The type of economics Marshall favoured involved the application of the tools of economic analysis to reality. Be it districts, trades or markets, his agents and markets were embedded in historically determined worlds. He devised the supply and demand apparatus not just as a mechanical tool designed to determine equilibrium price and quantity in each market, resulting from maximizing rules followed by consumers and producers. The apparatus was also a means to interpret situations in which expectations are fulfilled. Given their knowledge of the environment and the routines the various economic agents follow, on the basis of that knowledge, if they see no reason to expect a change, they behave in such a way that their expectations are confirmed. For Marshall it was not so much a matter of individual perfect foresight as the ability to adjust, through trial and error, to market twists and turns, assuming that individuals have varying decision-making skills.

While Marshall praised market mechanisms, albeit with many qualifications and footnotes to the contrary, the path was opened by the two intellectually leading figures of the group, Keynes and Sraffa, to expose the shortcomings of both the trust in markets and the faith in market theory inherited by Marshall.

Sraffa pursued the goal of exposing Marshall's inconsistencies arising from his method of representing the equilibrating forces of the market with a pricing mechanism of goods and factors of production based on marginal magnitudes. Keynes was more concerned with the inconsistency of expecting full employment of resources in the aggregate from individuals maximizing either utility or profit.

Kahn also accepted several Marshallian basic postulates, helped Keynes in proving that in general there is no level of effective demand sufficient to sustain full employment by forging the tools of the multiplier and the aggregate supply function and supported schemes to intervene in the market in the public interest.

On her part, while remaining a fierce Keynesian fighting against the 'bastard' (as she called it) progeny throughout her life, Joan Robinson was seduced by Sraffa's arguments favouring the classical (and Marx's) political economy as better equipped to explain capitalism, and took a more radical stance than the others in politics as well in academic debates.

Kaldor, owing to his economic growth models, theory of distribution and contributions to policy debates, became a leading figure of the postwar Cambridge economics and stood in the forefront of the fight against Monetarism in the 1970s.

This Cambridge group was embedded in what Mohit Sen called 'The Cambridge tradition of the equality of intellects, arrival at the truth through discourse and the careful nurturing of the minds of the young, encouraging without patronizing and guiding without compelling' (Sen 2003: 54). This 'Cambridge style' found expression both in the personal and professional lives of Cambridge dons and students, for whom public debate and discussion were founding elements in their life and in students' education.

What marked the Cambridge didactic system out was the personal relationship established with the students and the close attention given to their selection and education. Some of the personal rapports of respect and friendship that characterized the interaction between the Cambridge economists began as relations between supervisor and student (as in the cases of Keynes with Robertson and Kahn and of Robertson and Shove with Austin Robinson). Even the relationship of Marshall with Keynes and Pigou had begun as a relation between teacher and pupil.

Keynes gave form and finish to his ideas by submitting them to the others; his own contribution to the work of the others remaining far more modest. For him dialogue yielded the desired results only if it ran along the lines that he traced out, and apart from the occasional comments and consultation, it was hard to draw him out on other grounds, like the theory of value or imperfect competition.

The relationship between J. Robinson and Kahn epitomizes the kind of intellectual collaboration that was typical of Cambridge. In the first place, it was a sharing of time and space, which also entailed a sharing of knowledge and the habit of exchanging ideas and mingling together. From the post-war period, until the end of the 1970s, both had fundamental roles in shaping the Cambridge that attracted students and scholars in great numbers from all over the world.

Sraffa was involved in all the intellectually important happenings at Cambridge, but found no company along his solitary path in quest of an alternative economic theory. Although it was Keynes who drew him to Cambridge and both Kahn and Robinson attended his lectures, the impact of his criticism of the Marshallian theory and his efforts to gain acceptance for an alternative approach were surprisingly ineffective until the early 1960s. His 1926 suggestion – the assumption of imperfect competition – developed in directions departing far from the approach that had inspired them. This may explain why he did not share his research pursuits with any economists in Cambridge, with the exception of Maurice Dobb.

Kaldor, like Sraffa, with whom he became a close friend, was not a born-and-bred Cambridge economist, having got his education in economics at the LSE. Unlike Kahn and Robinson, he converted to the Keynesian Revolution only after the publication of the *General Theory*, but once he was made a fellow at King's and a member of the economic faculty he mingled with the group, although the rivalry with Joan Robinson was in more than one occasion a cause of bitterness and academic quarrels.

To sum up, the 'style' aspect of the Cambridge economists as a group lies in the particular type of communication – written and oral – that led to very close forms of interaction, not devoid of diversity and dissent, in the physical and temporal closeness, helped in part by relatively unconventional lifestyles upon which profound personal ties were threaded and woven.

In what follows, I will investigate the features of the approach to be identified as 'Cambridge' under the headings of divergences, differences and commonalities, concluding with a short review of its heritage in subsequent developments.

Divergences

'Marshall's *Principles* were the Bible' (Robinson 1951: vii), Joan Robinson flashed out recalling the time when she went to Cambridge as an undergraduate in 1922. With the arrival of Sraffa a few years later, the landscape changed. He came to Cambridge in 1927, upon Keynes's invitation, on the strength of two articles, only one of which was in English (Sraffa 1926). Joan Robinson was later to say, 'He was calmly committing the sacrilege of pointing out inconsistencies in Marshall' (Robinson 1951: vii).

Sraffa brought to Cambridge two new research programs: (i) a reappraisal of the theory of value of classical political economy as antagonist to the Marshallian 'fundamental symmetry' of supply and demand, and based on a definition of cost as 'physical' cost, which does not include any subjective factors, such as 'sacrifice' and 'waiting'; (ii) investigation into the exchange ratios between commodities that enable the exchanges between productive sectors which warrant reproduction of the economic system.

The first line of research would have been known only to those who were attending his lectures on 'Advanced Theory of Value' (as Kahn and Joan Robinson did), while the early formulation of the second line of research was shown to Keynes and Pigou, who like Kahn and Joan Robinson for the first, did not make much of it and was not disclosed until 1960.

The interwar years were dominated by Keynes who, between his first book, *The Treatise on Probability* (1921), and his major work, *The General Theory of Employment, Interest and Money* (1936), produced other landmark contributions including the *Treatise on Money* (1930), *A Tract of Monetary Reform* (1923) and the two collections *Essays in Persuasion* (1931) and *Essays in Biography* (1933).

The making of the *General Theory* and its aftermath marked a watershed in Cambridge economics, which was transformed by it at least for those, like Kahn, Robinson and Kaldor who fully endorsed the tenets: the rejection of the 'classical' conclusion that market forces are at work to bring the economic system to the full employment of resources while the individual's pursuit of self-interest does not – contrary to Smith's parable of 'the butcher, the brewer and the baker' – produce a social good, but the unemployment and waste of resources. Aggregate economic behaviour does not have the same outcome as individual economic behaviour, so what is good for the individual may not be good for the whole.

Keynes's approach to human behaviour rested on the two pillars of expectations and conventions provided the key to understanding how opinions are formed and how they can be transformed through the joint effects of persuasion and artfully designed institutions. His conception of probability, while offering the key to rational or rather reasonable actions, does not lead to the idea that we can overcome uncertainty by devising formulae to transform it into calculable risk.

Keynes saw the main task of economic policy as 'managing' rather than 'transmuting' human nature. In the last chapter of the *General Theory*, he concluded that it is 'wise and prudent statesmanship to allow the game to be played, *subject to rules and limitations*' (Keynes [1936] 1971: 374, emphasis added). He brought new arguments and strength to the tradition of thought which Marshall and Pigou upheld, in favour of some State intervention against exclusive reliance on market mechanism, tracing out the implications of individual behaviour for the welfare of society, admitting failures and suggesting ways of improving the working of society.

After Keynes's death, Kahn, Robinson and Kaldor were engaged in extending the *General Theory* to the long period and were faced with unsettled issues of determination of growth, income distribution and technological change. The question of the measurement of the value of capital and therefore the determination of the rate of profit cropped up and remained unsolved until the publication of *Production of Commodities by Means of Commodities* (PCMC) in 1960.

Sraffa provided the theory of prices and distribution alternative to neoclassical theory in general, and of Marshall in particular: given the quantities produced and the technical conditions of production for each commodity, the prices are determined by a system of simultaneous equations, under the assumption that in a capitalist society the rate of profit must be equal in all sectors. The distribution of the surplus is not made dependent exclusively on the technical conditions of production and the relative scarcity of productive factors, since one of the distributive variables is determined outside the system of prices and could be influenced by other economic, or even political and social causes.

By drawing an inverse relationship between rate of profit and wage, Sraffa shows that the interests of labourers and capitalists are antithetical. The substitution of labour for capital, when the rate of profit rises relatively to the wage loses any meaning after it is showed that the same technique could be adopted as the most profitable at different rates of wages (the so-called reswitching).

PCMC came out as a surprise inside and outside Cambridge, with the possible exception of Joan Robinson who said that she had seen the 'light' in Sraffa's Introduction to Ricardo's *Principles*, which led her to write her 1953 article, which anticipated the capital controversy.

Keynes had been dead for a decade when PCMC was published, but had he lived long enough to see Sraffa's project disclosed to the world, he would never have endorsed it. No matter how highly he regarded Sraffa or how strongly he felt the need to have him in Cambridge, he was reluctant to abandon his Marshallian tools, and he was allergic to Marx. On the other hand, no matter how much Sraffa felt for Keynes (both personally and intellectually), he considered him a 'bourgeois intellectual' whose 'mentality' prevented him from appreciating Marx and understanding the working class issues (P. Sraffa to R. Palme Dutt, April 19, 1932 in Marcuzzo 2005). On his part, Sraffa remained 'secretly sceptical of the new [Keynes's] ideas', (Robinson 1978: xii) as Joan Robinson had observed then and afterwards, isolating himself from the Keynesian revolution and, in turn, depriving it of his own contributions.

Since the late 1960s, many attempts have been made to argue for or against the compatibility of the approaches adopted by Keynes and Sraffa. Neo-Ricardians (Sraffa's followers accused Keynes and his followers [post Keynesians] of not sufficiently shaking off several neoclassical traits [for instance, acceptance of the inverse relationship – based on the marginal productivity of factors – between investment and the rate of interest]) and the post Keynesians retorted that in Sraffa's system there is no room for money and uncertainty, which are the distinct features of a capitalist economy.

In fact, the critique that Keynes, Kahn, Kaldor and Joan Robinson raised against the neoclassical paradigm went together with their apparently unquestioning acceptance – at least at a disaggregate level – of marginal analysis. True, Kaldor and Robinson in later years rejected the notion of equilibrium, but without severing the connection with supply-and-demand theories. Kahn championed the 'marginal principle' for the determination of price and output for the single firm and he was instrumental in persuading Keynes to adopt the marginal approach in the *General Theory*. Keynes never rejected increasing marginal costs in the *General Theory* and this led him to adopt assumptions, such as the inverse relationship between employment and real wages, which brought conclusions that he later admitted were at variance with facts.

Sraffa's estrangement from Cambridge economics and his refusal to engage in the discussion of his own work with those who were among his closest friends can be accounted for by a political, social and cultural gulf. In Cambridge, Sraffa remained an isolated intellectual figure, feared and admired rather than actually understood. An example of the difficulty or even impossibility of 'penetrating' the insularity of a body of doctrine remained, notwithstanding the Keynesian Revolution, far away from Sraffa's background and frame of mind.

Differences

Joan Robinson tried to incorporate Sraffa's prices into the Keynesian framework. Her encounter with Kalecki (who was in Cambridge during 1937–1939) and constant engagement with Sraffa made her more willing than Kahn to enlarge the Cambridge approach beyond the boundaries of Keynesian economics.

In her 1954 article, she drew attention to the 'profound methodological error' (Robinson 1954 [1964]: 120) connected with the concept of quantity of capital outside the short period. She pointed out the neoclassical failure to distinguish between changes in the conditions of producing a given output, when the quantity of physical capital is altered, from changes in the value of that capital, due to variations in wages and profits. The implication is that 'different factor ratios cannot be used to analyse changes in the factor ratio taking place through time', because over time the value of the quantity of capital may change as a consequence of a change in distribution, and we will not be comparing the same quantities. She concluded that 'it is impossible to discuss changes (as opposed to differences) in neo-classical terms' (Robinson 1954 [1964]: 129).

Robinson interpreted the 'points of view of difference and of change' as a distinction between legitimate and illegitimate comparisons between two equilibria, with different amounts of capital. Since changes in the value of capital may occur simply because of a change in the rate of profit, it is impossible to know whether the quantity of capital has changed in the transition from one position to another. Thus she drew the conclusion that equilibrium positions could only be compared as differences, and never described as changes from one position to another.

However, in the introduction to Ricardo's *Principles*, Sraffa takes the question of the measurement of the quantity of capital to pertain only to the question of measuring 'the magnitude of aggregate of commodities', i.e., to the *apparent* change in the quantity of output to be distributed whenever there is a change in its value due to a change either in wages or in profits.

Sraffa does not take it to pertain to the question of the impossibility of comparing two different aggregates of commodities at two different points in time because of the impossibility of singling out the effects of a change in distribution, as Joan Robinson seemed to take it. It is not the time element that makes the analysis of change impossible in neoclassical terms, but the circularity in the measurement of capital unless the rate of profit is determined simultaneously.

After the publication of *Production of Commodities*, Joan Robinson became aware of the misunderstanding of her reading of the introduction to Ricardo's *Principles*, but still defended her distinction between the 'two point of views of difference and of change' as resting on the distinction between logical and historical time, claiming that reasoning in logical time is common to both general equilibrium theory and Sraffa's system, while the language of Keynes is in historical time.

Joan Robinson's main line of attack on the neoclassical theory was levelled against the notion of equilibrium and the impossibility of dealing with historical time, rather than against the inconsistencies in the theory of supply and demand. She remained unconvinced by the theory of prices of production and objected to the method of *Production of Commodities*, because 'there is no causation and no change' and 'the argument is conducted strictly in terms of comparisons of logically possible positions' (Robinson 1980a: 132). She felt it to be more promising to rely on Keynes, who, 'at the opposite extreme to Sraffa, discusses only events' (Robinson 1980b: 139) and discusses them 'in terms of processes taking place in actual history' (Robinson 1979: xiv).

This issue gave rise to the controversy on the question as to where the dividing line of the alternative to neoclassical economics lay. There were those, like Garegnani (1979) who argued that the assumption of irreversibility in time was implicit only in the method of supply-and-demand analysis, in which the tendency towards equilibrium is described as movements along those curves. The same assumption is not made when comparing two long-term equilibrium positions determined by a 'classical' theory of prices and distribution. (Garegnani 1979).

Also K. Bharadwaj (1991), while agreeing that history, namely the process involving actual and irreversible changes as opposed to potential and reversible changes, has to be rescued from neoclassical theory and brought back into economic analysis, defended the method of comparison between long-term positions as a legitimate method of analysis of change. Robinson objected to the method of comparisons of classical political economy and to Sraffa's method as showing no substantial difference from the neoclassical equilibrium method in their neglect of disregard of uncertainty and disregard of expectations, which are the guiding forces of economic behaviour. K. Bharadwaj responded by making two objections to Robinson's criticism of the equilibrium (in the sense of the long-term position) method. First, the equilibrium concept does not entail that the corresponding prices and the uniform rate of profit actually rule at any particular moment in time. It is rather, the tendency towards it, driven by the forces that are believed to be persistent, that is argued for. Second, while not denying that uncertainty or expectations had a role to play, she followed Sraffa in defending an objective method of analysis, which does not to appeal to non-observable entities, such as individual utility functions, but instead to looks at customs, social norms and the like (see Marcuzzo 2014).

Commonalities

I have so far pointed to the divergences and differences among these economists who did not always share the same interests, background or attitudes, but nevertheless convey a sense of belonging to a common world. Where can we find those commonalities, which will allow us to define a Cambridge approach to economics? My answer will have two parts: the first relates to certain features which we can detect in the authors whom I have selected as representative of Cambridge economics, and the second concerns the heritage in the research development which have evolved since their time.

Marshall's works represented the major theoretical reference point for this group; all had to reckon with Marshallian theory, whether to go on to take a distance from it, as Marshall did, or to forge ahead along the most original and promising lines of research it offered. Marshall, who had 'acute awareness of its embeddedness in historically determined totalities' (Becattini 2006: 614) provided a framework which was distinct from the one embraced by other neoclassical economists. In his economics, expectations have an important role to play, so does the notion of the short period as a horizon defined by the nature of choices that the producer can make. His analysis, by assuming the *ceteris paribus* clause to hold, allows one to detect a chain of causes and effects in each individual markets. All these traits provided the fertile ground in which Kahn and Keynes's short period and partial equilibrium analysis developed.

We may also add that his version of the quantity theory, as a demand for money balances, by introducing the possibility of a variable, or even an unstable proportion of money held for transaction purposes, paved the way to the notion of liquidity preference. The notion of liquidity is at the centre of the

Cambridge critique of the quantity theory of money; it amounts to denying the separation between monetary and real factors and the determination of the level of price as the outcome of the interplay of a transaction demand for money and an exogenously given money supply.

In Chapter 21 of the *General Theory*, Keynes shows that the quantity theory results apply under very special conditions: far from being a general proposition, it can be applied in very special circumstances which rarely occur in the real world. The level of prices is shown, rather than the outcome of three factors, the level of money wages, technology and the level of demand.

On the demand side, the speculative demand for money, as a function of interest rate is another aspect worth noticing as a feature of the Cambridge approach. We need to be reminded that the liquidity preference is not a relationship, which can be assumed to be stable, as in IS–LM model; it follows that changes in the supply of money bring about changes in the interest rate only if the schedule of the liquidity preference can be thought of as a stable relationship. However – and this was Kahn's main point – it is unsuitable to think of 'a schedule of liquidity preference as though it could be represented by a well-defined curve or by a functional relationship expressed in mathematical terms or subject to econometric processes' and held Keynes responsible for giving way 'to the temptation to picture the state of liquidity preference as a fairly stable relationship' (Kahn [1954] 1972: 90).

These arguments are directed against the 'classical tradition' whereby thrift and capital productivity are the 'real forces' at work in determining the rate of interest, which are conceived as a highly conventional phenomenon, determined by the strength of the desire of individuals to hold money (as protection against an uncertain future) and the quantity of money provided by the banking system. However, the quantity of money necessary to bring about a fall in the rate of interest varies with the circumstances and the state and responsiveness of the market.

Kaldor challenged the alleged exogeneity that is the presupposition of the quantity theory equation. In his *Speculation and Economic Stability* (Kaldor [1939] 1960), he pointed out that the quantity of the money supply in a credit economy comes into existence as a result of bank lending and is extinguished through the repayment of bank loans. This volume of bank lending is limited only by the availability of credit-worthy borrowers. Accordingly, the money supply becomes a passive element varying automatically with the demand for credit. The increase in the supply of money in circulation is the response to increased demand and not an autonomous event. Without credit expansion, the Central Bank's willingness to expand the monetary base will not produce effects on the money supply. It is interesting to note that although we have only scattered passages testifying to Sraffa's monetary views, he certainly shared the idea of the rate of interest as a monetary and a highly conventional phenomenon.

Moreover there is a methodological aspect which make Keynes's and Sraffa's position very close to each other. As it is well known for Keynes in economics 'we cannot hope to make completely accurate generalisations' (Keynes [1936] 1971: 254) because the economic system is not ruled by 'natural forces'. The task of economics is rather to 'select those variables which can be deliberately controlled and managed by central authority in the kind of system in which we actually live' (*ibid.*).

In *General Theory*, while the liquidity preference, the propensity to consume, the marginal efficiency of investment, the wage unit and the quantity of money are presented as the 'ultimate independent variables', it is denied that this distinction could ever be general; on the contrary, the division is said to be quite arbitrary from any absolute standpoint (Keynes [1936] 1971: 247). *General Theory* explains why the level of employment oscillates around 'an intermediate position' below full employment and above the minimum subsistence employment (Keynes [1936] 1971: 254). However, Keynes added:

> we must not conclude that the mean position [of employment] thus determined by 'natural' tendencies, namely, by those tendencies which are likely to persist, failing measures expressly designated to correct them, is, therefore, established by laws of necessity. The unimpeded rule of the above conditions is a fact of observation concerning the world as it is or has been, and not a necessary principle which cannot be changed.
>
> (*ibid.*)

Keynes's stance is very similar to Sraffa's:

> I am convinced that the maintenance of the interest rate by the bank (or) the stock exchange has had its part in the determination of income distribution among social classes. . . . I did not want to commit myself much, and in general I only wanted to signal something in order to avoid the belief that the system is presented as 'foundation' for a theory of the relative supplies of capital and labour! It is *what is denied* that seems important to me: as to what is *affirmatively claimed*, I have no intention to put forward another mechanical theory which, in one form or another, states again that income distribution is determined by natural, or technical or even accidental, circumstances, which in any case are such that they make any action taken by either part, in order to modify, futile. . . . I do not see any difficulty in the determination of the rate of profit through a controlled or conventional interest rate, provided that the rate of profit will not be assumed to be determined by external unchangeable circumstances.
>
> (SP D3/12/111; quoted in Panico 2001: 301–302)

Finally, Sraffa's critique had implications for the contention that market forces always bring the system to the full employment equilibrium via changes in the wage rate. It was the same battle the Keynesians were fighting.

Heritage

There are least three research environments that purportedly draw and build upon the Cambridge tradition, that is, the Marshallian, Post-Keynesian and Sraffian approaches. I draw on Marcuzzo and Rosselli (2016) to present a short review of these developments.

Marshall's concept of 'industrial district, discussed in book IV of the *Principles*, describing 'the concentration of specialised industries in particular localities', pointed to a form of organization governed by trust and co-operation, which characterizes clusters of firms within well-defined regional boundaries in various parts of the world. The district can be seen, then, as a relatively stable community, which has evolved out of a strong local cultural identity and shared industrial expertise. (A recent assessment of the theoretical aspects of this literature can be found in Raffaelli et al. 2010). This attention to the social and historical embeddedness of the economic process within which firms operate is a far cry that has proved to be of great utility in interpreting the peculiarity of several contemporary industrial districts.

Another equally successful endorsement of the Marshallian apparatus draws on his evolutionary vision of the organic development of firms and society at large. Economic progress is seen as the cumulative result of increasing division of labour, of the development of specialized skills, knowledge and machinery and, at the same time, of the ability to coordinate them. Economic change is represented by concepts such as adaptive behaviour, variation and selection through industrial competition. The object of study is a population of firms, each different from the other and continuously evolving, through interaction among themselves and with their social environment. Although this evolutionary approach is not unique to Marshall, having its recognized forefather in Schumpeter, several interesting research trends in cognitive and industrial economics have exploited the richness of this Marshallian tradition.

However, nowadays the best-known and most widespread approach in economics associated with the Cambridge School is Post-Keynesianism, which emerged in the 1960s. In recent years, the insights of Minsky on the causes of the financial meltdown have given more visibility and credibility to an approach which had always stressed the role of uncertainty, as well as the importance of money and income distribution in capitalist economies. The role of effective demand in generating employment, rejection of the idea that public investment crowds out private investment, the monetary nature of the interest rate, mistrust in the flexibility of prices as a way to redress fundamental market imbalances and the importance of cost in generating inflation and of incomes policy in controlling it and fostering growth are the main ingredients of the Post-Keynesian approach.

There is indeed variety within the group of Post-Keynesians, in terms of emphasis and research agenda, while the (smaller) group of Sraffa's followers appears more cohesive and focussed. It is for expository purposes that the division is made here between the two approaches, since many heterodox economists would see no contradiction in endorsing both.

Sraffa's research programme has been carried forward along several different lines. One is the investigation into the properties of the so-called core, that is, the set of equations that determine long-period relative prices and the wage rate or rate of profit, under the assumption that outputs and the alternative techniques that produce them are given. The analytical complexities of the system when joint production is involved and/or the inputs include at least one natural resource have been explored. Another issue that drew the attention of Sraffian scholars is the convergence (or the non-explosive oscillations) of market prices to their long-run positions characterized by the uniformity of the profit rate. Important results have been reached in this field and the related literature is quite large (Kurz and Salvadori 1995).

Another line of research lies in the 'closure of the system' or the determination of the distributive variable which is assumed as given. The classical tradition of assuming constant real wage is rejected and attention is focussed on the rate of profit. Two routes have been pursued here. One, following Pasinetti and his Cambridge growth equation, is to consider the rate of profit determined by the rate of growth of the system, which, in turn, depends on the investment decisions of capitalists. The other route, following Sraffa's suggestion, is to assume the rate of interest to be equal to the rate of profit (allowing for differences in liquidity and risks). In this way, the possibility for monetary policy to impact income distribution – a clear case of non-neutrality of money – is posited.

Note that the two lines of research described previously represent what Pasinetti has labelled as the 'separation theorem', that is, the division between 'those investigations that concern the foundational bases of economic relations – to be detected at a strictly essential level of basic economic analysis – from those investigations that must be carried out at the level of the actual economic institutions' (Pasinetti 2007: 275). The separation concerns not only the objects, but the level of abstraction and generality that the analysis must and can achieve (Garegnani 2002).

Conclusions

At the end of this cursory excursus into the history of Cambridge economics, I have left out episodes and figures, such as Austin Robinson, C. Pigou, M. Dobb and D. Robertson, in the earlier period, and R. Goodwin, M. Kalecki and R. Stone, who also made significant contributions to what goes under the name of Cambridge economics. I have focussed on the five economists who epitomize the Cambridge approach to economics, by showing the divergences, differences and commonalities that make them a very composite group. I have also shown that their heritage can be found in contemporary research areas, which make this tradition alive and promising of further developments.

We may conclude by saying that the Cambridge tradition has handed down to us a legacy resting on two pillars. The first is the rejection of the 'classical' conclusion that market forces are always at work to bring the economic system to full employment of resources, implicated by the belief that there is no discontinuity between individual and aggregate behaviour, so that what is good for a single player in the market is good for the whole. The second is the Sraffian theme that the market, taken as synonymous with supply and demand, is a misleading arena for the representation of the rules of production and distribution. Both pillars are needed to travel the road towards an alternative economic theory and economic policy.

References

Becattini, G. 2006. 'The Marshallian School of Economics', in T. Raffaelli, G. Becattini and M. Dardi (eds.), *The Elgar Companion to Alfred Marshall*, Cheltenham, UK and Northampton, USA: Edward Elgar, pp. 664–671.

Bharadwaj, K. 1991. 'History Versus Equilibrium', in I. Rima (ed.), *The Joan Robinson Legacy*, Amok: Sharpe, pp. 80–103.

Garegnani, P. 1979. 'Notes on Consumption, Investment and Effective Demand: A Reply to Joan Robinson', *Cambridge Journal of Economics*, 3, 181–187.

Garegnani, P. 2002. 'Misunderstanding Classical Economics? A Reply to Blaug', *History of Political Economy*, 34, 241–254.

Kahn, R. 1954. 'Some Notes on Liquidity Preference', in *Selected Essays on Employment and Growth*, Cambridge: Cambridge University Press, pp. 72–96, 1972.

Kaldor, N. 1939. 'Speculation and Economic Stability', in *Essays on Economic Stability and Growth*, London: Duckworth, 1960.

Keynes, J. M. 1936. 'The General Theory of Employment, Interest, and Money', in E. Johnson and D. E. Moggridge (eds.), *The Collected Writings of John Maynard Keynes*, vol. VII, London: Palgrave Macmillan, 1971.

Kurz, H. and Salvadori, N. 1995. *Theory of Production: A Long-Period Analysis*, Cambridge: Cambridge University Press.

Marcuzzo, M. C. 2005. 'Piero Sraffa at the University of Cambridge', *European Journal for the History of Economic Thought*, 12(3), 425–452.

Marcuzzo, M. C. 2012. *Fighting Market Failure: Collected Essays in the Cambridge Tradition of Economics*, London: Routledge.

Marcuzzo, M. C. 2014. 'On Alternative Notions of Change and Choice: Krishna Bharadwaj's Legacy', *Cambridge Journal of Economics*, 38, 49–62.

Marcuzzo, M. C. and Rosselli, A. 2005. *Economists in Cambridge: A Study Through Their Correspondence, 1907–1946*, London: Routledge.

Marcuzzo, M. C. and Rosselli, A. 2016. 'The Cambridge School of Economics', in G. Faccarello and H. Kurz (eds.), *The Handbook of the History of Economic Thought*, Cheltenham: Edward Elgar, pp. 343–357.

Panico, C. 2001. 'Monetary Analysis in Sraffa's Writings', in T. Cozzi and R. Marchionatti (eds.), *P. Sraffa: A Centenary Estimate*, London: Routledge.

Pasinetti, L. L. 2007. *Keynes and the Cambridge Keynesians: A "Revolution in Economics" to Be Accomplished*, Cambridge: Cambridge University Press.

Raffaelli, T., Nishizawa, T. and Cook, S. eds. 2010. *Marshall, Marshallians and Industrial Economics*, London: Routledge.

Robinson, J. 1951. Introduction to *Collected Economic Papers*, Vol. I, Oxford: Blackwell.

Robinson, J. 1954. 'The Production Function and the Theory of Capital', reprinted 1964 in *Collected Economic Papers*, Vol. 2. Oxford: Blackwell, 1964.

Robinson, J. 1978. Introduction to *Contributions to Modern Economics*, Oxford: Blackwell.

Robinson, J. 1979. Introduction to *The Generalization of the General Theory and Other Essays*, London: Palgrave Macmillan.

Robinson, J. 1980a. 'Retrospect: 1980', in *Further Contributions to Modern Economics*, Oxford: Blackwell, pp. 131–134.

Robinson, J. 1980b. 'Misunderstanding in the Theory of Production', in *Further Contributions to Modern Economics*, Oxford: Blackwell, pp. 135–140.

Sen, M. 2003. *A Traveller and the Road: The Journey of an Indian Communist*, New Delhi: Rupar & Co.

Sraffa, P. 1926. 'The Laws of Returns Under Competitive Conditions', *Economic Journal*, 36, 535–550.

Sraffa, P. 1960. *Production of Commodities by Means of Commodities*, Cambridge: Cambridge University Press.

Chapter 10

Between theory and history

The structural dynamics tradition

Roberto Scazzieri[1]

Introduction

Structural change has been at the forefront of the economists' investigations into the dynamics of the wealth of nations since the formative period of political economy. This chapter argues that this line of research has provided an important link between economic theory and economic history since the earliest analytical explorations into the dynamics of economic systems. The second section considers pre-classical contributions to the study of structural economic dynamics, examining the writings of Antonio Genovesi and James Steuart. Then the chapter addresses Adam Smith's distinction between the actual and the hypothetical (which he calls 'natural') trajectory of structural change and argues that such a distinction is a fundamental analytical step in the structural dynamics tradition. The following section examines recent contributions to the theory of structural economic dynamics and highlights their character as analytical benchmarks for the causal investigation of historical trajectories. The chapter then concludes by discussing the criterion of relative structural invariance as the fundamental analytical principle common to the theoretical analyses of structural change.

The dynamics of the wealth of nations: historical trajectories and analytical principles

The formative stage of theoretical political economy is associated with the shift from a fund to a flow conception of national wealth (Pasinetti 1977). This shift provides the analytical background of the earliest attempts to formulate theoretical principles explaining the dynamics of national wealth along a sequence of compositional transformations (structural changes). The contribution by Antonio Genovesi (2013 [1765–1767]) and James Steuart (1966 [1767]) highlight the central role of production activities in determining the sequence of transformations in the composition of national wealth as the economy grows over time. At the core of Genovesi's and Steuart's analyses is the consideration of the 'hierarchies' internal to the production system as a system of interrelated production activities. In Genovesi's analysis, the consideration of 'hierarchies' follows from the distinction between 'political arithmetic' and 'political geometry'. The former (political arithmetic) provides *information* about the means available in a given state to support a population; the latter (political geometry) provides the *proportionality conditions* that any given polity should follow for those resources to support the corresponding 'just population' (*Lezioni*, I.5.iii, in Genovesi 2013 [1765–1767]: 50–51).[2] Political geometry directs attention to the proportionality requirements to be met by the different production activities and determines the sequence to be followed in their development. This sequence is based on the distinction between three categories of productive activities: (i) the 'fundamental arts' (*arti fondamentali*); (ii) the 'arts of improvement' (*arti miglioratrici*); and (iii) the 'arts of luxury' (*arti di lusso*). The first category (fundamental arts) includes activities delivering primary commodities, that is, commodities that do not derive from the transformation of raw materials (*Lezioni*, I.8.i, in Genovesi 2013 [1765–1767]: 80). The fundamental arts include hunting, fishing, husbandry, agriculture and metallurgy (*Lezioni*, I.8.i, in Genovesi 2013 [1765–1767]: 80). The second category (arts of improvement) includes the manufacturing activities that transform the products of fundamental arts into final consumption goods or in commodities needed to allow the practice of fundamental arts or their improvement (metal product manufacturing, textile production, carpentry and so on). A general principle governing the arts of improvement is that they should 'help and sustain the primitive [fundamental] arts' (*Lezioni*, I.9.ii, in Genovesi 2013 [1765–1767]: 93). As to the 'arts of luxury', they are manufacturing activities set in motion by needs that are only felt in a 'polite nation' (*Lezioni*, I.9.xi, in Genovesi 2013 [1765–1767]: 96). These activities are a consequence of the civilization process and should not be hindered unless otherwise harmful (*Lezioni*, I.10.vi–xiii, in Genovesi 2013 [1765–1767]: 94–95). The distinction between 'fundamental arts', 'arts of improvement' and 'arts of luxury' generates the sequence of stages that the economic system should follow along a dynamic trajectory of improvement. Fundamental arts are necessary for the reproduction of the means for material subsistence. However, the progress of material conditions and of civilization in general makes the 'arts of improvement' (the manufactures) indispensable, as progress involves the availability of goods that the fundamental arts cannot provide (*Lezioni*, I.8.xvii, in Genovesi 2013 [1765–1767]: 88). The requirements of fundamental arts (and of those employed in them) should regulate the proportions between the different 'arts of improvement' in the formation of a nation's wealth fund (see also Galasso 1977). This criterion suggests the sequence by which the different manufactures should be developed starting with the manufactures necessary to the fundamental arts, and only subsequently allowing the development of manufactures making products in demand with the 'other classes' (*Lezioni*, I.9.ii, in Genovesi 2013 [1765–1767]: 93). This criterion gives priority to the making of metal instrument, followed by the manufactures making textiles, carpentry and construction (*Lezioni*, I.9.viii, in Genovesi 2013[1765–1767]: 97). As to 'luxury arts' (the third category in the classification), we have seen that Genovesi takes a positive view of them, provided their development is not detrimental to the fundamental arts and the arts of improvement.

To conclude, Genovesi outlines an approach to economic dynamics that is grounded in the existing configuration of the economic system considered as a set of interdependent activities connected to one another by a well-defined hierarchy (his distinction between 'fundamental arts', 'arts of improvement' and 'arts of luxury'). This hierarchy determines the respective effectiveness of the different 'arts' at each stage of economic development for the maximization of each nation's wealth fund. In turn, this effectiveness ranking determines the *sequence* that each economic system should follow in transforming its structure (the relative proportions between its activities) as it moves from a primitive to an advanced state. In short, Genovesi outlines a type of structural analysis (his 'political geometry') that suggests a normative framework for development policy. On the other hand, Genovesi is ready to acknowledge that there may be physical or historical conditions in which the most effective sequencing of activities would be different (for example when a small territory makes the development of trade or manufacturing a priority relative to the growth of agriculture), or in which institutional constraints make it impossible to follow an effective dynamic trajectory for the maximization of national wealth (see also Bagchi 2014; Pabst and Scazzieri 2019).

Steuart's approach to the hierarchy between productive activities is different from Genovesi's, as it is steeped in awareness of the *interdependence* between agriculture and manufacturing and in the idea that the development of both requires the formation and extraction of net product from agriculture and the availability of sufficient numbers of 'free hands' (Steuart's expression for salaried workers) for employment in manufacturing (Steuart 1966 [1767]: 55). The formation of agricultural net product is central to Steuart's argument:

> The application of this net produce or surplus of the quantity of food and necessaries remaining over and above the nourishment, consumption, and expence, of the inhabitants employed in agriculture . . . must not this of necessity be employed in the nourishment, and for the use of those whom we have called the *free hands*; who may be employed in manufactures, trades, or in any other way, according to the taste of the times?
>
> (Steuart 1966 [1767]: 54)

Availability of agricultural net product is a necessary condition for manufacturing to develop, but this relationship leads to different consequences depending on the distribution of population between agriculture and manufacturing, and on the productiveness of the agricultural sector:

> [T]he raising of the rents of lands shows the increase of industry, as it swells the fund of subsistence consumed by the industrious; that is, by those who buy it. . . . [This] may denote either an increase of inhabitants, or the depopulation of the land, in order to assemble the superfluous mouths in villages, towns, etc., where they may exercise their industry with greater convenience. [Indeed] [while] the land rents of Europe were very low, numbers of the inhabitants appeared to be employed in agriculture; but were really no more than idle consumers of the produce of it.
>
> (Steuart 1966 [1767]: 55)

This argument leads to an important conclusion on the utilization of land in the development process:

> The more a country is in tillage, the *more* it is inhabited, and the smaller is the proportion of *free hands* for all the services of the state. The more a country is in pasture, the *less* it is inhabited, but the greater is the proportion of *free hands*.
>
> (Steuart 1966 [1767]: 55)

Steuart's focus on the relationship between agriculture and manufacturing makes him interested in the dynamics that may be triggered by improvements in agricultural technique:

> Which species of agriculture is the most advantageous to a modern society, that which produces the greatest quantity of fruits *absolutely* taken, or that which produces the greatest quantity *relatively* taken, I mean to the labour employed?
>
> (Steuart 1966 [1767]: 128)

This type of question finds no straightforward answer in Steuart. He highlights that the introduction of more effective agricultural techniques may enhance manufacturing, whose development may trigger further advances in agriculture:

> The natural and necessary effect of industry, in trade and manufactures, is to promote the increase of *relative* husbandry; which by augmenting the surplus, tends of course to increase the proportion of the free hands relatively to the farmers. . . . When lands are improved, the simplification of agriculture is a necessary concomitant of industry, because diminishing expence is the only method of gaining a preference at market. . . . When

industry is set on foot, it gives encouragement to agriculture exercised as a trade.

(Steuart 1966 [1767]: 132)

On the other hand, Steuart is aware of the shift of workers from agriculture to manufacturing this process involves, and of the need to achieve the shift in a gradual way in order to avoid farmers 'be forced to starve for hunger' (Steuart 1966 [1767]: 133):

[I]n every country where we see corn-fields *by degrees* turned into pasture . . . the change is gradual only, industry is not overstocked anywhere, and subsistence may be drawn from other countries, where the operose species of agriculture can be carried out with profit.

(Steuart 1966 [1767]: 133, added emphasis)

Steuart investigates both the 'natural' pattern of interdependence between agriculture and manufacturing and the exceptions that 'particular circumstances' may bring about:

The extensive agriculture of plowing and sowing, is the proper employment of the country, and is the foundation of population in every nation fed upon its own produce. . . . We commonly find agriculture disposed in the following manner. In the center stands the city, surrounded by kitchen-gardens; beyond these lies a belt of fine luxuriant pasture or hay-fields; stretch beyond this, and you find the beginning of what I call operose farming, plowing and sowing; beyond this lie grazing farms for the flattening of cattle; and last of all come the mountainous and large extents of unimproved or ill improved grounds, where animals are bred. This seems the *natural distribution*, and such I have found it almost every where established, when *particular circumstances* do not invert the order.

(Steuart 1966 [1767]: 134–135, added emphasis)

Steuart's distinction between 'natural distribution' and 'particular circumstances' is a central element of his analysis of the appropriate distribution of population between productive activities, and is at the root of his openness to considering the influence of context and the plurality of options for economic policy. At the same time, the exceptions to 'natural distribution' can be explained by the same causal mechanism associated with that distribution by virtue of *intervening factors* that modify its working and yet maintain it relevance:

The poorness of the soil near Paris, for example, presents you with fields of rye-corn at the very gates, and with the most extensive kitchen-gardens and orchards, even for cherries and peaches, at a considerable distance from town. Other cities I have found, and I can cite the example of this which I at present inhabit (Padoua), where no kitchen-garden is to be found near it, but every spot is covered with the richest grain; two thirds with wheat, and the remaining third with Indian corn. The reason of this is palpable. The town is of a vast extent, in proportion to the inhabitants; the gardens are all within the walls, and the dung of the city enables the corn-fields to produce constantly. Hay is brought form a greater distance, because the expence of distributing the dung over a distant field, would be greater than that of transporting the hay by water-carriage.

(Steuart 1966 [1767]: 135)

To conclude, 'natural' conditions highlight the fundamental mechanism of the social provision of material needs and suggest a hypothetical dynamic trajectory as analytical benchmark to explain a variety of historical paths. The latter could be significantly different from the 'natural' trajectory due to 'particular circumstances' which may influence the working of the fundamental mechanism depending on context.[3]

Natural dynamics and historical dynamics: Adam Smith

Book III ('Of the different Progress of Opulence in different Nations') of Smith's *Wealth of Nations* (Smith 1976 [1776]) is the *locus classicus* of the distinction between dynamic trajectories derived from analytical principles and dynamic trajectories reflecting the historical dynamics of economic systems. There Smith identifies the sequence of stages of structural transformation that can be derived from principles internal to the causal mechanism of economic growth as natural 'progress of opulence':[4]

As subsistence is, in the nature of things, prior to conveniency and luxury, so the industry which procures the former, must necessarily be prior to that which ministers the latter. The cultivation and improvement of the country, therefore, which affords subsistence, must, necessarily, be prior to the increase of the town, which furnishes only the means of conveniency and luxury. It is the surplus produce of the country only, or what is over and above the maintenance of the cultivators, that constitutes the subsistence of the town, which can therefore increase only with the increase of this surplus produce.

(Smith 1976 [1776], III.1.2, p. 377)

This structural constraint has an important consequence for the dynamic of transformation in a growing economy:

That order of things which necessity imposes in general, though not in every particular country, is, in every particular country, promoted by the natural inclinations of man. If human institutions had never thwarted those natural inclinations, the towns could no-where have increased beyond what the improvement and cultivation of the territory in which they were situated could support; till such time, at least, as the whole of that territory was completely cultivated and improved. Upon equal, or nearly equal profits, most men will chuse to employ their capitals rather in the improvement and cultivation of land, than either in manufactures or foreign trade.

(Smith 1976 [1776], III.1.2, p. 377)

In Smith's account, the 'natural' dynamics of an economic system undergoing structural transformation requires the development first of agriculture, then of manufacturing, and finally of 'foreign commerce':

According to the natural course of things, therefore, the greater part of the capital of every growing society is, first, directed to agriculture, afterwards to manufactures, and last of all to foreign commerce. This order of things is so very natural, that in every society that had any territory, it has always, I believe, been in some degree observed. Some of their lands must have been cultivated before any considerable towns could be established, and some sort of coarse industry of the manufacturing kind must have been carried on in those towns, before they could well think of employing themselves in foreign commerce.

(Smith 1976 [1776], III.1.8, p. 380)

Smith finds an instance of the 'natural course of things' applied in practice in the British colonies of North America:

In our North American colonies, where uncultivated land is still to be had upon easy terms, no manufactures for distant sale have ever yet been established in any of their towns. When an artificer has acquired a little more stock than is necessary for carrying on his own business in supplying the neighbouring country, he does not, in North America, attempt to establish with it a manufacture for more distant sale, but employs it in the purchase and improvement of uncultivated land. From artificer he becomes planter, and neither the large wages nor the easy subsistence which that country affords to artificers, can bribe him rather to work for other people than for himself. He feels than an artificer is the servant of his customers, from whom he derives his subsistence; but that a planter who cultivates his own land, and derives his necessary subsistence from the labour of his own family, is really a master, and independent of all the world.

(Smith 1976 [1776], III.1.8, pp. 378–9)

However, Smith is aware that many European economies had followed an inverse sequence developing first international trade, then manufacturing and finally the agricultural sector:

[T]hough this natural order of things must have taken place in some degree [in any society that had any territory], it has, in all the modern states of

Europe, been, in some respects, entirely inverted. The foreign commerce of some of their cities has introduced all their finer manufactures, or such as were fit for distant sale; and manufactures and foreign commerce together, have given birth to the principal improvements of agriculture.

(Smith 1976 [1776], III.1.8, p. 380)

Smith's distinction between the natural dynamics to be identified on the basis of a single causal mechanism (that is, the dynamics the economic system would follow if only that causal mechanism were in operation) and the historical dynamics generated through the interplay of a plurality of different causal mechanisms is an important contribution to the exploration of the working of analytical principles in explaining context-dependent growth-trajectories. For the inversion of the natural growth sequence is made possible by substituting the causal principles behind natural dynamics with different causal principles that perform the same function in a different context. For example, the commercial city states of medieval Europe had been able to reverse natural dynamics through surplus acquisition by means of international trade (which allowed those economies to skip the initial development of the agricultural sector). In turn, international trade triggered manufacturing growth, primarily in the form of import-substitution, and the surpluses generated through manufacturing growth eventually generated the type of demand for agricultural produce that triggered commercialization of agriculture and productivity increase in that sector. This inverted sequence of structural transformation calls attention to the rationale of Smith's analysis of natural dynamics. The natural sequence of transformation stages is not supposed to coincide with the historical evolution of economic systems. However, it is an analytical benchmark aimed at disentangling the causal mechanism at work along the growth process. Historical dynamics may be different from natural dynamics, but the difference itself can be explained in terms of the causal mechanism that natural dynamics brings to light. Smith's analysis of the growth process (his 'progress of opulence') is based on the distinction between the causal mechanism highlighting the necessary conditions for the increase of national wealth and the plural ways in which that mechanism may work under specific circumstances. This feature of Smith's analysis is a fundamental analytical step in the construction of a theoretical framework for the study of structural economic dynamics. The principal components of that framework are the following: (i) the distinction between a given causal mechanism and its mode of operation (so that a single mechanism may allow different modes of operation depending on context); (ii) the distinction between the 'natural' (that is, structurally determined) causal mechanism explaining the progress of national wealth and the historical trajectories that such progress may actually follow (see also Andreoni and Scazzieri 2014); (iii) the identification of relatively invariant principles regulating the hierarchy of motions of different sectors along the dynamic trajectory triggered by a given systemic goal (such as the full utilization of the economy's productive potential); (iv) the acknowledgement that the precedence pattern corresponding to the aforementioned hierarchy of motions may be changed or even reversed if the underlying causal mechanism finds alternative behavioural or institutional routes to work itself out (see also Cardinale and Scazzieri 2018).

Analytical benchmarks and historical trajectories: the structural dynamics tradition

In *A Theory of Economic History*, John Hicks argued that a *theoretical* account of any given historical trajectory should be construed by focusing on what he calls a '*normal* development' (Hicks 1969: 6), in terms of which 'exceptions' could be explained. However, the theoretical framework should be able to explain exceptions in terms of the causal mechanism from which the path of normal development derives:

> We are to classify states of society, economic states of society; we are to look for intelligible reasons for which one such state should give way to another. . . . It is only a *normal* development for which we are looking, so it does not have to cover all the facts; we must be ready to admit exceptions, exceptions which nevertheless we should try to explain.
>
> (Hicks 1969: 6)

Allowance for exceptions from the normal development extracted from a causal mechanism also entails that any natural development trajectory may be interrupted due to external or internal triggers:

> We are not to think of our normal process as one which, on being begun, is bound to be completed; it may be cut short from external causes, or it may encounter internal difficulties from which only sometimes there is a way of escape. All these possibilities will be admitted. Though we distinguish an underlying trend to which we may be willing to give the name of 'progress' or 'growth' or 'development', it is progress that is often interrupted, and which only too often takes disagreeable, even terrible forms. . . . We are accustomed to thinking of our last two centuries as a period of economic development, but it is a development that has been irregular ('cyclical') and has many dark places to it.
>
> (Hicks 1969: 6–7)

Reference to an analytical benchmark (Hicks's 'normal development') is a common feature of theories addressing the structural dynamics of economic systems. This benchmarking is also a common feature of attempts to investigate *historical trajectories* in terms of a theory of structural dynamics, as historical divergence from the benchmark is explained by the lack of certain conditions needed for the benchmark economy to follow the 'normal' or 'natural' path. However, the analytical benchmarking of historical trajectories takes a different character depending on whether we consider the 'normal' or 'natural' performance of the growth mechanism, or the *working out* of a new condition (such as a technical innovation, or the emergence of a resource bottleneck) within that mechanism. The former situation characterizes growth equilibrium literature starting with Roy Harrod's exploration of dynamic paths (Harrod 1939, 1948, 1973), the latter situation is the distinctive mark of traverse analysis, which deals with transitional paths from one growth equilibrium to another (Hicks 1973; Lowe 1976; Quadrio Curzio 1975, 1986; Quadrio Curzio and Pellizzari 1999, 2018; Hagemann and Scazzieri 2009; Scazzieri 2009).

The origin of growth equilibrium literature may be traced to Roy Harrod's 'Essay in Dynamic Theory' (Harrod 1939). There Harrod defines economic dynamics as 'the situation in which certain forces are operating steadily to increase or decrease certain magnitudes in the system' (Harrod 1939: 14). This definition suggests a cleavage between growth equilibrium theory and economic history, as in the latter steadily operating forces are seldom found.[5] In view of this, the aim of dynamic theory is described as that of providing 'a framework of concepts relevant to the study of change' (Harrod 1939: 14). Harrod's dynamic theory follows from the following set of propositions: (i) 'the level of a community's income is the most important determinant of its supply of saving', (ii) 'the rate of increase of its income is an important determinant of its demand for saving', (iii) 'demand is equal to supply' (Harrod 1939: 14). In Harrod's view, the consideration of steadily increasing or decreasing magnitudes requires '[a] new method of approach- indeed, a mental revolution' (Harrod 1939: 15). At the core of this approach is the idea of considering 'dynamic as referring to propositions in which a rate of growth appears as an unknown variable' (1939: 17). This approach leads Harrod to the following result:

> The dynamic theory so far stated may be summed up in two propositions. (i) A unique warranted line of growth is determined jointly by the propensity to save and the quantity of capital required by technological and other considerations per unit increment of total output. Only if producers keep to this line will they find that on balance their production in each period has been neither excessive nor deficient. (ii) On either side of this line is a 'field' in which centrifugal forces operate, the magnitude of which varies directly as the distance of any point in it from the warranted line. Departure from the warranted line sets up an inducement to depart farther from it. The moving equilibrium of advance is thus a highly unstable one.
>
> (Harrod 1939: 23)

In Harrod's dynamic theory, the 'warranted growth rate' (G_w) is endogenously determined as that rate of growth of the macroeconomy that would be consistent with a given macroeconomic propensity to save out of national income (s)

and with a given 'value of the capital goods required for the production of a unit increment of output' (C) (Harrod 1939: 16), thus leading to the following 'fundamental equation' (Harrod 1939: 17):

$$G_w = s/C$$

In Harrod's dynamic theory, there is a distinction between the warranted growth rate (G_w), as defined earlier, and that growth rate which the economy would be able to achieve under given conditions concerning population dynamics, technological progress, capital accumulation and 'propensity to work':

> Alongside the concept of warranted rate of growth, we may introduce another, to be called the *natural rate of growth*. This is the maximum rate of growth allowed by the increase of population, accumulation of capital, technological improvement and the work/leisure preference schedule, supposing that there is always full employment in some sense.
>
> (Harrod 1939: 30, added emphasis)

Finally, Harrod introduces, alongside the warranted growth rate and the natural growth rate, what he calls the *proper growth rate*, which he defines as 'that warranted rate which would obtain in conditions of full employment' (Harrod 1939: 30). The relationship between the three growth rates is set out as follows:

> The system cannot advance more quickly than the natural rate allows. If the proper warranted rate is above this, there will be a chronic tendency to depression; the depressions drag down the warranted rate below its proper level, and so keep its average value over a term of years down to the natural rate. But this reduction of the warranted rate is only achieved by having chronic unemployment. The warranted rate is dragged down by depression; it may be twisted upwards by an inflation of prices and profit. If the proper rate is below the natural rate, the average value of the warranted rate may be sustained above its proper level over a term of years by a succession of profit booms.
>
> (Harrod 1939: 30)

In short, Harrod's dynamic theory highlights the *growth condition* that would make a macroeconomy to meet the three following *and* distinct requirements: (i) the warranted growth condition allowing the economy to achieve a pattern of capital accumulation consistent with its capital needs per unit of output; (ii) the natural growth condition allowing the economy to achieve the maximum growth compatible with its population and technology dynamics, and with the existing propensities to present consumption versus future consumption, as expressed by the 'work-preference schedule' (Harrod 1939: 30) and the aggregate saving/income ratio; (iii) the 'proper growth' condition allowing the economy to grow at full employment.

Harrodian dynamics, as well as the growth-theoretical literature to which Harrod's paper gave rise, 'is not a theory of economic history' (Hahn 1971: vii). In fact, 'in almost all of the work the economy is always in equilibrium, and in much of it always in steady state. . . . If a historical theory ever comes to be formulated, the growth literature may be of some use; the bulk of the work will remain to be done' (Hahn 1971: vii). Macroeconomic growth theory provides a set of analytical benchmarks that leave scope to 'a great choice of behavioural postulates' (Hahn 1971: xv). Indeed, its determinateness results from its confinement to macroeconomic 'equilibrium paths' (Hahn 1971: xv). These equilibrium paths result from focussing on growth rates as endogenous variables determined by steadily operating forces and suitable behavioural assumptions (see earlier) to the exclusion of changes in the proportions between different sectors of the macroeconomy (structural economic dynamics), which are a distinctive feature of modern economic growth (Kuznets 1971). A seminal paper by Luigi Pasinetti and Luigi Spaventa noted the empirical inconsistency between the assumption of a continuously growing macroeconomy and the assumption of unchanged proportions between its constituent sectors (Pasinetti and Spaventa 1960). Building on this insight, Pasinetti investigated the conditions for the maintenance of full employment and full capacity utilization over time in a multi-sectoral economy subject to technical progress and increasing per capita income leading to changes in the per capita demand for different goods. The most important result of this analysis is that this type of economy can continue to grow along a path that satisfies both conditions provided certain changes in proportions between sectors take place (Pasinetti 1965, 1981). In this connection, Pasinetti distinguishes between what he calls 'natural dynamics' and the actual course of structural economic dynamics (Pasinetti 1981, 1993). The former is the trajectory of structural transformations the economic system should follow if changes associated with technical progress and the evolution of consumers' habits are to be consistent with the maintenance of full employment and full capacity utilization over time (Pasinetti 1981, Chapter VII). The latter is the historical transformation trajectory of the economic system, in which structural changes may be associated with phases of unemployment and idle productive capacity (Pasinetti 1981, Chapter X). In Pasinetti's view, the 'natural' level of investigation allows us to detect 'the "permanent" causes moving an economic system, irrespective of any accidental or transitory deviation which may temporarily occur' (Pasinetti 1981, Chapter VII: 'The "natural" features of a growing economic system', p. 127). Indeed, the analysis of the 'natural' properties of the economy 'has been developed independently of the institutional set-up of society, i.e. independently of the particular mechanisms which may in practice be put into operation in order to bring those "primary and natural" features into being' (Pasinetti 1981, ibid.). These 'primary and natural' features are 'the objective forces that are so basic as to be given prior to, and independently of, any institutional set-up' (Pasinetti 1981, cit., p. 149). In short, Pasinetti highlights the possibility of a dual approach to economic analysis:

> [t]he same economic variables may actually come under scrutiny at both levels of investigation, but in a quite different manner: at the *natural* level as ideal positions to be achieved; at the *institutional* level as actual positions that are in practice realizable, through particular institutional mechanisms; the latter having to be compared with the former, and to be gauged according to the speed with which they tend towards the former.
>
> (Pasinetti 1993, Chapter VIII: 'From the 'actual' towards the 'natural' economic system- the role of institutions', p. 147)

In particular, the 'natural' level of investigation is seen as leading to 'the analysis of the structural dynamics that is set into being by the fundamental forces that are at work, and that could not be perceived from the superficial observation of the actual market evidence' (Pasinetti 1993, *ibid.*). Economic investigation at the 'natural' level allows the detection of properties that may escape the analyst's attention when investigation is carried out at the institutional level. At the same time, detection of the 'natural' properties highlights the conditions that the economy should meet for it to be on a 'natural' growth path. Lack of these conditions makes it impossible for the economy to achieve full employment and full utilization of productive capacity (two fundamental properties of Pasinetti's 'natural' dynamics). As a result,

> the phenomenon of declining industries appears in all its clarity and simplicity, as the logical counterpart of the expanding industries. . . . [T]o have industries which are reducing their employment, and even industries which are compelled to shrink their production, is a necessary consequence of technical progress. In order to understand the process correctly, it is essential to look at it in the framework of the structural dynamics of the economic system as a whole.
>
> (Pasinetti 1981, Chapter X: 'The structural dynamics of a growing economic system', pp. 230–231)

In a different, but closely related, line of investigation there have been explorations into the structural dynamics of social classes generated along a growth equilibrium trajectory by the differentiated saving and bequest behaviour of different social groups (Baranzini 1991; Scazzieri et al. 2015). In this framework, it is possible to define the precise conditions according to which the various socioeconomic classes of the system may thrive, may disappear or may simply co-exist in the long period. This may be obtained by postulating a unique rate of interest, or a differentiated one which takes into account the different roles and attitudes to risk of the classes with different capital endowments. In short, analytical benchmarking through comparison between natural dynamics and historical dynamics makes it possible to outline a 'theory' of economic history built on *negative heuristics* (explanation in terms of missing conditions, rather than in terms of which conditions are fulfilled). Historical trajectories are explained by the *lack* of the type of structural dynamics (such as the reproportioning of sectors) that would make a 'natural' trajectory possible (see also Scazzieri 2012).

A different approach to analytical benchmarks is followed by the contributions addressing the working out of dynamic impulses along a causal path that is sequentially arranged over time (traverse analyses). The beginnings of traverse theory are in David Ricardo's investigation of the structural transformations triggered by 'sudden changes in the channels of trade' (Ricardo 1951[1817]: 263):

> [T]he demand for any particular manufactured commodity, is subject not only to the wants, but to the tastes and caprice of the purchasers. . . . In rich and powerful countries, where large capitals are invested in machinery, more distress will be experienced from a revulsion in trade, than in poorer countries where there is proportionally a much smaller amount of fixed, and a much larger amount of circulating capital, and where consequently more work is done by the labour of men. It is often impossible to divert the machinery which may have been erected for one manufacture, to the purposes of another; but the clothing, the food, and the lodging of the labourer in one employment may be devoted to the support of the labourer in another; or the same labourer may receive the same food, clothing and lodging, whilst his employment is changed.
>
> (Ricardo 1951 [1817]: 263–266)

Carl Menger called attention to the related issue of the complementarities across the time dimension in productive systems based on increasingly complex division of labour. The linkage between foresight and provision when goods of higher order (such as capital goods) are required draws Menger's attention to production as a fundamental attribute of provision:

> If the requirements of a people for grain for the current year were not directly covered in late autumn by the then existing stocks of grain, it would be much too late to attempt to employ the available land, agricultural implements, labor services, etc., for that purpose. But autumn would be the proper time to provide for the grain requirements of the following year by utilizing the above-mentioned goods of higher order. Similarly, to meet our requirements for the labor services of competent teachers a decade from now, we must already, at the present time, educate capable persons for this purpose.
>
> (Menger 2007 [1871]: 88–89)

This increasing dependence on time synchronization becomes the principal causal mechanism behind the transitional paths triggered by external or internal impulses in an industrial economy. Arthur Cecil Pigou's analysis of the repercussions of changes in a certain industry on other industries of the same production system shows this propagation at work by emphasizing the vertical linkages between the capital equipment industries and the final consumer industries of that system:

> [I]t is convenient to conceive industrial groups in the following abstract form. Industry A manufactures finished good, and has, subordinated to it and producing the materials and the machinery that it needs, sub-industries α_1 and α_2; the sub-industries in turn having other sub-sub-industries α_1' and α_2', which provide their material and machinery. Alongside of A there is another finishing industry B, with a similar series of sub-industries, and yet others, C, D, and so on. Of course this rigid division and specialisation of sub-industries does not exist in real life, but the conception is none the less of service for analysis.
>
> (Pigou 1929 [1927]: 65–66)

The vertical linkages embedded in a system of productive interdependencies such as the one described earlier determine the causal path followed by the repercussions of economic changes (such as a change in the demand for the product of any industry):

> When the demand for B's products in terms of A's stuff (for which we assume B has an elastic demand) expands, B, in order to increase his output so as to take advantage of the increased demand for his products, will need more materials and machines. It is plain, therefore, that a stimulus to expansion will be given to subindustries b_1, b_2, and to the sub-sub-industries below them. . . . So far, therefore, as the sub-industries b_1, b_2, and so on are concerned, it is true that A's prosperity propagates itself through B among further industries. But this propagation is, so to speak, analytic and not synthetic. That is to say, in its dealings with A, B is partly a principal and partly an intermediary for b_1, b_2, and so on, distributing what A pays between itself and its subordinates according to their respective contributions towards the final B product.
>
> (Pigou 1929 [1927]: 66)

Pigou's 'extraction' of a vertical causal path from within a set of horizontal relationships between industries highlights the working out of a given dynamic impulse (sectoral demand expansion) within a 'causal mechanism' that may lead to multiple trajectories depending on which impulse is at the origin of the dynamic path under consideration. John Hicks's investigation of transitional dynamics follows the vertical approach to causal paths by immediately focussing on a vertical representation of productive processes:

> We are now to define a productive process as a scheme by which a flow of inputs is converted into a flow of outputs. . . . We are not to think of the flows as steady flows, proceeding at a constant rate over time. . . . The process may then be expressed as a pair of flows, of inputs and outputs . . . varying over time. Any process, so expressed, has a distinctive time-shape, or *time-profiler*. Consider (as an example, but no more than an example) a process which consists in the construction of a plant, its operation over a period of years and its ultimate dismantling. . . . There is an initial construction period, with large inputs but no final output; it is followed by a running-in period, in which output rises from zero to a normal level, while input falls to its normal level (constructional labour being laid off while the labour force which is to work the plant is being built up). There follows a period, probably a long period, of normal utilization. Finally, as a result of a fall in the output curve or of a rise in the input curve, the process comes to an end.
>
> (Hicks 1973: 14–15)

This representation of the production system *directly* highlights the causal path generated by any given dynamic impulse without directly considering the repercussions of that impulse through a set of interdependent production processes (this is a critical distinctive feature of Hicks's analysis with respect to the analytical representation of production that Pigou adopts in the passage quoted earlier). Hicks's investigation of the dynamic trajectory followed by an economic system that is displaced from a given condition by 'some kind of disturbance' (Hicks 1973: 81) takes advantage of the 'one-way' point of view in the representation of production to focus on a specific causal path generated by that disturbance (thus avoiding consideration of alternative causal paths that the repercussions of the disturbance might take):

> [O]ut of the steady state, one point of time is not like another. In particular, it must have a beginning. The path which follows from that beginning is what we have to determine; so the state of the economy at the beginning (and its previous history, in so far as that is relevant) must be taken as given. . . . I propose to consider the problem as one of 'Traverse'. We begin with an economy which is in a steady state, under an 'old' technique; then, at time 0, there is an 'invention', the introduction of what, in some respects at least, is a new technology. . . . The new technique is adopted for new processes, but the old processes are continued, so long as it is profitable for them to be continued. . . . It cannot be taken for granted that the sequence, generated in this manner, will tend to a new equilibrium. It may or may

not. In most of the cases which we shall examine there will prove to be a tendency to equilibrium; so that our sequence can properly be considered as a *Traverse* from one steady state to another.

(Hicks 1973: 81–82)[6]

Hicks's traverse analysis traces the sequence of repercussions following the introduction of a new technique considering the transitional paths generated by two alternative assumptions on the 'law of motion' of the economic system. In one case (Hicks's 'full performance' trajectory) the economy is supposed to reinvest in production a constant proportion of profits (Hicks 1973: 89–90); in the other case (Hicks's 'full employment' trajectory) the economy is supposed to guarantee full employment of the labour supply under the condition of a variable wage rate (Hicks 1973: 101). In either case, traverse theory provides as analytical benchmark a transitional trajectory whose determinateness follows from the simplified 'one-way' representation of the production system and presupposes specific assumptions concerning, respectively, the accumulation of capital and the dynamics of employment. In Hicks's view, different assumptions on the time-profile of the productive process or rigidities due to intertemporal complementarities between the construction and utilization phases of each process are likely to make the traverse adjustments difficult and to bring about a 'jam' at which 'the processes that have been started cannot be carried through' (Hicks 1973: 137).[7]

The analysis of transitional dynamics presupposes the identification of causal paths of the sequential type in a system of interdependencies that link different processes both at any given time and across time. Sequential causality is immediately visible with Hicks's vertical representation of the productive process, but is also compatible with the consideration of interdependencies of the horizontal (circular) type. Quadrio Curzio's analysis of the dynamic trajectory followed by a circular economy subject to bottlenecks due to the limited availability of non-produced inputs (such as land) is a case in point (Quadrio Curzio 1975, 1986; Quadrio Curzio and Pellizzari 1999, 2018). Here an economy whose 'law of motion' is maximum accumulation follows a trajectory characterized by alternating phases of expansion and contraction under the influence of moving constraints due to a sequence of resource bottlenecks. The economic system is described as a set of distinct (and technologically self-contained) sub-systems where each sub-system is a circular sub-economy producing k commodities by means of k productive processes (the number of commodities is equal to the number of processes). In the complete economic system, on the other hand, the number of processes is greater than the number of commodities due to the need of using more than one process for producing commodities that require inputs whose availability is limited. In this type of economy, the linkage between different sub-systems is provided by capital accumulation, as the net products delivered by one subsystem are assumed to be invested in the sub-system next to it according to an efficiency ranking of sub-systems and to the extent that this 'transfer' of net products from one sub-system to another is compatible with the technical structure of the two sub-systems. Here the sub-systems are *connected in time*, in that they rely upon the means of production of techniques already activated. These disjointed, *but temporally connected* techniques, will give rise to composite technologies which ... represent a fair approximation to reality when account is taken of the non-produced means of production' (Quadrio Curzio 1986: 327; added emphasis). As in Hicks, complementarities over time characterize Quadrio Curzio's transitional dynamics. Here, however, the linkage between different time periods is provided by the dual influence of: (i) capital accumulation under a sequence of binding resource bottlenecks and (ii) of structural matches/mismatches between the technical structures of the different, and sequentially activated, subsystems. Capital accumulation requires activation of different subsystems as the economy grows over time; technical mismatches lead to the appearance in certain sub-systems of 'residuals' of net products that cannot be immediately invested but may be so in due course, thus leading to a surge of maximum growth that is independent of technical innovation even if it is entirely structural in its origin. In this case, transitional dynamics along the maximum feasible growth path may take a characteristically uneven character due to the above 'matching condition' on the utilization of residuals across different technical structures:

> Because of the presence of different types of non-reproduced means of production sequentially activated, the economy may pass from situations in which the entire net product can be accumulated to situations in which residuals are created, and back again to situations of total accumulation. . . . The intertwining of the above phenomena may give rise to various types of dynamics. The growth rates of production and net product may either increase or decrease and frequently change behaviour over time. For example, the activation of a less efficient process with NPMP [non-produced means of production], characterized however by a bundle of means of production much closer in quantity and quality with the available residuals, may bring about an increase in the growth rates rather than a dynamic slow down.
>
> (Quadrio Curzio and Pellizzari 1999: 83)

The dynamic trajectory described earlier follows from the maximum growth condition under the limited availability of non-reproduced means of production and the structural compatibility requirements between different techniques. It does not coincide with any particular historical trajectory, even if it provides an analytical benchmark for understanding actual transitional dynamics triggered by limited availability of non-reproducible inputs. In those dynamics 'lack of uniformity appears to be the rule' and can at least be partially explained by the lack of uniformity generated by alternating phases of structural matching and mismatching along the maximum feasible growth path (Quadrio Curzio and Pellizzari 1999: 83; see also Scazzieri et al. 2015).

Alternative representations of economic structure generate different analytical benchmarks for traverse analysis (Baranzini and Scazzieri 1990). As we have seen, the vertical representation adopted in the 'simple profile' of Hicks's *Capital and Time* draws attention to a relatively simple trajectory along which any given impulse works itself out. However, assumptions different from the 'simple profile' under a vertical representation of production highlight time asymmetries (lack of synchronization) that may lead a traverse to a halt (Hicks 1973: 137). A horizontal (circular) representation (as in Quadrio Curzio) may also generate 'vertical' trajectories of sequentially connected structural changes but the associated mismatches are of a different type. In his case, we may find that the production structure of one technique along the sequence does not fully fit the previous technique along the same sequence, but the reason is lack of structural compatibility (a proportionality issue) rather than lack of synchronization. The traverse theory outlined by Adolph Lowe combines horizontal and structural features and highlights the intertwining of the two types of mismatches along a transitional path (Lowe 1976). Lowe's representation of a production system (his 'schema of industrial production') shows a system 'vertically divided into two sectors: equipment-good industries . . . and consumer-good industries . . . described as Sector I and Sector II, respectively' (Lowe 1976: 31). This representation views production as the result of vertical and horizontal flows coordinated with one another:

> Vertically, natural resources flow in progressive transformation down to the level of finished consumer goods. The continuity of this vertical flow depends, however, on the simultaneous presence of a horizontal flow, from Sector I to Sector II, of certain quantities of finished fixed-capital goods large enough to replace at least the fixed-capital goods used in every stage during the vertical flow occurring in Sector II A corresponding vertical flow occurs in Sector I. At first glance, however, there is an important difference between the two sectors with regard to the horizontal flow. In sector II it is a horizontal flow from Sector I that replaces the worn-out equipment. In Sector I the currently used-up equipment is replaced from the output of that sector itself, more precisely, from the output of Subsector Ia. In other words, the horizontal flow consists of a portion of the vertical flow 'turned back', that is, it is a circular flow.

> (Lowe 1976: 33)[8]

Lowe's representation of a production economy highlights the complex intertwining of circular interdependencies and synchronization requirements that constrain transitional trajectories as the economy reacts to internal or external triggers of change. Traverses may be speeded up, slowed down, or become altogether impossible depending on the way in which the production system manages to overcome the horizontal and vertical bottlenecks embedded in its structure (see also Hicks 1985). This approach highlights Lowe's distinction between 'structure analysis' and 'force analysis', where 'structure analysis' investigates 'the configurations in which the elements of an economic system . . .

must be arranged if the transformation of the initial into the stipulated terminal state is to be achieved' (Lowe 1976: 17), while 'force analysis' studies 'the patterns of behaviour or motivation that initiate and sustain the motion of the system along the structurally determined path' (Lowe 1976: 17).[9] This distinction highlights the plurality of historical trajectories compatible with any given set of feasible transformation paths, and calls attention to the need of disentangling 'patterns of behaviour or motivation' specific to any given historical trajectory from the technological structure from which that trajectory is constrained (see also Bianchi 1984; Bianchi and Labory 2017).[10]

Relative structural invariance and the dynamics of economic structures

Classical and modern theories of structural economic dynamics are characterized by a common set of features that are set out here: (i) the identification of a given structural architecture for the economic system under consideration: this architecture highlights the deep structure of that system and is relatively invariant for the purposes of the analysis at hand; (ii) the consideration of dynamic impulses (such as technical change or resource bottlenecks) as generators of change of certain elements within that relatively invariant structure; (iii) the introduction of certain hypothetical conditions (such as full performance, full employment, maximum growth) as a device by which the sequence of changes prompted by any given dynamic impulse is made to engender a determinate trajectory. The principle of relative invariance of certain system elements, or of certain system motions, vis à vis other elements and/or motions is a fundamental characteristic of the economic theories of structural dynamics. The economic system reacts to any given impulse, or to any given operating force, by changing its original state under a limited set of feasible transformations (Landesmann and Scazzieri 1990: 96–97; Scazzieri 2018). Relative structural invariance presupposes a type of dynamic structure such that certain transformations are allowed and others excluded along the trajectory prompted by the impulse or force under consideration. This feature makes economic dynamics to reflect proportionality conditions between different subsystems (such as manufacturing versus the agricultural sector) as well as a given 'order of sequence' (Myrdal 1939: 27) between their movements. Hypothetical conditions make structural dynamics trajectories determinate but should not be taken as limiting the scope of structural economic dynamics. They should rather be considered as devices aimed at the formulation of analytical trajectories that highlight the causal mechanism of change that is at work even when the historical trajectory is different (see previous). Relative structural invariance provides a unifying framework for assessing the relationship between local dynamics and systemic conditions, which is central to the contemporary theories of structural change. This criterion also provides a clue into the relationship between short-, medium- and long-term dynamics, and into the possible alignments between the policy measures corresponding to the different time horizons.

Notes

1 I am grateful to Mauro Baranzini for enlightening comments and suggestions. The usual caveats apply.
2 Genovesi defines a 'just population' as the population adapted to the economy's carrying capacity in terms of food provision (Genovesi, *Lezioni*, I.5.iii, in Genovesi 2013 [1765–1767]: 50).
3 This point of view led Steuart to argue that different countries are likely to have different political economies in spite of the existence of 'universally true' principles: 'If one considers the variety which is found in different countries, in the distribution of property, subordination of classes, genius of people, proceeding from the variety of forms of government, laws, climate, and manners, one may conclude, that the political oeconomy in each must necessarily be different, and that principles, however universally true, may become quite ineffectual in practice, without a sufficient preparation of the spirit of a people' (Steuart 1966 [1767]: 17) (see also Skinner 1966; Reinert 2004)
4 Smith's account of the 'natural progress of Opulence' (Smith 1976 [1776], III.1.1) suggests a view of causality that is *prima facie* different from David Hume's approach to causal relations. For Smith's focus is on the internal structure of a relatively persistent system of interdependencies rather than on the uniformity of joint occurrences between series of events. Smith's 'systemic' view of causality closely resembles the approach to causality in terms of causal mechanism discussed in recent epistemological literature (Glennan 1996, 1997, 2010; Salmon 1984).
5 This is acknowledged by Harrod, who writes that a theory of economic dynamics 'would not profess to determine the course of events in detail' (Harrod 1939: 14).
6 Hicks also acknowledges that 'it is far from clear that [convergence to equilibrium] is generally true. There are other possibilities' (Hicks 1973: 82).
7 For example, '[i]f the typical process requires more input for its full development than it does at its beginning, then *either* fewer will be started to give continuous full employment *or* processes which have been started will have to be stopped, and cannot be carried through' (Hicks 1977: 194). This is because, assuming an initial full employment condition, fewer new processes sequentially arranged and partially overlapping over time would be compatible with continuous full employment. Otherwise, processes that have started will not reach completion due to shortage of labour.
8 Sector I (the equipment-good sector) is itself divided into two subsectors: subsector Ia, which produces equipment used in sector I (equipment-good sector) and sector II (consumer-good sector), and subsector Ib, which produces equipment used in sector II only.
9 This approach is related to Lowe's concept of 'instrumental analysis', which is a type of investigation that 'starts out not from an observed but from a postulated terminal state' (Lowe 1977: 146) and 'extracts' from knowledge of the internal structure of the economic system the means to achieve that state.
10 The distinction between a dynamic trajectory of *feasible* transformations and the actual dynamic path of structural change is also discussed in Scazzieri (1993, 2014).

References

Andreoni, A. and Scazzieri, R. 2014. 'Triggers of Change: Structural Trajectories and Production Dynamics', *Cambridge Journal of Economics*, 38(6), 1391–1408, November.
Bagchi, A. K. 2014. 'Contextual Political Economy, Not Whig Economics', *Cambridge Journal of Economics*, 38(3), 545–562, May.
Baranzini, M. 1991. *A Theory of Wealth, Distribution and Accumulation*, Oxford: Clarendon Press.

Baranzini, M. and Scazzieri, R. 1990. 'Economic Structure: Analytical Perspectives', in M. Baranzini and R. Scazzieri (eds.), *The Economic Theory of Structure and Change*, Cambridge: Cambridge University Press, pp. 227–333.

Bianchi, P. 1984. *Divisione del lavoro e ristrutturazione industriale*, Bologna: Il Mulino.

Bianchi, P. and Labory, S. 2017. 'Manufacturing Regimes and Transitional Paths: Lessons for Industrial Policy', *Structural Change and Economic Dynamics*, October 12, https://doi.org/10.1016/j.strueco.2017.10.003. Last accessed on 18 March 2018.

Cardinale, I. and Scazzieri, R. 2018. 'Political Economy as Theory of Society', in I. Cardinale and R. Scazzieri (eds.), *The Palgrave Handbook of Political Economy*, London: Palgrave Macmillan, pp. 787–815.

Galasso, G. 1977. 'Il pensiero economico di Genovesi', in *Nuove idee e nuova arte nel Settecento italiano*, Atti dei Convegni Lincei, n. 26, Roma, Accademia Nazionale dei Lincei, pp. 337–359.

Genovesi, A. 2013 [1765–1767]. *Lezioni di economia civile* [Lectures on civil economy], Edited by F. Dal Degan, Milano: Vita e Pensiero.

Glennan, S. S. 1996. 'Mechanisms and the Nature of Causation', *Erkenntnis*, 44, 49–71.

Glennan, S. S. 1997. 'Capacities, Universality and Singularity', *Philosophy of Science*, 64, 605–626.

Glennan, S. S. 2010. 'Mechanisms, Causes, and the Layered Model of the World', *Philosophy and Phenomenological Research*, 81, 362–381.

Hagemann, H. and Scazzieri, R. 2009. 'Capital Structure and Economic Transitions: An Introductory Essay', in H. Hagemann and R. Scazzieri (eds.), *Capital, Time and Transitional Dynamics*, Abingdon, Oxon and New York: Routledge, pp. 1–39.

Hahn, F. H. 1971. 'Introduction', in F. H. Hahn (ed.), *Readings in Theory of Growth: A Selection of Papers from the Review of Economic Studies*, London and Basingstoke: Palgrave Macmillan and St. Martin's Press, pp. vii–xv.

Harrod, R. 1939. 'An Essay in Dynamic Theory', *The Economic Journal*, 49(193), 14–33, March.

Harrod, R. 1948. *Towards a Dynamic Economics: Some Recent Developments of Economic Theory and Their Application to Policy*, London and New York: Palgrave Macmillan and St Martin's Press.

Harrod, R. 1973. *Economic Dynamics*, London and Basingstoke: Palgrave Macmillan.

Hicks, J. 1969. *A Theory of Economic History*, Oxford: Clarendon Press.

Hicks, J. 1973. *Capital and Time: A Neo-Austrian Theory*, Oxford: Clarendon Press.

Hicks, J. 1977. 'An Addendum to *Capital and Time*', in J. Hicks (ed.), *Economic Perspectives: Further Essays on Money and Growth*, Oxford: Clarendon Press, pp. 190–195.

Hicks, J. 1985. *Methods of Dynamic Economics*, Oxford: Oxford University Press.

Kuznets, S. 1971. *Economic Growth of Nations: Total Output and Production Structure*, Cambridge, MA: Belknap Press, Harvard University Press.

Landesmann, M. and Scazzieri, R. 1990. 'Specification of Structure and Economic Dynamics', in M. Baranzini and R. Scazzieri (eds.), *The Economic Theory of Structure and Change*, Cambridge: Cambridge University Press, pp. 95–121.

Lowe, A. 1976. *The Path of Economic Growth*, Cambridge: Cambridge University Press.

Lowe, A. 1977. *On Economic Knowledge: Toward a Science of Political Economics*, Enlarged edition, Armonk, New York and London: Sharpe.

Menger, C. 2007 [1871]. *Principles of Economics*, Introduction by F. A. Hayek, Foreword by P. G. Klein, Auburn, USA: The Ludwig von Mises Institute.

Myrdal, G. 1939. *Monetary Equilibrium*, London: Edinburgh and Glasgow, William Hodge and Company.

Pabst, A. and Scazzieri, R. 2019. 'Virtue, Production and the Politics of Commerce: Genovesi's "Civil Economy" Revisited', *History of Political Economy*, forthcoming.

Pasinetti, L. L. 1965. 'A New Theoretical Approach to the Problems of Economic Growth', in *Econometric Approach to Development Planning*, Amsterdam: North-Holland Publishing Company, pp. 571–696.

Pasinetti, L. L. 1977. *Lectures on the Theory of Production*, New York: Columbia University Press.

Pasinetti, L. L. 1981. *Structural Change and Economic Growth: A Theoretical Essay on the Dynamics of the Wealth of Nations*, Cambridge: Cambridge University Press.

Pasinetti, L. L. 1993. *Structural Economic Dynamics: A Theory of the Economic Consequences of Human Learning*, Cambridge: Cambridge University Press.

Pasinetti, L. L. and Spaventa, L. 1960. 'Verso il superamento della modellistica aggregata nella teoria dello sviluppo economico', *Rivista di politica economica*, 50, 1749–1781, September–October 9–10.

Pigou, A. 1929 [1927]. *Industrial Fluctuations*, London: Palgrave Macmillan.

Quadrio Curzio, A. 1975. *Accumulazione del capitale e rendita*, Bologna: Il Mulino.

Quadrio Curzio, A. 1986. 'Technological Scarcity: An Essay on Production and Structural Change', in M. Baranzini and R. Scazzieri (eds.), *Foundations of Economics: Structures of Inquiry and Economic Theory*, Oxford and New York: Basil Blackwell, pp. 311–338.

Quadrio Curzio, A. and Pellizzari, F. 1999. *Rent, Resources, Technology*, Berlin: Springer.

Quadrio Curzio, A. and Pellizzari, F. 2018. 'Political Economy of Resources, Technologies, and Rent', in I. Cardinale and R. Scazzieri (eds.), *The Palgrave Handbook of Political Economy*, London: Palgrave Macmillan, pp. 657–704.

Reinert, E. S. 2004. *How Rich Nations Got Rich: Essays in the History of Economic Policy*, Oslo: Centre for Development and the Environment, University of Oslo.

Ricardo, D. 1951 [1817]. *On the Principles of Political Economy and Taxation*, Edited by P. Sraffa with the collaboration of M. H. Dobb, Cambridge: Cambridge University Press for The Royal Economic Society.

Salmon, W. C. 1984. *Scientific Explanation and the Causal Structure of the World*, Princeton, NJ: Princeton University Press.

Scazzieri, R. 1993. *A Theory of Production: Tasks, Processes and Technical Practices*, Oxford: Clarendon Press.

Scazzieri, R. 2009. 'Traverse Analysis and Methods of Economic Dynamics', in in H. Hagemann and R. Scazzieri (eds.), *Capital, Time and Transitional Dynamics*, London and New York: Routledge, pp. 96–132.

Scazzieri, R. 2012. 'The Concept of "Natural Economic System": A Tool for Structural Analysis and an Instrument for Policy Design', in R. Arena and P. L. Porta (eds.), *Structural Dynamics and Economic Growth*, Cambridge: Cambridge University Press, pp. 218–240.

Scazzieri, R. 2014. 'A Structural Theory of Increasing Returns', *Structural Change and Economic Dynamics*, 29, 75–88.

Scazzieri, R. 2018. 'Structural Dynamics and Evolutionary Change', *Structural Change and Economic Dynamics*, 46, 52–58.

Scazzieri, R., Baranzini, M. and Rotondi, C. 2015. 'Resources, Scarcities and Rents: Technological Interdependence and the Dynamics of Socio-Economic Structures', in M. Baranzini, C. Rotondi and R. Scazzieri (eds.), *Resources, Production and Structural Dynamics*, Cambridge: Cambridge University Press, pp. 427–484.

Skinner, A. S. 1966. 'Analytical Introduction', in J. Steuart (ed.), *An Inquiry into the Principles of Political Economy*, edited and with an Introduction by A. S. Skinner, published for The Scottish Economic Society, Edinburgh and London: Oliver and Boyd, pp. lviii–lxxxiv.

Smith, A. 1976 [1776]. *An Inquiry into the Nature and Causes of the Wealth of Nations*, General Editors R. H. Campbell and A. S. Skinner, Textual Editor W. B. Todd, Vol. I, Oxford: Oxford University Press.

Steuart, J. 1966 [1767]. *An Inquiry into the Principles of Political Economy*, Edited and with an introduction by A. S. Skinner, Edinburgh and London: Oliver and Boyd.

Chapter 11

Buffer stock operations in history and economic thought

Romar Correa

Introduction

Banks emerged from warehouses of yore where first grain and then precious metals were stored for safekeeping (Donaldson et al. 2015). At the outset, we can observe a natural centralizing tendency. A farmer storing his/her rice or wheat in a granary at home is not analytically interesting. Warehouses tend to evolve through successive centralizing steps. The Food Corporation of India (FCI) is a nationalized body. It distributes grains when market prices are high, partly to bring them down and partly to ensure access to essential dietary staples. It acts as a public insurance mechanism when market mechanisms would undermine the livelihoods of farmers and poor consumers. The mechanism is not exempt from the forces of political economy. In the summer of 2014, India vetoed a proposed agreement on 'trade facilitation measures' under the aegis of the WTO that sought to challenge its food security infrastructure in the form of the FCI. In ancient Egypt, grain harvests were deposited in centralized warehouses and owners would write orders against their holdings of grain as a means of payment. These certificates could exchange as credit instruments. The principle of centralization would end with the sovereignty of the State, although blueprints for world buffer stock operations continue to be written. The authority of the State turned out to be the basis of a hierarchy of monies. The LoLR (Lender of Last Resort) function of central banks did not originate in the rescue of private banks but in the support of an entity adjacent in the hierarchy (Stockhammer 2015). They were set up to strengthen State finances.

John Maynard Keynes (JMK) postulated that private markets would not deliver the goods in storage and buffer stock operations in raw materials and foodstuffs and wrote extensively on the positive and normative facets of his thesis (Keynes 1971–1989a, b, c, d). He worked out the connection between commodities plans for governments and a remarkable scheme for the socialization of investment. The idea was to delete the vocabulary of lenders' risk and moral hazard from the lexicon of the functioning of these markets. Future prices would become less unpredictable and the liquidity premium of commodity stocks would increase. Monetary policy was instrumental to this end in lowering the liquidity premium of money. The state of long-term expectations would be managed and, as a byproduct, the rentier would be euthanized.

The next step in the development of early paper money, echoing the later gold standard, was the activity of Venetian goldsmiths. They extended credit, transforming gold deposits to the creation of liquidity. From ancient Egypt, warehouses/banks created 'funding liquidity', provided funds to entrepreneurs for investment in capital and labour. From the perspective of firms, they could not pay their suppliers of inputs or labour in credit because of the inability to pledge future output. They borrowed from warehouses. By extending credit through the issue of fresh receipts, warehouses/banks created liquidity for firms. The conclusion of this line in history would be the epoch of the gold standard. Recently, Jan Kregel (2016), has sought to retain the best features of that standard, dispensing with the dispensable in a reading of David Ricardo's 'Ingot Plan'. The mechanism was JMK's later 'bank money' via bank clearing houses through which payments were squared without the use of specie or paper notes. The modern rendition of the plan is based on central bank liabilities held by the public or by private banks as deposits. Private bank liabilities take the place of gold bullion as they are convertible into fiat money at the discount window. Instead of gold currency defined in terms of measures of that metal, the standard of central bank liabilities would be specified by the maturity and rating that make private liabilities eligible for discount, so-called standard debt.

JMK in the first half of the 1930s advised the abandonment of the gold standard and support of the exchange rate for monetary policy that put the state of the domestic economy, in this case a depression, first. FD Roosevelt (FDR) assumed the office of President of the US on March 6, 1933, inheriting the legacy of the ideas of JMK and four years of the Great Depression due, allegedly, to the paralysis of the Federal Reserve (Tavlas 2016). Between the presidential election in November 8, 1932, and inauguration day on March 4, 1933, the banking system spiralled downwards as depositors ran on banks and banks and firms develeraged. On his first full day in office, FDR closed all banks for three days and then added two more days. During his first week, he signed the Emergency Banking Act which extended his powers to close, liquidate, licence and reopen financially sound banks and empowered the Secretary of the Treasury to order all domestic gold holders to sell their gold to the Treasury. The bank holiday was a success. The banking crisis ended on March 13. The reason is the 'fireside chat' FDR delivered to the public on March 12. He explained, with great care, his plans for the reopened banks. The public was reassured of the safety of their deposits. In 1932, a Reconstruction Finance Corporation (RFC) had been established to bail out banks. In October 1933, FDR announced that the RFC would begin the purchase of newly minted gold for the purpose of raising the price of gold and the general price level. In January 1934, the US passed the Gold Reserve Act which gave FDR the authority to devalue the dollar against gold by up to 60%. The following day, FDR obliged by a devaluation of 59.06%. The increase in the price of gold resulted in $3 billion in profits for the Treasury. FDR went at it alone, against the other major countries of the world, in placing long-term domestic interests above the short-term objective of stabilizing the exchange rate (Edwards 2017b).

JMK's ideas evolved and turned subtle and nuanced to the point of his 1933 pamphlet, *The Means to Prosperity* (Edwards 2017a). Therein, he recommended a 'qualified return to the gold standard' based on an 'international note issue'. Thereby, individual countries would retain the freedom to counter deflationary tendencies. His 'international notes' would augment international liquidity and address central bankers' concerns about gold bullion over and above the requirement of backing their liabilities. Alongside a plan developed by James P. Warburg, an advisor to FDR, the new system would be flexible with no requirement for actual shipment of gold from place to place. Gold clauses would go. The new gold standard would stabilize exchange rates and enable traders and bankers and investors to make informed guesses about the future. Each country would declare a new parity and exchange rates would be related to each other. The impulse to competitive devaluations would be ruled out and the sharply reduced 'cover ratio' would enable central banks to undertake countercyclical policies.

JMK continued to flesh out his vision of multilateralizing international disequilibria (Carabelli et al. 2017). He sketched out the details of a proposed international organization, the International Clearing Union (ICU), with a new international unit of account, the bancor, that would serve as the ultimate world reserve asset. The currency would be held only by participating central banks and exchanged between themselves and the ICU. Central banks would continue to issue their domestic currencies but would open a current account in the new standard. The principle was to apply the banking principle of parity between assets and liabilities to international balance sheets. Deficits and surpluses were to be squared through centralized clearing accounts. Even more, creditor countries were enjoined to revalue their currencies and unblock foreign investments. Correspondingly, debtor countries were expected to devalue their currencies, sell gold and refrain from capital exports. JMK looked forward to the demise of the international rentier, an agent that profited from exchange rate differentials, and along with other agents form a critical mass as speculators that even generate the differentials. Creditor countries were compelled to use or make available to debtor countries resources that would otherwise be unutilised. They were free, on the other hand, to choose the surpluses to expand domestic credit and demand, increase wages and dismantle barriers to trade. The ICU would be an accounting, not a political, device and would not support capital market liberalization.

FDR's so-called second New Deal has been the basis for considering employment of millions of workers on large-scale public works like national road networks as the basis of buffer stock operations of workers over the cycle. Many detailed schemes, mostly green projects, along with costs, are being written up to employ large numbers of willing and able hands. These employment arrangements are meant to counter precarious work, activity that is temporary or part-time or means self-employment. In addition, job guarantee schemes that are being drawn up stem the downward spiral in job quality (Klosse and Muysken 2016). Work would be offered to provide collective goods and services, environmental projects, famously in short supply in private markets. Buffer stock operations in willing and able workers, then, are not new but Warren Mosler and Damiano B. Silipo (2016) have gone all the way in making the case for the superiority of the labour standard (the product of employed workers at a fixed wage) to a commodities/gold standard as a nominal anchor for an economy. For instance, employed workers are liquid and produce output. Employers would always be willing to draw down the stock of hires rather than advertise for the unemployed. Resistance to hiring is a positive function of the length of unemployment. Workers could always be 'sold' to the monetary authorities at the given price and, likewise, any potential employees on the existing list can be monetized at that price.

As a final modern embellishment, we note that Flavia Dantas and L. Randall Wray (2017) have recently proposed a new New Deal–type job guarantee. The scheme is comprehensive in that it creates jobs for all ready and able to work. On offer is an open-ended guarantee not confined by the labour input requirements of a specific string of projects. The principle is to create a 'reserve army of the employed'. The Great Recession has only accelerated the secular downward trend in labour force participation in the US. The broken working class has simply dropped out of the labour force and the statistics. In the recommended scenario, wages would increase with overall labour productivity pushing private sector wages. Why would productivity rise? By securing a secular employment regime, workers would maintain their skills and solidarity with working-class ideals. Hyman Minsky insisted on regular skill upgradation as the *sine qua non* of all such programs. To the issuer of legal tender would be the responsibility of funding a base wage.

A discussion point here is the centralization versus the decentralization of the scheme. FDR's New Deal programmes were centralized and that model might work in countries where regions and districts are way below the threshold of development to absorb the planning requirements of a massive job guarantee scheme. Elsewhere, the choice and implementation of schemes would naturally devolve to local governments and community groups. Continuing central support would depend on feedback from the fate of state schemes. The counter-cyclical effects of such a public spending programme would be powerful. The quality of the labour pool in the programme would be enriched as workers built up a history of characteristics. Hiring costs for private firms when the economy rebounded would, thereby, reduce. Dantas and Wray call their scheme a flow-price buffer stock programme. Since the base wage was uniform, private sector wages would not be bid up. Wage hikes in the programme would be policy calibrated and should match overall productivity. Private sector wages would move upwards for the best of reasons. The scheme could make a dent in closing the 'productivity gap'.

To conclude this section, the most important function of money in a fiat money world is the guarantee of final payment by the government (Thornton 2008). The rupee is the writ by the government that the unit can be used for the payment of private and public debt. Governments usually pledge final payments by issuing currency which is legal tender. Bank money exchanges at par with State money making currency and deposits perfect substitutes. The price level is the price of all commodities in terms of money. The central bank controls the price level by controlling the supply of base money. Without this guarantee, transactions may take place in an abstract unit of account with private agents underwriting final payments. There is no mechanism to constrain these institutions from buying goods by entering units of this account to claim against themselves. They can renege on their promises. Naturally, the private sector cannot determine the terms on which to accept fiat money. Rather, the monopoly issuer must set the terms of exchange. A job guarantee scheme is universal and can anchor the value of fiat currency. At the margin, it establishes how many rupees will exchange for an hour of ELR (employer of last resort) work.

From the past to the present

The next step in the dynamics of the circulation of money and commodities is the creation of financial instruments that evolve to grease the wheels of commerce. Money and finance have always been with us. Apostolos Fasianos et al. (2016) perform the service of placing the overworked word financialization in the context of US history. Finely calibrated regulation and intervention were the backdrop against which money and finance played their roles over 1933–1940. The outcome was the Golden Age of Capitalist Development, 1945–1973, where the boom in capital formation reflected the transition towards the long run in the planning orientation of firms. Furthermore, earlier periods, particularly in West Germany and Japan, were characterized as displaying a 'social compacting paradigm'. In contrast to the UK and the US, economic 'settlements' through formal bargaining were reached between capital and labour. The terms were more meaningful representation of labour in policymaking in return for wage restraint. In turn, expanding social wages motivated increased investment and rapid productivity growth.

In contrast, financialization today entails the untrammelled power of the State to underwrite production and finance under the guise of roll back and non-intervention (Fine et al. 2016). The stock market crash of 1987 has been shown to disprove the Black-Scholes-Merton (BSM) model (Brisset 2016). The BSM model is believed to be self-fulfilling. All traders acted on it and made it the 'true' model. An inter subjective volatility, however, does not imply a correspondence with actual stock market volatility. The crash of 1987 suggests that financial phenomena resist the theory because the components of the theory are not self-fulfilling. The subjective risk perceptions can be contradicted by objective price phenomena. Financial market equilibria are conventional, displaying mimetic behaviour.

In the realm of ideas, monetary policy was all of a piece with lending by central banks as a first or last resort all the while keeping the stability of the system uppermost in mind. Their balance sheets were always swollen. Later, the sway of a line of thinking began to regard monetary policy as the job of a specialist, only superficially resembling Keynes's dentist, and LoLR operations and even beyond, matters of financial stability were deemed to be random and rare events. The Bank of England's balance sheet was more than 10% of the nominal GDP through most of the last two centuries. In contrast, it was a little over 5% of the GDP just before the crisis (Haldane et al. 2016). Indeed, wars and financial crises have been occasions for large balance sheets expansions of many countries over the period. In particular, central bank balance sheets hovered around 40% of the GDP in a host of countries around the Second World War. Over the period 1719–1822, the expansion of the balance sheet in the UK was intended to meet the exigencies of the times, and the policy stance had no significant effect on prices and output. The difference with modern balance sheet expansions is that Japan and the US attempted to liquefy bank balance sheets. The Bank of England purchased commercial paper and acted as a market maker of last resort. In modern parlance, they were not monetary policy instruments but LoLR operations. In standard macroeconomic theory, they should have no effect on economic activity.

The modern Fed distinguishes between monetary policy with the conceptual apparatus of inflation targeting and the output gap, and LoLR policy. The classicals regarded LoLR policy as part of the central bank's remit to protect the stock of bank money from undue contraction and expansion. Only now has financial stability been added to inflation targeting in the job description of a central banker although a formal policy model connecting both has yet to be written. We have it on the authority of David Laidler (2016) that legally binding, constitutionally mandated constraints or goals assigned to monetary authorities like Henry Simons's (1936) price stability rule are without foundation. The reason is that the 'true model' is a theoretical fiction. Output could as well be a target as inflation, money an instrument for the interest rate. Each agent in a modern economy acts in an environment created by the actions of other agents. The monetary order is brought about by the coordination of individual plans. Coming to the LoLR function, in the first place, Henry Thornton (1760–1815) and Walter Bagehot (1826–1877) notably emphasized the importance of a clear preannouncement of a lending strategy against future panics (Humphrey 2013). The strategy would include lending for short periods only and a specified exit strategy. The Fed would lend freely to temporarily illiquid but solvent borrowers against the security of good collateral. Support would be denied to unsound, insolvent borrowers who would be allowed to expire. No bank was too big to fail. None other than Anat Admati (2016) has recently called 'wrong' the habit of tagging a risk term to banking models intended to depict liquidity shocks or unexpected panics. Risks are the outcome of the conflict of interest between parties with different control variables.

We will use the connection between bank money and central bank money, say ρ, to connect this section with the next. Rho is familiarly the reserves ratio, a number between zero and one, a familiar weapon in the armoury of central banks. However, the first section encouraged us to think of it as a number that potentially can exceed unity. Under depressed conditions, central banks can be proactive in providing reserves to banks. Finally, in a situation where loan granting and credit creation is dormant, the central bank can initiate activity by replenishing the stocks and bond holdings of market participants.

Modelling

Micro

The following notations and treatment are drawn from Duncan Foley and Thomas Michl (1999: 201–204). Consider a one-sector model of production but with land as an input in production. Land and land per worker are U and u, respectively. Capital goods are aggregated by measuring their value at market prices at the time they were constructed. The capital input is K, the sum of the real value of past gross investment minus the estimated sum of accumulated depreciation. The labour input is the number of employed workers, N. Capital stock per worker, $k = K/N$, is a measure of capital intensity. Real gross product in a period is output, X. Then $x = X/N$ is a measure of labour productivity. The ratio of the total wage bill, W, to employment is the average real wage, w. The price of the commodity in terms of gold say is p. Take as a unit of land the amount of land required per unit of capital so that $u = k$. A technique of production connects the flow of labour, capital and land with the flow of output, capital (after depreciation) and land. A model with gold would have two such techniques, one for output and one for gold.

Entrepreneurs organize production by renting land from landlords and capital from capitalists and hiring labour. Denote the profit rate on capital the amount of output the entrepreneur must pay the capitalist for use of capital by v_k. Similarly, the cost of the use of land as an input in production is land rent, v_u. In the familiar model without land, the capitalist had to choose between investing capital and consuming it. The asset price of land (in terms of output or capital) is p_u. Now, the entrepreneur has to choose between investing land as an input and holding it as an asset. An entrepreneur who chooses to be a landlord will earn rent on the land and be able to sell it. Assuming a unit period for returns to accrue, he/she will earn $v_{ut} + p_{ut+1}$ at the end of the period. If, on the other hand, he/she invests his/her money in capital, ignoring depreciation, the amount $(1 + v_{kt})$ would accrue to him/her. The no-arbitrage condition dictates that the two returns must be equal. We can express this equality in the form of a non-homogenous difference equation,

$$p_{ut+1} = \left(1 + v_{kt}\right)p_{ut} - v_{ut}$$

We may express the equation as a differential equation and observe that the equilibrium solution at the origin is a source when the rate of profit exceeds the land rent and is a sink when the rate of profit is less than the land rent. We have a bifurcation when the rate of profit equals the land rent.

We proceed to describe our agents. The entrepreneur is characterized by a profit function $\pi(p,r,w)$, landlord by an indirect utility function $v^u(p,r,u)$, and the worker by an indirect utility function $v^n(p,w)$. We define an equilibrium to be a market-clearing vector (x^*, u^*, n^*) in direct utility terms or (p^*, r^*, w^*) in indirect utility terms.

Now, suppose that our inputs land (and capital) and labour are 'restricted', $u \geq \bar{u}$ and $n \geq \bar{n}$. Profits would certainly increase in the event of the relaxation of the constraint on inputs since the profit function is strictly concave in the level of the inputs (assuming the production function is strictly concave). Indeed, let us assume that the monetary authorities of the previous section are able to relax the constraints in the direction of the starred values of the variables with their buffer stock operations. That is to say, $u* = \rho u \geq \bar{u}$ and $n^* = \rho n \geq \bar{n}$. Clearly, $\rho > 1$. The income of the landlord increases as does that of the worker. Social welfare, then, increases.

Macro

Before we proceed to a purely structural account of our theme, it is worthwhile to recall that the subprime mortgage crisis that fuelled the financial meltdown in 2008 invited buffer stock schemes in housing stock. A national mortgage bank was designed as a *macro* tool (De Koning 2016). The bank would be a home mortgage quality control and early warning system. It would be a LoLR only when a trigger was pulled in the form of the number of foreclosures exceeding a threshold. The bank would be a joint shareholder for working class households. It would ease their cash flow positions and reduce the pressure on them to sell their homes. Existing homeowners could turn a long-term borrowing position into favourable cash flows independent of the prevailing interest rate.

A seminal depiction of a capitalist economy through input-output categories is the so-called stock-flow-consistent (sfc) macroeconomics pioneered by the late Wynne Godley and Francis Cripps (1983) (hereafter G&C) at Cambridge, England. Nominal and real (expressed in widgets) variables are joined and dichotomies and neutralities between the two are absent. All the notations and equations that follow are drawn from G&C. Thus, the income-expenditure identity is $Y \equiv E$ and the latter breaks up into $FE + \Delta I$. Final expenditure, FE, is the sum of government spending, G, and private expenditure, PE. The notation for change from the last period to the present is illustrated with the accumulation (or running down) of inventories $\Delta I \equiv I - I_{-1}$. Fresh investment plans are absent but activity in the form of stockpiling and movement of goods to or from warehouses is incessant. Arthur Okun was eloquent on workers, even in recessions, being retained to perform routine tasks for the positive present value of long-term relationships. Money, *FA*, is created by private debt, *PD*, and government borrowing, *GD*. The fiscal authorities are represented by an income tax rate, theta. Thus, disposable income $YP = (1 - \theta)Y$. The movement from period to period is driven by so-called stock-flow (sfc) norms. Our first glimpse of a stock-flow norm is the steady-state money-income norm alpha. Outside of the steady-state, we have (G&C: 93)

$$FA = \alpha PE \qquad\qquad 1$$

A second sfc norm is beta, the debt-income norm (G&C: 149),

$$PD = \beta YP \qquad\qquad 2$$

We are ready to enter one of the fundamental theorems of macro, the equality of the private sector surplus with the public sector deficit (G&C: 105–106). We will confine ourselves to money financing of the deficit, although G&C provide a consistent account of the issue of Treasury bills.

$$YP - PE = G - YG = \Delta FA - \Delta PD \qquad\qquad 3$$

The extreme right-hand side expression can be decomposed into components of bank balance sheets as follows. Denoting bank reserves as *RA* and bank deposits as *BD*, we have (G&C: 151)

$$YP - PE = G - YG = \Delta BD - \Delta RA - \Delta PD \qquad\qquad 4$$

For reasons discussed in the previous section, we offer a norm of our own in the form of a reserves ratio, rho. Thus,

$$\Delta R = \rho \Delta BD \qquad\qquad 5$$

It is straightforward matter to combine all the norms and plug them into equation 4 to deliver

$$\alpha(1 - \rho)\Delta PE + PE = \beta \Delta YP + YP \qquad\qquad 6$$

In systems terms, and recalling our notations for change, we have

$$[PEYP] = \left[1 - \frac{1}{\alpha(1-\rho)}\,001 - \frac{1}{\beta}\right][PE_{-1}\,YP_{-1}] \qquad\qquad 7$$

Denoting the trace of the coefficient matrix by *T* and the determinant by *D*, it is only cumbersome to establish $T^2 - 4D > 0$ in the trace-determinant plane. In that case, both eigenvalues are real and distinct (Hirsch et al. 2013). The inequality holds independent of the value of rho. Recall that our imposition of a value of $\rho > 1$ in the previous section is surely unconventional, the famous 'reserves ratio' of equation 5 being a fraction. In either instance, it turns out that $D > 0$, $T < 0$, and we have a (real) sink.

Conclusions

The lessons of the past for the present suggested previously are as follows. Planted in the historical time of a recession, the central bank should frame a plan in coordination with capitalists in possession of environmentally friendly and labour-intensive projects. Workers on the unemployment rolls will be classified on the basis of actual and potential skills. Through the instrumentality of State investment banks, the central bank will cherry pick projects for credit disbursement. Banks will equally be entitled to underwrite the issuance of shares of such companies.

References

Admati, Anat R. 2016. 'It Takes a Village to Maintain a Dangerous Financial System, Graduate School of Business', Unpublished Paper, Stanford University.

Brisset, Nicolas. 2016. 'On Performativity: Option Theory and the Resistance of Financial Phenomena', GREDEG Working Paper No 2016–31.

Carabelli, Anna, Cedrini, Mario and Marchionatti, Roberto. 2017. 'J.M. Keynes, the Modernity of an Un-Modern Economist', *Annals of the Fondazione Luigi Einaudi*, 51(1), 17–54.

Dantas, Flavia and Randall Wray, L. 2017. 'Full Employment: Are We There Yet?' Levy Economics Institute of Bard College Public Policy Brief No 142.

De Koning, Kees. 2016. 'A Review of the Global Financial Crisis and Its Effects on US Working Class Households – a Tale of Vulnerability and Neglect', MPRA Paper No 73502, Last accessed on 6 September 2016.

Donaldson, Jason Roderick, Piacentino, Giorgia and Thakor, Anjan. 2015. 'Warehouse Banking', Unpublished Paper.

Edwards, Sebastian. 2017a. 'Keynes and the Dollar in 1933', NBER Working Paper 23141.

Edwards, Sebastian. 2017b. 'The London Monetary and Economic Conference of 1933 and the End of the Great Depression: A "change of regime" Analysis', NBER Working Paper 23204.

Fasianos, Apostolos, Guevara, Diego and Pierros, Christos. 2016. 'Have We Been Here Before? Phases of Financialization Within the 20th Century', Levy Economics Institute of Bard College Working Paper No 869.

Fine, Ben, Saad-Filho, Alfredo, Bayliss, Kate and Robertson, Mary. 2016. 'Things You Need to Know about Neoliberalism', FESSUD (Financialization, Economy, Society and Sustainable Development) Working Paper No 155.

Foley, D. K. and Michl, Thomas R. 1999. *Growth and Distribution*, Cambridge, MA: Harvard University Press.

Godley, W. and Cripps, Francis. 1983. *Macroeconomics*, Oxford: Oxford University Press.

Haldane, Andrew G., Roberts-Sklar, Matt, Wieladek, Tomasz and Young, Chris. 2016. 'QE: The Story So Far', Bank of England Staff Working Paper No 624.

Hirsch, M.W., Smale, Stephen and Devaney, Robert L. 2013. *Differential Equations, Dynamical Systems, and an Introduction to Chaos*, Oxford: Academic Press.

Humphrey, Thomas H. 2013. 'Arresting Financial Crises: The Fed Versus the Classicals', Levy Economics Institute of Bard College Working Paper No 751.

Keynes, John Maynard. 1971–1989a. 'Some Aspects of Commodity Markets', in J. M. Keynes (ed.), *The Collected Writings of John Maynard Keynes, Vol. XII*, London: Palgrave Macmillan, pp. 255–266.

Keynes, John Maynard. 1971–1989b. 'The Control of Raw Materials by Governments', in J. M. Keynes (ed.), *The Collected Writings of John Maynard Keynes, Vol. XIX*, London: Palgrave Macmillan, pp. 546–552.

Keynes, John Maynard. 1971–1989c. 'The Policy of Government Storage of Foodstuffs and Raw Materials', in J. M. Keynes (ed.), *The Collected Writings of John Maynard Keynes, Vol. XXI*, London: Palgrave Macmillan, pp. 456–470.

Keynes, John Maynard. 1971–1989d. 'Activities 1940–1946. Shaping the Post-War World', in J. M. Keynes (ed.), *The Collected Writings of John Maynard Keynes, Vol. XXVII*, London: Palgrave Macmillan, pp. 105–109.

Klosse, Saskia and Muysken, Jean. 2016. 'Inclusive Labour Market: A Role for a Job Guarantee Scheme', UNU-MERIT Working Paper No 2016–11.

Kregel, Jan. 2016. 'Financial Stability and Secure Currency in a Modern Context', Levy Economics Institute of Bard College Working Paper No 877.

Laidler, David. 2016. 'Economic Ideas, the Monetary Order and the Uneasy Case for Policy Rules', Department of Economics, Social Service Centre, Western University, Canada, Research Report #2016–4.

Mosler, Warren and Silipo, Damiano B. 2016. 'Maximizing Price Stability in a Monetary Economy', Levy Economics Institute of Bard College Working Paper No 864.

Russi, Luigi and Ferrando, Tomaso. 2016. '"Capitalism A Nuh" Wi Frien': The Formatting of Farming into an Asset from Financial Speculation to International Aid', Unpublished Paper, International University College of Turin.

Ryan-Collins, J., Greenham, Tony, Werner, Richard and Jackson, Andrew. 2016. *Where Does Money Come from?* London: Creative Commons.

Simons, Henry. 1936. 'Rules versus Authorities in Monetary Policy', *Journal of Political Economy*, 44(1), 1–30.

Stockhammer, Engelbert. 2015. 'Neoliberal Growth Models, Monetary Union and the Euro Crisis. A Post-Keynesian Perspective', Post Keynesian Economics Study Group Working Paper 1510.

Tavlas, George S. 2016. 'New Perspectives on the Great Depression: A Review Essay', Bank of Greece Working Paper 212.

Thornton, David L. 2008. 'Monetary Policy: Why Money Matters and Interest Rates Don't', Federal Reserve Bank of St Louis Working Paper 2008–011A.

Chapter 12

History of institutional economics

Phillip Anthony O'Hara

Introduction

The purpose of this chapter is to outline the history of institutional economics. We commence with the institutionalist tendencies of the Physiocrats in the
1700s through to the classical economists of the 1800s, and onto the 'founding
father' of institutionalism, Thorstein Veblen, in the late 1890s and early 1900s.
This is followed by the contributions of Joseph Schumpeter and John Maynard Keynes, then the neoinstitutional perspectives of John Commons, Wesley
Mitchell, Clarence Ayres, plus the later contributions of Gunnar Myrdal, and
J.K. Galbraith, in the mid- to late 20th century. Contemporary Veblenian institutionalists associated with the Association for Evolutionary Economics (AFEE)
and their European and other allies, are additionally explored; then there is an
introduction to the work of the so-called new institutional economics.

This history of institutional economics is analyzed through the prism of
some of the core principles of institutional and evolutionary political economy
(IEPE). IEPE is a mutation that has emerged through the 1990s, 2000s and
2010s from the heterodox work of selected evolutionary institutionalists, post
Keynesians, neo-Marxists, feminists, social economists and others who also take
an institutional view of socioeconomic systems (see O'Hara 2007 for details).
IEPE principles represent an emerging fusion of core institutional-evolutionary
elements of these schools of thought, associated with the work of, for instance,
Paul Dale Bush (1987), Daniel Fusfeld (1988), William Dugger (1988, 1995)
and James Ronald Stanfield (1995, 2011). Further work along these lines was
developed by scholars such as Phillip O'Hara (1999a, 2012a, forthcoming), as
well as Bhimo Samudro et al. (2014) plus Andrew Brennan and Jaslin Kalsi
(2015). In the contemporary environment, a multitude of other scholars are
eschewing rigid divisions between schools of heterodox institutionalism and
some of these seek conceptual development of institutionalism in a similar
fashion to that outlined here.

Our interpretation of institutionalism thus includes institutional political
economy more narrowly conceived (the 'American school of institutional economics'; see Anne Mayhew (1987) on this), plus an array of others who are also

centrally concerned with the workings of institutions and principles/concepts useful to the task of examining institutions. The philosophy of science that institutionalists employ is realistic, materialistic, pragmatic and policy-oriented. It seeks to understand the world as it exists and as it has evolved and changed, keeping 'close to the ground', and trying to generalize about the structure and dynamics of real social economies evolving through historical time. It essentially tries to comprehend the changing ways of life that groups of people operate within economic systems to solve problems of production, distribution, exchange and socioeconomic reproduction.

This generates a broad view of institutional-evolutionary trends, starting with the *principle of historical specificity and evolution*, where every serious problem or topic is required to be embedded in an historical inquiry into its emergence and evolution, since much can be learnt from historical and cultural analysis. This is especially the case for phases and stages of development and evolution, the relationship between culture and scholarship, path dependency and hysteresis. The history of institutional economics, broadly conceived, illustrates how the origins of the school start with the Physiocrats and the classical economists, through the early cultural origins of capitalism.

Institutionalism did not formally emerge until Veblen's work on institutions, habits and evolution at the turn of the 19th into the 20th century, during the time of the development of corporate capitalism, imperialism and financial dominance of industry. This immediately led to a flurry of new scholars taking on the task of developing the new school and impacting on policy through, for instance, the New Deal in the US. But it took until the long boom of capitalism of the 1950s and 1960s for the formal inception of an association of mostly Veblenian scholars to be formed – the Association for Evolutionary Economics (AFEE [1965]) – which continues even now to generate creative institutional scholarship in the *Journal of Economic Issues*. Into the 1980s and 1990s other trends developed and even orthodoxy recognized the importance of institutions, which stimulated the development of various forms of 'new institutionalism'.

This history of institutional economics also follows the evolution of several other principles of inquiry that are institutional in their origin but which also link to others in the IEPE mutation. For instance, the *principle of the nexus between institutions, habits and individuals* is linked to various institutional economists, but which had its origins in the work of Veblen. This broad principle links several levels of analysis to form a multilayered framework. More delimited in scope is the *principle of heterogeneous groups and agents*, which Veblen utilized to recognize the different roles that are played in the social economy, and the differential capabilities, skills and backgrounds of the various players in the institutions. Another high point of theory that formally started with Veblen, but which either in name or function was also associated with numerous other scholars who took an institutional direction, is the *principle of circular and cumulative causation* (CCC), including the notion of interdependency between spheres and amplified impact of changes.

The *principle of contradiction* is linked to various forms of heterodox institutionalism, including especially Veblenian institutionalism, some neo-Marxists, some feminists and post Keynesian institutionalists through the conflicts and instabilities associated with the institutionalized anomalies between capital and labour, industry and finance, men and women, national versus nation, business versus the environment, individual versus society, ethnic group versus ethnic group and capital versus the State/citizens. We also include the *principle of uneven development and hegemony*, developed by numerous schools of institutional and evolutionary political economy (starting with Veblen), as it applies to nations and regions, through which the received powers establish dominance, and where its elites benefit from this global source of power.

We reveal which *major* 'institutionalists' variously utilize or develop these principles as the chapter evolves, and which deviate from it somewhat and why.

Proto-institutionalism of the Physiocrats and the classical economists

The first generation of proto-institutionalists included the Physiocrats and some of the classical economists. The Physiocrats, most notably François Quesnay (1694–1774) and his *Tableau économique* ('graphic representation'), were active especially in France during the 1700s, and sought to comprehend the dynamics of the advanced economy of the time through the circuit of relationships between farmers (the productive class), landowners and the unproductive classes (industrialists, merchants and craftsmen). This first ever economic model of the economy, the *Tableau*, was institutionalist in the sense of being *realistic* and concentrating on the dominant sectors and classes of the economy interacting through time at the macro, meso and micro levels. This circuit of economic relations was probably fairly representative of the economy of its time, when agriculture in France was much more productive of the economic surplus than the manufacturing sector.

As productive agriculture *started* to promote industry and market capitalism, Adam Smith (1723–1790), much influenced by the Physiocrats, emerged as a proto-institutionalist in the sense that he placed a good deal of emphasis on historical specificity and the evolution of the institutions. It is also true, most notably, that he was the first to specifically illustrate the principle of CCC in the generation of the economic surplus. In this, productive investment in agriculture (Sector I) can stimulate cheap and steady supply of inputs to industry (manufacturing; Sector II), which in turn through greater division of labour and higher wages can stimulate trade (Sector III), expanding competition in foreign markets, thus increasing the potential surplus that can be used for further productive investment and expansions of the division of labour (see Prue Kerr 1993). Crucial for Smith were the interdependencies between sectors and the articulated development of the whole economy, in *The Wealth of Nations* (1776); as well as the role of ethics, trust and association in the *Theory of Moral Sentiments* (1759).

Thomas Malthus (1766–1834), especially in his *Principles of Political Economy* (1820), was also a proto-institutionalist in the sense that he scrutinized the distribution of the product between the major classes of capitalism, and explained how the economic surplus is generated through the process of effective demand interacting with production to realize value on the market. David Ricardo (1772–1823), notably in his *Principles of Political Economy and Taxation* (1817), had some elements of institutionalism in his method as he sought to comprehend the role of value, classes, distribution of income, accumulation, surplus and machinery.

As industrial capitalism expanded and evolved further throughout the 1800s, Karl Marx (1818–1883) deepened the institutionalist theme in political economy (see John Elliott 1978). In a whole series of innovative volumes, especially the 1857–1858 *Grundrisse*, and the three volumes of *Capital* (I: production [1867]; II: circulation [1887]; III: profit/competition/credit [1892]), he was an (unwitting) institutionalist because he analyzed the evolution of the political economy, especially 'capitalism', from the primitive phases of (i) mercantilism (simple commodity production) through to (ii) manufacture (handicraft workers under one roof), and then onto capitalism proper through (iii) competitive machine production (wage labour under the regime of capital), and onto (iv) large scale industry (greater concentration). These phases differ, of course, from area to area or nation to nation. He was also an institutionalist because he illustrated the workings of CCC whereby the economic surplus is produced, demanded and then reproduced through time within the institutions of the circuit of social capital. His third institutionalist thread was his tendency to be realistic in his analysis of the major heterogeneous agents and classes of capitalism, especially in his work on the different types of workers, industrial capitalists, money capitalists, merchants and others such as bookkeepers and transporters (O'Hara 2016). Lastly, he was institutionalist in the sense of developing a realist and materialist account of the rise and periodic as well as systemic decline of the institutions of capitalism; as well as the contradictory manifestation of the anomalous dichotomies of the capitalist system through recession, depression, cycles and evolutionary transformation.

Institutionalism of Thorstein Veblen

Thorstein Veblen (1857–1929) is well known to be the 'father' of institutional economics, through the development of a highly original theoretical schema, and under the influence of Darwinian evolution, pragmatism, the German historical school and Marxism (see Anderson 1932–1933; O'Hara 2002). Veblen sought to develop a social and political economy of capitalism in tune with the latest phase of its evolution *a la* imperialism, the robber barons, finance capital and corporate capitalism around the turn of the 19th into the 20th century. His first book, *The Theory of the Leisure Class: An Economic Study of Institutions* (1899), was an innovative self-conscious attempt to develop an institutional economics.

Veblen was an institutionalist, firstly, since he placed the economy firmly within a historical context; this is the *principle of historical specificity and evolution*. He studied the evolution of society from its primitive barbarian roots to the emergence of agriculture, then handicraft, later industrial capitalism, and still later the dominance of business. He concentrated on the capitalism of his day, especially that of US capitalism at the turn of the 20th century (1895–1905), and later on through to the early 1920s. *The Leisure Class* and most of his other works centred on how the economic surplus (net output) once produced by industry is often wasted on conspicuous consumption, financial wheeling and dealing, wars and mergers (oligopolies).

A *core principle of Veblen is the system-institutions-habits-individuals nexus*. Veblen was a systemist; i.e., one who concentrates on various systems of organization and behaviour. He recognized that there are different *levels* of organization in the social economy, which all exist emergently or in a *sui generis* fashion. They are qualitatively different, yet interactive, *systems*. At the most general level is (i) the world or planet Earth, including the geopolitical environment (see Veblen 1915, 1917); at a 'lower' level is (ii) capitalism, i.e., the system of production and distribution characterized by the existence of classes such as capitalists and workers (of various types) producing output, as well as managers, financiers and bookkeepers, plus consumers and merchants (Veblen 1919); at an even 'lower' level is the (iii) micro environment, including the sectoral workings of corporations, families, local communities and ecologies (Veblen 1899, 1904, 1923); and at a 'lower' level still are (iv) individual human beings, who exhibit various habits of thought and behaviour (Veblen 1899). These systems are all interconnected, but they operate at different levels and hence are qualitatively novel (i.e., emergent) (see Bunge 1974–1989).

Veblen focussed on all of these systems, but his main concern was to situate national forms of capitalism in a geopolitical, social and environmental setting, with the focus on the dominant institutions of the corporation, family, State and community, and how individuals through groups link into this fabric through their capabilities, skills, habits and instincts (O'Hara 1999b). The core thing for Veblen was that these institutions evolve through historical time, and that we must comprehend their changing form in these different historical contexts. In the process, we must not lose sight of the capitalist system within which the institutions operate, and the nature of the individuals in this nexus of interactions. For instance, Veblen (1904, 1923) developed the first detailed economic analysis of the corporation, which set the scene for later work, including that of Berle and Means (1932) on ownership and control (see O'Kelley 2011); plus, for instance, much work on economic power (e.g., J. K. Galbraith 1983; Tool and Samuels 1989); corporate hegemony (William Dugger 1989); and corporate finance (e.g., Karayiannis and Young 1991).

At the most general of these levels, Veblen (1915, 1917) was the first economist to develop the *principle of hegemonic dominance and uneven development* as he explored the global and regional evolution of capitalism, at a time when

Germany was seeking to replace Britain at the apogee of imperial power. Veblen also utilized the *principle of cumulative causation*, concerning the complex manner in which the institutions of capitalism interact with its various nations, classes, ethnic groups, genders and species (see Berger 2009). Such an interaction is not an equilibrium process, since ceteris paribus conditions do not prevail. Instead, an evolution in one area of the social economy will, more often than not, influence other areas, especially if the initial change is crucial, setting in motion (in many cases) a magnified or amplified impact on the system as a whole. In other words, the micro elements of the social economy (individuals, small groups) impact on the meso elements (sectors, institutions, organizations), which in turn affect the macro and global elements (nations, global system); while reverse causation also occurs as the macro and global constituents impact on the meso and micro levels, and the meso impacts on the micro as well. Each level (micro, meso, macro and global) is qualitatively different, so it is not possible, for instance, to reduce the macro from the meso or micro, or the micro from the macro or meso levels. Because of the *complexity* of the linkages between levels, the total impact of a change involving all levels tends to be magnified and amplified, resulting in qualitative as well as quantitative changes through historical time.

Veblen also developed the *principle of heterogeneous groups and agents*, wherein he was interested in the real human dynamics of groups of people and individuals who act out their roles through various norms, mores, agreements, accords and routines. The economy is a complicated system of arrangements comprising numerous roles, positions, strata, rankings, estates, divisions, sectors, institutions, ideologies and belief systems. This complexity manifests itself in various classes of occupations, skill sets, strata of status positions and officials. Much of Veblen's institutional economics sought to situate these different classes within the various institutions with a view to comprehending how real people contribute (or otherwise) to the reproduction of the system of arrangements. Veblen thus discussed the role of workers, capitalists, financiers, real estate agents, housewives, clerks and so on within the institutions of the corporation, the financial system, the State, family and world economy set within an ecological and biological environment (Veblen 1899, 1914, 1923).

It is clear that Veblen unwittingly utilized the *principle of contradiction*, under the influence of Marx, socialists and the classical economists, the various historical schools of political economy, and many other works. The main contradiction he examined was that between the 'vested interests and the common man' (Veblen 1919, 1921). In his works, the vested interests (elites) of the early 20th century in the US exploited the community's joint stock of knowledge and skills by controlling the main sectors or commanding heights of the economy; especially that of steel, railways, armaments, vehicles, construction and machinery. Corporate mergers, increasing concentration of industry, strategic alliances, interlocking directorships, and political interlocks were the main ways in which the vested interests accumulated power for the realization of their various aims and objectives. As the 20th century evolved into the 1920s he saw the formation of a *Great Union of Vested Interests* being created through various accords between business, State and labour. But the overriding power is held by those who control business, since they are better able to exploit the joint stock and manage sabotage (restricting output) through various means of upsetting the industrial system in the pursuit of industrial profit, through periodic redundancies, recessions, depressions plus financial and banking crises.

A core concern of Veblen was thus the contradictory tendency of capitalism towards periodic and structural crises, including financial crises, recessions, depressions, protracted dislocation, systemic bottlenecks and industrial strife. He sought to comprehend the anomalous workings of the system and to suggest *systemic* means for its amelioration. In *The Vested Interests and the Common Man* (1919) and *Absentee Ownership* (1923), for instance, he set the scene for the coming of the next major crisis. Much of his assessment made use of the distinction between instrumental (productive) and ceremonial (relatively unproductive) activities. The productive instrumental elements were those of workmanship, knowledge, skills and communication (the community's joint stock) embodied in production, innovation, transportation, education and community relations; while the unproductive ceremonial elements comprised much of corporate control, financial dominance of industry, the waste of conspicuous consumption, disinformational advertising and State spending of armaments for fighting wars for domestic and global business (exploiting the joint stock).

In Veblen's system, three main contradictions (unproductive ceremonial processes) can be seen to have led to the emergence of high levels of unstable finance, waste and sabotage by powerful corporations into the 1920s. The first was the increasing oligopolization of industry (monopoly capital), which often acted as a barrier to new innovators and productivity. The second was the increasing dominance of finance capital, especially through the equity and real estate markets generating unsustainable speculative bubbles. And the third was the combination of advertising and waste in the interests of the conspicuous consumption of the leisure class. He saw the transfer of economic surplus and national income from industry, workers and community development towards monopolies, finance/real estate and the upper class to be the source of increasingly low productivity, financial instability, and insufficient productive demand (Veblen 1923). In the late 1920s, these three anomalous tendencies merged to cause the greatest crisis in the history of capitalism: the Great Depression of the 1930s.

Keynes, Schumpeter and later institutionalists

Other than Veblen, John Hobson, John Maynard Keynes and Joseph Schumpeter certainly were the most well-known economists to develop certain institutional themes into the early and middle 1900s. Hobson (1858–1940) was a contemporary of Veblen who also authored a book on Veblen (Hobson 1936), and wrote some classic works on imperialism, unemployment and aggregate demand that took an institutionalist line. His work influenced Keynes, who also found aggregate demand antecedents in the work of Malthus and Marx. Keynes and Schumpeter contributed to the institutionalist concerns of being realistic, systemic and with a focus on the institutional and evolutionary dynamics of capitalism.

Keynes's (1883–1946) major contribution to institutional analysis concerned four themes. The first was in seeing capitalism as an evolutionary system that is subject to changing dynamics, periodic and structural crises, and the need for appropriate structural policies to (partially) rectify the anomalies. The second was the principle of aggregate effective demand (Keynes 1936), which was crucial to capitalism in order to evade and rectify problems of crisis, instability and depression. The third was the notion of uncertainty (Keynes 1937); namely, that industrial investment under capitalism is forever subject to a long-term horizon of prospective yield (relative to supply price), with partial funding of this based on debt-generating instabilities that perpetually subject the system to crises by undermining prospective yield and increasing supply price. And the fourth was Keynes's monetary theory of production, where money and aggregate demand are not mere veils but actually do impact on output (and also prices) in the short and long terms. Indeed, it is money and demand that, in Keynes's system, push the system forward and finance both innovation and general production as well as potentially enhancing prospective yield and hence expected profits, but also speculation, crisis and instability.

Schumpeter (1883–1950) had his own themes, buried temporarily by the Keynesian revolution and the neoclassical synthesis. It wasn't until the 1970s that his contributions and influences started to really take off in academic and policy circles; which has continued into the 21st century. His institutionalist themes were similar to those of Marx, Veblen and Keynes in being realistic in his formulations, being concerned with the evolutionary dynamics of capitalism through long historical time and especially being concerned with the cyclical and structural instabilities which he thought would lead capitalism to its grave. He emphasized the generation of surplus value from process, product, raw material, market and corporate forms of innovation. The early business cycle model of *The Theory of Economic Development* (1911) was developed much further in his two-volume work on *Business Cycles* (1939); while the process of creative destruction inherent in innovation was enunciated in some detail in his *Capitalism, Socialism and Democracy* (1942).

Schumpeter contributed three main proximate things to institutional economics. The first was the notion, first developed by Marx, that cycles are endogenously generated by the institutions of capitalism; specifically, through innovation activated by entrepreneurs or corporations via investment in new techniques, products and organizations. Some of the innovations help to generate short cycles, while others of a more durable and substantial nature engender longer cycles. Second, Schumpeter realized, as Marx, Veblen and Keynes had previously, that unproductive debt is the main generator of amplified cycles, which sets the scene for depression (such as the 1890s, 1930s and 2008ff). Third, he recognized that capitalism has inherent contradictions that contribute to short, medium and secular crises and instabilities, as well as to its eventual demise. Schumpeter (1942) situated capitalism's demise as being directly related to its successes – creative destruction – as capitalism becomes buoyant through innovation, but also wastes the resources of its success through institutionalizing innovation, protecting the system from excesses and reducing its destructive capabilities.

Keynes and Schumpeter were clearly very important institutionalists, even though many authors failed to include them in this camp due to their overly narrow vision of the 'school'. More obvious institutionalists, variously of the interwar, Second World War and postwar eras, include John Commons, Wesley Mitchell, Clarence Ayres, John Kenneth Galbraith and Gunnar Myrdal (see Allan Gruchy 1947, 1972; Geoffrey Hodgson 2004). Commons (1862–1945) was a key member of the 'Wisconsin branch' of institutionalism, and, along with some other institutionalists, made contributions to the New Deal. He developed not only general principles of collective action but also technical analyses of labour relations and public utilities. He was also a systemist in seeing *interconnections* between the relationships activated in the social economy – *the circular aspect of CCC* – which led him, especially in his two-volume *Institutional Economics: Its Place in Political Economy* (1934), to centre on transactions, such as those concerning bargaining, managing and rationing; and the nature of the working rules of laws, customs and going concerns, which enable such transactions to be undertaken to varying degrees of success.

Wesley Mitchell (1874–1948) was a student of Veblen at Chicago, and it was Veblen who engendered a lifelong concern in Mitchell with the contradictory and cumulative motion associated with business cycles, which Mitchell developed at the National Bureau of Economic Research (NBER). In numerous books and articles, such as *Business Cycles and Their Causes* (1941), his concern was with the *endogenous contradictions* which engendered rising costs and declining demand during the late upswing in the cycle, especially regarding factors which inhibit the profit of business enterprise. These contradictions tend to become *cumulative* (rather than equilibrium-tending) since the upswing sets in motion various conflicts and bottlenecks which impede continual growth. The downswing itself is also cumulative in that the declining profit and demand endogenously generates heightened uncertainty, leading to recession and often depression. However, forces of the downswing can also endogenously assist the recovery, especially the declining costs and the rising average propensity to consume, which can enable more optimism and thus initiate renewed upswing. For Mitchell, there were multiple types of cycles (or fluctuations, such as short cycles and long waves), in which the phases are interrelated or endogenously generated, and his analysis continues to inform even more contemporary theoretical and empirical analysis of cycles (e.g., Sherman and Kolk 1996).

Clarence Ayres (1891–1972) was the de facto leader of the Texas School of Institutionalism (the 'cactus branch'). His main contribution to institutionalism was in reformulating Veblen's basic dichotomy of the *instrumental and ceremonial functioning of institutions* for theory and policy. For Ayres, the progressive instrumental values are those of participation, knowledge, skills and tools (defined broadly) to enhance the enlightenment project of promoting and extending the human condition towards reason and quality of life for the common good. The ceremonial functions, for Ayres, sought the extension of inequality, invidious comparison and vested interests; basically supporting the elites in their quest for power and dominance over the common people. In a whole series of books, including *The Divine Right of Capital* (1946) and *The Theory of Economic Progress* (1962), Ayres developed his analysis of institutional political economy, involving greater participation of the population in the economy and politics; basically a contemporary New Deal (including a Global New Deal) involving welfare, innovation and inclusion for the greater good.

Gunnar Myrdal (1898–1987) developed what he called 'holistic' or 'institutional' economics and won a Nobel Prize for his efforts in 1974. His holistic – or systemic – economics was developed in works such as *The Political Element in the Development of Economic Theory* (1930), *An American Dilemma: The Negro Problem and Modern Democracy* (1944; 2 vols) and *Asian Drama: An Inquiry into the Poverty of Nations* (1968; 3 vols) and has much in common with Veblen. The *first sub-principle of holism or systemism* (see Myrdal 1978) is that the method of institutional economics must be open in the sense of including an array of factors, such as political, economic, cultural and environmental, in the causation of social problems. The *second sub-principle is that of a decentered totality*, in which no one basic factor overrides all others in the determination of socioeconomic dynamics. Myrdal castigates economic and technological determinism, arguing instead that 'base' and 'superstructure' are interrelated; it is through the multi-factorial approach that social problems should be viewed.

Myrdal's *third sub-principle posits the importance of circular and cumulative causation*: that every social problem has both a circular form of causation (interdependency) and, more specifically, operates through the process of cumulative causation. Thus, business cycles, poverty, inequality and world development should be viewed as being non-equilibrium in motion; subject to feedback processes, amplified or multiplied dynamics, and instability; as well as uneven development. The nature of these cumulations must be empirically scrutinized through an analysis of the interactions between the dominant forces at play in specific instances. The *fourth subprinciple is that of evolution*; that the world and its institutions continually change through long historical time, often in complex ways, sometimes going forward, and sometimes backwards, but always involving qualitatively different outcomes and institutions through various phases of metamorphosis.

John Kenneth Galbraith (1908–2006) was a post-Keynesian institutionalist who followed Veblen in analyzing capitalism as an institutionalized system of power. Being a prolific author of dozens of books, his better-known volumes include *American Capitalism* (1952), *The Affluent Society* (1958) and *Economics and the Public Purpose* (1973). His main contribution to institutional economics is the *principle of social balance* (Stanfield 1996), which we interpret as the processes necessary to *moderate the contradictions of corporate capitalism*. For Galbraith, the competitive sector of the economy is dominated by the administered sector, especially the large corporations, but also to some degree the State. The large power of the megacorp needs to be balanced by measures to increase the power of the common people. The expansion of automobiles, factories and warehouses especially over the past hundred years needs to be balanced by the collective provision of transportation networks, public transport and pollution control measures. The expansion of urban and city regions requires measures to service and protect these dispersed communities. The explosion of advertising and the consumer revolution needs to be balanced by proper waste disposal and recycling methods. The increasing number of two-wage couples requires appropriate resources to deal with the more complex issue of child support and family protection. Free market political systems tend to generate private affluence but public squaller. However, Galbraith recognized that many 'public services' support corporate interests and hence policy is more complex than the simple contradiction between public and private concerns.

Contemporary Veblenian and 'new' institutional economics

The past half a century has seen the development of two main types of institutional economics, one broadly following Veblen as a systemic science of the evolution of power within and between institutions, and the other seeking to graft onto institutional economics a neoclassical-type vision of property rights and corporate interests; although even the latter, neoclassical version, has occasionally moved in the Veblenian direction.

During the 1960s and 1970s long boom and start of the declining performance of global capitalism, institutional economics went through a revival. This was partly due to the Keynesian welfare state–type policies that were instigated during that time, and partly due to the booming university sector, including war veterans but especially the postwar generation which was looking for new and realistic types of economic theory to help explain the problems emerging in the social economy. These problems variously included the Vietnam War, consumerism, pollution, alienation, discrimination, inequality, sexism, exploitation, racism, underdevelopment and problematic performance. Feeling also that too many institutionalists and their themes were being left out of the pages of the *American Economic Review*, the Wardman Group (see Almeida 2016 for more details on this group) started having 'rump sessions' at the annual meetings of the American Economic Association, which eventually helped to form the Association for Evolutionary Economics (AFEE) in 1965, with their *Journal of Economic Issues* commencing publication in 1967. A sister organization, the Association for Institutionalist Thought (AFIT) emerged in 1979, with the initial aim of reflecting the 'traditional' theory and policy concerns of institutionalism, along the lines of the work of Thorstein Veblen, John Commons, Wesley Mitchell, Clarence Ayres and John Dewey (later it performed much the same role as AFEE, but with annual meetings in the West of the US). Institutionalism has a long history in Europe (see Waller 2001), and AFEE members helped to influence the formation of the European Association for Evolutionary Political Economy (EAEPE) during the 1990s, which led to the inception of the *Journal of Institutional Economics*, edited by Geoffrey Hodgson. Other journals, such as the *Forum for Social Economics*, have also become a vehicle for social and institutional economics. Also, most political economy and economics journals publish material on institutions and sometimes institutional economics per se. Numerous other groupings (formal and informal) were organized, such as in Japan as well as Eastern and Central Europe, China and some other Asian countries; while Latin Americans and Australians, as well as others, started to be involved in these institutional trends.

Generally, institutionalism seeks to comprehend the dynamics of economic systems, whether they are pre-capitalist socioeconomic formations; or different varieties of capitalism, fascism, socialism, dictatorship, Islamic forms of governance, and any hybrids or new forms that emerge. Within this framework, a key theme of the aforementioned scholarly organizations involves investigating the dominant socioeconomic and political institutions of modern capitalism and proposing alternatives or institutional modifications to capitalism. For instance, some varieties of capitalism that current exist include the (neo)liberal capitalist economies of the US, UK and Australia; the social democratic systems of Canada, Scandinavia and the Netherlands; the state capitalist economies of China, Vietnam and Russia; and the dependent semi-peripheral systems in Argentina, Brazil and Chile. They also seek to comprehend the different socioeconomic systems that variously operate in the core, semi-periphery and periphery at the global, regional, national and subnational levels; and especially the structural relationships that operate between these systems and which reinforce development and underdevelopment. Some of the institutionalists who sought to comprehend these 'world development' issues include Nobel Laureates W.A. Lewis (1915–1991), Simon Kuznets (1901–1985; a former student of Mitchell) and Gunnar Myrdal; and, more recently, James Dietz, Ilene Grabel, Ha-Joon Chang, Dilmus James, and James Cypher (among several others).

Institutionalists also seek to decompose these systems into their meso-components. This has manifested itself, for instance, in papers and books on the historically contingent evolution and transformation of institutional spheres – or institutional regimes – such as the Bretton Woods System (BWS: IMF, WB, etc), the trade regime, the Keynesian-welfare State (KWS), the international and national systems of financial regulation, the corporation, US hegemony (and decline), the system of industrial relations and the regimes of the family. As the 1950s and 1960s evolved into the 1970s, many of these institutions changed and, in some cases, underwent maturation and decline through the 1980s and 1990s onwards. The development of theory and empirics on *complexity, varieties of capitalism, experimental techniques* and *recent advances in extreme nationalism* in many core and semi-peripheral economies (in particular) have been other themes in the journals over recent years.

The French regulation approach and also the social structure of accumulation (SSA) school started to develop their own unique approaches to scrutinizing change within the institutions affecting socioeconomic performance; especially investment, growth and profit over different phases of evolution (see, e.g., O'Hara 2006). Veblenian institutionalists have made advances in developing (and extending) principles and concepts as applied to the real world. For instance, radical institutionalists (led by Bill Dugger, Ron Stanfield, Rick Tilman and Ted Wheelwright), instrumental institutionalists (following J. Fagg Foster, Marc Tool and Dale Bush), 'standard' institutionalists (such as Malcolm Rutherford, Warren Samuels and Anne Mayhew), feminist institutionalists (such as Deborah Figart, Janice Peterson and Janet Knoedler), postKeynesian institutionalists (following Nicholas Kaldor, Michal Kalecki, Hyman Minsky, Dudley Dillard and Wallace Peterson) and European institutionalists (such as K.W. Kapp, Geoffrey Hodgson and Wolfram Elsner) are just some of the influences advancing the state of Veblenian institutionalism (or 'original institutionalism' as some prefer to call it).

As the postwar era moved into the 1980s and so on through to the 2010s, the relative decline, metamorphosis and/or transformation of these postwar institutional spheres saw the emergence and then dominance of neoliberalism throughout much of the world. Neoliberalism has become a growth industry, but also impacting on institutional economics as well as the other schools of heterodoxy and other scholarly spheres. This has manifested itself as the emergence and evolution of corporate power (numerous merger waves, strategic alliances and flexible systems of production), financial dominance of industry (successive financial crises), the reconfiguration of the military–industrial State (numerous major wars), capital dominance over labour (stagnating real wages and rising un[der]employment), the rising relative power of Asia (deindustrialization of much of the core), climate change and declining ecological biodiversity plus diminishing social/cultural capital in the family and community, which have all became major themes in the institutionalist literature. Institutionalists have thus come to specialize on the major problems and institutional developments throughout the world; a major achievement in itself.

Following Veblen, the *concept of institutionalized culture and evolution* (see Hamilton et al. 2010) has become a major concern of Veblenians through an investigation especially of the rising power of corporate culture. As the power of the corporate sector has risen to new heights so too corporate hegemony has taken hold of other institutions such as the State, the family, finance, educational systems, world economy and industrial relations (Dugger 1989). Through the age of the Internet, corporate objectives and tendencies are more successfully being realized to extend the scope and reach of capital. All businesses and indeed interpersonal relations are developing through the Internet, as it becomes the main way of communicating in an increasingly global electronic system. Company accounts, financial systems, banking data, personal letters, advertising, sports, music, communication and even research are being conducted through the Internet. Computers, smartphones, robotics, artificial intelligence, medical science, surveillance methods, security systems, financial control systems, production methods, stocktaking and a host of other activities (including terrorism) are becoming more sophisticated as biotechnology and electronics mature as industries. Institutionalists have been especially interested in these cultural changes, including how workers and management in many sectors are losing employment, while other opportunities arise, as computers and robotics are taking over many of the production, distribution and exchange tasks. (See, e.g., Thierry and Poussing 2010).

Modern Veblenians have also advanced our understanding of the ways in which the vested interests – or the great union of vested interests – exploit the community's joint stock of knowledge, skills and institutional capabilities. Veblen's *concept of the joint stock of knowledge*, and the exploitation of the joint stock by the ruling classes – *a major contradiction* affecting people's livelihood – advances our understanding of the increasingly unequal share of capabilities, education, norms, mores and etiquette upon which control of productive capital, finance and economic surplus is based (Dugger 2019). It also provides a foundation for the vast wastage of socioeconomic resources through spending on capital, goods and services upon which conspicuous consumption, the military-industrial complex, political lobbying and private think tanks are based. This in turn provides a foundation for extensive systemic corruption in the form of institutionalized nepotism, fraud, embezzlement, bribery, State capture and extortion upon which much of the expropriation of the surplus and other resources are dependent (O'Hara 2014).

Following Veblen, they also seek to advance scholarship at the micro level of how individuals and groups of people can enhance their standard of living and quality of life through expanding their capabilities, skills, resources, networks and relationships. In terms of policy, they tend to promote an egalitarian framework of redistribution to inculcate more participation of the working classes in the economic, social and political framework of the community through a guaranteed minimum income scheme, a comprehensive universal healthcare system, and free primary, secondary and tertiary education. They also see the need for more democracy in the workplace through the institutionalization of worker cooperatives, workers being elected to the board of companies, and for fully fledged corporate responsibility to be incorporated in the articles of association as well as the habits and directives of companies. In general, they see the need for checks and balances to reduce negative externalities generated by business, the State and other organizations. They propose balancing material abundance with quality of life, ecological sustainability and standard of living institutional innovations throughout the community (see Stanfield 1995; Holt and Greenwood 2014; Forum for Social Economics 2017). Some Veblenians also develop a more reformist program through generous social safety nets, stringent regulations, demand and industry management techniques and other innovative policies to balance the numerous contradictions of contemporary capitalism (see, e.g., Olgen 2014).

One must, of course, recognize the rise of new institutional economics, since in a sense 'we are all institutionalists now', and it is hard for even orthodoxy to ignore institutions. New institutionalists have an eclectic pedigree, variously including some public choice, Austrian and neoclassical scholars. It includes (among others) Douglass North, Oliver Williamson, Mancur Olson, Friedrich Hayek, Elinor Ostrom, Richard Posner, and Andrew Schotter. While being hard to generalize, new institutionalists generally place emphasis on the exogenous nature of individual preferences, rather than the endogenous source of preferences *a la* Veblenians. They centre on the rational choice explanation of individual decisions rather than decisions being affected by the institutional environment as per Veblenians. The individual is thus the centre of their concern, whereas Veblenians believe that the micro, meso, macro and global levels are all emergent (novel). They centre on equilibrium rather than circular and cumulative change through long historical time. For new institutionalists, therefore, institutions tend to constrain individual choices and involve rules, norms and principles of action that help to structure (but not determine) the preferences of individuals. This is in contrast to the approach of Veblenians who recognized the importance of the institutional environment in not only constraining but also enabling and indeed helping to shape the habits of thought and behaviour of individuals and groups.

Some of these so-called new institutionalists have gone part of the way towards accommodating Veblen's approach, such as Nobel Laureate Douglass North (2005) in his *later* works, who includes analyses of ideology, historical specificity, evolution, path dependence and bounded rationality. Nobel Laureate Elinor Ostrom (2009) has had some influence from 'original institutionalism', including through John Commons's transaction economics; developing the concept of polycentric systems (State, market, community, etc); her analysis of trust, emergence and complexity and scrutinizing common pool resources; but counter to the Veblenian method, she seems to place a lot of emphasis on traditional microeconomic theory, individual agents and exogenous factors.

Many new institutionalists are very far removed from Veblen since they have as a basic theory the protection of private property rights, as they support the basic power structures of neo-liberal capitalism. They also tend to have a micro theory of agents within institutions with little regard for system-problems such as insufficient aggregate demand, recurring structural crises and endogenous cycles and waves. Their rational choice framework tends to ignore radical uncertainty, information problems and historical evolution (Rutherford

1994). Furthermore, they analyze inefficient institutions and emphasize functions rather than being concerned with the contradictions of capitalism. They emphasize transaction costs yet very often underplay the importance of many of the transactions analyzed by Karl Polanyi (1944) such as reciprocity, redistribution, informal marketing and householding, which are important to Veblenians.

Conclusion

This chapter has sought to analyze the history of institutional economics through the prism of institutional and evolutionary principles. The principle of historical specificity and evolution is crucial, and we utilize it to examine the broad contours of institutionalism through its variegated history. Evolution and transformation are ongoing, since the process of long-term historical change is forever having an impact on institutions and individuals, subjecting them to dislocations, which forever require the adjustment of skills, habits and new relationships, and leading to new phases of evolution. The combined principle of independency (circular) and of circular and cumulative causation (CCC) illustrates well the institutionalist concern for changes that are greater than the initial adjustment that set the process in motion. The principle of heterogeneous groups and agents seeks to inquire into the various groups and different types of individuals that impact on the social economy, including various segments of workers, capitalists and functionaries; different genders, ethnic groups and species; as well as numerous micro-groups that interact within the socioeconomic system.

The emergent principle of system, nation, institutions and individuals recognizes that there are various levels in the economy, and that each successive level constitutes a qualitatively different movement from micro to meso to macro to global as complexity and emergence come into play. The principle of contradiction states that there are various conflicts and tensions operating in the system that generate instability, war and anomalous reproduction of the system. These manifest in periodic and structural deep recessions, financial crises, social tension, crime, terrorism, climate change, and community dislocation. Such contradictions include those between capital and labour, finance and industry, competition and monopoly, men and women, ethnic group versus ethnic group, business and ecology, plus nation versus nation (or region). And the principle of uneven development and hegemony examines the differential power relations between nations and regions of the world as some periodically succeed in achieving world dominance in production, commerce and finance.

The major economists who followed many of these institutional-evolutionary principles include the Physiocrats, many of the classical economists, Marx, Schumpeter, Keynes, Commons, Mitchell, Ayres, Myrdal, Galbraith and others, especially those operating in the Association for Evolutionary Economics and the European Association for Evolutionary Political Economy. The so-called new institutionalists of course have their own journals, such as, among several others, the *Journal of Institutional and Theoretical Economics*, *The European Journal of Political Economy* and *Public Choice*; while the *Journal of Institutional Economics* is also publishing quite a few articles along these lines. Some contemporary institutionalists have modified the original Veblenian principles, while others deepened them and provided new insights into their workings in the new era. Others sought to apply Veblenian principles and provide insights into policy. Some (new) institutionalists have largely ignored Veblen's principles and sought instead to provide a support for private property, free markets and profit-oriented institutions. A minority of new institutionalists have sought to merge some Veblenian and orthodox concepts to form an eclectic framework of analysis. The present writer believes that Veblen's original insights were remarkable and that the best approach is to develop, extend and provide empirical as well as systemic-policy advice to enhance the common good and seek to improve the workings of institutions for the betterment of communities.

References

Almeida, Felipe. 2016. 'Inside the Organizational Institutions of Institutional Economics: Why Are There Two Institutionalist Associations?' *Journal of Economic Issues*, 50, 566–574.

Anderson, K. L. 1932–1933. 'The Unity of Veblen's Theoretical System', *Quarterly Journal of Economics*, 47, 598–626.

Ayres, Clarence. 1946. *The Divine Right of Capital*, Boston: Houghton Mifflin.

Ayres, Clarence. 1962. *The Theory of Economic Progress*, New York: Schocken.

Berger, Sebastian. ed. 2009. *The Foundations of Non-Equilibrium Economics: The Principle of Circular and Cumulative Causation*, London and New York: Routledge.

Berle, Adolf A. and Means, Gardiner C. 1932. *The Modern Corporation and Private Property*, Second Edition, New York: Harcourt, Brace and World, 1968.

Brennan, Andrew John and Kaur Kalsi, Jaslin. 2015. 'Elephant Poaching & Ivory Trafficking Problems in Sub-Saharan Africa: An Application of O'Hara's Principles of Political Economy', *Ecological Economics*, 120, 312–337.

Bunge, Mario. 1974–1989. *Treatise on Basic Philosophy*, 8 Vols, Boston and Dordrecht, The Netherlands: Reidel Publishers.

Bunge, Mario. 2009. *Political Philosophy: Fact, Fiction and Vision*, New Brunswick, NJ: Transaction Publishers.

Bush, Paul Dale. 1987. 'Theory of Institutional Change', *Journal of Economic Issues*, 11(3), 1075–1116.

Commons, John. 1934. *Institutional Economics: Its Place in Political Economy*, New Brunswick, NJ: Transaction Publishers, 1990. Two Volumes.

Dugger, William M. 1988. 'Radical Institutionalism: Basic Concepts', *Review of Radical Political Economics*, 20(1), 1–20.

Dugger, William M. 1989. *Corporate Hegemony*, New York: Greenwood Press.

Dugger, William M. 1995. 'Veblenian Institutionalism: The Changing Concepts of Inquiry', *Journal of Economic Issues*, 29(4), 1013–1028.

Dugger, William M. 2019. 'The Doleful Dynamics of Competition: Inequality and Fakery in Modernity', *Forum for Social Economics*, 48(1).

Elliott, John E. 1978. 'Institutionalism as an Approach to Political Economy', *Journal of Economic Issues*, 12(1), 91–114.

Forum for Social Economics. 2017. 'Policy Analysis Issue', *Forum for Social Economics*, 46(3), 221–317.

Fusfeld, Daniel. 1988. *Economics: Principles of Political Economy*, Third Edition, Boston: Scott, Foresman & Co.

Galbraith, John Kenneth. 1952. *American Capitalism*, Boston: Houghton Mifflin.

Galbraith, John Kenneth. 1958. *The Affluent Society*, Boston: Houghton Mifflin.

Galbraith, John Kenneth. 1973. *Economics and the Public Purpose*, Boston: Houghton Mifflin.

Galbraith, John Kenneth. 1983. *The Anatomy of Power*, Boston: Houghton Mifflin Company.

Gruchy, Allen G. 1947. *Modern Economic Thought: The American Contribution*, New York: Augustus M. Kelley, 1967.

Gruchy, Allen G. 1972. *Contemporary Economic Thought: The Contribution of Neo-Institutional Economics*, Clifton, NJ: Augustus M. Kelley.

Hamilton, David, Atkinson, Glen, Dugger, William and Waller, William. 2010. *Cultural Economics and Theory: The Evolutionary Economics of David Hamilton*, London and New York: Routledge.

Hobson, John A. 1936. *Veblen*, Fairfield, NJ: Augustus M. Kelley, 1991.

Hodgson, Geoffrey. 2004. *The Evolution of Institutional Economics: Agency, Structure and Darwinism in American Institutionalism*, London and New York: Routledge.

Holt, Richard P. F. and Greenwood, Daphne T. 2014. *A Brighter Future: Improving the Standard of Living Now and for the Next Generation*, Armonk, NY: M.E. Sharpe.

Karayiannis, Anastassios and Young, Allan. 1991. 'Transitional Economies and the Veblenian Financial Entrepreneur', in Allan Young, Ivan Teodorovic and Peter Koveos (eds.), *Economies in Transition: Conception, Status and Prospects*, Singapore: World Scientific Publishing Company, pp. 71–86.

Kerr, Prue. 1993. 'Adam Smith's Theory of Growth and Technological Change Revisited', *Contributions to Political Economy*, 12, 1–27.

Keynes, John Maynard. 1936. *The General Theory of Employment, Interest and Money*, London: Palgrave Macmillan.

Keynes, John Maynard. 1937. 'The General Theory of Employment', *The Quarterly Journal of Economics*, 14, 109–123.

Mayhew, Anne. 1987. 'The Beginnings of Institutionalism', *Journal of Economic Issues*, 11, 971–998.

Mitchell, Wesley. 1941. *Business Cycles and Their Causes*, Berkeley, CA: University of California Press.

Myrdal, Gunnar. 1930. *The Political Element in the Development of Economic Theory*, New York: Simon & Shuster, 1969.

Myrdal, Gunnar. 1944. *An American Dilemma: The Negro Problem and Modern Democracy*, 2 Vols, New York: Pantheon Books.

Myrdal, Gunnar. 1968. *Asian Drama: An Inquiry into the Poverty of Nations*, 3 Vols. New York: Twentieth Century Fund.

Myrdal, Gunnar. 1978. 'Institutional Economics', *Journal of Economic Issues*, 12(4), 771–783.

North, Douglas. 2005. *Understanding the Process of Economic Change*, Princeton, NJ: Princeton University Press.

O'Hara, Phillip Anthony. 1999a. *Encyclopedia of Political Economy*, 2 Vols, London and New York: Routledge.

O'Hara, Phillip Anthony. 1999b. 'Thorstein Veblen's Theory of Collective Social Wealth, Instincts and Property Relations', *History of Economic Ideas*, 7(3), 153–180. Reprinted in

Rick Tilman (ed), *The Legacy of Thorstein Veblen: Volume 3*, 330–358. Cheltenham, UK: Edward Elgar, 2003.

O'Hara, Phillip Anthony. 2002. 'The Contemporary Relevance of Thorstein Veblen's Institutional-Evolutionary Political Economy', *History of Economics Review*, 35, 78–103, Winter.

O'Hara, Phillip Anthony. 2006. *Growth and Development in the Global Political Economy: Social Structures of Accumulation and Modes of Regulation*, London and New York: Routledge.

O'Hara, Phillip Anthony. 2007. 'Principles of Institutional-Evolutionary Political Economy – Converging Themes from the Schools of Heterodoxy', *Journal of Economic Issues*, 41(1), 1–42.

O'Hara, Phillip Anthony. 2012a. 'Principles of Heterodox Political Economy Applied to Policy and Governance: Disembedded Economy, Contradictions, Circular Cumulation and Uneven Development', *Journal of Economic and Social Policy*, 15(1), 1–38.

O'Hara, Phillip Anthony. 2012b. 'Short-, Long-, and Secular-Wave Growth in the World Political Economy: Periodicity, Amplitude, and Phases for 8 Regions, 108 Countries, 1940–2010', *International Journal of Political Economy*, 41(1), 3–46.

O'Hara, Phillip Anthony. 2014. 'Political Economy of Systemic and Micro-Corruption Throughout the World', *Journal of Economic Issues*, 48(2), 279–307.

O'Hara, Phillip Anthony. 2016. 'The Contemporary Relevance of Karl Marx's Heterodox Political Economy', in Tae-Hee Jo and Fred Lee (eds.), *Marx, Veblen, and the Foundations of Heterodox Economics*, New York: Routledge, pp. 50–78.

O'Hara, Phillip Anthony. Forthcoming. *Principles of Institutional and Evolutionary Political Economy: Applied to Current World Problems*, 2 Vols.

O'Kelley, Charles R. T. 2011. 'Berle and Veblen: An Intellectual Connection', *Seattle University Law Review*, 34, 1317–1350.

Olgen, Faruk. 2014. 'How to Guide the Economy in a Socially Desirable Direction: Lessons from the 2007 Financial Turmoil', *Journal of Economic Issues*, 48(2), 575–583.

Ostrom, Elinor. 2009. 'Beyond Markets and States: Polycentric Governance of Complex Economic Systems', Nobel Prize Lecture in Economics. December 8. www.nobelprize. org/nobel_prizes/economic-sciences/laureates/ . . .

Penard, Thierry and Poussing, Nicholas. 2010. 'Internet Use and Social Capital: Strength of Virtual Ties', *Journal of Economic Issues*, 44(3), 569–595.

Polanyi, Karl. 1944. *The Great Transformation*, Boston: Beacon Press, 1968.

Rutherford, Malcolm. 1994. *Institutions in Economics: The Old and the New Institutionalism*, Cambridge: Cambridge University Press.

Samudro, Bhimo Rizky, Bloch, Harry and Salim, Ruhul. 2014. 'Global Investment Threshold and Long-Term Economic Growth 1960s – 2000s: Political Economy Perspective of Demand Regime', *Journal of Applied Economics in Developing Countries*, 1(1), 28–44.

Schumpeter, Joseph. 1911. *The Theory of Economic Development*, Cambridge, MA: Harvard University Press, 1934.

Schumpeter, Joseph. 1939. *Business Cycles: A Theoretical, Historical and Statistical Analysis of the Capitalist Process*, New York: McGraw-Hill.

Schumpeter, Joseph. 1942. *Capitalism, Socialism and Democracy*, New York: Harper & Row.

Sherman, Howard J. and Kolk, David X. 1996. *Business Cycles and Forecasting*, New York: Harper-Collins.

Stanfield, James Ronald. 1995. *Economics, Power and Culture: Essays in the Development of Radical Institutionalism*, New York: St Martin's Press.

Stanfield, James Ronald. 1996. *John Kenneth Galbraith*, New York: St Martin's Press.

Stanfield, James Ronald. 2011. 'Some Social Economics Concepts for Future Research', *Forum for Social Economics*, 40, 7–18.

Tool, Marc and Samuels, Warren J. eds. 1989. *The Economy as a System of Power*, New Brunswick, NJ: Transaction Publishers.

Veblen, Thorstein Bunde. 1899. *The Theory of the Leisure Class: An Economic Study of Institutions*, London: Unwin Books, 1970.

Veblen, Thorstein Bunde. 1904. *The Theory of Business Enterprise*, Clifton, NJ: Augustus M. Kelley, 1975.

Veblen, Thorstein Bunde. 1914. *The Instinct of Workmanship and the State of the Industrial Arts*, New Brunswick, NJ: Transaction Publishers, 1990.

Veblen, Thorstein Bunde. 1915. *Imperial Germany and the Industrial Revolution*, New Brunswick, NJ: Transaction Books, 1990.

Veblen, Thorstein Bunde. 1917. *An Inquiry into the Nature of Peace and the Terms of Its Perpetuation*, Los Angeles: Tutis Digital Publishing, 2008.

Veblen, Thorstein Bunde. 1919. *The Vested Interests and the Common Man*, New York: Kelley, 1964.

Veblen, Thorstein Bunde. 1921. *The Engineers and the Price System*, London: Transaction Publishers, 1983.

Veblen, Thorstein Bunde. 1923. *Absentee Ownership and Business Enterprise in Recent Times: The Case of America*, New York: Kelley, 1964.

Waller, William. 2001. 'Institutional Political Economy: History', in Phillip Anthony O'Hara (ed.), *Encyclopedia of Political Economy*, New York and London: Routledge, pp. 523–528.

Chapter 13

General equilibrium
A status report

Anjan Mukherji[*]

Introduction

It is generally accepted that general equilibrium analysis came to life with Walras almost 150 years ago, in 1874 when the famous, 'Elements of Pure Economics' was published, but it reached prominence when Arrow, Debreu and McKenzie presented their papers in the meetings of the Econometric Society in 1952, 80 years later. Debreu's theory of value (1959); Arrow and Hahn (1971) and, finally, McKenzie (2002) appeared much later. By the time McKenzie's book came out, the Nobel Prizes had been given and there was none for McKenzie.[1] It was mainly at the goading of some of his students that McKenzie's book finally came out. But the 1960s and the 1970s and the period even till the mid-1980s belonged to general equilibrium before it made way for industrial organization and game theory and allowed these areas to occupy centrestage. In a conference in France, to celebrate 50 years of the proof of the existence of equilibrium, Edmond Malinvaud (1993) mentioned several things that went wrong with the general equilibrium theory.[2] There were several things mentioned: however, they were mostly related to the unsatisfactory nature of results in the area of stability of equilibrium beginning with a re-iteration of Koopman's (1957) query: whose behaviour is expressed by the equation $\dot{p} =$ excess demand? There was also some disquiet about the treatment of uncertainty.

Quite distinct from the Malinvaud critique, is the discussion in Ackerman (2002), who interprets the death of general equilibrium not only due to the instability mentioned previously, but also to the 'individualistic model of consumer behaviour'. Hands (2009), clearly mentions and describes the failures of Walrasian general equilibrium to 'The features of Walrasian theory that are often suggested as its main failures, stability analysis and the Sonnenschein 1972, 1974-Mantel 1974; Debreu 1974 (SMD theorems on aggregate excess demand)'. Notice that Hands talks about Walrasian general equilibrium, whereas Ackerman talks about the death of general equilibrium. A more nuanced view is adopted by Guesnerie (2011) where he discusses the modernity of Walras and does not appear to consider the SMD theorems as being the final nail in the coffin. In fact, he dismisses the fact that these results as showcasing failures: 'However, concluding that the result kills the Walrasian program and dismisses its basic intuition is plainly wrong', Guesnerie (2011: 136).

Thus any reflection on general equilibrium would have to take up the matter of instability and the SMD theorems and this is what we propose to do. However we begin by indicating first of all the nature of general equilibrium analysis and we shall then draw your attention to the experiments of Plott and associates in Caltech; these and other results will provide some justification of the price adjustment processes. In short, what we shall attempt is the following: first, we shall explain what general equilibrium analysis is all about, the theory behind the approach, so to speak; second, we shall approach the question of instability, the SMD theorems and even the process of price adjustment: the main culprits behind the dissatisfaction with the state of general equilibrium theory; and finally, we discuss the second fundamental theorem of positive economics and its implications for the aforementioned. Before we proceed, we should point out that we shall carry out the entire discussion in the context of the classical model of exchange; this is because of our focus on the instability properties of equilibria and, for such properties, forces of production never trigger off destabilizing reactions; on the contrary, forces of production are always stabilizing.[3]

What is general equilibrium analysis?

In short, general equilibrium analysis is a method of analysis which takes into account the interconnections and feedbacks between markets. There are two distinct approaches to the study of markets: the partial equilibrium approach and the general equilibrium one. Partial equilibrium approach focuses attention on one market in isolation, assuming either that everything else is fixed or assuming that the interconnections between markets do not matter. We shall examine in this section the possible consequence of a partial equilibrium analysis.

We choose a rather well-known example due to Scarf (1960). The example is of the classic type that one may use for pedagogic purposes. There are three individuals (indexed by $h = 1, 2, 3$) and three goods (indexed by $j = 1, 2, 3$) and it is a model of pure exchange, with fixed endowments. The utility functions U^h and endowments w^h are as under:

$$U^1(q_1, q_2, q_3) = min(q_1, q_2); w^1 = (1, 0, 0)$$
$$U^2(q_1, q_2, q_3) = min(q_1, q_2); w^2 = (0, 1, 0)$$
$$U^3(q_1, q_2, q_3) = min(q_1, q_2); w^3 = (0, 0, 1)$$

Since these agents are taken to be competitive, given the price $P = (p_1, p_2, p_3)$ each agent solves the following maximization problem:

$$max\ U^h(q_1, q_2, q_3) \text{ subject to} \sum_{j=1}^{3} p_j q_j \leq P.w^h$$

Routine calculations lead first to demand functions and, since the supplies are fixed, also to excess demand functions, denoted by Z_j. We treat the commodity 3 as numeraire so that prices are of the type $P = (p_1, p_2, 1)$ and the prices of the first two goods are measured relative to the third. Thus we consider two markets; in the first, good 1 is exchanged with good 3 whereas in the second, it is good 2 which is exchanged with good 3.

$$Z_1(p_1, p_2) = \frac{p_1(1 - p_2)}{(1 + p_1)(p_1 + p_2)}$$

$$Z_2(p_1, p_2) = \frac{p_2(p_1 - 1)}{(1 + p_2)(p_1 + p_2)}$$

$$Z_3(p_1, p_2) = \frac{p_1 - p_2}{(1 + p_1)(p_1 + p_2)}$$

Solving the equations $Z_j(p_1, p_2) = 0 \ \forall j$, we note that there is a unique equilibrium $P^* = (1, 1, 1)$, at which $Z_j = 0$ for all j.

In such a context, suppose that we were to conduct a partial equilibrium analysis of market 1, for example; we shall need to fix the price of the second good at some level say $p_2 = q$. There are three possibilities $q < 1$ or $q = 1$ or $q > 1$. Of course, when we engage in a partial equilibrium analysis, we do so because we consider that prices elsewhere remain fixed at some level, here taken to be q.

Consider the excess demand in good 1 for each of the three cases mentioned previously, i.e., $q < 1$ or $q = 1$ or $q > 1$. Writing p_1 as p, the partial equilibrium excess demand for good 1 is given by:

$$Z(p) = \frac{p(1 - q)}{(1 + p)(p + q)}$$

For three values of q, which are representative of the three possibilities we have indicated, we have the[4] diagram shown in Figure 13.1.

First of all, notice that for $q = 1$, $Z(p) = 0$ for all p: **so any price is an equilibrium for market 1**. In the other two cases, we see that there are two equilibria in both of these cases, when $p = 0$ and when $p \to \infty$; thus the two equilibria involve one of the two becoming free relative to the other. But there are significant differences between the two cases $q < 1$ and $q > 1$.

To be able to discuss the differences between the cases we need to introduce the behaviour of prices in disequilibrium. We basically stick to the Walrasian hypothesis regarding the behaviour of prices in disequilibrium: viz., that the price moves in the direction of excess demand, i.e., with a positive excess demand, price rises and with a negative excess demand, price falls. And we shall call an equilibrium to be stable if it is approached by all prices in its vicinity which are not in equilibrium, because of this hypothesis. Now notice that

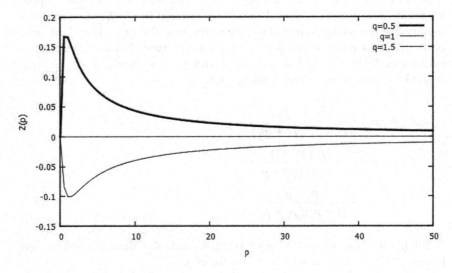

Figure 13.1 Partial equilibrium

when we take $q < 1$, the equilibrium $p = 0$ is unstable, whereas the price at infinity is the stable equilibrium; the situation is reversed when $q > 1$.

Thus notice that neglecting the influence of the second market, can lead to quite different conclusions about the market for good 1. In fact, these conclusions too may be quite misleading; exactly how misleading are these conclusions can be properly understood when we conduct a full-scale general equilibrium analysis of the example in the next section.

Examples of instability

To analyze stability properties of general equilibrium, the usual approach has been to study the behaviour of the solution to the following system of differential equations:

$$\dot{p}_j = \lambda_j Z_j(P) \text{ for all } j \neq n, \; p_n = 1$$

and to enquire whether the solution approaches an equilibrium (i.e., a price configuration P^* such that $Z_j(P^*) = 0 \forall j$). $\lambda j > 0$ are usually interpreted as the 'speed of adjustment' in the jth market and taken to be constant. Notice that these equations are a special form of the Walrasian hypothesis mentioned earlier and are generally referred to as the Walrasian *tâtonnement*.[5] We shall take these speeds to be unity in what follows. Walras in his original discussion assumed that such a process will always work without any further explanation; but he was aware that, in the two goods case, there may be problems.

The fact that we shall need strong conditions to ensure stability of equilibrium, or for the solution to approach equilibrium, was indicated by the very early examples due to Scarf (1960) and Gale (1963). The basic problem was that there was no way that one could counter the existence of unstable equilibrium: it was basically a question of the net seller's income effects being strong and wayward enough. And to bolster this feeling, two examples were provided where the substitution effects of price changes were non-existent and which led to unstable equilibria. We shall discuss these examples and indicate that there are ways of stabilizing the concerned equilibria by changing the endowment patterns, **without affecting the equilibrium price**; thus after transacting the trades at equilibrium, there is no difference between the pre-change and post-change status of the the concerned individuals. This will indicate the way we need to go to search for a meaningful resolution of the stability question.

Scarf example

We consider[6] the Scarf (1960) example first. In fact we have encountered this example in the last section. The *tâtonnement* process for this example is given by

$$\dot{p}_i = Z_i(p_1, p_2) \quad i = 1, 2 \tag{13.1}$$

Notice that equilibrium for this exchange model (and for the process defined earlier) is given by $p_1 = 1, p_2 = 1$. It would be helpful to transform variables by setting $x_i = p_i - 1$ for $i = 1, 2$. With this change in variables, our process becomes

$$\dot{x}_1 = -\frac{x_2(1+x_1)}{(x_1+2)(x_1+x_2+2)}, \quad \dot{x}_2 = \frac{x_1(1+x_2)}{(x_2+2)(x_1+x_2+2)} \tag{13.2}$$

In what follows, we shall analyze the answer to the following question: given an arbitrary $x^o = (x_1^o, x_2^o)$, how does the solution $x(t, x^o)$ to (Eq. 13.2) behave as $t \to \infty$?

Consider the function $v : R \to R$ by

$$v(x) = \frac{x^2}{2} + x - \ln(1+x)$$

which is continuously differentiable for all x such that $1 + x > 0$. One may show that[7]

13.1.1 $v(x) > 0$ *if* $x > -1, x \neq 0; v(0) = 0$.

Next define $V(x_1, x_2) = v(x_1) + v(x_2)$. We can now show:

13.1.2   *Along the solution $x(t,x^o)$ to (13.2), $\dot{V} = 0$ provided $x_i(t,x^o) > -1$ for $i = 1, 2$.*

We may next claim, using the above that

13.1.3   *Given $x^o = (x_1^o, x_2^o)$, $x_i^o > -1$, $i = 1, 2$ the solution $x(t, x^o)$ to (13.2) is such that $\exists a_i, b_i$ such that $-1 < a_i < b_i$ and $x(t, x^o) \in [a_1, b_1] \times [a_2, b_2] \; \forall t > 0$.*

For local stability, it may be of some interest to note the following

13.1.4   *For x small, $v(x) \approx x^2$.*

Proof. This follows since for x small one may use the following approximation:

$$\ln(1+x) \approx x - \frac{x^2}{2}$$

The above may be used to classify the solution to (13.2) when the initial point x^o is close to the equilibrium, i.e., the origin. It is approximately a circle with the centre origin and passing through x^o. Notice clearly, the unique equilibrium cannot be approached; however, since the figure cannot be taken as a proof, a complete demonstration is provided in Mukherji and Guha (2011: 269).

Formally, one may show:

13.1.5   *For any initial configuration x^o, the solution to (13.2), $x(t, x^o)$ is a closed orbit around the equilibrium $(0, 0)$.*

At this moment, one may recall the conclusion of the partial equilibrium analysis of the last section and see how vastly differing the conclusions about equilibrium and their stability are in the general case.

We introduce next a parameter, say b, which stands for the amount of second good which individual 2 owns completely. Thus the value of $b = 1$ would revert back to the example considered earlier. We continue to treat good 3 as the numeraire and then compute excess demand functions for the non-numeraire commodities for the case at hand; it turns out that these are given, using the same notation as earlier, by the following expressions:

$$Z_1(p_1, p_2) = \frac{p_1(1 - p_2)}{(1 + p_1)(p_1 + p_2)}$$

$$Z_2(p_1, p_2) = \frac{p_2(p_1 - b) + (1 + b)p_1}{(1 + p_1)(p_1 + p_2)}$$

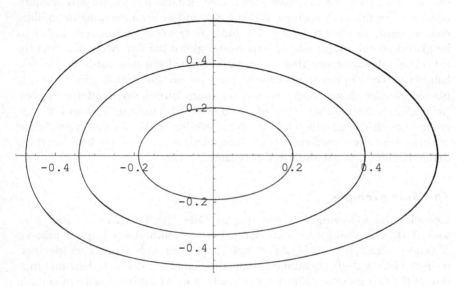

Figure 13.2 Orbits of the Scarf example
x_1 represented on the horizontal axis, x_2 on the vertical

Consequently the system (13.2) now takes the form:

$$\dot{p}_1 = \frac{p_1(1 - p_2)}{(1 + p_1)(p_1 + p_2)} \text{ and } \dot{p}_2 = \frac{p_2(p_1 - b) + (1 - b)p_1}{(1 + p_2)(p_1 + p_2)} \tag{13.3}$$

Once more standard computations ensure that the **unique equilibrium** is given by

$$p_1^* = \frac{b}{2 - b} = \theta \text{ say, } p_2^* = 1$$

Thus it may be noted that our choice of the parameter places a restriction on its magnitude to allow for a meaningful analysis, and we shall take it that this is met $0 < b < 2$. Notice also that when $b = 1, \theta = 1$ too, and we have the earlier situation. That there have been some changes to the stability property of equilibrium is contained in the next claim:[8]

We can show that:

3.1.6   *For the system (13.3), the unique equilibrium $(\theta, 1)$ is globally stable whenever $b < 1$. When $b > 1$ any solution with an arbitrary non-equilibrium initial point is unbounded.*

What the above means is that for the system (13.3), the value $b = 1$ is a point of Hopf bifurcation; on one side, when $b < 1$, we have global stability and on the other, when $b > 1$, we have unbounded behaviour. Thus an easy stability condition for the Scarf example is that $b < 1$; just as, for a meaningful equilibrium to exist, we need to have $b < 2$, and a more stringent requirement has to be placed on the magnitude of b to ensure global stability. More importantly, it is clearly demonstrated that income effects need not necessarily be the villain of the piece. In the Scarf example, there are no substitution effects, yet it is possible to have global convergence, if the **magnitudes involved are appropriate**. The contributions of Hirota 1981–1985 also indicate various different endowment holdings which lead to global stability in the Scarf example. Some of these leave the equilibrium prices unaltered, as we hope to show later. We shall establish a general result in this connection later.

The Gale example

Consider the following example due to Gale (1963). There are two persons **A,B** with utility functions defined over commodities (x,y) as follows: $U_A(x,y) = \min(x,2y)$ and $U_B(x,y) = \min(2x,y)$; their endowments are specified by $w_A = (1,0), w_B = (0,1)$; routine computations lead to the excess demand function of the first good (x), $Z(p)$, for $p > 0$, where p is the relative price of good x:

$$Z(p) = \frac{p-1}{(p+2)(2p+1)}$$

Thus the unique **interior** equilibrium is given by $p = 1$;[9] now notice that if the adjustment on prices is given by

$$\dot{p} = h(p) \tag{13.4}$$

where $h(p)$ has the same sign as $Z(p)$ and is continuously differentiable so that the solution to (13.4) say $p_t(p^\circ)$ is well defined for any initial point $p^\circ > 0$.

As Gale 1963[10] says, 'Arrow and Hurwicz have shown that for the case of two goods, one always has global stability. . . . Nevertheless, some queer things can happen even in this case'. To see the queer things referred to, consider the function $V(p_t) = (p_t - 1)^2$ and notice that along the solution to the equation (13.4), we have $\dot{V}(t) > 0$ for all t, if $p^\circ \neq 1$: so that the price moves further away from equilibrium and there is no tendency to approach the unique interior equilibrium. Notice that the excess demand curve in Figure 13.3 is upward rising at the interior equilibrium, and hence we have the aforementioned conclusion.

However, in this set-up, let us tinker with the distribution of resources. Suppose, for example, we interchange the endowments, i.e., **A** has $(0,1)$ while **B** has $(1,0)$. One may note that at equilibrium $p^* = 1$, the purchasing power has remained the same and hence so do the demands, but because endowments have changed the trades at equilibrium are different. Recomputing excess demand functions (see Figure 13.4, which plots the altered excess demand against price),

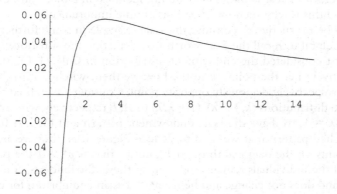

Figure 13.3 **Excess demand – the Gale example**

p represented on the horizontal axis, *Z(p)* on the vertical axis

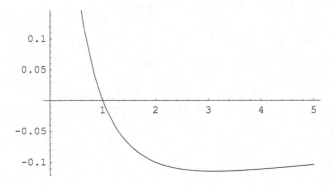

Figure 13.4 **Gale example with a switch in endowments**

p represented on the horizontal axis, *Z(p)* on the vertical axis

we note that the unique interior equilibrium is now globally stable. This follows since the excess demand function, for $p > 0$, is now given by:

$$Z(p) = \frac{2(1-p)}{(2p+1)(p+2)}$$

Notice now that the instability of the interior equilibrium noted earlier disappears. One may therefore say that we had instability of the interior equilibrium because the pattern of purchasing power, in relation to endowments had not been *right*. With the new pattern of endowments, excess demand curve becomes downward sloping. This should be the first indicator that, for stability, an appropriate distribution of endowments may be essential. Notice too that this is necessary because individuals are not identical in either tastes or endowments and this is why such investigations assume importance.

It may be instructive to consider the Gale example in some further detail. It may be helpful to recall the Edgeworth Box depicting the situation.

We first considered the endowment distribution in Gale: $(1, 0), (0,1)$ for A, B respectively, i.e., the point W in the box; we then switched it to $(0,1), (1,0)$ for A, B respectively, diagonally opposite point. Consider a weighted average of these two distributions $(\lambda, 1 - \lambda), (1 - \lambda, \lambda)$ to A, B respectively, where $0 \leq \lambda \leq 1$; thus for $\lambda = 1$, we have the Gale endowment pattern and for $\lambda = 0$ we have the switched pattern that we used to deduce Figure 13.4; thus we are considering points on the diagonal through W; notice that at $p^\star = 1$ the purchasing power of the individuals remains the same at these distributions; consequently the demand does not change and hence $p^\star = 1$ is an equilibrium for each such distribution; however, **the excess demand function changes**. Routine calculations yield:

$$f(p,\lambda) \equiv Z_x = \frac{2(\lambda(p-1)+1)}{2p+1} + \frac{p+\lambda(1-p)}{p+2} - 1.$$

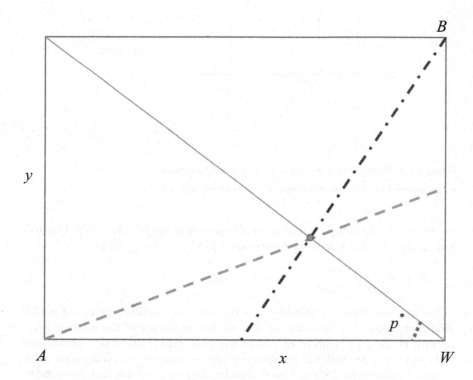

Figure 13.5 The Edgeworth Box

Consequently

$$Z_x = \frac{(p-1)(3\lambda - 2)}{(2p+1)(p+2)}$$

So that

Sign of $Z_{xp} | p = 1 = $ Sign of $(3\lambda - 2)$;

hence $p = 1$ for all values of $\lambda < 2/3$ is **stable**; when $\lambda = 2/3$, the derivative vanishes (in fact, $Z_x(p) = 0 \forall p$ if $\lambda = 2/3$). Our choice of $\lambda = 0$ worked to stabilize the equilibrium but clearly, as is evident, there are many other possible redistributions which will achieve the same end. Figure 13.6 may clarify how changes in the values of λ alters the excess demand function.

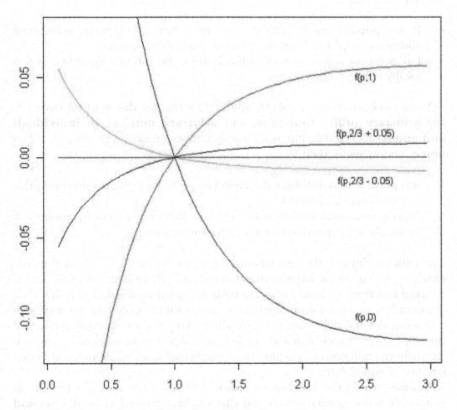

Figure 13.6 **Excess demands for alternative values of** λ
p represented on the horizontal axis; $f(p, \lambda)$ on the vertical

Notice that the excess demands $f(p, 0)$ and $f(p, 1)$ were drawn earlier; $f(p, 2/3)$ is a horizontal through the point $(0, 0)$: if $\lambda < 2/3$ the excess demand is downward sloping at $p = 1$, while for $\lambda > 2/3$ the excess demand is upward sloping at $p = 1$. Thus there are many endowment distributions which would render the interior equilibrium stable. We examine later how general this inference is.

Remark *The discussion of the previous two examples show that it may be possible to change the stability properties by redistributing endowments. We show that this claim is fairly robust. This is what we turn to in the next section.*

The second fundamental theorem of positive economics

Consider what we observed in the case of the Gale example in the last section. We observed that

- It was possible, in all cases except one (when $\lambda = 2/3$), to redistribute endowments and to keep the interior equilibrium constant.
- For some of these cases of redistribution, the interior equilibrium was locally stable.

What has been shown in Mukherji (2012) is that for **the general case**, i.e., **for arbitrary utility functions, and arbitrary number of individuals and goods**, if an equilibrium price configuration is unstable for some distribution of endowments, then

- It is possible to redistribute the endowments to keep the equilibrium price configuration unchanged.
- Among some such redistribution, the equilibrium price configuration will be locally stable provided a rank condition was met.

The rank condition is the general counterpart of the case $\lambda = 2/3$ for the Gale example; the condition requires that that the rank of the Jacobian of the excess demand functions evaluated at a zero trade Walrasian configuration is full. Thus it amounts to assuming non-degeneracy; clearly for the Gale case the argument will break down for the case $\lambda = 2/3$, when every price is an equilibrium and the slope of the excess demand curve is zero. Apart from such cases, one can redistribute endowments, keeping the equilibrium price unaltered, and obtain stability of equilibrium.

In other words, the conclusions obtained for the Gale example are true in general. It is this general conclusion that we have termed to be the **Second Fundamental Theorem of Positive Economics**.

Why *Tâtonnement*?

Preliminaries

One aspect of the dissatisfaction with general equilibrium theory has been the behaviour of prices in disequilibrium. It all goes back to what Walras described as the *tâtonnement* or the groping process: price moving in the direction of the excess demand. Samuelson (1947) was among the earliest to have written a set of differential equations to represent this process. One of the earliest critics was Koopmans (1957) when he enquired whose behaviour was being explained by these equations. There was some discussion that this was perhaps the behaviour of the invisible hand, and credit for this bit of fiction was attributed to Adam Smith in the celebrated *Wealth of Nations*. It turned out that this was not accurate since the invisible hand in that contribution did not appear when he was talking about markets, but in another context where it could not be interpreted as a means to bring about equilibrium. But yet the fiction continued and took some form of producing another bit of fiction, an auctioneer, who calls out prices and who called out higher prices in the face of positive excess demand whereas the auctioneer lowered prices whenever there was an excess supply, or a negative excess demand. Of course this does not answer why the auctioneer decided to follow this rule. Given the examples of instability, why would the auctioneer follow such a rule? We shall offer two routes to answer this question.

The Negishi conjecture

In one of the more celebrated surveys on the subject, Negishi (1962) proceeded to make a conjecture about the *tâtonnement*. He realized that one had to introduce an auctioneer, who calls out prices, and revises them in case there is a mismatch of demand and supply and suggested that the reason the auctioneer does so is because the auctioneer wants to arrive at an optimum for the economy. Thus instead of guiding the economy towards an equilibrium, the auctioneer is actually guiding the economy towards an optimum. Having said this, Negishi does not follow it up by asking whether the process would in fact solve an optimum problem. In Mukherji (2008), in a volume meant to honour Negishi, I began by asking the following question: 'What process would guide the economy to an optimum?' It turns out that the optimum can be written out as a solution to a concave pogramming problem, if the utility functions are taken to be concave. In such a situation there is a modified gradient process which we analyzed and which was the continuous form of a discrete process studied by Uzawa (1958), which always works, in the sense that it guides the economy to an optimum. I should add that the variables which were being revised along the process were the Lagrangean Multipliers, the so-called **shadow prices** of the optimization exercise.

What we showed in Mukherji (2008) was that this 'modified gradient process' reduces to the *tâtonnement*, provided the endowments are redistributed in a particular manner and that 'near' an equilibrium it was always possible to carry out such a redistribution. Thus one may defend the Walrasian process as a way of searching out the optimum, at least locally. Thus the 'auctioneer' was not merely trying to equate demand and supply but was trying to search out an optimum. Clearly this is a plausible answer for the question we posed at the beginning.

The Caltech experiments

In another line of approach, Charles Plott and his associates performed some experiments in Caltech to examine whether the predictions obtained from the Walrasian *tâtonnement* were robust. In particular, this aspect was examined in two papers, Anderson et al. (2004) and Crocket et al. (2011) where they put to test what would be the outcome if the Scarf and Gale examples were tested within the confines of the laboratories. What was also remarkable was that what happened within the confines of the lab was somewhat removed from the conditions of the Walrasian *tâtonnement*, yet the predictions put forward by Scarf (1960) and Gale (1963) and indeed our own tinkering thereof, held fast. Clearly, the conclusions from the experiments were unexpected, specially given the general disrepute that the *tâtonnement* had suffered.

Since the experiments with the two examples led to similar results, let us focus attention on the experience with the Gale example. First notice why Gale (1963) described the results as 'queer'. Here was a situation where while trading, unless one started with the fair price of unity, following the Walrasian rule, led to one person giving away the stock held by him/her for almost free and thus one person acquired the total gains from trade. An added aspect was that the particular person who gained all (and of course the particular person who lost all) was determined by whether the disequilibrium began with the price being greater than or less than the fair unity price. This aspect seemed to suggest that the Walarsian hypothesis about prices in disequilibrium, i.e., move in the direction of disequilibrium, was surely suspect. And of course, this contributed to a feeling that the general equilibrium theory of Walrasian fame had collapsed and died. We argue that such inferences are themselves suspect.

When all these discussions were going on, computers had not entered into the discourse and experiments were thought to be confined to other subjects. Plott and associates began to focus attention on the experiments to analyze price movements in the lab at the turn of this century, by which time computers were being widely used and helped make such experiments feasible. What they did in Crocket et al. (2011) was to consider the following questions within the context of the Gale Example:

- Is the interior equilibrium behaviourally stable?
- Are the price dynamics Walrasian?

- Do the prices reach corner equilibria?
- Can the primary phase price dynamics be reversed?

Some explanations are in order. Crocket et al. (2011) parameterize the Gale example keeping the basic spirit the same and show how specific values of the parameters provide the Gale example and derive a stability condition in terms of the parameters; they also consider a **discrete** version so that the unique interior equilibrium in the continuous case becomes a range of equilibria.

Further the researchers introduce an equal number of agents of each type, each preferring to consume the other's good in a greater proportion, and each type holding identical endowments. So there is a duplication, and, in each session, agents trade for three hours where trading occurs through a computerized **double auction**. Each session was divided into a sequence of thirteen to fifteen trading periods, each lasting six to fifteen minutes, beginning with longer periods and then followed by shorter periods, basically allowing traders to get acquainted to the trading environment. At the end of each period, subjects earned cash to be paid at the end of the session, depending on the allocation they ended with. Utility functions and endowments were reset to initial levels before the start of the next trading period. And the sequence of average prices at which trades occurred in the trading periods were noted. The behaviour allowed them to answer the earlier questions, respectively, thus:

- yes
- yes
- yes
- no

The Scarf example has been similarly tested in the Lab Anderson et al. (2004) and Hirota et al. (2005), and similar conclusions were obtained. What was remarkable was the complete robust support that the Walarsian hypothesis received even though the price formation was through a process of double auction; the *non-tâtonnement* aspect of trade actually occurring along the process was mitigated to ensure stationary repetition, so that the pre-conditions of the Walrasian hypothesis was adhered to.

Concluding remarks

We should point out another area where general equilibrium theory could have been faulted and that is the treatment of uncertainty and hence the treatment of money. This is something we have mentioned earlier. However that is a vast area and while some steps may be taken in that area as well (Mukherji 2018), we do not discuss these here.

It should be noted that studies relating the distribution of endowments to stability of equilibrium exist (e.g., Hirota 1981, 1985); however the results obtained in these papers are different from our results. For specific preference patterns, a weaker version of our result may be seen to follow from the Hirota studies. We should also point out that there have been some related studies which try to investigate the results that may be obtained by aggregating across individuals. Two such works are due to Hildenbrand (1983) and Grandmont (1992). These results show that aggregation will lead to stability of equilibrium, provided the distribution of endowments satisfy additional technical properties. Interested readers may refer to them for details.

What about the SMD theorems then? It may be recalled that what SMD theorems show is that the properties of homogeneity of degree zero in the prices and Walras Law do not tie down the nature of the excess demand functions adequately. The result we have named, the Second Fundamental Theorem of Positive Economics, shows, however, that the excess demand functions may be made to 'behave' by redistributing endowments **without affecting equilibrium prices**, provided a regularity condition holds. Such a redistribution is one that will alter the volume of trades at equilibrium as well as the distribution of the gains from trade. But post-trade, the situation remains unaffected.

What these redistributions achieve is to curb the magnitude of the net seller's income effects and thus reduce the impact of the wayward income effects, if there are any such. And this can be done whenever the given condition holds. The second fundamental theorem of *positive* economics has thus some structural similarities to the second fundamental theorem of *welfare* economics. While the SMD theorems have been categorized as an 'anything goes' result, it should be noted that while 'anything goes' alright, matters can still be held in check. Thus the properties of homogeneity of degree zero in prices and Walras law in the presence of continuity of excess demand functions do imply some nice properties, maybe after a possible redistribution. Guesnerie (2011:136–137), in fact, points out that what the SMD theorems do is to point out the really complex situations which may arise in reality, situations quite beyond our economic intuition, and these results are able to produce ' extraordinarily intriguing worlds from simple premises' and further demonstrate 'that our mind without the support of mathematics, cannot muster complex interactions'.

To sum up: instability of equilibrium was often taken to be a severe structural problem for the model of a competitive equilibrium; which is why the main criterion for stability has been either gross substitutes or dominant diagonals of the Jacobian or some technical condition on the distribution of endowments, if stability was to be ensured through aggregation. All of these are strong assumptions and rule out unstable equilibria. Additionally, the anything goes theorems (SMD results) were taken by many to be damaging to the structure; so much so that some made the mistake of taking the problems posed by the SMD theorem to be a fatal flaw to the entire construct. What we discuss and what we show may be interpreted thus: instability of equilibrium poses no significant, robust, structural problem to the model of general equilibrium. Whenever equilibrium appears to be unstable, we may take it that this very same equilibrium price configuration originated from an endowment configuration which would make it stable, given that the extreme situation does not occur; since the equilibrium configuration remains identical, one may consider instability to be a mis-specification of the endowments given the other specification of the model; and without changing preferences, or any other parameters, a redistribution would not only keep the equilibrium price unchanged, but change it to a stable price configuration if required.

It seems fair to end by applying Mark Twain's famous statement on rumours of his own death, 'The reports on general equilibrium theory's death are much exaggerated'. Consider our discussion in the second section; if we do not carry out general equilibrium analysis of the case, we would end up with quite erroneous conclusions about the market. Further, we have discussed why neither the examples of instability nor the nature of the Walrasian hypothesis are reasons why general equilibrium analysis should be discarded and written off. One other thing must be kept in mind: general equilibrium analysis seldom allows one to draw a clear-cut conclusion. Maybe that is where the dissatisfaction lies; but surely a clear-cut answer obtained by some other method which in fact may well turn out to be erroneous, since some interconnections were not correctly taken into account, is not the way to proceed.

Notes

* This report is based on 'Competitive Markets: Stability, Efficiency and Failures' prepared during the tenure of my Jawaharlal Nehru National Fellowship of the Indian Council of Social Science Research during 2011–2013. I am indebted to Ajit Sinha for the invitation to 'reflect' on the 'Status of General Equilibrium' at the Conference on the History of Economics held at Azim Premji University, Bengaluru, November 17–19, 2016. I am indebted to Roger Guesnerie and Hugo Sonnenschein for encouraging comments; Roger Guesnerie was kind enough to conduct a thorough audit and helped remove some deficiencies in the discussion. I am also indebted to Ajit Sinha for the interest he has shown from the very beginning in this project. The first version was written while I was an Honorary Visiting Professor at the National Institute of Public Finance and Policy in New Delhi and the facilities provided are gratefully acknowledged. For help in preparing this version, I am indebted to Arnab Mukherji and Soumya Datta.

1 For those interested in the background to what transpired, see Düppe and Weintraub (2014) for a detailed account.

2 General equilibrium theory may actually be a misnomer; see for instance, the titles of Arrow and Hahn (1971) or McKenzie (2002). The method of general equilibrium is a method of analysis applicable to many schools of thought.

3 See, for instance, Mukherji (1974).

4 To draw the diagram, we have taken $q = 0.5$ to represent $q < 1$ and $q = 1.5$ for the $q > 1$ case; clearly $q = 1$ represents the remaining case.

5 The word *tatonnement* is French and was used by Walras to describe a groping process, trying to locate the equilibrium.

6 The treatment follows Mukherji (2002). We actually analyze an example which is not quite the Scarf example since Scarf looked at the non-normalized version, whereas we look at the normalized case; we show of course that this normalization does not alter the Scarf conclusion but the robustness that Scarf claimed needs to be re-considered.

7 For the proofs of the following claims, see Mukherji (2002: 86–90).

8 See Mukherji (2002: 86–90) for proofs.
9 There are two other equilibria: equilibrium at infinity and an equilibrium at 0. The equilibrium at infinity follows since $\lim_{p\to\infty} Z(p) = 0$. The equilibrium at $p = 0$ has A consuming the bundle $(x_A, 0)$ and B consuming $(x_B, 1)$ where $x_A + x_B = 1$, $x_A, x_B \geq 0$, $x_B \geq 1/2$; further this equilibrium is locally asymptotically stable. To see how there is an equilibrium at $p = 0$, notice that at $p = 0$, the demand by A is any member of the set $\{x, 0\}$ such that $0 < x < 1$; while B's demand is any member of the set $\{(x, 1) : x > 1/2\}$; hence the claim follows. That $p = 0$ is locally asymptotically stable follows from the Figure 5.
10 There are two sets of examples in this contribution; we consider here the two-good example.

References

Ackerman, F. 2002. 'Still Dead After All These Years: Interpreting the Failure of General Equilibrium Theory', *Journal of Economic Methodology*, 9(2), 119–139.

Anderson, C. M., Plott, C. R., Shimomura, K-I. and Granat, S. 2004. 'Global Instability in Experimental General Equilibrium: The Scarf Example', *Journal of Economic Theory*, 115(2), 209–249.

Arrow, K. J. 1951. 'An Extension of the Basic Theorems of Classical Welfare Economics', in J. Neyman (ed.), *Proceedings of the Second Berkeley Symposium on Mathematical Statistics and Probability*, Berkeley: University of California Press, pp. 507–532.

Arrow, K. J. and Hahn, F. H. 1971. *General Competitive Analysis*, San Francisco: Holden-Day.

Chipman, John. 1954. 'The Nature and Meaning of Equilibrium in Economic Theory', in *Functionalism in the Social Sciences, Monograph no. 5*, Philadelphia: American Academy of Political and Social Sciences, pp. 35–64.

Crockett, S., Oprea, R. and Plott, C. 2011. 'Extreme Walrasian Dynamics: The Gale Example in the Lab', *American Economic Review*, 101(7), 3196–3220.

Debreu, G. 1959. *Theory of Value, An Axiomatic Analysis of Economic Equilibrium*, Cowles Foundation Monograph 17, New Haven, CT: Yale University Press.

Debreu, G. 1974. 'Excess Demand Functions', *Journal of Mathematical Economics*, 1(1), 15–21.

Duppe, T. and Roy Weintraub, E. 2014. *Finding Equilibrium: Arrow, Debreu and McKenzie and the Problem of Scientific Credit*, Princeton, NJ: Princeton University Press.

Gale, D. 1960. *The Theory of Linear Economic Models*, New York: McGraw Hill.

Gale, D. 1963. 'A Note on the Global Instability of Competitive Equilibrium', *Naval Research Logistics Quarterly*, 10(1), 81–87.

Grandmont, J-M. 1992. 'Transformations of the Commodity Space, Behavioural Heterogeneity and the Aggregation Problem', *Journal of Economic Theory*, 57(1), 1–35.

Guesnerie, R. 2011. 'On the Modernity of Walras', in P. Bridel (ed.), *General Equilibrium Analysis, A Century After Walras*, London and New York: Routledge, pp. 134–144.

Hands, D. W. 2009. 'The Rise and Fall of Walrasian General Equilibrium Theory – The Keynes Effect', presented at The First International Symposium on the History of Economic Thought the Integration of Micro and Macroeconomics from a Historical Perspective, University of So Paulo, So Paulo, Brazil, August 3–5.

Hildenbrand, W. 1983. 'On the "Law of Demand"', *Econometrica*, 51, 997–1019, July 1.

Hirota, M. 1981. 'On the Stability of Competitive Equilibrium and the Patterns of Initial Holdings: An Example', *International Economic Review*, 22(2), 461–467.

Hirota, M. 1985. 'Global Stability in a Class of Markets with Three Commodities and Three Consumers', *Journal of Economic Theory*, 36(1), 186–192.

Hirota, M. Hsu, M., Plott, C. and Rogers, B. 2005. 'Divergence, Closed Cycles and Convergence in Scarf Environments: Experiments in the Dynamics of General Equilibrium Systems', Caltech Social Science Working Paper, 1239, October.

Koopmans, T. C. 1957. *Three Essays on the State of Economic Science*, New York: McGraw-Hill.

Malinvaud, E. 1993. 'Existence Proofs of General Equilibrium, Looking Forty Years Back', anniversary lecture at CORE, June 3, commemorating the Arrow-Debreu-McKenzie contributions at the December 1952 meetings of the econometric society.

Mantel, R. 1974. 'On the Characterization of Aggregate Excess Demand', *Journal of Economic Theory*, 7(3), 348–353.

McKenzie, L. W. 2002. *Classical General Equilibrium Theory*, Cambridge: MIT Press.

Mukherji, A. 1974. 'Stability in an Economy with Production', in George Horwich and Paul Samuelson (eds.), *Trade Stability and Macroeconomics, Essays in Honour of L. A. Metzler*, New York: Academic Press.

Mukherji, A. 2000. 'Non-Linear Dynamics with Applications to Economics: Stability of Competitive Equilibrium Reconsidered', *Journal of Quantitative Economics*, 16(2), 93–144.

Mukherji, A. 2002. *An Introduction to General Equilibrium Analysis*, New Delhi: Oxford University Press.

Mukherji, A. 2008. 'The Stability of a Competitive Economy: A Reconsideration', *International Journal of Economic Theory*, 4(2), 317–336.

Mukherji, A. 2012. 'The Second Fundamental Theorem of Positive Economics', *International Journal of Economic Theory*, 8(2), 125–138.

Mukherji, A. 2018. 'Money and Market Failures: A Theoretical Perspective', in Ananya Ghosh Dastidar, Rajeev Malhotra and Vivek Suneja (eds.), *Economic Theory and Policy Amidst Global Discontent*, London and New York: Routledge.

Mukherji, A. and Guha, S. 2011. *Mathematical Methods and Economic Theory*, New Delhi: Oxford University Press.

Negishi, T. 1962. 'The Stability of a Competitive Economy: A Survey', *Econometrica*, 30, 635–669, October 1.

Samuelson, P. A. 1947. *Foundations of Economic Analysis*, Cambridge: Harvard University Press.

Scarf, H. 1960. 'Some Examples of Global Instability of the Competitive Equilibrium', *International Economic Review*, 1(3), 157–172.

Sonnenschein, H. 1972. 'Market Excess Demand Functions', *Econometrica*, 40, 549–563, May.

Sonnenschein, H. 1974. 'Do Walras Identity and Continuity Characterize the Class of Community Excess Demand Functions', *Journal of Economic Theory*, 6(4), 345–354.

Uzawa, H. 1958. 'Iterative Methods for Concave Programming', in K. J. Arrow, L. Hurwicz and H. Uzawa (eds.), *Studies in Linear and Non-Linear Programming*, Stanford: Stanford University Press, pp. 154–165.

Walras, L. 1877. *Elements d'economie politique pure*, Corbaz, Lausanne, Translated as *Elements of Pure Economics* by W. Jaffe. 1954, London: Allen and Unwin.

Chapter 14

Historical perspective of econometrics

K.L. Krishna[1]

1. Introduction

As pointed out by Nobel laureate Clive Granger (2006), econometrics began in the early 20th century as an 'offshoot' of the classical discipline of mathematical statistics because economic data had some distinctive properties. Economic data can be in the form of a cross-section, a time series or a panel (a time series of cross-sections). A set of economic variables can be related simultaneously, as in a simultaneous equations model (SEM) highlighted by the Cowles Commission (CC) researchers in the 1940s or dynamically, or both. Further, variables can be constrained in different ways, such as being discrete, positive bounded or censored or truncated. The time series data can have special properties, such as stochastic trends. On account of the distinctive properties of economic data, special methods of analysis have been developed since the birth of econometrics.

This chapter attempts a historical perspective of econometrics. Six broad phases/periods of the developments in econometrics may be demarcated: phases II to V are similar to those in Qin ed. (2013). Phases I and VI extend Qin's periodization backwards and forward, respectively.

Phase I: Before the 20th Century.
Phase II: Early 20th Century (Pre-1940).
Phase III: 1940s and early 1950s, when formalization of the discipline took place at the Cowles Commission, at the University of Chicago.
Phase IV: 1950s and 1960s, when consolidation and dissemination took place and the linear regression model came to be widely used for teaching and applied research.
Phase V: 1970s and 1980s, when Reformative Movements were launched to remedy the observed deficiencies/limitations.
Phase VI: 1990s and early 21st century, when different sub-disciplines of econometrics grew at a very rapid pace resulting in econometrics as a pace-setter for the economics discipline.

In terms of the nature of developments in econometrics, there is much overlap/continuity between the consecutive phases. The narrative in the chapter draws upon several books, collections of papers, handbooks and monographs cited at the appropriate places. Each phase mentioned is dealt in a separate section. Some subsections in a section provide supplementary relevant material.

The chapter is structured as follows: the developments in econometrics in the successive phases are outlined in Sections 2 to 7. Section 2 of the chapter is on pre-20th-century quantitative antecedents in economics. The early 20th-century (Pre-1940) developments are outlined in Section 3. The Cowles Commission's contributions during 1940–1953 are covered in Section 4. The historical accounts of econometric developments before 1950 in Morgan (1900), Hendry and Morgan eds. (1995) and Epstein (1987) are also reviewed in Section 4. Consolidation and expansion achieved in the 1950s and the 1960s, and the reviews by Spanos (2006), Gilbert and Qin (2006), Qin ed. (2013) and Epstein (1987) are also summarized in Section 5. The various reformative movements launched in 1970s and 1980s are reviewed in Section 6. The final phase (1990s and early 21st century) of rapid and diversified developments is covered in Section 7. The progress of econometrics teaching and research in India is outlined in Section 8. Appraisals of the contribution of econometrics to the advancement of economies are attempted in Section 9.

2. Phase I: pre-20th-century quantitative research in economics

Geweke et al. (2008) note that empirical analysis in economics dates at least as far back as the work of the 16th-century political arithmeticians, such as William Petty, Gregory King and Charles Davenant. The political arithmeticians led by Petty were the first group to make systematic use of facts and figures in their studies. Their primary interest was in practical issues of their time, such as taxation, international trade and finance. Their approach was quantitative and this distinguished them from the rest of their contemporaries.

Geweke et al. (2008) comment that the studies of Petty and King were perhaps the first examples of a unified quantitative/theoretical approach to economics. They refer to Schumpeter's (1954) comment that the working of political arithmeticians 'illustrate to perfection what econometrics is and what econometricians are trying to do' (Schumpeter) (p. 209). The first attempt at quantitative economic analysis is attributed to Gregory King, who attempted a linear regression of changes in corn prices on deficiencies in the corn harvest, reported in Charles Davenant (1698). King and others through their empirical work aspired to discover 'laws' in economics, like those in physics and other natural sciences.

The Newtonian revolution in physics had major consequences for 'the method as well as the objectives of research in economics' (Geweke et al. 2008: 4). Geweke et al. go on to state that the uncertain nature of economic relations was recognized after the birth of modern statistics in the late 19th century, and as more statistical data on economic variables became available.

The development of statistical theory by Galton, Edgeworth and Karl Pearson was promptly adopted by some economists of the time. The earliest applications of correlation analysis were carried out by Yule (1895, 1896) and Hooker (1901).

Spanos (2006) in the course of his retrospective on econometrics refers to economic methodology at the end of the 19th century. The methodological discussions during the 19th century concerning the proper method of economics focussed on whether the method of physical sciences exemplified by Newton's work could or should be applied to social sciences. There was a general consensus that the deductive approach was appropriate for economic theorizing. The disagreements during the 19th century were in regard to the nature and method of assessments of the initial postulates and the deductively derived economic laws. The 'inductivists', like Hume, Smith, McCllouch and Say, were pitted against the 'deductivists', like Ricardo, Senior, Torrens and Cairnes, who did not see the need for empirical testing of the premises or deductions.

Spanos (2006) further notes that there was consensus that economics differed from physics in some important respects, but there was no agreement as to how the deductive method should be modified to accommodate these differences. Mill (1874) was in both camps in arguing for inductively established initial postulates, but put the emphasis on deductively derived economic laws establishing 'tendencies' instead of exact predictions. He construed the empirical analysis of economic laws as establishing 'empirical uniformities'. Mill's attitudes influenced both Marshall (1890) and J.N. Keynes (1891), father of J.M. Keynes.

Jevons (1871, 1874) redressed the balance between induction and deduction in Mill's approach. J.N. Keynes (1891) attempted a synthesis of the two views by describing the consensus view in a manner that emphasized economics as a positive science, rather than as a normative art, and giving statistics a much greater role than hitherto (Spanos 2006).

2.1 Farebrother on early explorations

Farebrother (2006) describes the various procedures suggested for fitting a given mathematical relationship to a set of observations on the variables of the relationship. He notes that the maximum likelihood method was developed in the second half of the 18th century, and the Bayesian techniques were in common use in the 19th century.

Economists were reluctant to use the various Bayesian and non-Bayesian variants of the method of maximum likelihood, before R.A. Fisher reintroduced the method between 1912 and 1922, because they thought the stochastic elements in their observations were serially correlated and because of computational difficulties. These reservations were overcome after the Haavelmo (1944) breakthrough.

Farebrother reviewed a number of curve fitting methods for single and multiple equation models.

3. Phase II: early 20th-century (pre-1940) developments

The development and use of statistical tools for economic analysis began largely in the early part of the 20th century, when recasting of statistical induction into its modern form was propelled by R. A. Fisher (1922). As pointed out by Spanos (2006), Fisher's modus operandi was the notion of a statistical model in the form of a pre-specified 'hypothetical infinite population', and the data interpreted as a representative sample from that population.

Before Fisher, the notion of a statistical model was only implicit and the distinction between 'statistical description' and 'statistical induction' was nebulous until the 1920s.

Henry Moore was the first to undertake the statistical estimation of economic relations. Through his own work and that of his followers, such as Paul Douglas, Henry Schultz, Holbrook Working and Fred Waugh, Moore laid the foundation of 'statistical economics', the precursor of econometrics (see Geweke et al. 2008).

Epstein (1987) discusses the 'stirrings in Europe' in the early 20th century. In the late 1920s some young researchers in Europe turned their attention on the econometric problems first analyzed in the US. Two prominent scholars were Jan Tinbergen in Holland, Ragnar Frisch, in Norway. They saw much potential in econometrics to provide answers to a wide range of empirical questions. Their specific contributions are covered in Morgan (1990) (See sections 4.1 and 4.3 below). Epstein (1987) presents a highly perceptive account of the contributions of Tinbergen and Frisch in the pre-Cowles period.

4. Phase III: (1940–1953) formalization of econometrics by Cowles Commission's researchers

The Cowles Commission (CC) for Research in Economics created a revolution in econometric methods and practice. This section describes that revolution (see Carl Christ 1994). The CC was founded in Colorado Springs, Colorado, in 1932, with funding provided by Alfred Cowles, an investment counsellor. CC's objective was 'to advance the scientific study and development of economic theory in its relationship to mathematics and statistics'. CC moved, with Cowles himself from Colorado Springs to Chicago in 1939 and remained there till 1955, when it moved to Yale with change from 'Commission' to 'Foundation'.

The two main components of the Cowles econometric revolution at Chicago were (i) an explicit probabilistic framework and (ii) the concept of a simultaneous equations model (SEM). The Cowles programme was intended to combine economic theory, statistical methods and observed data to construct and estimate a system of simultaneous equations to describe the working of the economy. The aim was to learn from the system as to how suitable economic policies could improve the performance of the economy.

The programme required (i) the development of methods for solving the 'identification problem' and (ii) development of methods of estimation and hypothesis testing suitable for identified equations. In these two tasks, the Cowles programme was successful. However, the programme was not empirically successful in forecasting outside the sample.

The two chief architects of Cowles theoretical econometric work were Trygve Haavelmo and Tjalling Koopmans. Both received Nobel prizes in Economics. Haavelmo's pioneering contributions are contained in two papers (1943, 1944). The main body of Cowles's theoretical econometric results is contained in two CC monographs, Koopmans ed. (1950) and Hood and Koopmans eds. (1953).

The lasting contributions of the CC programme are less than what its econometric pioneers hoped for. Those contributions are principally in econometric theory rather than in applied econometrics: the probability approach, SEMs, the distinction between structural and reduced form equations, the distinction between endogenous and exogenous variables, the identification problem and its theoretical solution, methods of estimation of structural parameters, properties of estimators and testing of hypotheses. Other important aspects of modelling such as model specification, specification tests, endogenizing of policy variables, time-varying parameters, unit root problem in the case of time series data, heteroscedasticity and serial correlation etc. have been left to others to fill the gaps.

We now outline in subsections 4.1, 4.2 and 4.3 the critiques by Morgan (1990) and Hendry and Morgan eds. (1995) Epstein (1987) on pre-1950 developments in econometrics.

4.1 Morgan (1990), The History of Econometric Ideas

The book is a widely cited study of the early history of econometrics. When Morgan began her research in 1979 as a doctoral student at the London School of Economics (LSE) on the history of econometrics, she found that pre-1950 econometrics was notable for fundamental concepts and notions of the econometric approach. David Hendry was her main supervisor.

Morgan acknowledges advice from Dudley Baines, Meghnad Desai and Stephen Pudney, who were all at one time or another her supervisors along with Hendry at the LSE during 1979–1984. Morgan (1990) was based partly on her interactions with several 'founding fathers' of econometrics, namely, Haavelmo, Wold, Stone, Tinbergen, Reiersol, Kuznets, Koopmans, Sewall Wright and Holbrook Working, and second generation econometricians, Ted Anderson, Guy Orcutt, Lawrence Klein, Karl Fox, Arnold Zellner, Arthur Goldberger and Clive Granger.

Morgan (1990) consists of three parts: Part I: Business Cycles, Part II: Demand Analysis and Part III: Formal Models in Econometrics. Parts I and II trace the evolution of econometric practice up to about 1950. Part III deals with the history of formal econometric models of the data-theory relationship expounded by the CC group. This part draws on the earlier applied econometric work and on the theoretical econometrics which began to develop during the 1930s. By the early 1950s, theoretical developments and applied practice crystallized into modern econometrics of that time.

James Heckman reviewed Morgan (1990) in the *Journal of Economic Literature* in 1992. Heckman begins his review by complimenting Morgan for a carefully documented and lucidly written account of the evolution of econometric thought and practice from William Jevons through Trygve Haavelmo. He refers to the companion work, *The Foundations of Econometric Analysis*, edited by Hendry and Morgan and which got published in 1995. In this volume, more than fifty essays are assembled, summarized and commented. Heckman (1992) notes that Morgan (1990), Hendry and Morgan eds. (1995) and Roy Epstein's (1987) *A History of Econometrics* together constituted the foundation for an important field of knowledge: the history of econometric thought.

Part I of Morgan (1990) on Business Cycles discusses the evolution of macroeconometric model building from Jevons to Tinbergen, going up to Haavelmo's (1944) seminal paper, 'The Probability Approach in Econometrics'. Part II on Demand Analysis presents the evolution of modern understanding of the identification problem and the problem of estimating structural equations. The works of Henry Schultz, Sewall Wright, his father Phillip Wright, Tinbergen and Ragnar Frisch are discussed. The first chapter in Part III summarizes the main econometric issues of that era. The second chapter describes Haavelmo's econometric blueprint and the profession's immediate reaction to it.

In Part I, the contributions of Jevons, Moore, Mitchell, Burns and Perrons are discussed before those of Yule, Slutsky and Frisch. Yule and Slutsky are given credit for introducing random shocks into time series models. Part I concludes with a detailed discussion of business cycle analysis of Tinbergen and the professional reception. Tinbergen built on Frisch's work and developed the framework used by later macro-econometric model builders. Haavelmo's contribution added the probability structure needed for the development of the sampling theory of Tinbergen's estimators.

Morgan referred to the attack of J.M. Keynes on Tinbergen's first League of Nations model and the Keynes-Tinbergen debate which received much attention. Like many economic theorists, Keynes was sceptical of the notion that an econometric model could be a source of new economic ideas. She dismissed several of Keynes' comments as factually incorrect. Frisch found fault with the equations in Tinbergen's model for the lack of 'policy invariance'. Haavelmo drew attention to the idea of Slutsky that 'shock' could be a source of business cycles.

Heckman (1992), while giving credit to Morgan for presenting a lucid account of the evolution of econometric thought up to 1945, notes that a number of issues central to understanding the evolution of probabilistic and statistical thinking in empirical economics and econometrics remained unaddressed. According to Heckman, a clear statement of what constitutes econometrics is missing in Morgan's study. For this reason, the boundaries of Morgan's study are somewhat arbitrary. She confines herself to the work of econometricians. She separates econometricians from statistical economists by the former group's interest in *causal relationships*. She admits that, by the 1950s, the synthesis between economic theory and econometric methods had broken down. She too readily accepts the detachment of econometric theorists from data and too quickly dismisses a huge body of applied econometrics and the influence of empirical problems on the development of econometrics.

By way of conclusion, Heckman states that Morgan's book would have been strengthened had she taken a 'more restrained and balanced point of view' toward Haavelmo's actual achievements, deemphasizing his work on hypothesis testing in the Neyman-Pearson framework which is under attack in modern statistics.

4.2 Hendry and Morgan eds. (1995), The Foundations of Econometric Analysis

The book supplements the analysis of Morgan (1990). It is a major contribution to the history of econometrics of the pre-modern period: forty-two of the forty-five selected essays included in the volume originally appeared during 1900–1950. The volume of essays is largely the result of archival research on which Morgan (1990) was based. The editors of this volume had the benefit of discussing the history of econometrics with many of those who created it. The most important papers in the development of both structural and time series econometrics are included in the volume. The essays authored by ten pioneers, namely, Irving Fisher, Ragnar Frisch, Trygve Haavelmo, Tjalling Koopmans, Henry Moore, Henry Schultz, Jan Tinbergen, Abraham Wald, Herman Wold, Udny Yule and six other authors are contained in the volume. Hendry and Morgan note that progress in econometrics as a sub-discipline of economics up to 1940 was primarily due to innovative applied work and to critical appraisal. They point out that before the 1930s, there was very little work on econometric theory, and it was only in 1940s that theoretical work emerged.

The papers in the volume are classified under nine parts (subject areas). The titles of the parts provide an idea of the wide diversity of econometric research undertaken over different sub-periods of the first half of the 20th century with sub-period in parentheses are:

Part I: *The Emerging Role of Econometrics in Economics* (1891 to 1933)
Part II: *Early Time Series Analysis* (1862 to 1936)
Part III: *Applied Econometrics and the Identification Problem* (1914 to 1930)

Part IV: *The Evolution of Statistical Thinking in Economics* (1928 to 1945)
Part V: *Dynamic Models* (1925 to 1949)
Part VI: *The Tinbergen Debate* (1939 to 1940)
Part VII: *Structure and Simultaneity* (1942 to 1949)
Part VIII: *The Probabilistic Revolution* (1944 to 1947)
Part IX: *Exogeneity* (1950, 1952)

Hendry and Morgan (1995) also present the essential features of four Debates: (i) The Pitfalls Debate, (ii) Keynes–Tinbergen Debate (1939–1940), (iii) Measurement without theory debate between NBER and CC and (iv) Exogeneity Debate between Koopmans and Orcutt.

In the introduction to the volume (pages 1 to 82) the editors provide a six-page overview followed by commentary on the papers in each of the nine subject areas (parts). The interpretation/commentary on each paper is very insightful. In the concluding part of the Introduction, the editors remark that the conceptual structure of econometrics, its technical tool kit, its classes of models, its data structures, its empirical databases and its analytical methods grew vastly during the four decades since the early 1950s. The corresponding economic analysis tool kit too changed greatly. Hendry and Morgan conclude that the history of econometrics as of 1990s conforms to the standard pattern of scientific progress.

4.3 Epstein (1987), A History of Econometrics

The book is based on his PhD dissertation at Yale University completed in 1984. As stated by him, the book is neither a chronology of statistical methods nor an attempt at economic history. His emphasis is on the history of applications of the methods to macroeconomic problems, particularly on the debate's overt Keynesianism. Epstein claims several potential merits of his investigation. First, many writers in early 1980s specifically attacked the economic validity of the simultaneous equations model (SEM). Second, theoretical problems of equation specification was of interest to a number of econometricians of that period and the SEM provided a general framework for this type of analysis.

Epstein's interest in this area was stimulated by the intense debate among econometricians in the 1980s over the scientific foundations of contemporary methodology. He chose to focus on the SEM with exclusion restrictions. The recurrent theme in the literature as of the 1980s was the persistent gap between the theoretical and empirical achievements of structural estimation. Two different perspectives were employed by Epstein: (1) empirical experience and (2) estimation theory.

(1) Empirical experience

The founders of structural estimation were all optimistic about the usefulness of econometric business cycle investigations by Tinbergen in the mid-1930s. This work was expected both to provide accurate economic forecasts and to guide government policies for controlling the business cycle. Although Tinbergen's work was not entirely successful, the Cowles group was convinced that his approach was sound and only needed improvement to avoid simultaneity bias and the identification problem.

Epstein presents evidence to show that the work of the Cowles group between 1946 and 1952 was no better than Tinbergen's in accurately forecasting beyond the sample period. The goal of providing useful analysis of 'structural change' appeared beyond reach. The CC then decided to devote their attention to other areas in mathematical economics, particularly activity analysis. The next generation of applied econometricians too were disappointed.

(2) Estimation Theory

There was much success in the derivation of formal statistical properties of SEM estimators. The CC solved the basic identification problem and derived the asymptotic results for statistical tests. The research on estimation given up by CC staff in early 1950s was taken up by other researchers and brought to fruition in the 1970s and 1980s.

Epstein was able to draw on valuable but previously unknown manuscript material from the archive of the CC stored at Yale University for the period of 1933–1954.

The comparative sections in Epstein (1987) on British and Dutch research were not based on similar archival sources, records of the Department of Applied Economics (DAE), Cambridge and documents relating Keynes' views on the significance of econometrics were not available. Epstein could not cover three important topics: Bayesian methods, time series techniques and the perceptions of prominent English econometricians, particularly Denis Sargan and David Hendry.

Carl Christ (1994) notes that Cowles Commission's contributions are principally theoretical rather than applied econometrics. Alfred Cowles's objective of predicting the stock market and Marschak's dream of predicting the effects of economic policy variables in order to control business cycles were not realized.

5. Phase IV: (1950s and 1960s) consolidation and applications

Gilbert and Qin (2006) and Qin ed. (2013) describe the process of consolidation around the linear regression model as the dominant tool in econometrics during 1950s and 1960s. The consolidation came about through econometric applications, government sponsored macro-econometric model building and the growth of econometric teaching in almost all universities in developed countries and in leading universities in the developing countries.

Haavelmo (1943, 1944) established the simultaneity bias of ordinary least squares (OLS) estimator. New estimation methods, namely, LIML (limited information maximum likelihood) and 2 SLS (two-stage least squares) estimates, were suggested as consistent estimators in place of OLS. The LIML method was used for estimating the equations in the Klein-Goldberger (1955) macroeconometric model for the US. When the model was re-estimated by OLS, Haavelmo bias was found to be smaller than expected. Christ relied on Monte-Carlo experiments to compare the LIML and OLS estimates in finite samples and found the differences to be small.

Stone et al. (1954) found that the Cowles Commission exaggerated the importance of simultaneity in the estimation of consumer demand equations and was led to believe that OLS estimates were likely to be more accurate than LIML estimates. By 1960, it was clear that LIML or other sophisticated estimations were not superior to 2 SLS estimates.

A solution to the problem of residual serial correlation was developed at the department of applied economics (DAE) in Cambridge, where the Cochrane-Orcutt (1949) transformation for estimation and Durbin-Watson (1950) test of serial correlation as a model diagnostic were proposed and applied.

The US researchers tended to look for specification of dynamic models implied by economic theory. The adaptive expectations formulation of the Permanent Income Hypothesis for time series data was due to Friedman (1957). The partial adjustment hypothesis developed by Nevlove in the context of agricultural supply response too implied the Koyck's geometric distributed lag model. The distributed lag models of Almon, Solow and Jorgenson were also developed and applied extensively from the 1960s.

5.1 Responses to the Cowles Commission approach

Haavelmo's 'Probability Approach to Econometrics' (1944) marks the beginning of modern econometrics. Before Haavelmo, a long tradition was sceptical of the applicability of probability models to economic data. Economics was not unique in this respect. But in other fields, controlled experimentation was used to generate data that could be related to probability models. Ronald Fisher's work on experimental design, especially for agricultural applications, dominated statistical thinking in the first half of the 20th century. Fisher's view was that without a controlled experiment, a probability model was inappropriate.

The absence of an acceptable methodological foundation for their empirical work undermined confidence in the results produced by applied econometricians. Haavelmo's insight was that properly accounting for the naturally occurring variations in economic factors could act as a surrogate for the missing explicit controls. If a regression equation is properly specified, then the disturbances will conform to an appropriate probability distribution, enabling a test of the specification.

Economic theory guides the specification of the relationship to be estimated. The implication of the Haavelmo paradigm is that when account is taken of the relevant observed factors, repeated, controlled experiments are not necessary even in a time series context.[2] In Haavelmo's probabilistic approach, the emphasis is on the link between economic theory and statistical modelling of data. Different econometric methodologies can be distinguished according to the relative roles they assign to economic theory and data. Koopmans in the 'measurement without theory' debate with Vining strongly maintained that theory must be prior to data (Hendry and Morgan 1995, ch. 43). Data could not be interpreted without theoretical pre-supposition. From the 1950s through the 1970s, the profession followed Koopmans's prescription in applied econometrics. Theoretical econometrics focussed on developing appropriate estimators.

5.2 Textbook econometrics

By the middle of the 1950s, the CC programe had become the dominant econometric methodology. The focus of econometric research had shifted away from conceptual issues to concerns with the development of estimators and tests.

CC attitudes continued to dominate econometric thought, even in the face of the failure of systems estimation of macroeconometric models and of microeconomic demand systems to live up to the promise of the CC methodology. Econometric textbooks and many of the econometric applications reverted to the single equation regression model. Much of the applied work was atheoretical or weakly theoretically justified. The robust-estimation approaches that were part of the post-CC developments dominated textbook econometrics.

The problem of least squares bias was addressed through the application of instrumental variables estimators to obtain consistent estimators.

5.3 Macroeconometric modelling before 1980

The work at the Cowles Commission in 1940s and early 1950s on identification and estimation of the simultaneous equations model and the development of time series techniques since 1950s facilitated the widespread application of econometric methods to economic and financial issues. Rapid expansion of computing facilities, advances in macroeconomic and financial modelling, and the increased availability of economic data sets, times series, cross-section data and panel data contributed to econometric applications in different braches of economics across the globe. In this sub section the history of macroeconometric modelling will be reviewed. Simultaneous structural macro econometric modelling in the Cowles Commission research framework was perhaps the most important research area in econometrics until 1970s.

Bodkin et al. eds. (1991) attempt a comprehensive review of macroeconometric model building undertaken in several countries across the globe between the 1930s and 1970s. The book contains seventeen chapters in all: three chapters are on the experience in the US, in the 1950s, the 1960s and the 1970s; comparative experiences in the Netherlands, the UK, France, Canada, Japan, India and Latin America are presented in the next seven chapters. The project LINK and multi-country modelling is described in Chapter 14. Chapter 15 is on the history of computation in econometrics. Chapter 16, on lessons or generalizations from half a century of macro-econometric modelling, is based on Nobel Laureate L.R. Klein's Jan Tinbergen Lecture, 'Carrying Forward the Tinbergen Imitative in Macroeconometrics'; delivered in 1987 at the Hague.

The chapter in the book on lessons from macroeconomic modelling concludes that many lessons were absorbed in the course of over a half century. The profession's knowledge of the real world macroeconomy was considerably better at the end of 1970s. Chapter 17 is on future prospects and response to the major critiques of the traditional modelling practice.

The relatively unsatisfactory forecasting performance in the 1970s, and various critiques by Lucas (1976), Sims (1980), Hendry (1980) and Leamer (1983) brought about several important changes in the development and the use of large-scale SEMs in the 1980s and subsequently.

In response to the various critiques, new generation large-scale SEMs have incorporated desirable features, namely, equilibrium conditions, expectations formation and dynamic adjustments. However, these models are subject to a number of limitations arising primarily from their large and complex structure. A full integration of theory and measurement has proved elusive in large scale modelling. (See Section 6.2.)

6. Phase V (1970s and 1980s): reformative initiatives

Geweke et al. (2008) highlight the emergence of a new phase in econometrics since 1970s, as a response to significant changes in the world economic environment, and as a result of the breakdown of the Bretton Woods system and the quadrupling of oil prices. Macroeconomietric models built during the 1950s and 1960s in an era of economic stability were found to be ill-suited for the 1970s. A fundamental reappraisal of econometric modelling as a tool of forecasting and policy analysis took place.

It was argued that the equations in the macro models, invariably lack the necessary microfoundations and cannot be derived from the optimizing behaviour of individual economic agents. Also, the Cowles Commission approach to the indentification and estimation of macro-econometric models was questioned by Lucas and Sargent and by Sims for different reasons Lucas (1976), Lucas and Sargent (1981) and Sims (1980). There was a shift of attention from macroeconometrics to microeconometrics with an emphasis on models derived from individual decisions. Some of these will be covered in Section 7.

It was realized that economic theory could not be relied upon for the complete specification of the econometric model (Leamer 1978). The emphasis in applied work gradually shifted from estimation and inference to diagnostic checking, specification searches, model uncertainty, model validation, structural breaks, semi-parametric and nonparrmetric estimation. The choice of the methodology for a study depends on the purpose of the study, the nature of the economic application, data base, computing and software technology.

The rational expectations hypothesis (REH) first advanced by Muth in 1961 was brought to prominence by Lucas, Sargent, Sargent and Wallace in the early 1970s in terms of the New Classical explanation of the breakdown of the Phillips Curve. The REH raised serious doubts about the invariance of structural parameters of the traditional macroeconometric models in the face of changes in government policy. This was highlighted by Lucas's (1976) critique of macroeconometric policy evaluation. The implication of the Lucas critique was that traditional econometric models and methods were not suitable for policy evaluation. There have been a number of reactions to the REH and the Lucas Critique.

While the 1960s saw the consolidation of standard econometrics through the textbooks of Johnston (1963), Goldberger (1964) and Malinvaud (1966), there were growing signs in research, of deviation from, as well as dissatisfaction with the standard approach. The SEM framework built by the CC was intended as an interface with economic theories of the most general kind (both simultaneous and dynamic). But its practical execution was hampered by the paucity of both data and testable theories.

During the 1970s and 1980s, diverse research strategies were advanced as alternatives or supplements to the SEM-based standard econometrics. Developments in Bayesian econometrics, theory-led dynamic models, microeconometrics and revival of data-based modelling from the 1960s to 1980s have been reviewed by Gilbert and Qin (2006).

In their final comment on the process of development of econometrics in the 20th century, to become a separate discipline within economics, with its own journals and with dedicated faculty teaching a range of courses in econometrics, Gilbert and Qin highlight the formation of a standard paradigm. This process took place over the 1950s to 1970s, building on the foundations laid in the interwar period and their consolidation over the wartime period, when European econometricians came to the US to escape Nazi terrorism.

Many of the advances in econometrics were in statistical theory relating to the linear regression model, developed in response to the specific problems encountered in analyzing non-experimental data. Since the early 1960s, these advances were facilitated by advances in computing which eliminated a most serious constraint on applied econometric analysis.

The Cowles structural tradition, which evolved in the context of macroeconometric applications in 1940s, has survived to a larger extent in microeconometrics (see Heckman 2000, 2001).

6.1 'Credibility Revolution' in econometrics: post 1980

In the early 1980s, a trio of prominent econometricians Sims (1980), Hendry (1980) and Leamer (1983) advanced staunch critiques of contemporary econometric practice. They offered different reformative remedies for improvement in econometric practice, as pointed out by Stock (2010). The three solutions shared the same key message: more attention has to be paid to identification of the causal effect of interest, and inference should be robust to auxiliary modelling assumptions.

Sims (1980) argued in his paper 'Macroeconomics and Reality' that the 'incredible' exclusion restrictions imposed for estimating large scale macroeconometric models reduced the reliability of policy advice based on such models. He suggested using as few identifying assumptions as possible and proposed a new approach: vector auto regressions (VARs) as an alternative to SEM modelling strategy.

In his inaugural lecture in 1980 at the London School of Economics (LSE) 'Econometrics: Alchemy or Science?' Hendry highlighted the pitfalls of regression studies which are threats to the identification of the effect of interest; he suggested a research strategy with minimum of identifying restrictions which corresponds to an error correction/cointegration model.

In 'Let's take the Con Out of Econometrics', Leamer (1983) criticized the 'whimsical' nature of assumptions made in regressions and the sensitivity of results to the choice of control variables; he then proposed extreme bounds analysis (EBA) as a tool for quantifying the sensitivity of regression estimates.

These two objectives − first, credible identification of key causal effects and, second, statistical inference that is robust to auxiliary assumption − have guided much of applied and theoretical econometric research since these three papers appeared, as pointed out by Stock (2010). The quality of research outcomes relying on the prescriptions of the three papers has improved since early 1980s.

According to Stock (2010) and Stock and Watson (2015), in the 1980s the standard undergraduate curriculum focussed on the estimation and inference in the model in which all regressors were treated symmetrically. In contrast, the current focus in teaching is more on specific causal effects, and less on the estimation of the model.

Stock (2010) points out that Angrist and Pischke (2010) highlight one aspect of the first of the two research strands specifically the rise of experiments and quasi-experiments as credible sources of identification in microeconometric studies. Stock highlights some important developments in the second research strand. Robust standard errors, inference with weak instruments, the use of control variables and non-parametric and semi-parametric methods belong to the second strand of new methods.

6.2 Macroeconometric modelling since 1980s

Garratt et al. (2006, 2012) provide a recent overview of the main approaches to macroeconometric modelling, with focus on long-run implications. The approaches considered are these:

1   Large-scale simultaneous equation models
2   Unstructured and structural VARs
3   Dynamic stochastic general equilibrium (DSGE) model
4   The structural cointegrating VAR approach

(1) Large-scale simultaneous equation models

The pioneering efforts of Tinbergen in 1930s and 1940s and of Klein and his associates in the 1950s to 1970s were discussed in Bodkin et al. (1991), a short account of which was given in Section 5.3. That traditional approach was amended in later decades.

(2) Vector auto regressions (VARs)

Following the methodology developed by Doan et al. (1984), Litterman (1985) and Blanchard and Quah (1989), unrestricted Bayesian structural VAR (SVAR) specifications have been used extensively. VAR and Bayesian VAR (BVAR) are primarily used for forecasting. The SVAR approach aims to provide the VAR framework with structural context through the imposition of restrictions on the covariance structure of the different types of shock. Its application is limited to relatively small models where the distinction between the two types of shock is sufficient to bring about identification.

(3) DSGE methodology

This methodology was originally employed in the Real Business Cycle (RBC) approach developed by Kydland and Prescott (1982) and Long and Plosser (1983), and provides an explicit intertemporal general equilibrium model of the economy based on optimizing decisions made by households and firms. Some of the DSGE models can be approximated by the restricted VAR models, which also renders them more comparable with other modelling approaches.

(4) Structural cointegration VAR (SCVAR) approach

Garratt et al. (2006, 2012) have elaborated and implemented this approach for the UK economy. The approach seeks to develop a macroeconometric model that has transparent foundations, providing insight on the behavioural relationships. Implicit in the approach is the conviction that economic theory is most informative about the long-run relationships.

The approach shares common features with many applications of cointegration analysis. By beginning the analysis with an explicit statement of the underlying macroeconomic theory the SCVAR approach employed by Garratt et al. places the macroeconomic theory centrestage in the development of the macro-econometric model.

7. Phase VI (1990s and early 21st century): significant advances in diverse areas

During the past twenty-five years or so, econometrics has grown at a very rapid pace and has come to play a major role in the development of economics. Palgrave's *Handbook of Econometrics* edited by T.C. Mills and K. Patterson in two volumes: *Volume 1: Econometric Theory* (2006) and *Volume 2: Applied Econometrics* (2009), each volume with ten parts and 29 chapters, bears testimony to the diversified growth of both econometric theory and applied econometrics.

The Handbook of Macroeconomics, Volumes 2A and 2B edited by J.B. Taylor and H. Uhling in 2016 contain several chapters focussing on recent advances on macroeconometric modelling. The symposium on Recent Ideas in Econometrics published in the *Journal of Economic Perspectives*, Spring 2017 issue, covers six themes: one in econometric theory, four in applied econometrics and one on undergraduate econometrics instruction.

It needs to be emphasized that econometrics, especially empirical econometrics has grown phenomenally in recent decades, thanks to availability of new data sets and advances in computing techniques and computing power. This is an important aspect of the recent history of econometrics.

In this section, a highly selective review of the new literature of the past twenty-five years will be outlined.

Taylor and Uhlig eds. (2016) attempt to survey the state of knowledge and major advances during the past two decades in the field of macroeconomics. It covers empirical and econometric issues in addition to theoretical, methodological and policy issues dealing with unemployment, economic growth and crises, taking account of research developments, before, during and after the global financial crisis (GFC) of 2007–2009. As the editors of the *Handbook* point out, the field of macroeconomics has grown significantly since the advent of rational expectations, microeconomic foundations, dynamic optimization and general equilibrium models. The thirty-three chapters of the *Handbook* are divided into five sections. In all the five sections, there are chapters focussing on developments in econometric methodology including parameter estimation and model selection. Section 2 on methodology of macroeconomics covers dynamic factor models (DFMs), factor-augmented vector autoregressions (FAVARs) and structural vector autoregressions (SVARs) among other things. Section 5 on macroeconomic policy presents a thorough review of models used by Central banks for conducting monetary policy and the analysis of regulatory policy.

7.1 Contributions in microeconometrics

In his Nobel Lecture, Heckman (2001), summarizes the contributions of microeconometrics to economic knowledge. Four main themes are mentioned:

1   New tools of microeconometrics have been developed to respond to econometric problems raised by new sources of micro data produced after the Second World War.
2   Microeconometrics are to improve on aggregate time series methods by building models that linked economic models for individuals to data on individual behaviour.
3   An important empirical regularity detected by the field is the diversity and heterogeneity of behaviour. This heterogeneity has profound consequences for economic theory and econometric practice.
4   Microeconometrics has contributed substantially to scientific evaluation of policy.

Heckman notes that microeconometrics emerged since 1970s to aid economists in providing accurate description of the economy, in designing and evaluating public policies and in testing economic theories and estimating the parameters of well-posed economic models.

In recent decades economics has been enriched by vast new sources of micro data, recognition of social problems and evaluation of social programmes. These new data challenged the traditional econometric methodologies. The field of microeconometrics has flourished and substantial progress has been made. A more robust approach to policy evaluation has been developed.

According to Heckman, the field will continue to flourish if it renews itself by tackling new econometric problems that arise from new problems in economics.

Important challenges to the field include the development of microeconomic data-based general equilibrium theory for testing theory and evaluating impacts of large-scale policies.

Cameron and Trivedi (2005), Wooldridge (2010) and Greene (2018) provide good coverage of developments in microeconometrics.

7.2 Hendry on the methodology of empirical time series data modelling

David Hendry, a student of Denis Sargan at the London School of Economics, has made seminal contributions in theoretical and applied econometrics for more than four decades Hendry (2009) discusses the role of applied econometrics (AE) in an historical context, develops a theory of AE, discusses the important problem of model selection, offers suggestions on the teaching of AE and discusses two applications using the Autometric Software developed by (Doornick). The first application extends the work of Magnus and Morgan (1999) on the US food expenditures, which was itself an update of a study by Tobin (1950) on demand function for food. The second application relates to a multiple equation vector auto regression (VAR) of four variables, namely, industrial output per capita, number of bankruptcies, patents and real equity prices, with twenty-five lags using data for the UK for years 1757 to 1989. Hendry claims that most of the empirical results presented in the chapter make sense.

Hendry (2009) is of paramount significance to researchers and students in applied time series econometrics. It is an authoritative essay on the methodology and real world application of a major modern approach to empirical econometric modelling, namely, general to specific modelling approach.

7.3 *Palgrave* Handbook of Econometrics

The Palgrave *Handbook of Econometrics* in two volumes edited by T.C. Mills and K. Patterson *Volume 1: Econometric Theory* published in 2006 and *Volume 2: Applied Econometrics* published in 2009, bring out the 'breadth and depth' of the field of econometrics at the turn of the century. Each volume with ten different themes (parts according to the editors) and twenty-nine chapters per volume provides a comprehensive and authoritative account of the developments in econometrics from the 1970s to 1990s. Various topics in macroeconometrics or time series econometrics, in microeconometrics using cross-section data or panel data, Bayesian econometrics, computational aspects of econometrics receive well-rounded treatment in the handbook. At the beginning of Volume 1, one part is devoted to a retrospective view of econometrics by Spanos another to methodology and history of econometrics. At the end of Volume 1, spatial econometrics and non-parametric econometrics are covered.

Volume 2: Applied Econometrics is a rich collection of themes. It begins with a detailed and insightful essay on empirical modelling by David Hendry, a consummate econometrician, intimately associated with the London School of Economics (LSE) approach to econometrics, which has evolved since the 1980s. This essay is covered in Section 7.2.

Mills and Patterson (2006, 2009) emphasize the fact that at the beginning of the 21st century, the development of economics is closely associated with the development of econometrics. The first Noble Prize in Economics was awarded in 1969 to Ragnar Frisch and Jan Tinbergen who made significant contributions to applied econometrics. In the award of Noble Prize to Clive Granger, Robert Engle, James Heckman and Daniel McFadden and others in recent decades, the influential role of econometrics both theoretical and applied, in advancing economic knowledge was recognized. Each of the ten themes covered in Volume 2 – namely, (i) the methodology and philosophy of applied econometrics, (ii) forecasting, (iii) time series applications, (iv) cross section and panel data applications, (v) microeconometrics, (vi) economic policy applications, (vii) financial econometrics, (viii) econometrics of economic growth, (ix) spatial econometrics and (x) applied econometrics and computing – is of considerable significance and interest in the advancement of economics. The twenty-nine chapters in each volume have been specially commissioned. They were subjected to a rigorous referring process.

Together, the total of fifty-eight contributions in the two volumes are encyclopedic. The editorial introduction at the beginning of each volume reviewing each contribution provides valuable guidance to the reader.

7.4 Stock and Watson (2017), Twenty Years of Time Series Econometrics

There has been significant progress in time series econometrics during the past two decades in six broad areas, as documented very recently by Stock and Watson (2017). The nature of progress in the six areas is as follows:

1   estimations of dynamic causal effects,
2   estimation of dynamic structural models with optimizing agents (DSGE models),
3   methods for exploring information in big data that are specialized to economic time series,
4   improved methods for forecasting and monitoring the economy,
5   tool for modelling time variation in economic relationships, and
6   improved methods for statistical inference.

7.5 The role of theory and evidence in macroeconomics

Juselius (2011) examines the recent literature on empirical macroeconomics. Her central thesis is that the theory-first approach that currently dominates empirical macroeconomics should be replaced by the more data-based approach of cointegrated vector auto regressive (CVAR) model that gives the data rich opportunity to reflect the reality. The theory-first approach starts with a static mathematical model and then expands it to include stochastic components, while the CVAR starts with a statistically well-specified model that is more capable of dealing with disequilibrium and the non-stationary data. In addition to being more true to the data than the dominant approach, Juselius argues that the CVAR methodology is more falsificationist (and less verificationist) oriented and more effective in detecting regime shifts. She is critical of the real business cycle (RBC)–based models of Peter Irealnd that employ a VAR approach to empirics. She also argues that the data is more consistent with the theoretical framework offered by imperfect knowledge economics (IKE) than with most rational expectations (RE)–based models. She defends CVAR as a partial solution to the poor performance of DSGE-based models in predicting or explaining the recent global financial crisis (GFC).

The brief accounts of the developments described in this section have not done justice to rapid strides in the methodologies and applications during the past quarter century.

8. Progress of econometrics teaching and applied practices in India

In this section, a brief account of the progress of econometrics teaching and applications in India will be attempted. This account draws partly upon Pandit and Shanmugam (2008b).

Indian Statistical Institute (ISI) established by P.C. Mahalanobis in the early 1930s contributed much to teaching and research in statistics, both theoretical and applied. Several Indian universities developed facilities for post-graduate teaching in statistics by the 1950s. Delhi School of Economics founded in 1949 by V.K.R.V. Rao introduced a two-year diploma course in Economic Statistics in the early 1950s, which was converted into a Master's programme in the mid-1950s. Thanks to the far-sightedness of Prof. Mahalanobis, properly designed National Sample Surveys were launched soon after independence to collect data on socioeconomic subjects. An active Research and Training School was set up in ISI, Kolkata, with Prof. C.R Rao as the Head. Many young mathematicians and statisticians from different parts of India took advantage of the training and research facilities at ISI. Many university statistics departments in the US have on their faculty, statisticians who migrated from India.

In 1951, the Econometric Society (International) held two joint sessions in India, one jointly with ISI in Delhi and the other with the Indian Economic Association Conference in Palla. In 1960, the Mathematics Division of the Indian Science Congress organized a special symposium on statistical methods in economics. The symposium was chaired by Prof. C.R. Rao, while Prof. Mahalanobis delivered the inaugural address.

With the encouragement and support of Prof. C.R Rao, Annual Conferences of econometricians were regularly held across the country. The Indian Econometric Society (TIES) came into existence in 1970 in Madras, where the 10th Annual Econometrics Conference was held. TIES was registered in Hyderabad in 1971 under the Registration of Societies Act. Prof. C.R. Rao served as the first president of TIES from 1971 to 1976. Thereafter he continued to guide the Society as its Chairman. Dr N.S. Iyengar, a product of ISI, took active interest in the activities of the society for 15 years, 1970–1985, as its Secretary. V.M. Dandekar, S. Chakravarty, A.L. Nagar, T.N. Srinivasan and B.S. Minhas played vital roles in the early growth phase of TIES.

Since its very inception, TIES has pursued the objective of promoting professional competition among budding econometricians and more widely among economists engaged in teaching and research. This has been done in different ways over the past nearly five decades with considerable success. Activities of the Society have included well-attended annual conferences, orientation courses, workshops and training programmes from time to time. TIES has provided a most conducive forum to young and promising researchers for interaction and dissemination of their research work with peer groups. The regularly held annual conferences attended by senior as well as younger academics have played an important role in this endeavour.

8.1 Three major landmarks

Three major landmarks in the growth of TIES over the past five decades will be highlighted in the following subsections: (i) JQE; (ii) Mahalanobis Memorial Medal (M3) and other awards and (iii) TIES TRUST for supporting Society's activities.

(1) **JQE (Journal of Quantitative Economics)**

JQE as an organ of TIES was established in 1983 with A.L. Nagar as the Editor-in-Chief, K.L. Krishna as the Managing Editor and Kaushik Basu as the Joint Managing Editor. The Editorial Board comprised of eminent academics from India and abroad. K.L. Krishna edited JQE till 1997. R.K. Das and TCA Anant served as editors in the next five years. They were succeeded by Profs. D.M. Nachane and M.J. Manohar Rao of Bombay University. After Prof. Nagar's demise, Prof. Nachane became the Editor-in-Chief. The journal's office is now in IGIDR with P. G. Babu as the Managing Editor. JQE is now published by Springer. The Presidential address delivered at the Annual Conference of TIES is published in JQE. Some of the presidential addresses of earlier years are included in Pandit and Shanmugam (2008b).

(2) **Mahalanobis Memorial Medal for Scholars under forty-five years was instituted in 1974 for high quality quantitative research in economics! National award once in two years; international award once in four years**

About thirty economists have received the National Award and about twelve have received the International Award.

(3) **TIES Trust was registered in 2001 with Prof. V.R. Panchamukhi as the chairman. The trust is providing the funds for the M3 awards and the publication of JQE**

Prof. A.L. Nagar Fellow award for an economist in the age group forty-five to sixty-five was instituted by the Trust with funds provided by A.L. Nagar's family, and Prof. Nagar's students. Kaushik Basu received the first award for 2015. Bhaskar Dutta received the award for 2016. Dilip Mookherjee received the award for 2017. Prof. M.J. Manohar Rao also received award for the best research paper by young econometricians for the past five years.

8.2 Databases, computing facilities and institutions

Growth of econometrics in India has been facilitated by the expansion of databases, and greater availability of computing facilities and econometric software. Quality of papers presented at the Annual Conferences of TIES has been steadily improving. The number of papers in a variety of subject areas too has been on a steady increase.

TIES has become more active in the past decade in organizing/participating short-term refresher courses and training programmes in different parts of India. Members of the Indian Statistical Service and the Indian Economic Service have benefited from such training progammes: ICFAI University in collaboration with TIES has also contributed to such an effort.

The late K. Krishnamurthy and Prof. V. Pandit, PhD students of the Nobel Laureate L.R Klein, contributed significantly to macroeconometric modelling of the Indian economy. In the next generation, the late B.B. Bhattacharya was active. Currently Prof. Pami Dua and Prof. N. R. Bhanumurthy are associated with the Indian component of the World Link Project. Considerable research in the areas of microeconometries has been undertaken by many scholars in recent years. The volume of work in empirical econometrics by young scholars has been increasing steadily, thanks to the availability of computational facilities including econometric software.

The research output in the different branches of applied economics relying on econometric techniques presented at the Annual Conferences of TIES by relatively young scholars has been steadily growing over the years and the quality, on average, has shown much improvement.

Delhi School of Economics, Bombay School of Economics, Indian Statistical Institute, University of Hyderabad, Jadavpur University, Pondicherry University, Jawaharlal Nehru University, Madras School of Economics, Indira Gandhi Institute of Development Research, the IITs at Kharagpur, Kanpur, Delhi and Mumbai, among others, have facilities for the teaching of econometrics at the post-graduate level and for doctoral research. In a few universities and colleges, econometrics is being taught at the UG level also. However, an unfortunately large proportion of universities and colleges in India do not have the facilities for training or teaching of the subject, even at the Master's level.

Some important collections of papers on econometric themes relating to India edited by Krishna (1997) Kalirajan and Bhide (2003), Pandit and Krishnamurthy (2004) Parikh (2009), CDE-DSE (2014), Dhar (2014) and Kamaiah et al. (2014) provide an idea of the diversity and richness of applied econometric research in India during the past two decades. The Department of Economic Policy and Research in the Reserve Bank of India, Mumbai, has been a major promoter of applied econometric research.

Econometrics has become an integral and dominant component of the economic discipline worldwide. It is to be hoped that more and more colleges in

India will be enabled to teach econometrics right from the undergraduate level, so that the country as a whole will catch up with developed countries in the next few decades.

9. Appraisals of the contributions of econometrics

In this final section of the chapter, some brief appraisals of the contributions of econometrics in the light of the vision of its founding fathers will be presented. The aims of econometrics have been to give empirical content to economic relations for testing economic theories, forecasting and policy evaluation. Econometrics calls for a unification of theory and measurement in economics. As a unified discipline, econometrics has evolved since 1930s and has expanded very rapidly over the past few decades. A comparison of the entries on econometrics in the first (1987) and second (2008) editions of *New Palgrave Dictionary of Economics* reveals the rapid transformation and expansion of this sub-discipline of economics.

Section 9.1 presents Heckman's (2000) appraisal. Section 9.2 mentions the pace-setting role of econometrics as a sub-discipline of economics. Section 9.3 contains the appraisal of Geweke et al. (2008). The critical appraisals of Spanos (2006), Summers (1991) are summarized in Section 9.4, before endorsing the assessment of Geweke et al. (2008).

9.1 Heckman on contributions of 20th-century econometrics to knowledge

James Heckman of the University of Chicago was awarded the Noble Prize in Economics in 2000 for his work in the area of microeconometrics. Heckman (2000) documents the major trends in econometrics in the 20th century and highlights its 'enduring' contribution to knowledge. He provides an unambiguous definition of and the identification of causal parameters in economics and describes their role in econometric policy analysis.

Heckman notes that at the beginning of the 20th-century economic theory was mainly intuitive, and empirical basis was largely anecdotal. At the end of the century, economics has a rich set of formal models and considerable empirical literature.

Fundamental work on a causal framework necessary for economic policy evaluation was done at the Cowles Commission located at the University of Chicago, 1939 to 1955 as noted before. The 'lasting legacy' of the Cowles research programme includes the concepts of exogenous and endogenous variables and the nature of 'policy invariant parameters and structural parameters'.

Heckman assesses the responses of the economic community to the CC research programme. The Cowles team developed the linear simultaneous equations model (SEM), and analyzed the identification problem. Subsequently, much work was done on estimation of the Keynesian macro models. Bodkin et al. (1991) provides a history of this work. However, by the mid-1960s, the CC programme was widely perceived to be an intellectual success but an empirical failure. Epstein (1987) is a good critique of the CC programme.

According to Heckman, there were two radically different responses. The first was the VAR or 'innovation accounting' associated with the work of Sims (1972, 1980) objection to the 'incredible' nature of the identifying assumptions. The VAR approach systematically incorporated time series methods into macroeconometrics and produced more accurate descriptions of macro data than did the Cowles group.

The second response is in terms of the dynamic stochastic general equilibrium (DSGE) models. This approach has been applied extensively.

In the 1980s, the calibration approach, non-parametric research program, 'natural experiments' approach have been proposed (see Heckman 2000 for more details).

Heckman (2000) concludes by arguing that the different approaches to empirical research in economics have much to learn from each other. More recent appraisals are found in Sections 9.2 and 9.3.

9.2 Mills and Patterson (2006, 2009)

Mills and Patterson (2006, 2009) draw attention to the fact that, at the beginning of the 21st century, the development of economics is closely associated with the development of econometrics. The first Nobel Prize in Economics was awarded in 1969 to Ragnar Frisch and Jan Tinbergen who made significant contributions to applied econometrics. In the award of Nobel Prize to Clive Granger, Robert Engle, James Heckman and Daniel McFadden and other econometricians in recent decades, the influential role of econometrics in advancing economic knowledge was recognized.

9.3 Geweke et al. (2008)

In the assessment of Geweke et al. (2008), both in theory and practice, econometrics has more than fulfilled the expectations of its founders. Much progress has been achieved in the compilation of economic data, cross-section, time series and panel, and in the development of concepts, theories and tools for the construction and evaluation of a wide variety of econometric models. Econometric methods have been applied in most fields of economics, econometric models have been widely used by government agencies, international organizations and commercial enterprises. Macroeconometric models of differing sophistication and size have been constructed for a large number of countries.

Econometrics emerged in the 1930s and 1940s in the belief that economic theory and statistical inference could be adapted for providing empirical content to received economic theory. This optimistic view of the interaction between economic theory and measurement in econometrics turned out to be somewhat illusory.

In the specification of economic models for econometric analysis, institutional features and accounting conventions have to be allowed for. Auxiliary assumptions about functional forms, dynamic specifications and latent variables have to be made. But economic theory provides insufficient guidance on these aspects.

Economic data are not the result of designed experiments. There are also problems of aggregation over time, commodities and individuals that further complicate the testing of economic theories that are microbased (see Geweke et al. 2008).

9.4 Spanos (2006) and Summers (1991)

Spanos (2006) offers a thought-provoking account of the retrospect and prospect of econometrics. He argues that despite impressive advances in the development of econometric techniques, the vision of the founding fathers remains largely unfulfilled. The 'quantification of theoretical relationships' perspective and the economic-theory dominated approach to empirical modelling has produced evidence that lacks reliability and robustness.

Some twenty-five years ago, Lawrence Summers (1991) argued that applied econometric work in macroeconomics always failed. According to Summers, 'the only empirical research that has contributed to thinking about substantive issues and the development of economics is pragmatic empirical work'. This criticism is often referred to in the literature.

9.5 Balanced verdicts

In spite of the limitations of econometrics highlighted by Spanos (2006) and Summers (1991), the overall contribution of econometrics to the advancement of economics is substantial and it is on the increase. Geweke et al. (2008) and Mills and Patterson (2006, 2009) appear to be balanced verdicts.

Notes

1 I am grateful to Professor Ajit Sinha for inviting me to the workshop in November 2016 and for asking me to contribute a chapter to the volume. I have benefitted from discussions with Prof. V. Pandit, Prof. S. Bhide, Prof. J.V. Meenakshi, Prof. N.R. Bhanumurthy, Dr Seshadri Banerjee and Dr A. Sri Hari Naidu. I thank Mr. Rajesh Papnai and Ms. Anitha Simon for typesetting the chapter.
2 This section draws upon Hoover (2006).

References

Anderson, T. W. and Rubin, H. 1949. 'Estimation of Parameters of a Single Equation in a Complete System of Stochastic Equations', *Annals of Mathematical Statistics*, 20, 46–63.

Angrist, J. D. and Pischke, J-S. 2010. 'The Credibility Revolution in Empirical Economics: How Better Research Design in Taking Ion Out of Econometrics', *Journal of Economic Perspective*, 24(2), 3–20, Spring.

Banerjee, S. 2017. *Application of DSGE Models and Bayesian Estimation for Mainstream Macroeconomic Modeling in India*, Mimeo.

Basmann, R. L. 1957. 'A Generalized Classical Method of Linear Estimation of Coefficients in a Structural Equation', *Econometrica*, 25, 77–82.

Bhanumurthy, N. R. and Kumawat, L. 2014. 'External Shocks and the Indian Economy Analysing Through a Small Structural Quarterly Macroeconomic Model', in B. Kamaiah, S.V. Seshaiah and G. R. K. Murty (eds.), *Select Issues in Macroeconomics: A Quantitative Approach - A Festschrift in Honour of Dilip Nachane*. Hyderabad: IUP Publications.

Blanchard, O. J. and Quah, D. 1989. 'The Dynamic Effects of Aggregate Demand and Supply Disturbance', *American Economic Review*, 79, 1146–1164.

Bodkin, R. G., Klein, L. R. and Marwah, K. eds. 1991. *A History of Macroeconometric Model-Building*, Aldershot: Eedward Elgar.

Box, G. E. P. and Jenkins, G. M. 1970. *Time Series Analysis: Forecasting and Control*, San Francisco: Holden Day.

Burns, A. F. and Mitchell, W. C. 1947. *Measuring Business Cycles*, New York: Columbia University for the NBER.

Cameron, A. C. and Trivedi, P. K. 1998. *Regression Analysis for Count Data*, Econometric Society Monograph No. 30, Cambridge: Cambridge University Press.

Cameron, A. C. and Trivedi, P. K. 2005. *Microeconometrics: Methods and Applications*, Cambridge: Cambridge University Press.

Christ, C. F. 1960. 'Simultaneous Equations Estimation: Any Verdict Yet?' *Econometrica*, 28, 835–845.

Christ, C. F. 1994. 'The Cowles Commission's Contribution to Econometrics at Chicago 1939–1955', *Journal of Economic Literature*, 32, 30–59.

Cochrane, P. and Orcutt, G. H. 1949. 'Application of Least Squares Regression to Relationships Containing Auto-Correlated Error Terms', *JASA*, 44, 32–61.

Davenant, C. 1698. *On the Public Revenues and on the Trade of England*, Vol. 1. London.

Davis, J. B. and Hands, D. W. eds. 2011. *The Elgar Companion to Recent Economic Methodology*, Cheltenham: Edward Elgar.

Dhar, Arpita. ed. 2014. *Themes on Quantitative Economics*, New Delhi: Allied Publishers Private Limited.

Doan, T., Litterman, R. and Sims, C. A. 1984. 'Forecasting and Conditional Projections Using Realistic Prior Distributions', *Econometric Reviews*, 3, 1–100.

Durbin, J. and Watson, G. S. 1950. 'Testing for Serial Correlation in Least Squares Regression I', *Biometrica*, 37, 409–428.

Durbin, J. and Watson, G. S. 1951. 'Testing for Serial Correlation in Least Squares Regression II', *Biometrica*, 38, 159–178.

Dua, P. 2017. 'Macroeconomic Modeling and Bayesian Methods', *Journal of Quantitative Economics*, 15, 209–226.

Epstein, R. J. 1987. *A History of Econometrics*, Amsterdam: North Holland.

Farebrother, R. W. 2006. 'Early Explorations in Econometrics', in T. C. Mills and K. Patterson (eds.), *Palgrave Handbook of Econometrics*, Vol. 1. New York: Palgrave Macmillan.

Fisher, R. A. 1922. '"On the mathematical foundations" of Theoretical Statistics', *Philosophical Transaction of Royal Society A*, 222, 309–368.

Fox, K. A. 1989. 'Some Contributions of US Agricultural Economists and Their Close Associates to Statistics and Econometrics", Oxford Economics Papers, 41, pp. 53–70.

Friedman, M. 1957. *A Theory of the Consumption Function*, Princeton, NJ: Princeton University Press.

Frisch, R. 1934. 'More Pitfalls in Demand and Supply Curve Analysis', *Quarterly Journal of Economics*, 48, 749–755.

Garratt, A., Lee, K., Pesaran, M. H. and Shin, Y. 2006, 2012. *Global and National Macro Econometric Modelling: A Long-Run Structural Approach*, Oxford: Oxford University Press.

Geweke, J., Horowitz, J. and Pesaran, H. 2008. 'Econometrics', in S. N. Durlauf and L. E. Blume (eds.), *The New Palgrave Dictionary of Economics*, Second Edition, New York: Palgrave Macmillan.

Gilbert, C. L. and Qin, D. 2006. 'The First Fifty Years of Modern Econometrics', in T. C. Mills and K. Patterson (eds.), *Palgrave Handbook of Econometrics, Volume I: Econometric Theory*, New York: Palgrave Macmillan.

Goldberger, A. 1964. *Econometric Theory*, New York: Wiley.

Granger, C. (2006), 'Foreword', in T. C. Mills and K. Patterson (eds.), *Palgrave Handbook of Econometrics, Volume I: Econometric Theory*, New York: Palgrave Macmillan.

Greene, W. H. 2018. *Econometric Analysis*, Eighth Edition, Noida: Pearson Education.

Haavelmo, T. 1943. 'The Statistical Implications of a System of Simultaneous Equations', *Econometrica*, 11, 1–12.

Haavelmo, T. 1944. 'The Probability Approach in Econometrics', *Econometrica*, 12, supplement, 1–118.

Heckman, J. J. 1992. 'Haavelmo and the Birth of Modern Econometrics: A Review of the History of Econometric Ideas by Mary Morgan', *Journal of Economic Literature*, 30, 876–886.

Heckman, J. J. 2000. 'Causal Parameters and Policy Analysis in Economics: A 20th Century Perspective', *Quarterly Journal of Economics*, 115, 47–97.

Heckman, J. J. 2001. 'Micro Data, Heterogeneity and the Evaluation of Public Policy', *Journal of Political Economy*, 109(4), 673–748.

Hendry, D. F. 1980. 'Econometrics – Alchemy or Science?' *Economica*, 47(188), 387–406.

Hendry, D. F. 2009. 'The Methodology of Empirical Econometric Modeling: Applied Econometrics Through the Looking Glass', in T. C. Mills and K. Patterson (eds.), *Palgrave Handbook of Econometrics, Volume 2: Applied Econometrics*, Berlin: Springer.

Hendry, D. F. and Morgan, M. S. eds. 1995. *The Foundations of Econometric Analysis*, Cambridge: Cambridge University Press.

Hood, W. C. and Koopmans, T. C. eds. 1953. *Studies in Econometric Method*, Cowles commission monograph No.14, New York: John Wiley.

Hooker, R. H. 1901. 'Correlation of the Marriage Rate with Trade', *Journal of the Royal Statistical Society*, 44, 485–492.

Hoover, K. D. 2006. 'The Methodology of Econometrics', in T. C. Mills and K. Patterson (eds.), *Palgrave Handbook of Econometrics, Volume I: Econometric Theory*, London: Palgrave Macmillan.

Jevons, W. S. 1871. *The Theory of Political Economy*, London: Palgrave Macmillan.

Jevons, W. S. 1874. *The Principles of Science*, London: Palgrave Macmillan.

Johnston, J. 1963. *Econometric Methods*, New York: McGraw-Hill.

Juselius, K. 2011. 'In the Role of Theory and Evidence in Macro-Economies', in J. B. Davis and D. W. Hands (eds.), *The Elgar Companion of Recent Economic Methodology*, Cheltenham: Edward Elgar.

Kalirajan, K. and Bhide, S. 2003. *A Disequilibriums Macroeconometric Model for the Indian Economy*, Aldershot: Ashgate Publishing Company.

Kamaiah, B., Seshaiah, S. V. and Murty, G. R. K. eds. 2014. *Select Issues in Macroeconomics: A Quantitative Approach – A Festschrift in Honour of Dilip Nachane*, Hyderabad: IUP Publications.

Keynes, J. N. 1891. *The Scope and Method of Political Economy*, London: Palgrave Macmillan.

Keynes, J. M. 1939. 'Professor Tinbergen's Method', *Economic Journal*, 44, 558–568.

Keynes, J. M. 1940. 'Statistical Business – Cycle Research: Comments', *Economic Journal*, 50, 154–156.

Keynes, J. M. 1944. 'The Probability Approach in Econometrics', *Econometrica*, 12, 1–118.

Klein, L. R. and Goldberger, A. S. 1955. *An Econometric Model of the United States, 1929–1952*, Amsterdam: North Holland.

Koopmans, T. C. 1937. *Linear Regression Analysis of Economic Time Series*, Netherlands Economic Institute, Publication No. 20, Harlem F. Bohn.

Koopmans, T. C. ed. 1950. *Statistical Inference in Dynamic Economic Models*, Cowles commission Monograph No.10, New York: John Wiley.

Krishna, K. L. ed. 1997. *Econometric Applications in India*, New Delhi: Oxford University Press.

Kydland, F. and Prescott, E. 1982. 'Time to Build and Aggregate Fluctuations', *Econometrica*, 50(6), 1345–1370. doi:10.2307/1913386

Leamer, E. E. 1978. *Specification Searches: Adhoc Inference with Non-Experimental Data*, New York: Wiley.

Leamer, E. E. 1983. 'Let's Take the Con Out of Econometrics', *American Economic Review*, 73(1), 31–43.

Litterman, R. B. 1985. 'Forecasting with Bayesian Vector Autoregressions: Five Years of Experience', *Journal of Business and Economic Statistics*, 4, 25–38.

Long, J. and Plosser, C. 1983. 'Real Business Cycles', *Journal of Political Economy*, 91(1), 39–69.

Lucas, R. E. 1976. 'Econometric Policy Evolution: A Critique', in K. Brunner and A. M. Meltzer (eds.), *The Pillips Curve and Labour Markets*, Amsterdam: North Holland.

Lucas, R. E. and Sargent, T. J. 1981. *Rational Expectations and Econometric Practice*, London: George Allen & Unwin.

Malinvaud, E. 1966. *Statistical Methods of Econometrics*, Chicago: Rand Mc Nally & Company.

Marshall, A. 1890. *Principles of Economics*, London: Palgrave Macmillan.

Mill, J. S. 1874. *Essays on Some Unsettled Questions of Political Economy*, Second Edition, London: Longmans.

Mills, T. C. and Patterson, K. eds. 2006. *Palgrave Handbook of Econometrics Volume 1: Econometric Theory*, London: Palgrave Macmillan.

Mills, T. C. and Patterson, K. eds. (2009). *Palgrave Handbook of Econometrics: Volume 2: Applied Econometrics*, Berlin: Springer.

Morgan, M. 1990, *The History of Econometric Ideas*, Cambridge: Cambridge University Press.

Morgan, M. S. and Magnus, J. R. 1999. *Methodology and Tacit Knowledge: Two Experiments in Econometrics*, New York: John Wiley and Sons.

Nerlove, M. 1958. *Distributed Zags and Demand Analysis*, Washington, DC: USDA Agriculture Handbook No.141.

Pandit, V. and Krishnamurthy, K. eds. 2004. *Economic Policy Modelling for India*, New Delhi: Oxford University Press.

Pandit, V. and Shanmugam, K. R. 2008a. 'The Indian Econometric Society: A Saga of Growth and Achievements' in V. Pandit and K. R. Shanmugam (eds.) *Theory, Measurement and Policy: Evolving Themes in Quantitative Economics*, New Delhi: Academic Foundation.

Pandit, V. and Shanmugam, K. R. eds. 2008b. *Theory, Measurement and Policy: Evolving Themes in Quantitative Economics*, New Delhi: Academic Foundation.

Parikh, K. S. ed. 2009. *Macro-Modelling for the Eleventh Five Year Plan, Government of India: Planning Commission*, New Delhi: Academic Foundation.

Pesaran, M. H. 2015. *Time Series and Panel Data Econometrics*, Oxford: Oxford University Press.

Qin, D. ed. 2013. *The Rise of Econometrics: Critical Concepts in Economics*, 4 Vols., London: Routledge.

Schumpeter, J. A. 1954. *History of Economic Analysis*, London: George Allen & Unwin.

Sims, C. A. 1980. 'Macroeconomics and Reality', *Econometrica*, 48, 1–48.

Spanos, A. 2006, 'Econometrics in Retrospect and Prospect', in T. C Mills and K. Patterson (eds.), *Palgrave Handbook of Econometrics, Volume I: Econometric Theory*, London: Palgrave Macmillan.

Stock, J. H. 2010. 'The Other Transformation in Econometric Practice: Robust Tools for Inference', *Journal of Economic Perspectives*, 24(2), 83–94.

Stock, J. H. and Watson, M. 2015. *Introduction to Econometrics*, Third Edition. Pearson.

Stock, J. H. and Watson, M. 2017. 'Twenty Years of Time Series Econometrics in Ten Pictures', *Journal of Economic Perspectives*, 31(2), Spring.

Stone, J. R. N. et al. 1954. *Measurement of Consumers Expenditures and Behaviour in the U.K., 1920–38*, Vols. 1–2, London: Cambridge University Press.

Summers, L. H. 1991. 'The Scientific Illusion in Empirical Macroeconomics', *Scandinavian Journal of Economics*, 93(2), 129–148.

Taylor, J. B. and Uhlig, H. eds. 2016. *Handbook of Macroeconomics*, Vol. 2 A–Vol. 2 B, Amsterdam: Elsevier.

Tobin, J. 1950. 'A Statistical Demand Function for Food in the USA', *Journal of the Royal Statistical Society. Series A (General)*, 113(2), 113–149.

Wooldridge, J. M. 2010. *Econometric Analysis of Cross Section and Panel Data*, Second Edition, Cambridge: MIT Press.

Yule, G. 1895, 1896. 'On the Correlation of Total Pauperism with Proportion of Out-Relief', *Economic Journal*, 5, 603–611, 6, 613–623.

Yule, G. 1921. 'On the Time Correlation Problem, with Special Reference to the Variate-Difference Method', *JRSS*, 84, 497–526.

Zellner, A. 1971. *An introduction to Bayesian Inference in Econometrics*, New York: Wiley.

Zellner, A. 2008. 'Bayesian Econometrics: Past, Present and Future', in S. Chib et al. (eds.), *Bayesian Econometircs*, Bingley, UK: Emerald.

Chapter 15

Writings of Indian economic history since independence

Tirthankar Roy

Economic history of India was formally born around 1900, with an ideological debate about patterns of economic change in India during British colonial rule (1858–1947). The field gained a theoretical perspective in the 1960s and the 1970s with the rise of global Marxism, and the rediscovery or rehabilitation of turn-of-the-century Nationalist writings. Even as the influence of Marxism declined, evidence-based research in the field revived in the wake of the 'great divergence' debate in the 2000s.

While these global discourses encouraged innovations in method, they used India as an instrument to solve a problem – explaining the genesis of economic inequality between nations – which essentially derived from Europeanist roots. If we stand back from the inequality problem, from the Europeanist perspective, and study Indian economic history as a field in its own right, what questions should we be asking? The chapter surveys the evolution of the field in the last seventy years, and addresses this task.

Prehistory

In 1902–1904, a book was published in London with the title *Economic History of India in the Victorian Age*. This was probably the first time the phrase 'economic history' was used in a work on India. The author Romesh Dutt (1848–1909) was a civil servant, a well-known writer in Bengali and a critic of British rule. The book illustrated the two main points of his criticism: the land was taxed too much, and 19th-century free trade policy practised by the British colonial rulers ruined India's artisans. Another turn-of-the-century work, *Poverty and Unbritish Rule in India* (1901), written by the Parsi merchant-scholar-parliamentarian Dadabhai Naoroji (1825–1917), came to be bracketed with Dutt's *Economic History*. *Poverty* was less historical in structure, but made a comparable claim about the economic consequences of the Raj. The British-Indian State paid a large sum of money every year to Britain for factor services like interest on public debt or salaries of expatriate officers. Naoroji treated the payment as a tribute reflective of India's colonial status, and called it a 'drain'.

Though their methods differed, the two writers shared a common goal. Both wanted to show that the 19th-century globalization and the British Empire's commitment to openness had made India poorer. One of them targeted free trade and the other targeted open borders to capital and labour. This message would appeal to the mid-20th-century Indian Nationalists who advocated import-substituting industrialization under high tariffs, and ended free factor mobility across borders.

Between 1900 and 1947, economic history moved in two directions. One of these was a critique of the Dutt-Naoroji line. Charles Joseph Hamilton, Minto Professor of Economics at the Calcutta University, wrote *The Trade Relations Between England and India 1600–1894* (1919), among other reasons, to show how trade had brought gains and not costs to India. William Harrison Moreland (1868–1938), a Cambridge-trained civil service officer, wrote a series of books with 'Economic History' in the titles. Moreland was an officer of the land registry in a northern Indian province in the 1890s, and discovered that concepts and practices of property were embedded in Mughal institutions. The discovery made him interested in history. Moreland's work was many-dimensional and left a varied legacy. Some of it had the implication that the Mughal Empire, which preceded the British, was a despotic and extractive State, implicitly suggesting that the British created a more benign rule.

Criticisms of the Dutt-Naoroji brand of nationalism was not the mainstream in historical research, however. The mainstream was a positivist mode of enquiry that shunned political presumptions, big debates, pored over government papers and produced in-depth but descriptive studies on institutions and economic structures. To a large extent, Moreland too belonged to this tradition. However, its emergence owed mainly to the professionalization of economics teaching, as more universities set up chairs in the subject. In the late-interwar period, several university professorships in economics were held by individuals who had published historical works, or displayed a historical sense in their writings on contemporary economic trends. The three significant names in this set were the Madras University professor Gilbert Slater (1864–1938), his successor to the chair, P.J. Thomas (1895–1965), who wrote a substantial history of Indian public finance, and, perhaps most importantly, Radhakamal Mukerjee (1889–1968) of Lucknow University. Mukherjee's forty odd books on subjects ranging from demography to environment, agriculture, planning, distribution, humanism, community, labour and comparative politics were steeped in the belief that institutions mattered to economic change, and since institutions did not change easily, history mattered to economic change.

There was not yet any sign of a serious methodological debate on economic history. In contemporary economics textbooks, the relevance of history was introduced contextually. Economists of this time, who wrote textbooks and syntheses, including G.B. Jathar, S.G. Beri, K.T. Shah, K.J. Khambatta, P.A. Wadia, G.N. Joshi and C.N. Vakil, seemed to believe that history was important to shed light on particular problems of economics. They also shared some version of the

Dutt-Naoroji criticism of openness (except one offbeat text by the LSE-trained economist and League of Nations officer P.P. Pillai), and advocated protectionist industrialization based on the understanding that openness had been damaging for India. But political critique was not the impetus behind this discourse. In fact, economic history did not yet represent a distinct field, one with its own core questions, and its own preferred methods of analysis.

The first twenty years after 1947 continued in much the same way. During these years, the positivist tradition entrenched itself, and on a few occasions the debate on colonialism and development flared up. Still, these were peaceable and unchallenging years for the field, as we see next.

The staid 1947–1967

The 1950s and the 1960s witnessed the shaping of two big intellectual movements, and a minor one, with implications for Indian economic history scholarship.

The first one of these occurred in the nascent field of enquiry, development economics. With few exceptions, the architects of the new discipline were preoccupied with investment planning, and displayed a remarkable lack of historical knowledge of the countries they were giving advice to. The exchanges that followed these early writings, those of Ragnar Nurkse, Paul Rosenstein-Rodan, Albert Hirschman or Paul Streeten among others, turned into debates on the correct application of investment, rather like a team of doctors debating the dosage of a medicine to be given to a sick patient without regard for the medical history. The disease was imagined, the medicines would fail and the field would sink into obscurity within thirty years.

The effect of W.A. Lewis, another pioneer of development economics in this time, was of a different kind. Lewis's model of economic development with unlimited supplies of labour was as ahistorical as any of the other big ideas being used in this time to understand and solve the problem of underdevelopment. However, it resonated well with a neo-Marxist historiography that saw, in the manner of Friedrich Engels, Karl Kautsky and Maurice Dobb, the emergence of an underemployed labour force as an outcome of the 19th-century trade and a globalization process. In policy implications, the Lewis model would endorse the investment and statist fetish of the rest of the discipline. The key weakness of all of development economics in this time was the assumption that indigenous private enterprise and investment did not exist or did not count in the development process, a premise reinforced by modernization theory (see later). Lewis was as much a subscriber to this absurd premise as any of the other founders of development economics.

The new field, development economics, had an indirect link with another, sociological, approach to development that followed Max Weber, who had apparently invented the very phrase 'Economic History'. The North American modernization theory represented this. Broadly speaking, these theorists believed that the spread of industrial capitalism in regions like India was con-strained by a scarcity of entrepreneurial culture and a shortage of efficient and committed workers. The message implied that the government rather than the capitalists should take the lead in economic transformation and indirectly endorsed the kind of investment-management that the development econo-mists made a fetish of.

The third debate was more Indianist in scope, at least as yet. In 1952, a Wharton-educated Indian economist Surendra J. Patel (1923–2006), published a pamphlet-size book *Agricultural Labourers in Modern India and Pakistan*, which showed that widespread distress among peasants and artisans due to colonial interventions in property and trade had led to the emergence of a rural prole-tariat in India from the 19th century. Patel used census occupational statistics to show this. Later research by Daniel Thorner, Dharma Kumar and J. Krishna-murty would reveal fundamental flaws with the evidence used in the book. Still, this was evidence-based research, and, as such, the first occasion that the Dutt-Naoroji critique found a professionally acceptable restatement.

These twenty years did see the publication of several important research monographs in the field, most of the corpus was produced in the positivist his-torical tradition. Doctoral students trained in India and in the leading British, American and Japanese universities, and they produced their most important research works during these years. A short list would include Binay Chaudhuri, Kshitimohan Mukerji, V.D. Divekar, Amalendu Guha, Dharma Kumar, Irfan Habib, Hiroshi Fukazawa, Robert Frykenberg, Peter Harnetty, Bipan Chandra, K.N. Chaudhuri, Arun Banerji, Morris David Morris and, towards the end of the 1960s, M.J.K. Thavaraj, Radheshyam Rungta, Amiya Bagchi, Sabyasachi Bhattacharya and S. Ambirajan. The subjects ranged widely, from agricultural production and agrarian relations to business history, trade history, balance of payments statistics, industrialization and the ideological foundations of the Brit-ish raj. Holden Furber, Charles Boxer and Tapan Raychaudhuri carried forward the Hamiltonian tradition with books on the Portuguese Estado da India, and the Dutch and the English East India companies (see Roy 2014 for a survey).

What connected this corpus together was the mainly British tradition of source-based research. But in small steps, these works were beginning to open new frontiers of interpretive economic history. For example, Morris's doctoral research (University of California, Berkeley, 1954) on the history of textile labour in Bombay city challenged the modernization story that factory work-ers in India were insufficiently committed to industrial work. Dharma Kumar's doctoral research (University of Cambridge, 1965) on agricultural labour in South India questioned Patel's conclusion by showing that caste-based labour servitude was a part of Indian tradition, and showed up better in the census caste data than in the census occupation data that Patel had used.

Notwithstanding these interventions, the field was yet to see its paradigmatic moment. The evolution of economics teaching and research in India 'under-lines the view that Economic Theory is rooted in Economic History'. With these words, the editor of the first-ever reader published in Indian economic history concluded the editorial introduction (Singh ed. 1965: 19). Other than this broad claim, little else in the book hinted at a historiographical tension of any kind. In 1961, Burton Stein and Morris D. Morris did a survey of the field (Morris and Stein 1961); and, in 1972, Dharma Kumar published a survey (Kumar 1972). Both were rather insipid in tone.

This was to change from the late 1960s.

The historiographical turn

The Indian economy, which had grown at a small but respectable average rate in the first twenty years after independence, faced a deep crisis at the turn of the 1970s. The crisis came from a collapse of balance of payments and trade, repeated harvest failure, gathering distress among the rural population of eastern India that lived on too little land resources, industrial stagnation and two successive wars with Pakistan. These were temporary shocks. But were there structural reasons why so many people had to suffer at the same time? When India became independent in 1947, its leaders made a promise to deliver rapid and radical economic transformation. What went wrong? Where did the failure of the Indian State to achieve the promised transformation derive from?

It was not an accident that the radical left asked such questions more insistently than did mainstream economics. Within the mainstream tradition in economics, long-term changes in living standards tended to be explained with reference to unique features of individual nations. The rise of global Marxism in the 1960s changed that by suggesting that poverty and prosperity were outcomes of surplus appropriation on a worldwide scale. The rich countries became richer not because they were exceptional, but because they exploited the poor countries. For some, the crisis of the 1960s signified a crisis in the world capitalist system, which had originated in colonial exploitation.

There was a prehistory to the study of the methods of exploitation. The crudest of methods, plunder, followed Karl Marx's own depiction of primitive accumulation closely. 'These methods depend in part on brute force, e.g., the colonial system. But, they all employ the power of the state' (volume I of *Capital*, Ch. 31). Unequal exchange – a concept derived from the labour theory of value – explained the transfer of surplus on a world scale via normal trading relationships. The process would ordinarily entail structures of collaboration between international capital and local agents like moneylenders, landlords and industrialists. And these structures persisted after the formal end of colonialism. Bagchi (1983) contains an exposition on how trade-mediated surplus appropriation and transfer occurred worldwide. A paper published by V.M. Dandekar in the *Economic and Political Weekly* in 1980, and an exchange that followed, showed the influence of unequal exchange on contemporary thinking on trade.

Finally, there was fiscal transfer, Naoroji's drain. The Polish-American economist Paul Baran (1909–1964), author of *The Political Economy of Growth* (1957), rehabilitated Indian Nationalist writings when he wrote about how British rule engineered Indian poverty, and thus joined Indian history with a global Marxist account of how the world became so unequal since the 19th century. In this way, the idea that European colonialism impoverished tropical regions via trade, plunder and drain became the new canon of economic history.

Before it became a canon in India, a rather innocuous article published in 1963 generated an unusual degree of interest. Morris D. Morris, then a faculty member at the University of Washington, published an article in the *Journal of Economic History* in 1963. Morris's target was not the Marxists, who had yet to get their act together, but the modernization school popular in the US among Morris's own colleagues. Based on the evidence that he thought there was, he argued that India's persistent poverty and underdevelopment could not be explained by trade, colonial repression or cultural backwardness. The roots were more structural and geographical, poor conditions of agriculture or high costs of trade, for example. The colonial State, on the other hand, was too minimalist (Morris's words were the 'night-watchman state' or 'Nachtwächterstaat', coined by Ferdinand Lassalle) to matter either as an agent of growth or an agent of decline.

Morris in this piece and other historiographical essays did not necessarily marshal new data. He raised questions, pointed out where the crucial data gaps were and used stylized facts with great effect. Two such questions left a deep legacy upon future scholarship in the field. First, if free trade had been so damaging to the Indian handicrafts (see discussion of Dutt and Patel earlier), how was it that ten million artisans survived in 1950? Second, if the whole purpose of the colonial State was to enrich Britain at the expense of India, why did the colonial rulers allow the world's fourth largest cotton textile mill industry to appear in Bombay and Ahmedabad in direct competition with Manchester? With questions like these, Morris seemed to suggest that Indian economic history in the colonial times presented a series of paradoxes rather than a decline-and-fall story. The principal paradox was the yet unexplained combination of extraordinary enterprise, illustrated by Bombay's industrialists, with persistent and degrading poverty in much of the countryside. Neither a pure exploitation and immiseration story in the Marxist fashion, nor a pure cultural backwardness story after the modernization theory, did a good job explaining the combination.

Let us consider the point of a paradox with a few more pieces of evidence, because this is an important point for the present article. In the 19th century, the main commercial cities experienced an extraordinary process of growth led by private enterprise, or capitalist growth, and that in a region where the cost of capital was exceedingly high, several times that in the western European money markets. The physical volume of traded goods, much of it passing through the cities, increased from roughly 1 million tons in 1840 to 100 million in 1940. The cities became sites where modern industry emerged even as capital markets were undeveloped. As profits in trade were invested, India led the contemporary developing world in two leading industries of the industrial revolution, cotton textiles and iron and steel. In 1910, 55% of the cotton spindles installed outside Europe, North America and Japan were in India. In 1935, 50% of the steel produced outside Europe, North America and Japan was produced in India. At the time of independence in 1947, the port cities were home to some of the best schools, colleges, hospitals, universities, banks, insurance companies and learnt societies available outside the Western world. A big part of that infrastructure had been created by the Indian traders and industrialists.

On the other side, the record of colonial India in creating public goods, including universal healthcare and education, was truly appalling. In 1933, the UK government spent on average £4.5 per person on social welfare, including education. The Indian government spent £0.05 on social welfare. Literacy rate on average was 5% in the Indian subcontinent in 1900, and rose to 19% in 1951 in the Indian Union. UNESCO data for 1957 showed India's illiteracy rate to be one of the highest in the world. Only a few regions, such as Haiti, Sarawak, North Borneo and Portuguese Guinea, exceeded this rate. Parts of North Africa came close to it. Agricultural yield was almost everywhere significantly smaller than comparable European and American levels. How do we make sense of such divergent conditions inside a country? On the face of it, the economic system would seem to consist of a robust market and a weak State. This peculiar combination might have been the source of the paradox Morris identified. I will return to this point.

Morris (1963) article was republished in the New Delhi journal *Indian Economic and Social History Review* in 1968 (Morris et al. 1968), along with three critical reviews of the piece. Without exception, the critics – Bipan Chandra, Toru Matsui and Tapan Raychaudhuri – rebutted Morris with great energy, restated the case for colonial exploitation and in the process missed noticing the main point of the article, the paradox that Morris had pointed out.

The symposium energized Indian economic history. In the 1970s and the 1980s, Marxism and the Morris debate made it possible for students of history then doing their doctorate to start with a more solid analytical reference point than before. Globally, the rise of Marxist offshoots like the dependency theory had helped the emergence of the so-called periphery's own story of imperialism, whereas imperial history until then had been mainly written from the perspective of Europe. Revolutions in China (1949) and Cuba (1959) had strengthened the hope that socialist revolution was possible without a 'bourgeois revolution', whereas the world of the industrial bourgeoisie, being an imperialist creation, carried little promise for social change. A direct effect of the new radicalism, therefore, was interest in class relations in agriculture. The blend of Marxist-Leninist theory, world history and Indian evidence is best represented by the 'mode of production' in Indian agriculture debate (see essays in Patnaik ed. 1990). Major contributors to this literature, including Utsa Patnaik, Jairus Banaji, Hamza Alavi and Alice Thorner, interpreted colonial legacy while trying to interpret contemporary conditions.

In the 1980s, economic history found its brief moment of glory, as the positivist tradition of archival work joined forces with the new analytical narratives. In the somewhat easier economic conditions of the 1980s, a larger number of Indian students of history than before travelled offshore to do doctorates. The facility for doctoral research within India had grown under new funding schemes that led to the establishment of a string of research institutes. A great deal of the research was in economic history. The Oxford University Press in India captured the top end of the monographic output, and started a series dedicated to the field. The publication of the two-volume *Cambridge Economic History of India* was recognition of the growing prestige of the field within history scholarship and an impetus to new work, funding, seminars and conferences (Habib and Raychaudhuri ed. 1983; Kumar ed. 1983). It was easy to publish and easy to find a teaching job in India by doing economic history in the mid-1980s.

Inspired by the Marxist literature on development, agrarian history was by far the largest field of publication (see, for example, contributors to the four anthologies, Guha ed. 1992; Ludden ed. 1994; Bose ed. 1994; Stein ed. 1992). The direct legacy of the Morris debate was an interest in national income studies, which had produced its best output independently of the debate (S. Sivasubramonian, Alan Heston). Other subfields more distant from the mainstream historiography or tangentially related to it would include business communities (Thomas Timberg, Ashok Desai, Amalendu Guha, Raman Mahadevan, see also Ray ed. 1992), Indian Ocean studies (Om Prakash, S. Arasaratnam, Sanjay Subrahmanyam), colonial monetary policy (B.R. Tomlinson, Dietmar Rothermund), industrialization (Rajat Ray), business–politics interaction or the process that later became known as 'decolonization' (Claude Markovits, Tomlinson) and demography (Ira Klein).

I came into the study of Indian economic history during this efflorescence. At that time, economists took history seriously. There was even a certain glamour attached to doing economic history. Fired as they were by a growing interest in analytical narratives, historians seemed to know more and were more interesting to talk to than the policy analysts. I was swayed by that glamour. My mental makeup was influenced by a neo-Marxist paradigm, as well as respect for the positivist tradition, which valued source-bound research.

Troubles began when my doctoral work on the handicrafts was published in 1993. In the positivist tradition, I had to faithfully report what the data told me. And the data told me that Morris may have been right to notice a paradox. His conjecture that free trade had a mixed effect upon the Indian artisans rather than a uniformly damaging one as Romesh Dutt contended, seemed to me to be closer to the facts. I soon discovered that a direct conflict between narrative history and the ruling sentiment on colonialism was a dangerous thing for an early-career researcher. Stalwarts in the field who sat on job selection committees and refereed applications did not like it.

I was not wrong to sense that a dysfunctional attitude had set in. The early sign of intolerance had showed up during the Morris debate of 1968. The three critics of Morris saw him to be trying to defend colonialism. Twenty years later, a Marxist historian would again accuse Morris of trying 'to exonerate the colonial regime from any culpability throughout' (Habib 1985). From 1970 onward, to say that we should rethink the story that the British ruined India amounted to being an admirer of the Raj, and, by implication, an admirer of the lack of political liberty that colonial rule embodied. That, of course, was a terrible thing to be! It was safer to conform to political correctness, believe in a straight and narrow story and not bother with any paradox. The 1968 debate in this way marked the beginning of the end of serious and dispassionate discussions on patterns of Indian economic history in the colonial times. In my time, the leading figures of the field working in India displayed a barely concealed hostility towards views other than their own.

That there was a growing problem was soon proved by metrics that showed that the field was growing steadily weaker.

A time of decline: 1990s

The number of research publications suffered a sharp fall, slightly relieved by a cluster of works in environmental history after 1990 (Figure 15.1). The fall characterized mainly research published in the area journals. On the other hand, research published in the leading economic history journals did not see a fall. But then these papers never formed the main body of Indian economic history. There was a parallel fall in research emerging *from India*. The proportion went from 62% in 1991–1995 to 19% in 2011–2013 (Figure 15.2).

The decline owed to several factors. Intolerance was one of these. Postcolonialism was another. Worldwide, historians lost faith somewhat in positivist history under the influence of postmodernism, its criticism of sources and skepticism about 'grand narratives'. The reaction against sources was quite fierce in the postmodernist offshoot called postcolonial studies. Economic historians faced outright hostility in this milieu. They tried to explain how economic growth and inequality emerged in the modern world, a project that implicated as many as three wicked habits: belief in colonial documents, belief in modernization and belief in grand narratives. Economic history became an untouchable in history schools, a situation that has not changed much since then, especially in North America. By and large, historians still shun dialogues with economists with a hostility that is returned in full measure.

The link between global Marxism and economic history was becoming weaker than before. Agrarian history scholarship, for example, moved away from studies of markets and property rights towards political processes, best embodied in the 'subaltern studies' school, initiated by Ranajit Guha. Initially a small collective that tried to revise the narrative of Nationalist movement in India,

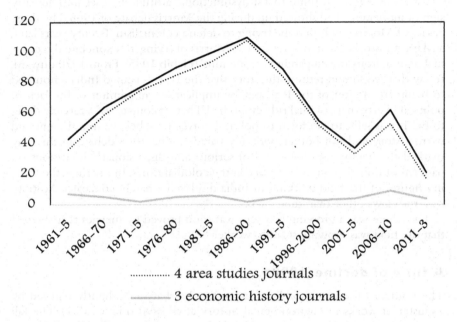

.... 4 area studies journals

―――― 3 economic history journals

Figure 15.1 Articles on Indian economic history published in leading journals, 1961–2013

Notes: The four area studies journals are *Modern Asian Studies* from Cambridge University Press, *Journal of the Economic and Social History of the Orient* from Brill, *Indian Economic and Social History Review* and *Studies in History*, both from Sage. The three economic history journals are *Journal of Economic History*, *Economic History Review*, and *Explorations in Economic History*.

Source: *Author's calculation.*

the school received international attention in the 1980s with the emergence of resistance studies from elsewhere in the world, one of the more popular being the work of James Scott of Yale University. Like the Marxists, the subalterns explored struggle and displayed a keen interest in the prospect of a revolution or the absence thereof, but, unlike the Marxists, avoided dependence on the problematical category of class.

Within India, reduced university funds for research in the mid-1990s allowed practitioners of 'hard' economics to drive out 'soft' ones like economic history. The situation in Delhi School of Economics was symptomatic of this. When I finished my doctoral research (1989) there were four full professorships in economic history here. In the next fifteen years, with the retirement of the incumbents, other subfields happily cannibalized the economic history chairs.

I should not say that new works in the positivist tradition stopped flowing altogether. While the journals fielded fewer articles in economic history, publications of monographs continued, if with reduced frequency. Path-breaking

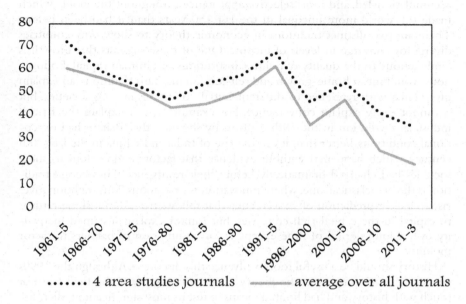

Figure 15.2 Articles on Indian economic history published in leading journals and originating in India (% of total), 1961–2013

Source: *Author's calculation*

research was published, for example, in six themes. These were, the experience of the artisan industries (Tirthankar Roy, Douglas Haynes), monetary and financial history (G. Balachandran), labour and environmental history (Rajnarayan Chandavarkar, Ramachandra Guha, Madhav Gadgil, among others), economic change in the 18th century (Rajat Datta, Neeraj Hatekar, Prasannan Parthasarathi) and, in the light of that literature, reinterpretation of the link between State formation and the economy in the 18th century. The Cambridge historian Chris Bayly's work was influential in framing the 18th-century research agenda, and connecting it to global tendencies and processes.

Already, economic history, banished from the history schools, was beginning to find a new home in the economics schools in North America. This reentry into the mainstream happened via two more recently charted roads, institutional economics and the 'great divergence' debate. Both reshaped the India-bound scholarship in novel ways.

New global movements and a revival

Economic theory had long been interested in the problem of the origin of modern economic growth, 'modern' meaning productivity-led rather than accumulation-led, and in its selective appearance throughout the globe, which made the world more unequal in the last 150 years than it had been before. There are two distinct traditions in economic theory to show why countries diverge or converge in levels of income. One of these suggests that growth is 'endogenous' to the quality of politics, institutions and human capital. Endogenous would mean home-grown and self-reinforcing. This tradition can explain divergence with reference to different initial conditions among societies, but it cannot easily explain convergence. For example, it can explain the British industrial revolution in the 19th century, by showing that Britain had exceptional conditions, better than it can the rise of India and China in the late 20th century, which happened without evidence that factors endogenous to these societies had changed dramatically before their resurgence. The second tradition is the 'neoclassical' one, where innovation is exogenous. This tradition gives rise to a clear prediction of convergence that follows from diminishing returns to capital in the capital-rich countries, but cannot explain sustained inequality over a long period of time except via an assumption of barriers to factor mobility.

History should be a useful tool to advance this discourse. Although the 1990s saw some developments in the theory of economic growth, the field had lost touch with history, and had limited means to test its most significant predictions. The rise of the new institutional economic history – an intellectual programme that belongs in the endogenous growth tradition – breathed new life in the field mainly by having one foot in theory and another in history. The central proposition of the institutionalist school is that, rules (institutions) that reduce the costs of market exchange (costs that arise from risk, uncertainty, opportunism or predation) encourage market exchange and foster growth. These rules do not appear at the same time everywhere, among other reasons because people in power who make rules have an incentive to bend these in their favour. Douglass North's empirical works showed that Britain experienced modern economic growth before the rest of the world thanks to exceptional checks on the exercise of power after 1688. If this were true, and because institutions tend to be persistent, we should expect to see the basic pattern of world inequality to have emerged hundreds of years ago, at least from the 1600s.

Although this is a theory meant to explain inequality in the whole world, the test of the theory stayed Europe-centred until 2000, while being generously speculative about Asia, Africa and Latin America. A 2000 book by Kenneth Pomeranz (now in University of Chicago) changed that. Pomeranz's *The Great Divergence* (2000) challenged the key prediction of institutionalist history that the roots of world inequality took shape in the 1600s, or earlier, by showing that livings standards in a large deltaic region of China and those in England displayed more similarity than difference as recently as 1800. A similar point was earlier advanced by Parthasarathi (1999) with South Indian data. Pomeranz's account of why the two regions diverged thereafter is not relevant here. The 2000s saw a battle unfold between institutional economics and its critics, and forced both camps to seriously engage with India, China, Africa and Latin America.

The debate was global and comparative, and drew attention to a whole range of historical processes and variables that had a potential effect upon world inequality. These included geography and environment, technology, law, consumption, State formation and globalization, in addition to institutional quality measured in diverse ways. The availability of a ready audience for such works in the economics schools encouraged economists to test some of the predictions of the institutionalist and other models of long-term patterns of change, often with surprisingly offbeat datasets (relevant examples might include a joint work by Abhijit Banerji and Lakshmi Iyer on public goods, David Donaldson, Latika Chaudhary and Dan Bogart on railways, and Anand Swamy's co-authored works on contracts, strategy and law). At the same time, new debates started on measurement of living standards, in which Stephen Broadberry, Robert Allen, Bishnupriya Gupta and Prasannan Parthasarathi took part. A recent anthology (Chaudhary et al. eds. 2016) contains a selection of writings inspired by some of these global debates.

One of the more significant works to emerge from this discussion is Studer (2015), which argues that geographical influences on trade costs mattered a lot to which region would see a commercial revolution earlier than others. The book takes the discourse, refreshingly, away from the uncomfortably overgeneralized assumptions about societal differences made by institutional economics. Furthermore, Studer's work pays more attention to regional inequality within India, which complicates the discussion in a necessary way.

For many economists, the reason to get into the divergence debate was the availability of Angus Maddison's international dataset on per capita income, which became fully operational in the 1990s. The field became obsessed with international differences in average incomes, implicitly assuming an identity between one country and one institution. In the process, the method of narrative history retreated somewhat, and quantitative history of the kind published in economics journals became popular. The two methods did not live happily together. Economists, or at least some economic writings, tested causal models, usually with a single explanatory variable. If the cause could be placed in the past, they called this 'history'. Historians did not define history in this way. They studied processes of change, typically processes entailed many mutually interacting causes for the same effect. Econometric technology cannot handle such complexity, and yet, real life history is complex in exactly this way. The results drawn using one type of method would rarely persuade those with more faith in the other method.

All this is rather absurd from the perspective of an Indianist. To see how, let us return to Morris's paradox. Whether India became more like Europe or less like it depended on whether we study Bombay's industries or the forested tribal zones of central India, because their experiences were fundamentally dissimilar. The point of doing Indian history should be to explain inequalities like these that emerged within India. A preoccupation with per capita income would obscure rather than reveal the causes of *this* inequality. Neither the divergence debate nor its institutional underpinnings even recognized the existence of a problem here, blithely testing models of why 'India' fell behind.

The big unfinished business, then, is to explore why divergent tendencies developed in 19th-century India.

Back to India

In a survey of the field, I used the title 'flourishing branches, wilting core' (Roy 2004a). The implication was that the field was doing well when we looked at narrow questions, but it had lost touch with paradigmatic debates. I followed up in the same year with a piece in the *Economic and Political Weekly*, suggesting that the overwhelming dominance of a Marxist-Nationalist narrative of history in the Indian academia around the sole question – how did British rule ruin India? – served the field badly, narrowed its scope, squeezed other questions out of range and made fresh students afraid of falling foul of political correctness (Roy 2004b). The paper met with thoughtful yet critical response from four leading global historians of the time, André Gunder Frank, Roy Bin Wong, Kaoru Sugihara and Kenneth Pomeranz, and a bad-tempered dismissal from Indian stalwarts. Aditya Mukherjee called my work 'revisionism', and as revisionism went, 'bad economic history and even worse political history', 'return of the colonial' (Mukherjee 2008); Arun Banerji called it 'far-fetched' (Banerji 2005) and Amiya Bagchi 'the acme of neocolonial historiography' (Bagchi 2010: li). Banerji treated the symposium in the journal as a pointless conversation between 'four foreign economists'.

I stick by my belief that the discourse needs to change, not just towards revisionism about the historical process, but about what questions we should be asking about the historical process. Why is this necessary and what should be the building blocks of an alternative mode of discussing economic history?

It is necessary quite simply because Morris's point about a paradox is still a valid one, and it has not been addressed adequately. Let me show why the paradox is the heart of the problem. In Figure 15.3, I rearrange the national income statistics for the years 1900 and 1946 taken from the most acceptable estimates available (of S. Sivasubramonian) into three main heads: agricultural production, government and everything else. The residual is dominated by trade, transportation and finance. A simple designation for the three sectors could be peasants, government and capitalists. I make the further assumption that peasant agriculture was constrained, among other factors, by natural resource endowment like soil and water; whereas capitalist business enterprise was particularly responsive to free markets in goods and services.

Figure 15.3 shows that during these years, (i) peasant agriculture grew slowly, or that the geographical influence on economic change was significant and negative, (ii) capitalists did well, or that the open economy encouraged private

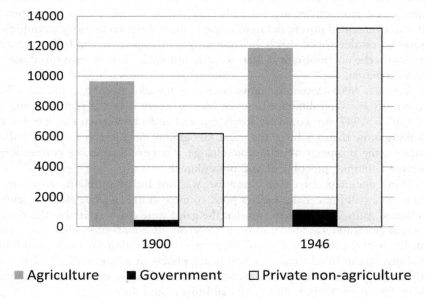

Figure 15.3 GDP by major activities (Rs Billion, in 1938–1939 prices)
Source: *Compiled by author*

investment and entrepreneurship and (iii) the State was weak as an economic agent. The aggregate of the three heads, national income, did not grow fast because of the weight of peasant agriculture, and when normalized by population, did not grow at all. But the trend in income is not the main point of the graph, it is the inequality between peasants and capitalists, and the seeming irrelevance of the State. I should add that Sivasubramonian's data that the graph draws on underestimate commercial profits by a huge margin. He assumed unchanging productivity in trade during these years, whereas tonnage of goods carried by the transport system per head of worker in commerce and transport increased manifold.

Why did openness make India more unequal? I end with three broad propositions in answer to that question.

First, whereas Marxist, Nationalist and institutionalist paradigms place undue stress on the role of the State as an agent in development or underdevelopment, a State-centric analysis of economic change in India cannot go very far because the State had been so small in the past. The State is always important, but long-term patterns of change need to be seen also as a joint outcome of geography and world economy. A simple example will illustrate this point. The State-centric analysis of Indian agricultural problems tends to be preoccupied with private property in land. Those familiar with Indian agricultural conditions would consider that private property in water was more critical to raising land productivity in a tropical climate. Unlike landed property, property in water remained poorly defined by the State, and the technology to improve water access developed slowly because they were expensive and had uncertain effects on the environment. A State-centric history is likely to miss this dimension altogether.

Second, a State-centric narrative overstates the discontinuity more than the continuity between different times in history. Every time the politics changes, as it did in 1947, we would see a dark age end and a new dawn rise. But this is nothing more than a habit of the mind. Geography having such enduring influence on the prospects of economic change, it is necessary to see connections between colonial, precolonial, and postcolonial.

Third, openness, forced or otherwise, was not India's problem. British free trade policy did not make India a poor country. Trade and free factor markets delivered gains. The problem was that the gains were concentrated in the commercial cities, and had little spill-over effects on the countryside. Here again, the smallness of the State, its limited contribution to bridging inequality, and limited investment in education or healthcare, played an indirect role. We have to recognize, however, that public investment is not a magic solution to structural inequality, as the record of postcolonial India would show.

Conclusion

I suggest in this chapter that the mode of argumentation in Indian economic history has been influenced, in different times, by Marxism, institutionalism, development economics, Nationalist sentiments and debates on world inequality. In each case, along with some freshness, some distortions came in. India became an illustration for broader theses about colonial oppression, surplus appropriation or origins of the great divergence. It is a good idea to remind ourselves that none of these starting points allows us to see India itself as a composite and a contradictory bundle of growth and stagnation. The task of the India-bound scholar is to bring that contradiction, or Morris's paradox, to the centre.

There is a contemporary resonance to all this. India remains a country of paradoxes. Its agriculture has run out of momentum and is in a crisis, even as trade and services do fantastically well. The return of liberalism since the 1990s has had a deep transformative impact, but limited spread effect. Regional inequality, and possibly personal inequality, are growing. It would be a pity if the economic historian cannot adapt the tools of trade to show why stagnation and dynamism could co-exist in the present, seeing how normal this condition was in the past.

References

Bagchi, A. K. 1983. *The Political Economy of Underdevelopment*, Cambridge: Cambridge University Press.

Bagchi, A. K. 2010. 'Introduction. Colonial Rule as Structural Adjustment: Expropriation, Agency, and Survival', in A. K. Bagchi (ed.), *Colonialism and Indian Economy*, New Delhi: Oxford University Press, pp. xv–lii.

Banerji, Arun. 2005. 'White Man's Burden', *Economic and Political Weekly*, 40(27), 2973–2978.

Bose, S. ed. 1994. *Credit, Markets and the Agrarian Economy*, New Delhi: Oxford University Press.

Chaudhary, Latika, Gupta, Bishnupriya, Roy, Tirthankar and Swamy, Anand. eds. 2016. *A New Economic History of Colonial India*, London and New York: Routledge.

Guha, Sumit. ed. 1992. *Growth, Stagnation or Decline: Agricultural Productivity in British India*, New Delhi: Oxford University Press.

Habib, I. 1985. 'Studying a Colonial Economy – Without Perceiving Colonialism', *Modern Asian Studies*, 19(3), 355–381.

Habib, I. and Raychaudhuri, T. eds. 1983. *The Cambridge Economic History of India, v. 1, 1200–1751–1970*, Cambridge: Cambridge University Press.

Kumar, D. 1972. 'Economic History of Modern India', *Indian Economic and Social History Review*, 9(1), 63–90.

Kumar, D. ed. 1983. *The Cambridge Economic History of India, v. 2, 1751–1970*, Cambridge: Cambridge University Press.

Ludden, D. eds. 1994. *Agricultural Production in Indian History*, New Delhi: Oxford University Press.

Morris, M. D. 1961. 'Economic History of India: A Bibliographic Essay', *Journal of Economic History*, 1(2), 179–207.

Morris, M. D., Matsui, Toru, Chandra, Bipan and Raychaudhuri, T. 1968. *Indian Economy in the Nineteenth Century: A Symposium*, New Delhi: Indian Economic and Social History Association.

Morris, M. D. and Stein, Burton. 1963. 'Towards a Reinterpretation of Nineteenth Century Indian Economic History', *Journal of Economic History*, 23(4), 606–618.

Mukherjee, A. 2008. 'The Return of the Colonial in Indian Economic History: The Last Phase of Colonialism in India', *Social Scientist*, 36(3–4), 3–44.

Parthasarathi, P. 1999. 'Rethinking Wages and Competitiveness in the Eighteenth Century: Britain and South India', *Past and Present*, 158, 79–109.

Parthasarathi, P. 2012. 'The History of Indian Economic History', Economic History Seminar, London School of Economics and Political Science.

Patnaik, U. ed. 1990. *Agrarian Relations and Accumulation: Mode of Production in Indian Agriculture*, New Delhi: Oxford University Press.

Ray, R. K. 1992. *Entrepreneurship and Industry in India: 1800–1947*, New Delhi: Oxford University Press.

Roy, T. 2004a. 'Flourishing Branches, Wilting Core: Research in Modern Indian Economic History', *Australian Economic History Review*, 44(3), 221–240.

Roy, T. 2004b. 'Economic History of India: An Endangered Discipline', *Economic and Political Weekly*, 39(29), 3238–3243.

Roy, T. 2014. 'The Rise and Fall of Indian Economic History', *Economic History of Developing Regions*, 29(1), 15–41.

Singh, V. B. ed. 1965. *Economic History of India 1857–1956*, Bombay: Allied.

Stein, Burton. ed. 1992. *The Making of Agrarian Policy in British India 1770–1900*, New Delhi: Oxford University Press.

Studer, Roman. 2015. *The Great Divergence Reconsidered. Europe, India, and the Rise to Global Economic Power*, Cambridge: Cambridge University Press.

Chapter 16

On the evolution of heterodox economic thinking in India

Sunanda Sen[1]

Dispelling the official line of thinking in colonial India as a guide to economic policies in the country and deviating from the passive role on part of the general public regarding their acceptance, dissenting voices like Dadabhai Naoroji, Madan Mohan Malaviya and M. Govind Ranade could be heard in India, from as early as the end of the 19th century. Opposition to the ongoing British policies in India emerged from a group of intellectuals with broad leanings to ideas which came to be identified as nationalism.

Spanning the period between the late 19th century and the interwar years, opposition in India to British economic policies covered three major issues. Those included, *first*, the unilateral and unrequited transfers of both tax revenue as well as the sterling proceeds of net export earnings of India – to meet what Britain charged on India as overseas expenditure (or 'home charges') related to colonial administration of the country. A *second* aspect of official policy, questioned by the Nationalists, related to tariffs as well as exchange rates, in relation to the deleterious effects on the upcoming industries in India. The *third* issue was related to the management of credit as well as of external payments, especially during the years of the Great Depression. While the Nationalists continued to cover a number of related aspects in Colonial India, our analysis, in the rest of this chapter, is confined to the three specific aspects we mentioned above. In this, attention is drawn to the ability of the early thinkers in India to anticipate and incorporate many of the heterodox ideas under the banner of economic nationalism, which provided later the basis of industrialization strategies in independent India. As we point out, the perceptions also come close to anticipating the Keynesian aggregate demand analysis, which was yet to be formulated fully in the coming years.

The early years

Tracing back the early beginning of the dissenting voices in India, one can revisit the last two decades of the 19th century, when a group of Nationalists started questioning the ongoing British policies in the country. Attention was drawn to the transfers of tax revenue as well as net export earnings from India to meet overseas expenditure in Britain, legitimized as 'home charges' on colonial India by the British. Policies of such expropriation, as pointed out by the Nationalists, could be held responsible for the impoverishment of the Indian economy. Arguments as above, as we point out in the next section, mark the early beginning of a discourse on political economy in India along heterodox lines of thinking.

References to transfers of resources from India can, however, be noticed even earlier in the context of the rule of the East India Company in the country. Thus Adam Smith in 1776 (Smith 1776: 719) mentioned the East India Company as 'plunderers of India' during 1757 to 1858, the years when India was under its control. Criticisms of the East India Company can also be found in Karl Marx's writings (Marx and Engels 1968:143). As pointed out by Marx, it was possible for the Company to appropriate the entire revenue from trade by monopolizing the merchandise trade of India. Much later, Rajni Palme Dutt, subscribing to the left wing group in England, pointed out that there were 'opportunities of direct plunder in addition to profits on trade' on part of the East India Company (Dutt 1983: 101–102). As elaborated by R.P. Dutt, one third of India's total revenue raised by the Company was sent out as 'clear gain' from India during 1765–1773, corroborating the unfair activities of the East India Company.

Unpaid transfers from India and the macroeconomic impact – the Nationalist critique

Opposition to the continued transfer of funds under British rule mounted up in India in the late 19th century, by when the Nationalist groups within the country were in a position to articulate their views and to mobilize public opinion. One can, in these protests, identify the rising political consciousness of intellectuals in a colonized nation – in turn sharing the basics of economic nationalism.

Economic arguments articulated by the Nationalists also captured the elements of a macroeconomic framework which anticipated the Keynesian frame of analysis, a theory to be developed later in the context of the Great Depression of 1929–1930. For Nationalists, the goal was one of making India free from foreign rule, not only by having more Indians in local administration, but also with economic sovereignty – both denied under British rule.

Nationalist interrogations, on what they considered as the illegitimate appropriation of resources from the country, deviated from the mercantilist notions developed earlier by authors like Thomas Munn and Josiah Child, defending the treasure flows on the part of the East India Company (Mun 1713). Instead, their arguments were directed against the self-justifying assertions by the ruling British power aiming to provide legitimacy for the ongoing, transfer of resources from India. Writings by the Nationalists were effective in generating public opinion and controversies among the contemporaries, which included both Indians and the British. Among the latter were the British officials John Shore, a civilian in Bengal who was writing in 1837, and C.J. Hamilton, an economist writing in 1919, both in astute defense of the empire (Banerji 1982 :177–78,198). In opposition were British officials like George Wingate who made the statement that

> tribute paid to Great Britain (is) . . . the most objectionable feature in our existing policy. Moreover, . . . the cruel, crushing effects of the tribute upon India . . . with taxes raised in one country and spent in another. . . (imply) an absolute loss and extinction of the whole amount withdrawn from the taxed country.
>
> (Royal Commission on Indian Currency 1898:
> Minutes of Evidence Part III)

However, while commentaries from British quarters brought to the fore questionings of the transfer, most other writings in Britain stopped short of such criticisms. Their position was obviously in line with the prevailing official view on British rule in India. Such views had approvals from eminent writers in England like John Maynard Keynes (Keynes 1913) and Theodore Morrison (Morrison 1911:186,197,202), providing further justifications of the empire with empirical research.

For Nationalists at turn of the century and thereafter, the recognition itself of the transfer, notwithstanding the justifications by the British, provided the background to reassert their charter of demands – which included a reduction of home charges along with the Indianization of civil services in the country (McLane 1963). Those demands, however, were wholly rejected by the British government (McAlpin 2007).

Prominent among Nationalists during the period was Dadabhai Naoroji, an academic turned politician. Naoroji founded the Indian National Congress in 1885 and was its President – while continuing as a member of the British Parliament. His attacks on official policies centred on the transfer of resources from India on a unilateral basis, which he considered as politically illegitimate and economically damaging for the country. The transfer, as viewed by Naoroji, was both financial as well physical. As for the financial, Naoroji drew attention to the tax revenue in India's fiscal budget – a part of which was earmarked as 'expenditure abroad' to meet official expenses in Britain (also described as home charges). The latter included what Britain considered as India's liabilities on account of the overseas expenses of British rule in India. As for the financial and the physical counterparts of the transfer, the two respectively related to the tax revenue and the net merchandise, with the sterling proceeds of the latter kept back in London to meet the home charges. According to Naoroji, the twin extractions constituted the 'drain' from colonial India. As for estimates of the latter, he drew attention to the rising transfers of tax revenue as 'expenditure abroad', which had risen from an annual value of £5mn in 1800 to £30mn in

1901. Adding the charges levied on freight, profits and insurance on trade, the amount transferred could be around £40mn (Naoroji (ed)Grover 1982: 5–8); a sum which was enormous as related to the current national income or net export earnings of the country.

Analyzing the economic basis of the arguments related to the drain from India, as formulated by Dadabhai and his followers (which included G.K. Gokhale, M.G. Ranade, etc.), their analysis, in our judgment, narrates the sequence of a *negative multiplier* exercising a dampening effect on the country's income and output. The reasoning lies in the use of a part of domestic revenue to finance overseas expenditure, which was considered as the liability of the colony to meet the home charges. Points formulated by Naoroji can be viewed as precursors of heterodox ideas having a close resemblance to what came up later as Keynesian macroeconomic analysis of effective demand.

The Nationalists, however, did not spell out the actual process of transfer which relied on institutions and instruments set up by British administration. Those involved, as we have pointed out in an earlier study (Sen 1992:71–82), institutions like the Treasury in India, Exchange Banks and the Secretary of State (SOS) in London.

As for the stages of the financial and the physical transfer, it included the transfer of the sum earmarked in the domestic budget in rupees, as 'expenditure abroad', from the Treasury to the SOS in England in sterling. Above was with the inter-mediation of the exchange banks, thus meeting the liabilities towards the home charges. Back in India, trade bills were submitted (by agencies) against the net trade surplus to Exchange Banks, which, cashed in sterling, was used to purchase the Council Bills issued by the SOS. The Council Bills, cashable in rupees, were drawn on the Treasury, which in turn handed over such sums to Exchange Banks to pay the agencies for the sum due on trade bills for net exports. As already mentioned, the sum extracted from the domestic budget as 'expenditure abroad' was thus transferred to the SOS in sterling (and via the Exchange Banks) as home charges. And it was the sterling proceeds from the sale of Council Bills which were retained by the SOS, to be handed over to the financial districts in the London City.

It is understandable from the aforementioned that while the transfer of revenue (earmarked in the budget as expenditure abroad) provided for the payments to the SOS in sterling, the home charges claimed by the British administration as the sterling proceeds of India's net export earnings, were retained in the City, while the counterpart in rupees was paid to exporters in India. I have provided a schematic flow chart in my earlier study to explain the network of transactions as explained previously (Sen 1992:22).

While Naoroji and his followers did not work out the details, as above, of the network of transactions; the implications of the transfer was well understood by them as a clever device on part of Britain to extract resources from India by using the institutions and its political power over the colonized nation. The process ended up, as described by Naoroji, in none other than an 'act of bleeding' (see Naoroji 1901: 73)!

Leaving out a narration of the actual process of financial transfers, the Nationalists emphasized instead on what they viewed as 'unpaid' export surpluses, which, technically, was *not* the reality. Rather the process was one where the sterling counterpart of those surpluses was never brought back to India while its rupee counterpart was, of course paid out to exporters against the trade bills. To complete the story of the transfers, one has to consider the parallel process of transferring to the SOS the rupees earmarked as expenditure abroad via exchange banks. That was the sum which certainly was the tribute India paid as a colony. The details mentioned earlier on the stages of transfer are provided to avoid possible confusions on the process (Sen 1992: 22).[2]

Naoroji's approach to the drain, however, was further enunciated in his other writings as he identified such extraction of the surplus as 'the main cause of famine and mass poverty' of the Indian people. As pointed out,

> It was a pure matter of fact that Great Britain, during the whole period of her connection with India, had never spent a single farthing of British money on the Eastern Empire. . . . Now the amount taken away was officially admitted to be 30 million sterling annually. The result had been to reduce the bulk of Indian population to extreme poverty, destitution and degradation. . . . There could only be one ending to this continual bleeding of India. . . . Famine following upon famine.
>
> Naoroji (ed) Grover 1992:78–79

The statement clearly relies on a macroeconomic argument that extractions of resources, from the domestic budget and from the trade account, generated a contractionary process in the economy, marked by famines and other related consequences (see Bagchi 1989: 92).

Rise of economic nationalism: interwar debates on tariffs and exchange rates

Taxes currently levied on people in India, as pointed out by Dadabhai, was excessive, especially as compared to countries like Britain. As he mentions,

> Now the UK pays 48s.9d from an income of £35.2 per head which makes the incidence or pressure of 6.92% per head of income. British India pays 5s.8d out of an income of 40s which makes the incidence or pressure of 14.3 per cent of the income. Thus, while UK pays for its gross revenue only 6.9 per cent out of its rich income of £35.2 per head, British India pays out of its scantiness and starvation a gross revenue of 14.3 per cent, of its income.
>
> (Naoroji (ed) Grover 1992: 30)

This was also considered by Naoroji as one of the causes of the related distress conditions in the economy. Interestingly, as claimed by him, 'The capacity to bear a burden, with ease or to be crushed by it, is not to be measured by them as percentage of taxation, but by the abundance or otherwise, of the means of income from which to pay it from' (Naoroji (ed)Grover 1992: 85). The point well indicates an endorsement for progressive taxes, which in those days were a far cry from the prevailing practices. A related distinction, between poverty in the context of intra-national and international inequality, as pointed out in a recent study, displays one more original contribution of Naoroji. The notion, for the first time, highlighted the distinction between poverty in the colonies as distinct from that in the context of the imperialist countries (Bhattacharya 2017). Discarding the 'palliative' notion of poverty and famine relief as held by the colonial rulers under the influence of the Benthamite utilitarian explanation relating poverty to inefficiency, Naoroji introduced a macroeconomic causal explanation, with the low level of income providing the causal link (Bhattacharya 2017).

Naoroji also related the state of poverty and the related destitution of people in India to levels of poor consumption on an by average, with the level of food and clothing, as pointed out, was not even enough 'for such food and clothing as a criminal obtains' (Naoroji 1887: 190). In other words, it was even worse than the bare minimum of food and clothing a criminal was entitled to in the prison. The low level of purchasing power in India was also a cause, as Naoroji held, for the rather small value of the country's imports from Britain and other countries. Moreover, imports were low despite the rather free access in India, contrasting the protectionist barriers in Europe and the US. Relating the small imports to the low income levels in India, Naoroji observed,

> only a small proportion of British exports went into that country. Why was it that a small amount was exported to India? Simply because the process of bleeding had been carried onto such an extent that the people had literally, no money left with which to bring British produce.
>
> (Naoroji (ed) Grover 1992: 81)

One clearly notices an early idea of the Keynesian consumption function in these explanations.

Following Dadabhai, his followers took an active interest in articulating their reservations on the colonial policies, especially those concerning the upcoming industries during the period. One here recalls the changed set-up of the economy during the war years of 1914–1918 when a few industries came up. It seemed the colonial government was even ready to offer protection to a few of those, including steel and cotton textiles, primarily to meet wartime demand. The new developments led to further concerns in the country regarding policies regulating the tariff duties and also the exchange rate. Much of those arguments, as we point out later, foresaw the basics of economic sovereignty, a notion yet to take shape.

Among the Nationalists concerned about tariffs included M.G. Ranade, a follower of Dadabhai. In a set of letters written in a pseudo-name, Ranade made a strong case for protection (Datta 1978: 62). He wanted protection along the infant industry argument as advocated in 1841 by Frederick List of the German Historical School (List 1841). While much used in the US and Germany to build up their industries, the plea for infant industry protection remained unheeded in Colonial India.

With the few industries already set up in the country by end of the First World War, a need was felt, even in official circles, to formulate policies concerning those. The Industrial Commission of 1918 was one such indication. In this an Indian member in the Industrial Commission, Madan Mohan Malaviya, submitted a separate note requesting positive State action for industries. Earlier than that, and back in the 1880s, Nationalist demands for protection of Indian industries faced further hurdles when the government had introduced the countervailing excise duties on domestic cotton products (Datta 1978:63-64). As demanded by the Manchester merchants, the measure sought to balance the competing power of imported British cotton goods, which were facing customs duty in India. Since the latter was a good revenue earner, the government could not tamper with it. A solution, thus, was found in the countervailing duties, which took care of the demands by the Manchester group. The step naturally raised added concerns on part of the Nationalists who protested against the measure. Protectionist demands in the country spread to activism by Nationalists in 1905 as the *swadeshi* (national origin) movement gave a call to ban the use of imported goods, primarily of textiles (Sarkar 2011).

The Industrial Commission set up by the British government in 1918 was followed by the Indian Fiscal Commission, 1921–1922 – suggesting, for the first time, a tariff policy for India which, however, was on a discriminatory basis. It included prominent Indian members like Jahangir Coyaji who was in full agreement with the majority position and subscribed to the cautious approach of discriminating protection. Similar sentiments were expressed by H.L. Dey, an economist who pointed at the possible adverse effects of protection on consumers, largely sharing the accepted theories on tariffs in British textbooks. (Dey's analysis, however, provided useful analysis of individual industries in the context of protection).

The Fiscal Commission, guided by Jahangir Coyaji, recommended 'discriminating protection' for selected industries which included steel, matches, cotton textiles and sugar. Objecting to the Nationalist demand for what was viewed by the as 'indiscriminate protection', the Fiscal Commission wanted a cautious approach to tariff protection. However, the 'discriminating protection' as recommended by the Commission was only for selective industries which fulfilled certain conditions, and that too on a temporary basis. In effect the regulation of the duties was left to the Tariff Boards, which were empowered to decide on such issues. Selective approaches to tariff protections, as above, set an agenda for Indians to put up once again, the case for protection *in general*, of domestic industries – providing arguments which later proved influential in shaping the import-substitution strategy of independent India in its first two plans. The Commission also discussed the issue of 'Imperial Preference' which later took a shape in India and other countries within the British Commonwealth area in terms of the Ottawa Agreement, which offered reciprocal tariff concessions in 1932.

Proposals, as mentioned previously, for tariff protection on a selective basis as well as the opposition by Nationalists seeking wider coverage of protection, were, by and large, based on the competitiveness of industries at a micro level. Some members of the Fiscal Commission, backed by the rising industrial groups in India, provided a minority view which opposed the preferential tariffs. With debates on tariff policies in British India, attention was drawn, for the first time in India, to industry-specific issues relating to tariffs.

Nationalist demands for protection consolidated further over next few years, with conceptual clarity as was provided in Adarkar's 1941 book based on the Keynesian view relating to aggregate demand and protection (Adarkar 1941). As pointed out by the renowned teacher and scholar, Bhabatosh Datta, in an exhaustive survey of Indian Economic Thought, while Keynesian ideas were yet to take roots fully in Indian economic writings, an exception included the work by B.N. Adarkar 'who stood as a strong advocate of protection for stimulating industrial growth' (Datta 1978: 64–65,69). Refuting the plea for discriminating protection along the lines suggested in the 1921 Fiscal Commission Report, Adarkar tried to lay the ground for protection as a means to achieve industrialization in the underdeveloped economies like India under colonial rule. As held by Professor Datta, 'By the time Adarkar wrote, the Keynesian ideas had enthralled those who favoured state regulation with a view to achieving further employment and output, and they had added respectability to some of the basic principles of mercantilism' (Datta 1978: 71).

Official policies in the Indian economy, which by the 1920s witnessed the early beginning of specific manufacturing industries, generated further debates on aspects of official policies as mentioned earlier. In addition to tariffs, those related to exchange rates and gold exports from the country. Tariffs and exchange rates were both of importance for domestic manufactures in terms of their competitive position *vis a vis* foreign products; while gold exports, especially during the Great Depression years of 1929–1931, were attributed to the distress sales on part of the impoverished peasants, much used by the British administration to manage external payments.

As with the opposition related to discriminating tariff and the demands for overall protection, the sterling value of the rupee also came up as a major point of controversy between the colonial and the contesting voices in the country. It may be recalled here that the exchange rate of the silver rupee, as officially managed, was never allowed to find its level in terms of purchasing power parity or the market price of the metallic content of the silver coin. The official rate of 1sh 4d during 1893–1914 was, however, considered as overvalued by the Indians when silver prices started falling in world market with the switch-over to gold standard all over. For Britain, however, it suited them to pitch the rupee rate high for transferring more easily the sum abroad to meet the home charges. As for India, the country never was given an opportunity to be on gold standard, in spite of the fact that the country earned, as export surpluses, large sums in gold-backed sterling. Rather, the country was subject to shortage and stringency of credit, much of which was related to inadequate silver imports from Britain, while silver trade was monopolized by the London-based merchants (Sen 1992:93–146).

As the First World War broke out in 1914, the rupee was set to float as a part of wartime measures by the ruling government. With rising silver prices during the war, the initial spurt in the rupee rate led it to reach unprecedented highs. In the following years, Britain went back to the gold standard in 1925 and fixed the sterling at the pre-war rate in gold. These changes initiated further adjustments in India's exchange rate policy as a Committee was appointed under Hilton and Young in 1926. The latter recommended the rupee rate to be determined in terms of the gold price of sterling. The procedure ended up in fixing the rupee at 1sh 6d, a rate considered by the Indian critics as too high, even compared to the earlier rate at 1sh 4d. The move, in particular, was opposed by exporters (Indians as well as European export houses) while it was also pointed out by Indian industrialists that the higher rate would ease the entry of British imports by making them cheaper within India (Sen 2002 in Bagchi (ed.) 2002: 189–194). However, the higher rate was providing benefits to the government by reducing the rupee cost of home charges (accounted in the budget as expenditure abroad), and to the expatriates in India fetching higher sterling value of the remittances they sent home, by using the overvalued rupee. Jahangir Coyaji, the loyalist who was a member of the 1926 currency committee as well, was on defense of the 1sh 6d rate – on the grounds that prices in the country had already adjusted to exchange rates. The notion however, was conceptually incorrect in terms of the prevailing purchasing power parity theory already developed by Cassel (1918: 413–415), explaining exchange rate variations by relative prices between countries which determine the purchasing power of countries. As protests came up from concerned circles within the country more arguments came up in a book (Vakil and Muranjan 1927) from Western India (Datta 1978: 78–82) Dwelling on the Casselian purchasing power parity doctrine in the context of the floating exchange rates in India, the authors questioned the official position (subscribed by Coyaji) that prices in India had *already* adjusted to the (higher) exchange rate of the rupee. They pointed out the relevance of prices determining the exchange rate rather than the other way out. An analysis close to a Keynesian approach on exchange rate effects on aggregate demand was also there in Ganguli's theoretical attack on the deflationary impact of an overvalued currency as in those days (Ganguli 1977: 72–73).

Ottawa Imperial protection 1932

The global scene, however had fast changed as India was facing, along with the rest of world, the Great Depression of 1929–1932. For Britain, a way out was to enter into a reciprocal preferential agreement covering India and other Commonwealth countries in the Ottawa Agreement in 1932. It laid the basis for the introduction of Imperial Preferences, which implied for India a 10% duty concession for goods traded between India and Britain (Bagchi 1978: 85–92). The issue, as discussed by the Fiscal Commission of 1922, was opposed in a minority note of dissent by five Indian members, who declined to consider the move till the country got a self-governance status (Datta 1978 :64–66). That Ottawa Agreement on Imperial preferences was of little benefit to India was pointed out in two major studies by Indian authors B.K. Madan and D. Ghosh, both decrying the unequal trade relations between India and the ruling nation, Britain (Datta 1978:66).

The points raised on tariff protection as well as the exchange rates were also close to the position of a group which was described later as the 'Bombay School'. It was subscribed by the upcoming industrial groups in Western India. Prominent among the group was Purshottamdas Thakurdas, an industrialist who drew attention to the contractions faced by the Indian cotton textile industry on account of the overvalued exchange rate. On the whole, the macroeconomic reasoning of the Keynesian variety was slowly entering the discourses, especially in academic circles the contemporaries among whom were, as already mentioned, B.N. Adarkar and also M. Visvesvaraya (M. Visvesvaraya 1936: 3–4).

Managing the Great Depression in India: Nationalist critiques of distress sales of gold and their exports from India

Studies by Indian authors also questioned the large outflows of gold from India to Britain which, as it was argued, negated the possibility for the country to ever have a gold-based currency. As for the outflows of gold from the country, the official position rested on the prevailing price disparity with gold fetching lower prices in India as compared to what prevailed in Britain. Analysis offered in Indian writings covered more grounds. As pointed out by Sinha, a contemporary, the sharp fall in world prices of primary products during the depression years of the 1930s led peasants in the Indian countryside face acute financial problems (Sinha 1938). This led to some distress sales of gold in the local market, of which a large part made way as exports from the country. In the aforementioned study, Sinha provided, for the first time, a sectoral analysis of the distress in India's agricultural sector which bore the major brunt of the Great Depression (Datta 1978: 87–88).

Of the others active in countering the British position on gold exports from India, there was N.R. Sarkar, the President of the Bengal Chamber of Commerce. Sarkar, along with other members of the Chamber of Commerce, was keen on retaining gold as reserves located in India, to be used as a base for gold currency in the country (Mukherjee in (ed.) Bagchi 2012: 149–163).[3] Pointing at the fallacy advanced by Britain that gold exports from India were needed to pay for India's imports, as pointed out by the British Finance Minister Schuster, Sarkar pointed at the adverse consequences of those imports on indigenous production and industry within the country (Mukherjee 2002). The position was clearly one which tallied with the arguments for economic nationalism and industrialization, as developed in what was formulated by industrialists as the Bombay Plan, which later turned out as a harbinger of independent India's Five Year Plans.

The use of India's export earnings in sterling along with the official policy on silver imports to the country as needed to sustain credit flows therein, generated resentments within the country. Interestingly, the latter included the Anglo-Indian banking community and even the government officials in India. Given the shortfall in silver imports to the country and the credit stringency that resulted, protests were lodged from those quarters opposing the British authorities. The situation was one with interest rates in the economy hitting extremely high levels which, along with the fiscal strategy to siphon off tax revenue abroad, were responsible to a state of acute contractionary process in the country. For Britain, policies to limit imports of silver suited their interests, both in the interest of sterling accumulations and the silver lobby in the city. Incidentally, the impact felt in India also included the collapse of a large number of domestic banks and also bankruptcy of the local silver traders (Sen 1992: 93–119). Protests and disagreements mentioned previously, as voiced by the local banking community, also indicated their heed to achieve a state which was not far from economic nationalism.

Concluding remarks

This chapter seeks to draw attention to the much-neglected early economic thinking in India. As we emphasize in this chapter, the ideas came up in opposition to British economic policies and the macroeconomic implications of the prevailing policies of the colonial government. Those included the unilateral transfer of resources from the country resulting in famines and poverty, the discriminatory tariff duties and an absence of protection in general which violated the inception of industrialization, the use of the overvalued exchange rate of the rupee having similar consequences, the credit stringencies in the economy as resulted from shortage of silver imports and, finally, the continued transfer of net export earnings from the country under the guise of the so-called home charges (including distress sales of gold in depression years). All of these indicate an early beginning of unconventional ideas based on economic nationalism.

Opposition to ongoing policies, as formulated earlier in colonial India provided the groundwork for policies in independent India, especially in the first two five-year plans. Earlier than that, in 1944, eight major industrialists in the country drafted what came to be known as the Bombay Plan, relying much on the arguments developed earlier in the frame of economic nationalism. The Plan emphasized the role of the State and of the public sector, while discouraging imports financed by foreign capital. The group later allied with the Congress Party, protesting against British rule. The emphasis in the Bombay Plan on the State as a harbinger of growth and on the role of basic industries for industrialization with little role of foreign capital shaped policies in the first three of India's Plan models.

On the whole, the rise and the development of ideas in pre-independent India, shaping economic nationalism, provided a framework which also suited big capital in framing plans to ensure a domestic market for independent India. Much of those were carried forward in the country's planning exercises, bent on industrialization and an import-substituting strategy. The pattern, however, has changed over time, giving way to a collaborative regime where domestic capital (both in industry and finance) as well as the State have accepted the predominance of overseas finance and State powers over the national economy. Much of the earlier notions of economic nationalism as developed in colonial India have thus been buried under dust in the process.

Notes

1 The author thanks Ajit Sinha and Alex Thomas along with other participants at the 'Economics and its History' conference at Azim Premji University in November 2016 for their comments on an earlier version of this chapter.

2 We notice, in a recent paper, a claim that my interpretation of the transfer, in my 1992 book *Colonies and Empire: India 1890–1914* was wrong in 'faulting' the Nationalists on the ground of their argument that net exports of India remained unpaid during the colonial period. As I point out in this chapter, and also earlier in my book mentioned previously, the institutional arrangement which provided for the transfer of rupees under the budgetary head of 'Expenditure Abroad' to the SOS went, side-by-side, with the appropriation of the sterling proceeds of India's net trade surpluses by the ruling country. The two acts were separate, and signified, between them, the home charge–related 'financial' and the trade balance–related 'physical' transfers constituting the 'drain' from India as held by the Nationalists. The latter, by overlooking the process, merged the two-part process as one, which inevitably fails to capture the stages including the payments to exporters. In other words, the fact remains that the sterling proceeds of the trade surplus were retained in England does *not* capture the rest of the transfer relating to the transfer abroad of the earmarked budgetary expenditure. Hopefully the confusion in interpreting the analysis in my 1992 book will be over by the present analysis.

See Utsa Patnaik, "Revisiting the "Drain" or the Transfer from India to Britain in the context of Global Diffusion of Capitalism in S. Chakrabarti and U Patnaik (Chakrabarti and Patnaik 2017: 288–289).

3 Speech of N.R. Sarkar, Bengal National Chamber of Commerce (BNCC) 5 February 1932, Purushottamdas Thakurdas Papers, press clippings f 1 11 Nehru Memorial Museum and Library, New Delhi. Cited in Aditya Mukherjee (Mukherjee in Bagchi (ed) 2004: 157–159).

References

Adarkar, B. P. 1941. *The Indian Fiscal Policy*, Allahabad: Kitabistan.

Bagchi, A. K. 1989. *The Presidency Banks and the Indian Economy, 1876–1914*, Oxford: Oxford University Press.

Bagchi, A. K. 1972. *Private Investment in India: 1900–1939*, Cambridge: Cambridge University Press.

Banerji, A. K. 1982. *Aspects of Indo-British Economic Relations, 1858–1898*, Oxford: Oxford University Press.

Bagchi, A. K. (ed.). 2012. *Money and Credit in Indian History: From Early Medieval Times*. New Delhi: Tulika Books.

Bhattacharya, S. 2017. 'The Concept of Poverty in Colonial India', in S. Chakrabarti and U. Patnaik (eds.), *Agrarian and other Histories*, New Delhi: Tulika.

Cassel, G. 1918. 'Abnormal Deviations in International Exchanges', *The Economic Journal*, 28(112), 413–415.

Chakrabarti, S. and Patnaik, U. eds. 2017. *Agrarian and Other Histories*, New Delhi: Tulika.

Datta, B. 1978. *Indian Economic Thought: Twentieth Century Perspectives, 1900–1950*, Tata McGraw-Hill.

Dutt Palme, R. 1983. *India Today*, Calcutta: Manisha Granthalaya.

Ganguli, B. 1977. *Indian Economic Thought*, Tata McGraw Hill Publishing Co. Ltd.

Grover, V. ed. 1992. *Dadabhai Naoroji*, Vol. 12. Deep and Deep Publications.

Keynes, J. M. 1913. *Indian Currency and Finance*. Palgrave Macmillan.

List, F. 1841. *National System of Political Economy*, Philadelphia: JB Lippincott & Company.

Marx, K. and Engels, Friedrich. 1968. *On Colonialism*. Progress.

McAlpin, M. B. 2007. 'Price Movements and Fluctuations in Economic Activity', in D. Kumar and M. Desai (eds), *Cambridge Economic History of India, Vol II*. Cambridge.

McLane, J. 1963. 'Drain of Wealth and Indian Nationalism at the Turn of Century', in T. Roychoudhury (ed.), *Contributions to Indian Economic History, Vol II*, Calcutta, p. 40.

Morrison, T. 1911. *Economic Transition in India*. London: John Murray.

Mukherjee, A. 2012. 'The Depression Years', in A. K. Bagchi, *Money and Credit in Indian History*, pp. 157–159.

Mun, T. 1713. *England's Treasure by Foreign Trade: Or, the Balance of Our Foreign Trade Is the Rule of Our Treasure*, J. Morphew.

Naoroji, D. 1887. *Essays, Speeches, Addresses and Writings, (on Indian Politics,) of the Hon'ble Dadabhai Naoroji*.

Naoroji, D. 1901. *Poverty and Un-British Rule in India*, London: Swan Sonnenschein & CO.

Sarkar, S. 2011. *The Swadeshi Movement in Bengal, 1903–1908*, New Delhi: Orient Longman.

Sen, S. 1992. *Colonies and the Empire: India, 1890–1914*, New Delhi: Orient Longman.

Sen, S. 2012 'Money and Finance in the Periphery – A Tool of Expropriation in Colonial India', in A. K. Bagchi (ed.), *Money and Credit in Indian History: From Early Medieval Times*. New Delhi: Tulika Books.

Sinha, J. C. 1938. *Indian Currency Problems in the Last Decade. 1926–36*, New Delhi: University of Delhi.

Smith, A. 1776. *The Wealth of Nations, Book 1*, London: Methuen & Co.

Vakil, C. N. and Muranjan, S. K. 1927. *Currency and Prices in India*. London: P. S. King & Son.

Visvesvaraya, M. 1936. *Planned Economy for India*, Bangalore: Bangalore Press.

Chapter 17

Two sides of the colonial coin

British and Indian women's engagements with colonialism and patriarchy

Sheetal Bharat[1]

Introduction

In the early centuries of recorded history in India, slaves and other underprivileged groups made up a majority of the subcontinental population. Women, as in almost any time or place in history, made up a half; they did not enjoy the same freedoms that men did. Lepers and other physically deformed people added to the numbers. These proportions of the population that may be referred to as marginalized are so large that they almost challenge the definition of marginality.

There is no such thing as fair history that is representative of the concerns of these marginalized groups. That said, given the abundance of literature produced by various groups of people in the colonial period, it is possible to construct a more democratic account of historical events that does not appear to have been written by the winners. This chapter looks at the literature produced by women who lived in colonial India to gain an understanding of the various and opposing forces at play with regard to the British occupation of India, and related aspects of these women's lives.

The British women who lived in India and, to an extent, called it home, represent one side of the colonial coin. They helped maintain the government machinery in ways that are not adequately acknowledged in modern scholarship, nor indeed by the dominant thinking of the colonial times. The Nationalist leadership and the tens of thousands of women who participated in the freedom struggle represent the other side. With the help of the material that both these groups of women wrote, this chapter brings out their respective positions with regard to the perceived legitimacy of foreign rule, and their impressions of specific government actions or inactions. They also yield an insight into the considerations that informed their decisions.

The texts

There is plenty of evidence in literary works from all ages and geographies of the maltreatment meted to underprivileged groups.[2] These works are almost always written by the sufferer rather than the perpetrator of the indignities. In the context of colonial India, the perpetrators were British officers of the East India Company, and, later, the officers appointed by the India Office in London. In this sweeping statement, the role of the British women who accompanied officers or travelled alone is hidden. They were not direct perpetrators of any crimes. In fact, they were sometimes critical of the maladministration that colonialism entailed (Raza 2006: 216), and many British women served the Indian population by providing education and vocational training. Yet, their complicity in colonialism, and, in some cases, even in the associated violence is starkly reflected in their writings. The roles they played through their writings and actions were essential to the sustenance of British rule in India. The sufferers, on the other hand, were, in one way or another, all Indian nationals. Women faced the double burden of being second-class members in a patriarchal society as well as being second-class citizens in a country under foreign rule. They were simultaneously engaging in two fights: as feminists, they fought patriarchy, and as Nationalists, they fought colonialism. Each had important influences on the other. Particularly, the fight against patriarchy played a crucial role in mobilizing women against colonialism, to an extent setting back the clock on feminism.

The literature that forms the resource base for this chapter is authored by women from a range of cultures, languages, religions and perspectives. British women wrote their memoirs, letters to personal friends, guide books on living in India and popular novels. Their memoirs and letters reveal their innermost sensibilities about their precarious political position in a colony. The guide books they authored were ever-practical and invaluable for new officers and ladies visiting the new continent. Their novels reflected their interpretation of the politics in and culture of their adopted home. At least one Indian woman, Cornelia Sorabji, sympathized with British rule in India and did all in her power to support it. The Nationalist literature produced by Indian women and cited here appears mostly as journal articles[3] and speeches to bring alive to the masses the consequences of continued foreign rule and to incite them to action. Feminist literature by Indian women is in the form of novels[4] and newspaper articles. Since patriarchy was a more chronic issue, it did not demand urgent measures like speeches as colonialism did. Public speeches touched on feminism only to the extent that it would help the Nationalist cause.

A lot of these writings were based on a cultural exchange between British and Indian women. Both sides learnt a great deal about a new culture, a new kind of social arrangement and tried to place their own in comparison. Naturally, the freedom to appear and move about in public that British women enjoyed would have seemed incredible to the homebound Indian woman. Further, 'the possibility of a female ruler constantly fascinated Indian women. The awareness that there were other social models began to create a sense of the limitations of their own customs' (Raza 2006: 159). British women, on the other hand, were astonished by the illiteracy and superstitions that Indian women lived with.

> Women's texts force us to confront, even as they help us chart, the awesome historical texturing that situates and governs feminist initiatives in

our time. Read thus, stories and poems that might otherwise appear to be concerned only with an existential agony or with spiritual endurance, lay bare their politics.

(Tharu and Lalita, Vol II 2006: 70)

With this justification for choosing to look at the political institution of colonialism through women's literature, this chapter now proceeds to discuss how some women – mostly British, and Cornelia Sorabji – undergirded the British administration in key ways while also criticizing it and advocating for rights for Indians. The latter section, after briefly discussing women's – mostly Indian, and some British – Nationalistic efforts, looks at how these efforts interacted with the feminist agenda.

Women who oiled the colonial machinery

British women were not permitted by the East India Company to accompany the officers who came to the new tropical colony throughout the 17th century, since the mortality rate for the European population in South Asia was high. It was only in the later decades of the 18th century that a few officers' wives and sisters and some missionaries braved the new environment and culture. Throughout the 19th century, the female population from England grew steadily so that there was a unique British–Indian domestic and social culture, as distinct from British culture.

The Indian custom of *pardah* required women, at least those from the higher castes, to remain in the *zenana*, secluded from all males not immediately related. This meant that British men could never find out how upper caste Indian women lived, and so could never exercise control over zenana activities like they were able to control the larger political and economic environment in India (Ghose 1998: 52). It was a dangerous 'unexplored and uncolonised' space (Forbes 1998: 97). This was an important consideration because each zenana was a world by itself: larger zenanas had their own special markets and schools. Zenanas were easily accessible to interested British women 'due to the asymmetry of opportunity derived from Indian social custom' (Raza 2006: 152). They were able to visit zenanas, write about them and so open up a world of information to the male officers of the government. By the late 19th century, the India Office realized the necessity of instituting a Court of Wards, a special court to manage properties in cases when the 'proprietors shall be held disqualified to manage their own property'. This could be assumed if the proprietors were 'incompetent' women, minor heirs who lived with their mothers in the zenana or persons 'of unsound mind' (Court of Wards Act 1879: Part H; Sorabji 1934: 118). Once a property fell into the hands of any person who may have been described in this manner, it was difficult for the regular courts to investigate or at all intervene because of pardah norms. The Court of Wards needed special powers to manage such properties, or, to put it another way, it needed special provisions to divest the woman or child of his/her ownership of the property and gain control of it. Cornelia Sorabji (1934), an Indian lawyer who served as the Lady appointed to the Court of Wards, provides instances, much to her displeasure, of British officers mistreating wards and misappropriating properties. An understanding of what was needed, legally, to extract revenues or control zenana properties would not have been possible without an understanding of what went on inside and who wielded what kind of power. This was afforded by the British women who visited and reported from within zenana quarters.

The quality of description of any new culture is often coloured by the general perception of the age. In the 18th and early 19th centuries, British scholarship tended to be appreciative of Indian religion and culture, as it provided a contrast to the seemingly shallow industrial culture of new Europe. By the mid-19th century, this perception was visibly changing, as utilitarian thought differently coloured the same India. The descriptive language changed from appreciative and curious, to insulting and parochial.

> The rise of utilitarian thought led to the rejection of the orientalist celebration of Indian culture. James Mill's *History of India* (1818), which became a key text, denigrated Indian achievement, especially Hindu, while Macaulay's notorious Minute on Education (1835) claimed the superiority of European literature and culture. . . . The belief that the Hindu religion 'surpasses all others in depravity' shaped the way many later women presented India to the Western world.
>
> (Raza 2006: 187–188)

Early British women writers were trying to make Indian culture more accessible by popularizing Indian scholarship, and writing about and creating art based on dying Hindus, dashing Sikhs, exotic *fakirs* and adventurous traders (Raza 2006: 10, 181–182, 185). In line with Macaulay's Minute on Education, the early 19th-century British women who formally worked in India were 'restricted [by the British manifestation of patriarchy] to teaching in well-to-do homes, where their introduction of English language and mores ran parallel to the administration's policy of anglicisation' (147). That said, the restriction of women to the teaching occupation did not restrict their influence. From their place in the domestic and social sphere, women shaped the values which their men carried to their offices (67). Several British women thought that 'you can only rule Asiatics by fear' (Ghose 1998: 100) because they were 'comparatively unenlightened people' (Raza 2006: 200) who did not deserve political freedom (212). 'The association of dark colour with negative qualities created a vocabulary of abuse which rose in intensity as the nineteenth century progressed. Women's writing unconsciously reflected this' (203). Katherine Harris, soon after the first war of independence in 1857,[5] called for Delhi 'to be razed to the ground' since it was an 'everlasting memorial of the galling insult offered to England's honour' (Ghose 1998: 100). Mrs. Coopland celebrates the 'privilege of living in a country where freedom reigns', but does not reveal an appreciation of the fact that her own free country was eliminating political freedom in India (101). A similar sentiment was held by several other British women writers, though there was no evident inconsistency. They were serving Indian women most diligently by providing education and vocational training. They also held that British rule was benevolent (Forbes 1998: 4, 120; Raza 2006: 211). 'By defining the other as backward, English women were able to define themselves as emancipated, civilised and rational creatures' (Ghose 1998: 61). This, according to Emily Eden, legitimized 'continued colonial rule over a people so obviously unfit to take up responsibility for itself' (63).

Apart from performing the acceptably feminine tasks for the empire, like working as teachers and nurses, and providing secretarial and medical assistance (Raza 2006: 126–127), British women ventured out to a particularly unorthodox area of enterprise for a woman. They travelled to parts of the subcontinent that were till then unknown in Britain (180). Julia Harvey travelled with a retinue of Indian servants in 1850 to Kashmir, Ladakh and Tibet (162). Emma Roberts's personal accounts of her experience of living in India were published as a series of articles, and when the demand for her guide grew, the articles were published as a book (7). She wrote in detail about the clothes, food, skills and equipment needed for comfortable living in India. An anonymous woman wrote about how to care for children in India and also some recipes for women of modest means (15). Ann Elwood gave detailed time tables for the travel between India and England with 'copious practical recommendations in the appendix' (14). Several of these publications became standard references for those planning a career or life in general in the subcontinent (25). They remained in print and widely circulated for decades. Published in London, Edinburgh and Calcutta (15), these books and articles by British women in India opened a whole new world of experience for those who were learning about the new colony back in England (5, 147). What made women's works particularly popular was 'a personal tone, lightness of touch, vivacity [and] deft treatment of themes' (7), apart from the publications also being 'cheap' and 'authentic' (24). Interpreted another way, these women were performing the characteristically feminine task of oiling the machinery on mundane tasks so that the running of the empire, a male prerogative, was smoother.

Apart from British women supporting British rule in India, colonization drew strength from other women too. Katherine Mayo came as a formidable voice justifying British rule, and that, well into the 20th century when the imperial power itself had started negotiating a respectable exit. She was an American who spent six months in India and wrote her book *Mother India* 'in a vivid, popular style and filled with gruesome details and anecdotes' (Teed 2003: 37). Her thesis was that Indians were exhausted from over exposure to sexuality from too young an age and too given to superstition and unproductive pursuits to be able to contribute productively to the progress of their lives and their country. She connected the high level of political activism in Bengal, itself an accepted idea, and Bengal being a 'stronghold of strict purdah', also a justifiable statement, with a claim that Bengal was 'among the most sexually exaggerated regions in India' (Mayo 1937: 122). She was suggesting that the custom of pardah led to sexual frustration, which in turn led men to seek gratification in 'eccentric crime[s]'.[6] '[W]ith strong racist overtones' (Gooptu 2006: 173), *Mother India* presented the worst in Indian culture. By Mayo's own admission, she 'never intended to make a rounded picture of India' (*ibid.*). The immense popularity of the book meant that India was being shown in an unfavourable light the world over, in several languages, over several editions and, later, in technicolour. Mayo carried her views to the political arena and 'insisted that India's independence should be resisted by all informed Westerners so long as the society's rampant sexuality and its brutal suppression of women and low-caste Hindus continued unchecked' (Teed 2003: 37). She was referring to the practices of child marriage, *sati* and untouchability.

One such 'informed Westerner' was Cornelia Sorabji, an Indian woman who lived in England for extended periods for her legal studies and to recover her health. Sorabji's favourable review of *Mother India* made her even more unpopular in Nationalist circles than she already was (Gooptu 2006: 173). The manifestation of 'mid-Victorian British conservative political thinking' (182) in her interactions led her to nurse a 'disdain for the "rabble" and for "excesses of democracy"' (67). She felt that the British administration had brought 'co-operation and unity' through and after the First World War, and that the Indian National Congress was responsible for a lot of 'disruption' (Sorabji 1934: 261). She was certain that Mohandas Gandhi and his public image were being abused by the Congress's propaganda machine (271), and fighting the essentially benevolent British rule was unwise. Even though she was aware that the British men she encountered at the Bar had no professional ethics (Gooptu 2006: 143), even though her professional requests to the administration were too often ignored, and she was repeatedly insulted (119–120), she allowed herself to be used by the administration as the Lady appointed to the Court of Wards, to extend and strengthen their control of property and their authority over the colony in general (95). Her appointment was meant to ensure smooth administration, rather than good administration (103–104). The First World War provided another opportunity for the British administration to use Sorabji's efficiency to its advantage. Since the Indian language news reports seemed to be using the same word for the English and the Germans, listeners were confused about world events. Sorabji wrote a series of War Letters and made a series of War Talks to clarify issues for her 'illiterate charges' (aristocratic women whom she represented in the Court of Wards and towards whom she had developed a deep sense of responsibility). Her letters were then circulated by the administration to all the presidencies of the colony (Sorabji 1934: 255) to clarify the positions and so justify India's war contributions.

In addition to Sorabji's imperialist sympathies, her reservations against the Nationalist struggle warrant elaboration to bring out her position on the rights of the underprivileged. Gandhi had chosen *swadeshi* (that of one's own country) as a preferred tool in the Nationalist struggle. The recognition that the Indian population had of the economic exploitation of the colony, made the Nationalist insistence on swadeshi convincing. The solution, then, as proposed by Gandhi was to revive the traditional arts and occupations of the Indian villages – primarily, the art of hand-spinning cotton threads and hand-weaving coarse fabrics – for three reasons: to provide a livelihood to the unemployed and underemployed millions, to instil a sense of pride in the national heritage and, if enough people participated, to ensure that India does not need to rely on imported machine-made fabric. Sorabji had a problem with the idea of swadeshi, not because it was an unwise strategy, but because it was followed for political rather than economic reasons (Sorabji 1934: 264). She personally inquired into the difference in price between Lancashire and hand-made cloth and found that the Lancashire variety was half as expensive as the local one. Under such circumstances, it was ridiculous to expect poor people to purchase the more expensive cloth. On further inquiry, she found that it was impossible to make the local produce any cheaper either: so the entire swadeshi movement was bound to fail. Sorabji was, of course, taking the conservative view of economic policy, and looking at the economic rights of producers and consumers, rather than human rights. Granting consumers the right to purchase cheap fabric was effectively granting British industrialists the right to manipulate international trading rules to benefit themselves over their much poorer competitors in India. Sarojini Naidu captures the human rights view in a powerful speech (further discussion of her role in the Nationalist struggle belongs in the following section):

> [E]very inch spun of this stuff (pointing to her *saree* [made from course hand-spun, hand-woven fabric, *khadi*]) there is the benediction of a women who knows that her hands are buying bread for her little children. . . . The women behind the *Pardah*, who cannot go out as their Hindu sisters do, have blessed the spinning wheel because it has saved them from the reproach that they are idlers hanging on the one solitary wage earner.
>
> (Naidu 1925: 294–295)

Yet another instance of Sorabji finding herself 'unfortunately on the wrong side of history' (Gooptu 2006: 6) was with the Temple Entry Bill of 1934. She was certain that permitting lower caste people to enter temples would cause 'bloodshed on a scale unknown since the British Occupation of India', and that the proponents of the Bill were only using it as an election 'stunt' (Sorabji 1934: 275). Sorabji held the orthodox Hindu sentiment as sacred and went to great lengths to protect it from attack.[7]

History recognizes the Governors-General as the heroes of empire, but the women's roles in supporting and sustaining British rule for as long as it survived was crucial, though largely invisible.

Women who fought colonialism

Indian nationals formed the mass of the Nationalist movement. Powerful political speakers spoke relentlessly about freedom from British rule as India's birthright. Madam Bhikaji Cama pointed out the irresponsibility in the expenditure pattern of the colonial government as one of several reasons (Sharma 2011: 97). Naidu's speeches electrified thousands of students in each rally. She made references to Gandhi in many of her speeches, claiming to spread his message of non-violence and *satyagrah* (insistence on the truth). One of Gandhi's most fundamental beliefs in Indian culture derived from the village economy. Naidu highlighted India's tradition of administration through village councils as an institution to be revived and strengthened (Naidu 1925: 136). Some of her most powerful words were reserved for encouraging the common person to do his/her part to build healthy institutions. These speeches by her and others played a big role in informing the masses about the injustice of foreign rule and gathering support to oust it. The freedom struggle was a collective action problem – few people's efforts hinged, for success, on the dedicated support of the masses, and the dedicated support for politics was a tall call on a people who lived on the edge of poverty. The magnitude of the collective action problem was multiplied by the cultural and linguistic diversity in the country (Bardhan 1999: 17). Naidu spoke passionately about the need for unity among the many religious and caste groups in India (Naidu 1925: 37, 85, 243). She suggested that the true greatness of a country is not measured by its greatest people – by its Gandhis and Tagores, but rather by the greatness of its 'average' people (39–40). These efforts were critical to incite the masses to struggle against British rule.

A movement cannot take on a mass characteristic without the participation of women. The use of religious symbolism played an important role in encouraging women to step out of their homes and participate in the struggle. India was imagined as a woman[8] (the inspiration for Mayo's book title – *Mother India*) who was in danger of being violated by a foreign male – the British (Thapar-Bjorkert 2006: 83). This imagery derived directly from, as well as challenged, the 'colonial discourse which hinged on the feminised subordination of the whole nation, femininity associated with retrogressive rather than progressive qualities' (91). In response, the Nationalist rhetoric imagined girls and women as 'the powerful Durga [warrior goddess in Hindu mythology] in disguise' (Thapar-Bjorkert 2006: 86). This strategy of using 'an incredibly effective deployment of gods and goddesses' to justify certain actions has long had currency in India: Emperor Asoka employed this strategy effectively in the 3rd century BCE (Lahiri 2016: 137).

> In highlighting women's roles as mothers, wives and nurturers, women were often exalted to the status of devis or goddesses. . . . [This] helped to 'Hinduise the tone of nationalism'. . . . Participation in the Congress agitation also meant performing one's religious duty and the interdependence

and mutability of the two ideas 'enabled nationalism to transcend the realm of politics and elevate itself to a religious domain!

(Thapar-Bjorkert 2006: 87)

This Hinduized nationalism pervaded all the media that women were being exposed to, including magazine run by women themselves – Mokshodayani Mukhopadhyay's *Banga Mahila* (Tharu and Lalita Vol I 2015: 217), Swarna-kumari Devi's *Bharati* (237), Kalyanamma's *Saraswati* (394) and *Punjabi Bhain* (Bharti 2014: 4) to name a few. But this symbolism did not motivate the Muslim population, who were not idol-worshipers (Ray 2005: 445). Nonetheless, *Khatun* and *Tehzib un-Niswan* were popular Urdu language magazines that tried to broaden the horizons of their readers and, to an extent, succeeded (Minault 1988: 4).

Literary figures too contributed to raising awareness and bringing about a national consciousness. The Progressive Writers' Association had several women members who held rigid anti-capitalist and anti-imperialist views and reflected these in their fictional works – Razia Sajjad Zaheer, for one, had assertive women protagonists in her works (Tharu and Lalita Vol II 2006: 144). Rokeya Shekhawat Hossein envisioned, in her popular utopian fiction, *Sultana's Dream*, science being used in the service of humanity, rather than to gather power or profits, and the country is run by women with aplomb (Tharu and Lalita Vol I, 2015: 340). Some of these writers participated actively in the political struggle, like Subhadra Kumari Chauhan, who was the first woman *satyagrahi* (419).

There were several British women too who sympathized with the Nationalist cause. 'With the publication of *Hartly House* [novel by Phebe Gibbs] we see that a woman writer exploring female themes of empire can establish forms of female solidarity with native women as well as expose the forms of colonial violence that masculine histories try to hide' (Joseph 2006: 31). Gibbs[9] employs a 'scene of violence against the female body . . . as a continued allegory for the plunder of India' (87). Emily Eden, though convinced of the legitimacy of British rule, shows an appreciation of the opposition's argument or motivation. A decade and a half before the watershed year of 1857, she writes in a letter about the Indians attending to the amusements of 105 Europeans on a pristine hillside: 'I sometimes wonder they do not cut all our heads off, and say nothing more about it' (Eden 1867: XXXVIII, letter dated May 25, 1839). Sister Nivedita and Annie Besant were other politically active British women who charged Nationalist sentiment in India through a nuanced analysis of Indian culture and imperial policy respectively.

The critical mass might simply not have been achieved without the participation of half the population, and the use of religious symbolism in speeches and writings was meant to not just get women to participate in the struggle, but also ensure that society accepted the stepping out of women.

That said, the contribution that the feminist movement made to the Nationalist struggle was not returned in equal measure. Cama suggested that since 'independence alone could resolve women's subordination, they should concentrate on nationalism' (Sarkar 2005: 548). 'Nationalists saw rape as an example of imperialist barbarism, but they saw it as a violation of national honour rather than as an act of violence against women' (Basu 1995: 98). The freedom of movement that women were granted and any other privileges that they won during the Nationalist movement were only temporary (Sarkar 2005: 552). Since women had proved through their participation in the Nationalist struggle that they were evolved political beings, they were given the vote at independence, but real changes in the lives of common women did not materialize. Dayani Priyamvada, a participant in the Telangana peasant struggle said in 1948:

> We were full of firm confidence. . . . [W]e began to appreciate what a new society would be like with equality for men and women. After the police action and the elections to Parliament, these dreams were smashed. Crushed like an egg. . . . After the elections you know how we were – we were like the proverbial blanket which, when asked, 'where are you?' replied 'I'm lying exactly where I was thrown'.
>
> (Tharu and Lalita Vol II 2006: 64)

To add to the tensions between nationalism and feminism, the British government too was blowing hot and cold on women's issues. It attempted, maybe half-heartedly, to ban barbarous customs through the Sati Regulation Act of 1829, the Widow Remarriage Act of 1856, the Age of Consent Act of 1860 and the Prohibition of Female Infanticide Act of 1872 (Ray 2005: 6). Though well-intentioned, the desired results cannot be expected to materialize if the proposed improvements are completely foreign to the local culture and imposed suddenly. A woman holds up her 'the shrivelled-up little finger on her right hand':

> Ever since I was three years old I was taught to be *Suttee*. We stirred boiling rice with a bare finger, to learn how to bear fire when our time should come. But when my Lord died, there was a law which said that I must not be *Suttee*.
>
> (Sorabji 1934: 185)

Judges in the lower courts were often sympathetic listeners and ruled with a sense of humanity. But their decisions were overturned in the higher courts and the new rulings were used as precedents in all the presidencies in the colony, regardless of local custom (Ray 2005: 6–7). The most famous instance of this was Rukhmabai's case. She was married as a child, but refused to live with her husband because he had not grown to be a responsible man. Since she had property to her name, the husband went to court demanding that his wife be made to live with him. Rukhmabai, in a then-anonymous newspaper article, published, cleverly, the morning of her first hearing, wrote a stinging piece on the grievances of women due to the various impositions of patriarchy and how they had the right to expect redress from the government (Chandra 2008: 32). The judge ruled in her favour without hesitation, but the ruling was overturned at appeal. The reason for the reversal was the confusion between the applicability of two distinct legal systems – British and Hindu.

> [H]ere, for us, is an *exposé* of the fiction on which rested the powerful mystique of a transcendental legal system unvitiated by personal factors. The fiction that judges simply administered the existing laws, ... underlined the Victorian conception of judicial objectivity.
>
> (Chandra 2008: 85)

Rukhmabai went to prison (Sorabji 1934: 79) and several unnamed women suffered under the 'combined tyranny of indigenous social authority and colonial legal dispensation' (Chandra 2008: 1). An Indian character in an early 20th-century novel by Josephine Bell says:

> If it were a man insulting me ... I would use all the strength I have of muscle and sinew to resist and defeat him. ... But O! Madam, when you know that that man ... has the House of Lords, the *Queen*, the *Law*, all at his back, you feel as if your heart died within you.
>
> (Twells 2007: 213)

In the rare occasion when disputes involving women went to court, it was found that several women wanted to claim non-Hindu status because patriarchy in orthodox Hinduism tended to deprioritize women's rights, and so their hopes rested with British law. But over decades of adjudicating family disputes, somehow, whatever few provisions Hindu tradition made for women's welfare were diluted or entirely removed (Ray 2015: 9), so that more and more control went into men's hands. It is in this context that the efforts of a few women stood out. A writer for the *Bombay Gazette* admitted that:

> In the great masses of the people a practical recognition of the woman's rights has been obtained by the force of circumstances helped out by feminine self-assertion, which on some points might make an American lady of the newer and freer states die of envy.
>
> (Chandra 2008: 33)

A concluding remark

Economic motivations underlie colonization. Britain needed access to cheap inputs for its industrial-age machinery and, given that these machines ran most efficiently when producing much larger quantities than were needed on the island, they needed a market. These exchanges might not have been to the obvious advantage of any potential trading partner. Having a monopsony buyer of the most important agricultural products of a country might put the seller in a rather insecure position, with low bargaining power, especially in contrast with a sustenance, low-productivity-low-risk model of production. Since most of the raw produce of the country was being sold abroad instead of being used domestically for consumption, the basic necessities had to be purchased. Only political pressure or, better still, complete political control could persuade a country to enter into such an agreement.

The women who participated in picketing of shops selling foreign cloth were trying to resist the negative influences of Britain's expansionist urge. These negative influences were plain for them to see – famine-hit districts saw grain being exported by hoarders, while people starved; Indians were being physically abused and emotionally demoralized in their own country. The agricultural pattern and all associated economic relations in the country underwent a change within less than a century – too fast by historical standards. The impact of the swadeshi movement in economic terms may have been little, but it made a loud and clear point on principle. These women were taking a principled stance: the British government had to leave, so that Indian-elected representatives could decide on economic and social policy in India.

The principles that motivated the British women in India were different, not just in that they supported British rule, but even in the strength of their conviction. The British, at least the classes that travelled to India, were never threatened by the spectre of death the way Indians were. In fact, due to the legendary success of the East India Company, the lives of the common people were getting perceptibly better, through the London Stock Exchange, and there was no need for any fundamental rethinking of life and public events. 'Well, I am sure it is all for the best – I make no objection – I like to see things take their course' (Eden[10] 1867, Chapter I, letter dated October 21, 1837). What was needed was a justification for the exploitation, and that was easily found in the shape of the civilizing mission that the British officers and their wives claimed to be carrying out in India.

This civilizing mission was the support that incipient Indian feminism grabbed at. British feminism may have had its own reasons for fighting, but, to Indian eyes, the respect that British women seemed to enjoy with their men, and their freedom of movement were what they had not thought possible for themselves. With the close observation of British women's lives, Indian women had something concrete to fight for in their society. It was a hard fight, well fought, as evidenced by the *Bombay Gazetteer* article from earlier, but change did not come easy. Williamson (2000: 596) says that the most deeply embedded informal institutions – patriarchy is one – 'display a great deal of inertia – some because they are functional; others take on symbolic value with a coterie of true believers; many are pervasively linked with complementary institutions' (597). The 'coterie of true believers' in patriarchy was composed of men who were the obvious beneficiaries, and women themselves, to the extent that they were 'socialized' to accept an inferior status (Papanek 1990: 176). This made the feminist struggle more difficult than the struggle for independence: the struggle for independence had clearly identifiable opposing sides, and both benefited from the struggle against patriarchy.

Notes

1 The author is grateful to Ranjini, Vivek and Divya for permitting use of their libraries, and to the editors for their comments.
2 Bharat 2019 looks at Indian women's fight against patriarchy through the lens of Indian women's literature from around the 5th century BC till pre-colonial times. It adds to an existing mountain of African American slave literature, Dalit literature, feminist literature, etc.
3 Tens of journals mushroomed around the country in the last few decades of the 19th century and early decades of the 20th to coincide with the inclusion of the district *daak* in the system of Imperial post, a move which increase the availability of postal services to the remotest parts of the colony (Bharat 2012).
4 Tharu and Lalita list several women and their novels in their exhaustive two-volume anthology of women's writings: Muddupalani (*Radhika Santwanam*), Hannah Catherine Mullens (*Phulmani O Karunar Bibaran*), Savitribai Phule, Tarabai Shinde, Sarat Kumari Chaudhurani, Rokeya Sakhawat Hossain, Nazar Sajjad Hyder, Sudha Chauhan, Geeta Sane, Mahadevi Varma, Lalitambika Antherjanam, M.K. Indira (*Phaniyamma*), Razia Sajjad Zaheer, among several others.
5 British history recalls the event as the Sepoy Mutiny, while Indian Nationalists refer to it as India's First War of Independence.
6 There seems to be a mismatch between Mayo's claims that Bengal was 'sexually exaggerated' and 'the unspeakable flatness of their purdah-deadened home lives' (Mayo 1937: 122).
7 The Temple Entry Bill faced opposition from some quarters of the Nationalist side as well. Dr Bhimrao Ambedkar, the lower caste leader, to name one, opposed the bill, though for drastically different reasons. He believed that education and employment opportunities were what the depressed classes needed. It was not appropriate for them to beg the patronage of the upper caste Hindu for something as inconsequential as entry to a temple. In contrast, Sorabji's rationale for opposing the Bill was that it would hurt upper caste Hindu sentiments.
8 For various representations of the map of India as a woman, see Ramaswamy (2001).
9 Gibbs never visited India. The descriptions of India in her novel were based on letters from her son (Joseph 2006: 90).
10 The immediate motivation for Eden making this statement was some waste of materials during her travels, but she expresses the general sentiment that her expectations from life were rather different from her current position anyway, and she was willing to see where it took her.

References

Bardhan, P. 1999. 'Democracy and Development: A Complex Relationship', *Democracy's Value*, 93–111.

Basu, A. 1995. 'Feminism and Nationalism in India, 1917–1947', *Journal of Women's History*, 7(4), 95–107.

Bharat, S. 2019. 'Indian Women's Agency through Indian Women's Literature', pp 13-32, in ed. Madden, K. and Dimand, R.W. *Routledge Handbook of the History of Women's Economic Thought* Oxon: Routledge.

Bharat, S. 2012. *Where the Runners Went: British Motivations Behind Postal Policy and Allocation in Colonial India*, Riverside: University of California.

Bharti, S. 2014. 'Living Patriotism: The Experience of "freedom" Among the Muslim Women of Colonial Punjab', *Pakistan Journal of Women's Studies, Alam-e-Niswan*, 21(2), 1.

Chandra, S. 2008. *Enslaved Daughters: Colonialism, Law and Women's Rights*, Oxford: Oxford University Press.

Eden, E. 1867. *'Up the Country': Letters Written to Her Sister from the Upper Provinces of India*, R. Bentley.

Forbes, G. 1998. 'Women in Modern India', *The New Cambridge History of India*, IV(2), 157–159.

Ghose, I. 1998. *Women Travellers in Colonial India: The Power of the Female Gaze*, New Delhi: Oxford University Press.

Gooptu, S. 2006. *Cornelia Sorabji: India's Pioneer Woman Lawyer*, Oxford: Oxford University Press.

Joseph, B. 2006. *Reading the East India Company, 1720–1840: Colonial Currencies of Gender*, Orient Blackswan.

Lahiri, N. 2016. *Ashoka in Ancient India*, Ranikhet: Permanent Black.

Mayo, K. 1937. *Mother India*, New York. http://arrow.latrobe.edu.au:8080/vital/access/manager/Repository/latrobe:34585. Last accessed on November 2017.

Minault, G. 1988. 'Urdu Women's Magazines in the Early Twentieth Century', *Manushi*, 48, 2–9.

Naidu, S. 1925. *Speeches and Writings of Sarojini Naidu*, GA Natesan & Company.

Papanek, H. 1990. 'To Each Less Than She Needs from Each More Than She Can Do: Allocations Entitlements and Value', in I. Tinker (ed.), *Persistent Inequalities*, New York: Oxford University Press.

Ramaswamy, S. 2001. 'Maps and Mother Goddesses in Modern India', *Imago Mundi*, 53(1), 97–114.

Ray, B. ed. 2005. *Women of India: Colonial and Post-Colonial Periods*. London: Sage.

Raza, R. 2006. *In Their Own Words: British Women Writers and India, 1740–1857*, New Delhi: Oxford University Press.

Sarkar, T. 2005. 'Political Women: An Overview of Modern Indian Developments', in B. Ray (ed.), *History of Science, Philosophy and Culture in Indian Civilization. Women of India: Colonial and Postcolonial Periods*, pp. 541–563, New Delhi: SAGE Publications.

Sharma, H. D. 2011. *100 Significant Pre-Independence Speeches*, Rupa Publications.

Sorabji, C. 1934. *India Calling: The Memories of Cornelia Sorabji*, Nisbet and Co. Ltd.

Teed, P. 2003. 'Race Against Memory: Katherine Mayo, Jabez Sunderland, and Indian Independence', *American Studies*, 44(1–2), 35–57.

Thapar-Bjorkert, S. 2006. *Women in the Indian National Movement: Unseen Faces and Unheard Voices, 1930–42*. London: Sage.

Tharu, S. J. and Lalita, K. eds. 2006. *Women Writing in India: The Twentieth Century*, Vol. 2. New Delhi: Oxford University Press.

Tharu, S. J. and Lalita, K. eds. 2015. *Women Writing in India: Volume I, 600 BC to the Early Twentieth Century*, New Delhi: Oxford University Press.

Twells, A. 2007. *British Women's History: A Documentary History from the Enlightenment to World War I*, Vol. 44. IB Tauris.

Williamson, O. E. 2000. 'The New Institutional Economics: Taking Stock, Looking Ahead', *Journal of Economic Literature*, 38(3), 595–613.

Name index

Note: Page numbers followed by 'n' denote notes.

Aaranovitch, S. 55
Ackerman, F. 191
Adarkar, B. P 11, 263
Admati, A. R. 165
Akhtar, M. A. 34, 36, 38n18
Alavi, H. 245
Allen, R. 251
Almeida, F. 181
Anderson, C. M. 204
Anderson, K. L. 174
Andreoni, A. 143
Angrist, J. D. 223
Armstrong, P. 111
Arrow, K. J. 3, 14, 18, 191, 207n2
Asimakopulos, T. 108
Aspromourgos, T. 24–26, 36, 37n6, 38n16
Ayres, C. 171, 180

Bagchi, A. K. 138, 243, 252, 260, 264, 266, 268
Banaji, J. 245
Banerji, A. K. 252, 258
Baran, P. A. 56, 89
Baranzini, M. 148, 154
Bardhan, P. 276
Barna, T. 29
Basu, A. 278
Baumol, W. 57
Bayly, Chris 249
Becattini, G. 129
Beer, Max 55
Berger, S. 176
Beri, S.G. 240
Bharadwaj, K. 24, 38, 114, 117, 129, 134
Bharat, S. 269, 281n2, 281n3
Bharti, S. 277

Bhattacharya, S. 261
Bhide, S. 231
Bianchi, P. 155
Blanchard, O. J. 224
Blankenburg, S. 113
Bodkin, R. G. 220, 224, 232
Boisguilbert, P. 24
Bortis, G. 106
Bortkiewicz, L. V. 3, 55, 61
Bose, S. 246
Boulding, K. 109
Bowles, S. 57
Boxer, C. 242
Brennan, A. J. 171
Brewer, A. 24, 26, 32, 36
Brisset, N. 164
Broadberry, S. 251
Bunge, M. 175
Bush, P. D. 171

Cameron, A. C. 226
Cantillon, R. 3, 24–27, 37n7, 78; circular view of the economy 24; consumption 24–27, 29–37; social classes 24, 25, 26; prices 38n17
Carabelli, A. 162
Cardinale, I. 144
Carter, C. 104
Cassel, G. 264
Chakrabarti, S. 267, 268
Chandra, B. 245
Chandra, S. 279
Child, J. 257
Cochrane, P. 219
Cohen, J. 107
Commons, J. 171, 179

Cord, B. 99
Correa, R. 2, 8
Corry, B. 109
Coyaji, J. 262
Cripps, F. 167

Dandekar, V.M. 243
Dantas, F. 163
Dasgupta, A. K. 68, 75, 113
Das Gupta, C. 67, 80, 82
Datta, B. 262–265
Davenant, C. 9, 211
Davidson, P. 4, 87, 93, 108
Davis, A. 76
Deane, P. 16
Debreu, G. 14, 18, 191
De Koning, K. 167
De Leo, M. 2017 74
Desai, M. 2, 3, 55, 63
Dhar, Arpita 231
Dixon, R. 102
Doan, T. 224
Dobb, M. 24, 49, 55, 124, 133, 241
Donaldson 160
Duesenberry, J. 37
Dugger, W. M. 171, 175, 183, 184
Dumenil, G. 64
Dunlop, J. T. 103, 114n9
Duppe, T. 207n1
Durbin, J. 219
Dutt, R. P. 257, 268
Dutt, R. 239, 246

Eagly, R. V. 34
Eatwell, J. 93
Eden, E. 277, 280
Edwards, S. 162
Eichner, A. S. 107
Einstein, A. 21
Elliott, J. E. 174
Eltis, W. 24, 28, 29
Ely, R. T. 94
Engels, F. 80, 81, 241, 257
Epstein, R. J. 211, 213–215, 217, 218, 233

Farebrother, R. W. 212
Farmiloe, T. 109
Fasianos, A. 164
Fedorenko, N. P. 103, 114n9
Fisher, R. A. 9, 212, 213
Flaschel, P. 63
Foley, D. K. 166

Forbes, G. 271, 273
Frank, A. G. 252
Freedman, C. 108
Friedman, M. 219
Fullbrook, E. 21
Furber, H. 242
Fusfeld, D. 171

Galasso, G. 137
Galbraith, J. K. 94, 171, 180
Ganguli, B. 264
Garegnani, P. 128, 133
Garratt, A. 224, 225
Genovesi, A. 6, 136–138, 156n2
Geweke, J. 211, 213, 221, 232–234
Ghose, I. 271–273
Ghosh, D. 265
Gilbert, C. L. 211, 218, 222
Gintis, H. 57
Glennan, S. S. 156
Glyn, A. 57, 64
Godley, W. 167
Gokhale, G.K. 259
Goldberger, A. S. 219, 222
Goodwin, D. 109
Goodwin, R. M. 63, 102, 133
Gooptu, S. 274, 275
Grafl, L. 95
Grandmont, J-M. 206
Granger, C. 210
Grant, J. McB. 99
Greene, W. H. 226
Greenwood, D. T. 185
Groenewegen, P. D. 24, 28, 33, 38n13
Grover, V. 260, 261
Gruchy, A. G. 179
Guesnerie, R. 191, 192, 206
Guha, R. 247
Guha, S. 196, 246
Gupta, B. 251
Gupta, C. D. 2, 3

Haavelmo, T. 9, 212, 214, 215, 219
Habib, I. 246, 247
Hagemann, H. 145
Hahn, F. H. 62, 147, 191, 207n2
Haldane, A. G. 165
Halevi, J. 112
Hamilton, C. J. 188, 240, 258
Hands, D. W. 191
Harcourt, G. C. 2, 5, 87, 88, 95, 99–115
Harkin, M. 71

Harrod, R. 7, 145, 146, 156n5
Harvey, J. 273
Hayes, M. 95
Heckman, J. J. 215, 216, 222, 226, 232, 233
Hein, E. 95
Henderson, D. 102
Hendry, D. F. 211, 214, 215, 217, 220, 221, 223, 226, 227
Hicks, J. R. 114n2, 144, 145, 150–152, 154, 156n6, 156n7
Hildenbrand, W. 206
Hilferding, R. 76
Hill, C. 56
Hilton, R. 56
Hirota, M. 198, 205
Hirsch, M. W. 169
Hirschman, A. 241
Hobsbawm, E. J. 56, 76
Hobson, J. A. 76, 177
Hodgson, G. 179
Hollander, S. 58
Holt, R. P. F. 185
Hood, W. C. 214
Hooker, R. H. 212
Hoover, K. D. 234n2
Hudson, P. 107
Humphrey, T. H. 165

Itoh, M. 57

Jathar, G. B. 240
Jevons, W. S. 17, 19, 212
Johnston, J. 222
Joseph, B. 277, 281n9
Joshi, G. N. 240
Juselius, K. 228

Kahn, R. 6, 123–127, 129, 130, 134
Kaldor, N. 6, 100, 122–127, 130, 135
Kalecki, M. 4, 88–90, 102, 107, 112, 114n3, 133
Kalirajan, K. 231
Kamaiah, B. 231
Karayiannis, A. D. 34, 35, 175
Karmel, Peter 104
Kaur Kalsi, J. 171
Kautsky, K. 241
Kenyon, P. 107
Kerr, P. 109, 115n15, 173
Keynes, J. M. 6, 85, 93, 94, 99, 123–127, 129–131, 160, 171, 177–181, 258; consumption function 261; *Economic*

Activity 105; *General Theory* 85–86, 112; ideas 2, 11, 36, 89, 90, 95, 263; IS-LM model 86; post Keynesian economics 93–95
Khambatta, K. J. 240
Kinda-Hass, B. 112
King, G. 9
King, J. E. 2, 3, 86, 87, 89, 90, 92, 93, 95, 109
Klein, L. R. 56, 219
Klosse, S. 163
Kolk, D. X. 179
Koopmans, T. C. 9, 14, 20, 203, 214
Kowalik, T. 89
Kozo Uno 57
Kregel, J. 161
Kriesler, P. 95, 112
Krishna, K. L. 2, 9, 210, 231
Krishnamurthy, K. 231
Krishnamurty, J. 242
Kuczynski, M. 28–30
Kumar, D. 242, 243, 246
Kurien, C. T. 2, 3, 13
Kurz, H. D. 24, 133
Kuznets, S. 147
Kydland, F. 224

Labory, S. 155
Lahiri, N. 276
Laidler, D. 165
Lalita, K. 271, 277, 278
Landesmann, M. 155
Lange, O. 86
Lavoie, M. 95
Leamer, E. E. 221–223
Lee, F. 94
Lenin, V. I. 56, 76
Lerner, A. 107
Levy, D. 64
Lewis, W. A. 241
List, F. 262
Litterman, R. B. 224
Lowe, A. 146, 154, 155, 156n9
Lucas, R. E. 221, 222
Luchtenberg, S. 63
Ludden, D. 246
Luxemburg, R. 56, 62
Lydall, Harold 102

Madan, B. K. 265
Maddison, A. 251
Magnus, J. R. 227

Malaviya, M. M. 256, 262
Malinvaud, E. 191, 222
Mandel, E. 64
Mantel, R. 191
Marcuzzo, M. C. 2, 5, 122, 126, 129, 132
Marshall, A. 18, 86, 101, 122–126, 212
Marx, K. 77, 78, 80–82, 123, 126, 243, 257
Mathews, R. 99
Matsui, T. 245
Matthews, R. 103
Mattick, P. 56
Mayhew, A. 171
Mayo, K. 274, 281n6
Mazat, N. 28
McAlpin, M. B. 258
McKenzie, L. W. 8, 191, 207n2
McLane, J. 258
Means, G. C. 175
Meek, R. L. 28–30, 37n9, 37n11, 37n12, 38n15, 55
Menger, C. 17, 18, 149
Michl, T. R. 166
Miliband, R. 64
Mill, J. S. 48, 49, 212
Millmow, A. 93
Mills, T. C. 225, 227, 233, 234
Minault, G. 277
Minhas, B. S. 103
Minsky, H. P. 4, 90–93, 132, 163
Mirrlees, J. 102
Mitchell, W. 171, 182
Mohun, S. 58, 60
Moreland, W. H. 240
Morgan, M. S. 211, 213–217, 220, 227
Morishima, M. 60
Morris, M. D. 10, 243–245
Morrison, T. 258
Mosler, W. 163
Mukherjee, A. 252, 266
Mukherji, A. 2, 191, 196, 202–205, 207n3, 207n6–207n8, 266–268
Mun, T. 257
Munn, T. 257
Muranjan, S. K. 264
Murphy, A. E. 24, 26, 27, 37n3
Muysken, Jean 163
Myrdal, G. 155, 171, 180

Naidu, S. 275, 276
Naoroji, D. 11, 239, 256, 258, 259, 261
Negishi, T. 203
Nevile, J. W. 112

North, D. 11, 185, 250
Nurkse, R. 241

Obst, T. 95
O'Hara, P. A. 2, 171, 174, 175, 183, 184
O'Kelley, C. R. T. 175
Okun, A. 167
Olgen, F. 185
Onaran, O. 95
Opocher, A. 5, 100
Orcutt, G. H. 219
Ostrom, E. 185

Pabst, A. 138
Pandit, V. 229–231
Panico, C. 131
Papanek, H. 281
Parikh, K. S. 231
Parthasarathi, P. 250, 251
Pasinetti, L. L. 7, 122, 133, 136, 147–148
Patel, A. 113
Patnaik, U. 245, 267
Patterson, K. 225, 227, 233, 234
Pellizzari, F. 145, 152
Penard, T. 184
Perlman, M. 105, 106
Petty, W. 9, 24
Pigou, A. C. 124–126, 133, 150
Piketty, T. 107
Pischke, J-S. 223
Polanyi, K. 186
Pomeranz, K. 252
Poussing, N. 184
Prescott, E. 224
Pressman, S. 111
Prest, W. 105

Qin, D. 210–211, 218, 222
Quadrio Curzio, A. 145, 152, 153
Quah, D. 224
Quesnay, F. 3;; net product 27–31; sectors 33, 34; social classes 31; *Tableau Economique* 28, 173; theory of economic growth 28, 29

Raffaelli, T. 132
Ramaswamy, S. 281n8
Ranade, M. G. 256, 259, 261
Randall Wray, L. 163
Ray, B. 277, 278
Ray, R. K. 246
Raychaudhuri, T. 242, 245, 246
Raza, R. 270–273

Reinert, E. S. 156n3
Ricardo, D. 19, 41, 46–50, 67, 73–76, 126, 128, 149, 174
Richardson, G. B. 107
Robertson, D. 124, 133
Robinson, E.A.G. 124, 133
Robinson, J. 6, 55, 56, 90, 93–94, 99, 100, 103, 106, 107, 114n3, 122–129, 133, 135
Roemer, John 57
Rogers, C. 95
Roosevelt, F. 8
Rosenstein-Rodan, P. 241
Rosselli, A. 122, 132
Rothschild, K. W. 99
Rowthorn, B. 57
Roy, T. 2, 10, 239, 242, 252
Rutherford, M. 1994 185, 186

Salmon, W. C. 156n4
Salter, W. E. G. 101
Salvadori, N. 24, 133
Samudro, B. 171
Samuels, W. J. 175
Samuelson, P. A. 56–57, 203
Sardoni, C. 111
Sargent, T. J. 221
Sarkar, N.R. 266
Sarkar, S. 262
Sarkar, T. 278
Saville, J. 56, 64
Say, J-B. 14
Scarf, H. 8, 192, 195, 204
Scazzieri, R. 2, 6, 138, 143–145, 149, 153–155, 156n10
Schumpeter, J. A. 18, 19, 24, 56, 171, 177–181, 211
Sekine, T. 57
Sen, M. 123
Sen, S. 2, 11, 259, 268
Serrano, F. 28
Shackle, G. 109
Shah, K.T. 240
Shanmugam, K. R. 229, 230
Sharma, H. D. 276
Shaw, G. B. 85
Sherman, H. J. 179
Shore, John 258
Shove, G. 124
Silberston, A. 103
Silipo, D. B. 163
Sills, D. 108
Simons, H. 165

Sims, C. A. 221, 223, 233
Singh, A. 114
Singh, V. B. 243
Sinha, A. 2, 6, 24, 45, 48–50, 53, 74, 75, 99–115
Sinha, J. C. 265
Skinner, A. S. 34, 35, 156n3
Smith 73, 78
Smith, A. 2, 3, 7, 14, 21, 24, 41–46, 67, 69, 72–74, 141–143, 156n4, 257
Smith, S. 71; GDPs 42–46; Man and Nature 42; natural dynamics and historical dynamics 141–144; rate of profits 45; 'real' and 'nominal' price 43; world of utopia 68–73
Smolensky, E. 87
Solow, R. M. 103
Sonnenschein, H. 191
Sorabji, C. 271, 274, 275, 279
Spanos, A. 211–213, 232, 234
Spaventa, L. 7, 147
Spengler, J. J. 27
Sraffa, P. 1, 3, 6, 41, 48–53, 53n3, 76, 104, 122–133, 135; classical economics, reinterpretation 41–53; commodities 51; commodity residue 50; hypothesis 51; Man versus Nature 50; mathematical reasoning 52; rate of profits 50; standard commodity 53
Stanfield, J. R. 171, 181, 185
Steedman, I. 5, 60, 100
Stein, B. 243
Steindl, J. 89
Steuart, J. 3, 7, 33–36, 136, 138–141, 156n3; aspiration effect 36; effectual demand 35–36; sources of aggregate demand 35
Stirati, A. 24, 35
Stock, J. H. 223, 228
Stockhammer, E. 95, 160
Stone, D. 109, 133
Stone, J. R. N. 219
Streeten, P. 241
Studer, R. 251
Sugihara, K. 252
Summers, L. H. 232, 234
Sutcliffe, R. 64
Sweezy, P. M. 55, 56, 89

Targetti, F. 112
Tarshis, L. 108
Tavlas, G. S. 161
Taylor, J. B. 225
Taylor, T. 107

Teed, P. 273, 274
Thakurdas, P. 265
Thapar-Bjorkert, S. 276, 277
Tharu, S. J. 271, 277, 278
Thirlwall, A. P. 93
Thomas, A. M. 3, 24, 26, 37n2, 38n14, 40, 71, 113–114
Thorner, A. 245
Thorner, D. 242
Thornton, D. L. 164
Tobin, J. 227
Tool, M. 175
Toporowski, J. 88, 89
Toye, J. 71
Tribe, K. 107
Trivedi, P. K. 226
Truger, A. 95
Turgot, A. R. J. 3, 31–33; saving and accumulation 31; social classes 31; theory of value 31
Twells, A. 279

Uhlig, H. 225
Uzawa, H. 203

Vaggi, G. 29
Vakil, C. N. 240, 264
van den Berg, R. 37n3
Veblen, T. B. 171, 174–177

Velupillai, K. V. 99
Veneziani, R. 58, 60
Visvesvaraya, M. 265

Wadia, P.A. 240
Wallace, B. 104
Waller, W. 182
Wallich, H. C. 86
Walras, L. 14, 17, 86, 191
Warburg, J. P. 162
Watson, G. S. 219
Watson, M. 223, 228
Weber, M. 241
Weintraub, R. E. 109, 207n1
Weintraub, S. 4, 86
Whalen, C. 92, 95
Wicksell, K. 86
Williamson, O. E. 280
Wilson, A. 108
Wingate, G. 258
Wong, R. B. 252
Wood, A. 107
Wood, E.M. 81
Wooldridge, J. M. 226
Wray, L. R. 92

Yang, H-S. 34–36, 38n18
Young, A. 175
Yule, G. 212

Subject index

Note: Page numbers in *italic* indicate figures on the corresponding page.

'Accountant in a Golden Age, The' 5, 102, 103
accumulation: agricultural profits and 28; of capital 27, 28, 31–34, 36; social structure of 8
Accumulation of Capital, The 56, 62, 99
activity levels: aggregate 26, 27; sectoral 26, 27; theories of 24–38
activity levels, theory of: in Cantillon 24
act of bleeding 259
advanced theory of value 6
Age of Consent Act of 1860 278
aggregate activity levels 3
aggregate demand: composition of 25; consumption 26; domestic 30–31; foreign 27, 35; investment 33; as an outlet 34; size of 25; state spending 37n5; sufficiency of 27, 29; and underconsumption 30; widening of the market (Quesnay) 30
Aggregate Demand-Aggregate Supply (AD-AS) model 87
aggregate economic behaviour 125
aggregate expenditure 99
aggregate income 88
aggregate output: theory of 37n6
aggregation 206
agrarian history scholarship 247
Agricultural Labourers in Modern India and Pakistan (Patel) 242
agricultural rents 27
agricultural sector 142
agricultural surplus 35
agriculture 28, 33–36
Altro Polo. Italian Economics Past and Present (Halevi) 105
analytical descriptions 16

Analytical Foundation of Marxian Economic Theory (Roemer) 57
analytical narrative, pedagogic challenge 22
Anglo-Indian banking community 266
animal spirits 93
Anti-Duhring 55
Arrow, Chenery, Minhas and Solow (ACMS) 103
arts of improvement 137
aspiration effect: in Steuart 36
asset price of land 166
Association for Evolutionary Economics (AFEE) 171, 172, 181, 186
assumptions: implicit (decision to save is one and the same as a decision to invest) 30; special 30, 32
asymmetry of opportunity 271
auction: double 205
auctioneer 203, 204
Australian Labor Party (ALP) 108
average commodity 74

balancing proportion, labour production 52
Banga Mahila 277
bank lending 130
Bank of England 165
Bharati 277
biotechnology and electronics 184
Black-Scholes-Merton (BSM) model 164
Bombay Plan 267
'Bombay School' 265
bon prix: in Quesnay 28, 30, 37n11, 38n14; and workers' consumption 30
borrowing: by Cantillonian landowners 25, 32
box diagram: Edgeworth 200
British economic policies 266

buffer stock operations 160–169; macro modelling 167–169; micro modelling 166–167
Bulletin of the Conference of Socialist Economists 57

caltech experiments 204, 205
Cambridge, economics in 6, 89–90, 93
Cambridge approach to economics 5, 122–134; commonalities 129–131; differences 127–129; divergences 125–127; heritage 132–133
Cambridge Capital Theory 107
Cambridge Economic History of India 246
Cambridge group 122–124
Cambridge Journal of Economics 94
capital: accumulation of 27–29, 31–34, 36, 76, 153; first analysis of (in Quesnay) 27; meaning of 27; net accumulation of 28, 34; quantity of 127, 128; and stationary economy 28
Capital (Marx) 55, 59, 77, 81
Capital and Time (Hicks) 154
capital endowment 148
capital investments 50
capitalism 58, 67–82, 89, 90, 92, 93, 172–183, 185, 186; dynamics 62; market utopia of 82; Marx's theorization of 67
capitalist accumulation 78
capitalist market economy 5
capital-labour ratio 75, 76
capital-output ratio 63
caste 271, 274–276, 281n7
chain of reasoning 16
child marriage 274
circular and cumulative causation (CCC) 172, 173, 186
circular flow: saving as a leakage 30, 34
circular view of the economy: in Cantillon 24; in Quesnay 27; in Steuart 34; demand should validate supply 36; production and consumption 24, 27, 29
civilizing mission 280
classes 173–176, 184
classical economics: Boisguilbert 24; Cantillon 24–27; Malthus 174; *versus* marginalist economics 27; Marx 24; Petty 24; Quesnay 27; Ricardo 24, 46–50; Smith 24–38, 41–46, 141–144; Sraffa's reinterpretation of 41–53; Steuart 33–36; Turgot 24, 31–33
classical economists 24–37, 171–174, 176, 186; *see also* classical economics

classical political economy (CPE) 67–82; Marx's utopia and critique 77–82; utopia to dystopia, Ricardo's departures 73–76; *see also* classical economics
classroom situation 13
climate change 183, 186
collective action problem 276
colonial coin: two sides of 269–281
colonialism 71, 270, 271, 276–279
colonial machinery 271–275
colonial policies 261
colonial trade 71
colonization 273, 279
commodities: creation and expansion of 70; exchange-ratios of 47; 'nominal price' of 42; residue 50
commodity supplies: commodity demands adapt to 26, 37
community's joint stock of knowledge 176, 184
competitive capitalist economy 3
competitive economy 19
complexity 176, 183, 185, 186
concept of institutionalised culture and evolution 183
concept of the joint stock of knowledge 176 184
Congress Party 267
conjecture 203, 204
conspicuous consumption 175, 177, 184
consumption: borrowing 25, 32; expenditure 91; luxury 25–27, 32–34; necessary 28, 31, 33, 34, 36
consumption, in Cantillon: across sectors 26; autonomous 25, 30, 33, 36; and composition of aggregate output 27; conspicuous 26; and consumption 24–27, 29–37; and demonstration effects 27; imitation and 26; induced 25, 30; by landowners 24–26, 30, 32; luxury 25, 26, 32–34; necessary 28, 34; non-necessary 25; and saving 25, 31–33; and size of aggregate output 27; subsistence 25, 26; by workers 30, 31
consumption, in Quesnay: autonomous 30, 33; induced 30; landowners 28–30, 32; workers 30–32
consumption, in Steuart: agricultural and manufacturing 34–35; luxury 34; foreign 35; effectual demand 35–36; taste 36; landlords 36
consumption, in Turgot: customary subsistence 32; landowners and luxury

consumption 32; effect on capital
  accumulation 33
contradictions of capitalism 186
*Contribution to the Critique of Political
  Economy, The* (Marx) 55
core, periphery and semi-periphery 182
Corn Laws 74
corporate hegemony 175, 183
corporate power 183
corporation 175–178, 181, 182
cost-push inflation 86
Council Bills 259
court of Wards 271, 272, 274
Cowles Commission 9
creditor countries 162
credit rationing 92
credit stringency 266
crises 177–179, 183, 185, 186
critical proportion, labour production 52
Critique of the Gotha Programme (Marx) 81
crucial reform 89
'Crucial reform' of capitalism, Kalecki on 89

debt, non-neutrality of 92
decentered totality 180
decolonization 246
demand-pull inflation 86
development and underdevelopment 182
dialectic movement 78
discriminating protection 262
distress conditions 260
distress sales of gold 265–266
division of labour (DOL) 16, 69; in Turgot
  33, 38n16
double auction 205
'drain' from colonial India 258
Durga 276
*Dynamics of a Capitalist Economy, The:
  A Multi-Sectoral Approach* (Goodwin) 113
dynamic stochastic general equilibrium
  (DSGE) models 95, 224
dynamic theory 145, 146
dynamic trajectory 151, 153

East India Company 257, 270, 271, 280
econometrics 9; appraisals of contributions
  232–234; consolidation and applications
  218–221; contributions to knowledge,
  Heckman 232–233; Cowles Commission
  approach, responses 219–220; databases,
  facilities and institutions 231–232;
  diverse areas, advances 225–229;
  empirical experience 217–218;

empirical time series data modelling,
  Hendry 226–227; formalization, Cowles
  Commission (CC) 213–218; Geweke
  et al. 233–234; Hendry and Morgan,
  econometric analysis foundations
  216–217; historical perspective of
  210–234; history, Epstein 217–218;
  macroeconometric modelling 220–221,
  224–225; Morgan, econometric ideas
  history 214–216; Palgrave *Handbook
  of Econometrics* 227–228; pre-20th-
  century quantitative research 211–212;
  reformative initiatives 221–225; teaching
  and applied practices, India 229–232;
  theory and evidence, macroeconomics
  228–229
Economic Activity (Harcourt, Karmel and
  Wallace) 104, 105
Economic and Political Weekly 243, 252
economic dynamics 138
economic goods 18
economic growth 3; constraints in Cantillon
  and Quesnay 28, 29; labour and land
  constraints 28; necessary conditions
  28, 31, 33; negative effects of luxury
  consumption 33; role of adequate demand
  33; sufficient conditions 27, 29, 32
Economic History of India in the Victorian Age
  (Dutt) 239
economic inequality 239
economic nationalism 260–264, 266
Economic Record 101, 102, 104, 109
economic 'settlements' 164
economic systems 172, 182
economy: as a circular process 27, 34;
  circular view of the 24
Economy and Society 57
effective demand, principle of 87, 88, 93
effectual demand 35; and agricultural surplus
  33–36; role of income 36; Steuart 35, 36
egalitarian framework 184
emergence 172, 175, 177, 183, 185, 186
employment: machinery and 38n18
endogenous contradictions 179
endogenous cycles and crises 185
endowments 192, 198–200, 202, 204–207
entrepreneurs 32, 166; in Cantillon 24–26,
  31, 32
equilibrium: price 13; theory 3
equilibrium: general 191–208; partial 192,
  193, *194*, 196
equilibrium, competitive: existence of 191;
  instability of 199, 206; stability of 191

ergodicity 87
Essai sur la Nature du Commerce en General
   (Cantillon) 24, 25
'Essay in Dynamic Theory' 145
Euclidian geometry 1
European Association for Evolutionary
   Political Economy 182, 186
European Journal of Economics and Economic
   Policy (EJEEP) 94
excess demand: properties of 206
exchange banks 259
exchange rates 263, 265
'Existence of an Equilibrium for a
   Competitive Economy' (Arrow and
   Debreu) 18
expectations 87, 91, 93, 123,129
expenditure abroad 258, 259
exports 35, 162, 256, 259
extensive agriculture 140
extreme bounds analysis (EBA) 223

fallacy of composition 87
famine and mass poverty 260
FD Roosevelt (FDR) 161
feminism 270, 278
finance capital 174, 177
financial dominance of industry 172, 177,
   183
financial fragility 4, 90–91
financial instability hypothesis (FIH) 4,
   90–93
financial market equilibria 164
financial market regulation vulnerability
   hypothesis (FMRVH) 92
financial transfers 258, 260
First War of Indian Independence 272,
   281n5
First World War 262, 274
Fiscal Commission 262
fiscal transfer 243
food and clothing, criminal 261
Food Corporation of India (FCI) 160
foreign capital 267
foreign commerce 142
foreign trade: role in economic growth
   (Steuart) 34
Forum for Social Economics 182, 185
freedom struggle 276
free hands 138
French Regulation Approach 8, 183
full employment 85, 87, 89, 93, 95;
   equilibrium 131; no tendency towards
   35, 37

Full Industry Equilibrium (Opocher and
   Steedman) 100
fundamental arts 137
fundamentalist Keynesians 4, 86–87, 92
"fundamental symmetry" of supply and
   demand 125
fundamental theorem, second: of positive
   economics 192, 202, 206; of welfare
   economics 206
fundamental uncertainty 5
funding liquidity 161

Gandhi, Mohandas 274, 275
GDP 42
general equilibrium 191–207; analysis
   192–194; theory 8
General Theory of Employment, Interest and
   Money, The (Keynes) 4, 6, 58, 85–88, 93,
   124, 125, 127, 131
General Theory of Exploitation and Class
   (Roemer), *A* 57
global Financial Crisis 92, 95
global Marxism 243, 247
gluts: in commodity 35; in labour 35; *see*
   also aggregate demand
gold-based currency 265
'Golden age' of capitalism 89
gold exports from India 266
Great Depression 91, 177, 256, 263,
   265–266
Great Divergence, The (Pomeranz) 11
Great Recession 1, 163
Great Union of Vested Interests 177, 184
gross substitution 87
guide books 270

Hartly House 277, 277
hedge finance 91
heterodox economics 8, 94, 95
heterodox economic thinking: early
   beginning 256–257; economic
   nationalism 260–264; evolution in
   India 256–267; Great Depression, India
   265–266; macroeconomic impact,
   Nationalist critique 257–260; Ottawa
   imperial protection, 1932 265; tariffs
   and exchange rates, interwar debates
   260–264; unpaid transfers, India
   257–260
hinduism: orthodox 279
hinduized nationalism 277
History of India (Mill) 272
History of Political Economy 106

hoarding 34
holistic economics 180
home charges 256, 257, 264, 266
homogeneity 206
hypothetical infinite population 213

ideology 89
illiteracy 270
imperfect competition, 124
imperfectionism 87
Imperialism (Lenin) 56
Imperial Preference issue 263
income: uncertainty 25
income-expenditure model 88
incomes policy 86, 93
India: British 271; colonial 269, 270
Indian economic history 10
Indian economic history writings:
   historiographical turn 243–247; new
   global movements and revival 249–252;
   prehistory 239–241; staid, 1947–1967
   241–243; time of decline, 1990s
   247–249
Indian Fiscal Commission 262
Indian National Congress 258, 274
Indian Nationalists 240
India's Five Year Plans 266
Industrial Commission 262
industrial revolution 74, 245
industriousness of societies 71
infanticide: female 278
inflation 86, 87, 93, 99
'Ingot Plan' 161
*Inquiry into the Nature and Causes of the
   Wealth of Nations, An* (Smith) 14, 24
*Inquiry into the Principles of Political
   Oeconomy, An* (Steuart) 33
instability examples 194–202
institution: colonial 271; informal 280
institutional and evolutionary political
   economy (IEPE) 8
institutional economics 8; history 171–187;
   history of 171–187
institutional environment 185
institutionalism 172; of Thorstein Veblen
   174–177
institutional regimes 182
institutions of capitalism 174, 176, 178
instrumental and ceremonial functions of
   institutions 180
interest rate 130, 131, 132
International Clearing Union (ICU) 162
Internet 184

inter-sectoral relations: equilibrium 29;
   in Quesnay 33, 34; in Steuart 33, 34,
   138–140; *see also* sectors
intolerance 247
inverse relationship between profit and
   wage 126
investment *see* accumulation
investment expenditure 4, 89
investment-management 242
invisible hand 203
IS-LM model 4, 86–87, 130

Japanese Marxism, schools 57
job guarantee scheme 164
John Maynard Keynes (Minsky) 90–93, 95,
   160, 162
Journal of Economic History 10
Journal of Economic Issues 172
Journal of Economic Literature 57
JQE (*Journal of Quantitative Economics*) 230
judicial objectivity 279

Kaleckian economics 89, 90 89, 90
Kalecki version 87–90
Karl Marx and the Close of His System
   (Bohm-Bawerk) 56
Keynesian aggregate demand analysis 256
Keynesian consumption function 261
Keynesian ideas 2, 11, 36, 89, 90, 95, 263
Keynesian revolution 124, 126
Khatun 277

labour: expenditure 44; productivity 44, 45,
   63, 76; theory of value 55, 60, 88
labour, in Cantillon: as a constraint 28,
   37n8; demand 26, 27; employment 37;
   induced consumption 30; and population
   26; supply 26–28, 37; supply adapts to
   demand 37n8; and technological progress
   25, 26; utilization of 26
labour-time ratios 46, 47
Lagrangean multipliers 203
land: in Cantillon, primary use of 25; as a
   constraint 28, 29; utilization of 26
landowners, in Cantillon: luxury
   consumption 25, 32
large-scale simultaneous equation models 224
Late Capitalism (Mandel) 64
law of motion 152
Lectures on Jurisprudence (Smith) 78
legal systems: British 279; Hindu 279
Leverhulme Exchange Fellowship 106
liquidity 129, 130

liquidity preference 131
literature: feminist 270; nationalist 270
local silver traders 266
LoLR (Lender of Last Resort) function
    160, 165, 167
London Stock Exchange 280
long waves 179
luxuries: effect on economic growth 36;
    manufactured 26, 27

Macaulay's Minute on Education 272
macroeconomic growth theory 147
Mahalanobis Memorial Medal 230
Manchester merchants 262
Man *versus* Nature 50
Marchand calculating machine 100
marginal analysis, 127
marginalism: versus classical economics
    37; tendency to the full employment of
    labour 37
marginal productivity 127
marginalized 269
market utopia 73, 82
Marshall-Pigou tradition 6
Marxian economics 3, 88, 93, 94; Adam
    Smith's utopia 68–73; business cycle
    model 63; capitalism, dynamics of 62;
    CPE and 77–82; history of 55–64;
    quantitative Marxism 63–64; Ricardo,
    utopia 73–76; teaching 60–62; three
    circuits 62–63
Marxian Economics (Desai) 62
Marxian Economic Theory (Desai) 60
Marxist-Leninist theory 245
Marxist political economy 67
Marx's Economics (Morishima) 60
materialist theory 88
mathematical reasoning 52
Maturity and Stagnation (Steindl) 89
Means to Prosperity, The 162
memoirs 270
microeconometrics 9
microfoundations of macroeconomics 87
military-industrial complex 184
minority note of dissent 265
modified gradient process 203, 204
Modigliani-Miller theorem 5, 92, 93
monetarism, 123
monetary policy 160
monetary theory of production 178
money, non-neutrality of 92
Money and the Real World (Davidson) 93

monopoly capital 177
Monopoly Capital (Baran and Sweezy) 56, 89
monopsony buyer 280
moral philosophy 67
Mother India 273–274, 276
multiplier, 123

National Bureau of Economic Research
    (NBER) 179
nationalism 256, 276–278
nationalist interrogations 257
Nationalist movement 278
nationalists 256, 257, 261, 270
nationalist struggle 275
nationalist struggle 274, 275, 277, 278
natural dynamics (Pasinetti) 147–148
natural economy 7
natural path of development 137–144
natural rate of growth 146
necessaries: manufactured 26
negative heuristics 149
neoclassical economics 2, 14, 20, 21, 90,
    181, 185; *see also* marginalism
neoclassical synthesis 86, 87
neoliberalism 183
neo-Ricardian economics 87
net product: agricultural rents and 27; in
    Quesnay 27–31
neutrality of money 87, 92
new Deal 172, 179, 180
new institutional economics 171, 181–186
'new' institutional economics:
    contemporary Veblenian and 181–186
new Keynesian economics 86, 87, 95
new Neoclassical Synthesis 87
non-ergodicity axiom 87
non-neutrality of debt 92
non-neutrality of money 5
non-violence 276

'Observations on a paper by Saint-Peravy
    on the Subject of Indirect Taxation'
    (Turgot) 38n13
old Keynesian synthesis 86
old neo-classical synthesis (ONS) 86
opulence 141, 143
Origins of Family, Private Property and Law
    (Engels) 58
Ottawa Agreement 263
Ottawa imperial protection, 1932 265
output: aggregate 27, 37n6; necessary 37n6;
    sectoral 29; surplus 34, 37n6

overvalued exchange rate 265
ownership of resources 19
Oxford Economic Papers 102, 103

parallel process of transfer 260
pardah 271, 274, 275
Pareto optimality 19
patriarchy 269, 270, 272, 279–281
pedagogy: analytical narrative 22; history, logic
    and narrative in 13–23; traditions and logic
    19–22; traditions in economics 14–19
Perron-Frobenius theorem 51
physical transfer 258
physico-mathematical science 17
physiocracy 27
Physiocrats 171–174, 186; Marx on 27;
    proto-institutionalism of 173–174
political economy 58, 136
Political Economy of Growth, The (Baran) 243
political geometry 6, 137
political thinking 274
Ponzi finance 91
poor laws 74
positive economics: second fundamental
    theorem of 202
postcolonialism 247
post-Keynesian economics 5
post Keynesian economics: in 1970s and
    2018 93–95
post Keynesian macroeconomics: *General
    Theory,* ambiguity of 85–86; origins of
    85–95
post-Keynesian themes 3
poverty 261; famines and 266
Poverty of Philosophy, The (Marx) 77, 78
power 173, 175–177, 180, 181
predator-prey model 63
preferential tariffs 263
prices: 'classical' theory of 128; of
    commodities 16; and consumption 33;
    formation 205
prices, in Cantillon: intrinsic value 38n17
prices, in classical economics: natural price 32
prices, in Quesnay: fundamental value and
    bon prix 38n14
prices, in Steuart: 'prime cost' 38n17
prices, in Turgot: fundamental value 32
principle of aggregate effective demand 178
principle of circular and cumulative
    causation 172
principle of contradiction 172, 173, 176,
    186

principle of heterogeneous groups and
    agents 172, 176, 186
principle of historical specificity and
    evolution 172, 175, 186
principle of nexus between institutions,
    habits and individuals 172
principle of social balance 181
principle of uneven development and
    hegemony 173, 186
Principles of Economics (Marshall) 18
principles of institutional economics 180,
    181, 183
Principles of Political Economy (Malthus) 173
Principles of Political Economy and Taxation
    (Ricardo) 73, 173
Principles of Political Oeconomy (Steuart) 33
private bank liabilities 161
private sector wages 163
'Probability Approach to Econometrics' 9,
    219
*Production of Commodities by Means of
    Commodities* (Sraffa) 6, 126, 129
productive: expenditure 28; sector 28, 29,
    34, 37n7
Productivity and Technical Change
    (Salter) 101
productivity gap 163
profits: net capital accumulation and 28, 29,
    33; proportional to capital advanced 32;
    and realization of the social surplus 32;
    source of accumulation 27–29, 32
profit share in national income 89
Progressive Writers' Association 277
Prohibition of Female Infanticide Act of
    1872 278
proper growth rate 146
proportion: of necessaries to non-
    necessaries (in Cantillon) 26
proto-institutionalism 173–174
proto-institutionalist 173, 174
public expenditure: role of 35
public insurance mechanism 160
Punjabi Bhain 277
purchasing power parity doctrine 264

quantitative Marxism 63–64
quantity Theory of Money 93, 129, 130

rape 278
rate of profits 50, 75, 167
rate of surplus value 61
rate of taxation 76

rational expectations hypothesis (REH) 87, 222

realism 181

real life activities 14

real-life issues 22

Reconstruction Finance Corporation (RFC) 161

Reflections sur la Formation et la Distribution des Richesses (Turgot) 31

reformist program 185

relative structural invariance, principle of 155

rentier forms 80

rent of land 45

reproduction schemas 3, 32

Rethinking Economics – Reflections Based on a Study of the Indian Economy (Kurien) 23n1

reverse causation 176

Review of Keynesian Economics (ROKE) 94, 95

Review of Political Economy 111

Review of Radical Political Economics (RRPE) 56, 94

Review of Social Economics (ROSE) 94

rising relative power of Asia 183

Robinson Crusoe 2, 14, 15

robotics 184

sabotage 177

Saraswati 277

Sati 274, 278

Sati Regulation Act of 1829 278

satyagrah 276, 277

saving: in Cantillon 25, 32, 34; and capital accumulation 29, 31–34; and consumption 25, 29–32, 34; by entrepreneurs 25, 31, 32; by farmers 29; and hoarding 34; and investment 29, 30, 32; is investment 29, 30, 32; by landlords 31; leakage from the circular flow 34; and output and employment levels 34; from profits 29, 31–34; in Quesnay 29–32, 34; from rents 34; as source of capital accumulation 29, 31, 32; and thrift 32; from wages 31, 32

scheme of expanded reproduction (SER) 62

secretary of state (SOS) 259, 260

sectoral analysis, distress 265

sectors: consumption of 26; output supplies across 28, 29, 34; productive, sterile, and proprietary 28

self-interest 68, 73

self-love 68, 69

separation theorem 133

sepoy Mutiny 281n5

Shann Memorial Lecture 106

shortage of silver imports 266

short cycles 178, 179

short period 127, 129

silver coin 263

simultaneous equations model (SEM) 210, 217

SMD (Sonnenschein-Mantel-Debreu) theorems 9, 191–192, 206

social classes, in Cantillon: fixed-income earners 24; labourers 26, 28; landowners 25; uncertain-income earners 25

social classes, in Turgot: disposable 31; productive 31; sterile 31; stipendiary 31

social conflict 74

social/cultural capital 183

social economies 172

socialism 85, 88

Socialist Register 64

socially necessary labour time (SNLT) 79

social reproduction 76

social structure of accumulation (SSA) school 183

social surplus: agriculture 33–36; its definition 32; and its realization 32; and net produce 33; and net product 34; in Cantillon 33

social wealth 17–18

societal nature of economics 15

Solow-Swan growth model 86

Sonnenschein-Mantel-Debreu theorems 2

Speculation and Economic Stability (Kaldor) 130

speculative finance 91

standard of living and quality of life 184

state-centric narrative 254

state intervention 126

stationary economy 28

sterile: classes (Turgot) 31; expenditure 28; sector 28, 30

sterile expenditure 28

stock-flow-consistent (SFC) macroeconomics 167

stock-flow-consistent modelling 8

stock market volatility 164

structural change 136

structural cointegration VAR (SCVAR) approach 224–225

structural dynamics tradition 136–156; analytical benchmarks and historical trajectories 144–155

structural dynamics trajectories 155
structural economic dynamics 136–155
structuralist dynamics 2
Structure of Social Accumulation (Bowles and Gintis) 57
subprinciple of evolution 180
'substantive' approach 14
substantive logic 21
Sultana's Dream 277
surplus value 178
swadeshi (national origin) movement 262, 275, 280
systemic corruption 184
system-institutions-habits-individuals nexus 175
system-problems 185

Tableau Economique (Quesnay) 28, 173; inter-sectoral equilibrium in 29; stability of equilibrium 29
Tariff Boards 262
tariff protection 265
tariffs 263
tariffs and exchange rates, interwar debates 260–264
tâtonnement 194, 195, 203–205, 207n5; Caltech experiments 204–205; Negishi conjecture 203–204; preliminaries 203
taxation 78
taxes 260
tax revenue 258
technological progress: 146; in Cantillon 25, 26, 38n16
Tehzib un-Niswan 277
Temple Entry Bill 275, 281n7
Texas School of Institutionalism 180
The Indian Econometric Society (TIES) 230
theoretical tension: between consumption and investment 33
Theories of Surplus Value, The (Marx) 55, 77
Theories of Value and Distribution since Adam Smith (Dobb) 24
Theory of Capitalist Development, The (Sweezy) 55
theory of consumption: Duesenberry 37
theory of economic growth: and aggregate demand 29, 31, 33, 34, 37; and moveable wealth 31; and net product 27, 34; and saving 25, 29, 31, 32; 'simple reproduction' and

'expanded reproduction' 32; and workers' consumption 31
theory of economic growth, in Quesnay: *bon prix* 28, 30; negative impact of saving 29
Theory of Economic History, A (Hicks) 144
Theory of Moral Sentiments (Smith) 68, 69, 173
theory of value and distribution: in classical economists 24; and rate of profit 31
time, logical and historical 128
trade facilitation measures 160
Trade Relations Between England and India 1600–1894, The (Hamilton) 240
transactions 179, 186
transfer of revenue 259
transformation problem 3
Treasury in India 259
trial and error method, 123

uncertainty 178, 179, 185
underconsumption: in Quesnay 27, 30
uneven development 173, 175, 180, 186
unilateral and unrequited transfers, tax revenue 256
Union of Radical Political Economists 56
universality 16, 20
Universities and the Left Review 57
Uno School 57
'unpaid' export surpluses 260
unproductive debt 179
unproductive labour 80
untouchability 274
utilitarianism 272

value of commodities 42
value price transformation problem (VPTP) 55, 58, 59
value–profit relationship 59
varieties of capitalism 182, 183
veblenian institutionalism 173, 183
vector auto regressions (VARs) 224
vested interests *versus* the common good 176, 177
vocational training 270, 273
vulgar economists 77

wage fund 75
wage-led growth 95
wages 75
'Wages and Profits' 56
wage share in national income 89

Walrasian general equilibrium 191
Walrasian hypothesis 193, 194, 205, 207
Walras Law 206
Wardman Group 181
war letters 274
warranted growth rate 145
war talks 274
waste 175, 177, 179, 181
wealth effect 4
wealth of nations: dynamics of 136–141;
    historical trajectories and analytical
    principles 136–141
Wealth of Nations, The (Smith) 14, 15, 48,
    67–69, 141, 173
Weintraub-Davidson approach 4

Wicksell effects 105
widow remarriage 278
Widow Remarriage Act of 1856 278
women: aristocratic 274; British 269–273,
    277, 280; colonialism and 276–279;
    colonial machinery and 271–275; Indian
    270, 271, 273, 274, 280; literature/
    writing 270–273, 277; subordination
    276, 278
workers' consumption 30
work-preference schedule 146
*Works and Correspondence of David Ricardo,
    The* 6

zenana 271, 272